# A Textbook of
# Microeconomics

# A Textbook of
# Microeconomics

**Dr. Priyanka Murria**

Ph.D. (Eco.), MPhil. (Eco.), U.G.C.-N.E.T.,
M.B.E., P.G.D.B.M., C.A.-P.E.-II, B.Com (H)
*Associate Professor (Economics)*
Institute of Innovation in Technology and Management
Affiliated to G.G.S.I.P. University
New Delhi

NEW DELHI

*Published and Printed by*

Techsar Pvt. Ltd.
4435-36/7, Ansari Road, Daryaganj
New Delhi–110 002 (India)
E-mail: tech_info@techsarworld.com
Website: www.techsarworld.com

ISBN: 978-81-948676-9-2



Reprint 2025

*Dedicated to*

My family especially my mother
with reverence and respect

# Preface

The environment of the present-day business is turbulent and is changing fast. This volatile environment needs careful understanding and consideration as it not only affects the concerned business but also the various stakeholders. Keeping this in mind, the nations around the world are increasingly adopting Business Economics as compulsory subject in their curriculum for their undergraduate or postgraduate courses. In this regard, the present book has been authored in such a manner that it is likely to prove beneficial to the students of management, commerce, economics and other allied disciplines. This book is targeted for the students of MBA, MBE, MCom, MA (Economics), BBA, BCom (Hons), BBM, BBE, LLB (Hons) and the like courses. Some distinguishing features of the book include:

- Coverage of subject matter in simple language with lucid explanation of topics covered.
- Pedagogical features such as outline of the chapter, learning objectives, summary, and review questions.
- Chapter outlines give a snapshot of subject matter covered.
- Learning objectives specify the objectives that would be achieved after the completion of each chapter.
- Chapter summarization at the end promotes easy comprehension of the subject matter.
- Review questions act as tool in assessment of reader's progress after reading the book.
- Extensive use of tables, flowcharts, and diagrams to simplify the concepts.
- Case studies to ensure better understanding of concepts and stimulate innovative thinking of readers.

The above-mentioned value additions would not only consolidate the theoretical framework of the students but would also provide the application-oriented approach to the book. The present book utilizes a mix of pedagogical devices that make it useful.

**Dr. Priyanka Murria**

# Acknowledgements

"In the name of Almighty God, the most merciful, the most beneficent"

Though words are often inadequate to express the feelings of gratitude, one must acknowledge the help and support received from those who helped in completion of particular task. I am extremely thankful to all who inspired me to write this book.

With immense pleasure, I extend my deepest gratitude and sincere thanks to Shri J.C. Sharma (Chairman, IITM Group of Institutions) for his persistent encouragement and support for writing research papers and inspiring the faculty members to enhance focus on research. In addition, I also want to thank Shri Ravi Sharma (Chairman, Institute of Innovation in Technology and Management) for his encouragement to the faculty members to author books and conduct webinars. I am also thankful to Prof. (Dr.) C.P. Chawla (Director General, Institute of Innovation in Technology and Management) for his constant motivation and blessings. I am thankful to the librarians Mr. Nagender and Ms. Poonam for being supportive and helpful. In addition, I acknowledge all my teachers who have taught me and helped me in shaping my academic career.

I express my profound respect and regard to my father Late Shri Anil Kumar Murria. He always inspired me to work hard and author books on economics.

I would be failing and becoming ungrateful if I do not place on records my sincere thanks and gratitude to my mother Smt. Rita Murria for being a constant source of inspiration to me. The book would not have seen the light of the day had she not suggested, inspired and provided overall guidance for authoring a book on microeconomics. Her constant support and guidance from the beginning till the end is one of the foundation stones of this book. This study is the result of her joint efforts and guidance. I would not have been what I am today, without her support, encouragement and blessings.

I also acknowledge my elder sister, Dr. Deepti Murria, Gold Medalist in M.D. (Homeopathy) who was regular source of hard work and inspiration to me. She deserves special mention for patiently listening and providing valuable suggestions for improvement in the subject matter and presentation of contents of the book. I am really thankful to her for her great support to me since the commencement of my academic career till now. I would like to express my deep regards to her for being the role model for me.

I would like to express profound gratitude to the numerous authors who have enriched the literature on the subject that has helped me in developing the framework of the book. I am also grateful to all my colleagues and staff members for being supportive. I also want to acknowledge my students of previous and current batches who always encouraged me to author a book on microeconomics.

Moreover, to say the least, this work could not have been given the final shape without the blessings of the Almighty.

**Priyanka Murria**

# Contents

1 CHAPTER

# Introduction to Economics

**LEARNING OBJECTIVES**

After going through this chapter, reader would be able to understand:

- ✓ The meaning and the economic literature in relation to the definitions to explain the concepts of economics.
- ✓ The economic issues being confronted by each segment and sector of the economy.
- ✓ Three fundamental economic questions.
- ✓ Nature and scope of economics specifying the area of functioning of economics.
- ✓ Branches or dimensions of economics.
- ✓ Comparison between microeconomics and macroeconomics.

## 1.1 INTRODUCTION

In this chapter, we will examine the concepts and definitions of economics. We begin with the meaning and move to various definitions of economics propounded by contributors of economic thought. Thereafter, the economic issues have been discussed in terms of limited economic resources that require optimization and the problem of scarcity and choice. Further, three fundamental economic questions have been discussed. This is followed by a discussion on the nature and scope of economics. Then, we examine the branches of economics in terms of microeconomics, macroeconomics, international economics, labour economics, agricultural economics, industrial economics, developmental economics, etc. Finally, the points of difference between the two major branches, viz., microeconomics and macroeconomics have been discussed and elaborated.

## 1.2 MEANING OF ECONOMICS

The word 'economics' derives from two Greek words, viz., *oikos* and *nemein.* The meaning of *oikos* is *a house* and *nemein* means *to manage*. Thus, the collaborative word means 'managing a household'. It means managing the economy of house with the limited available funds and in the most efficient manner.

However, this is a narrow connotation of economics. In the wider perspective, economics is defined more appropriately as 'political economy' by the classical economists in the wake of rise of industrial capitalism in Great Britain (1760-1820). Among the classical economists, Adam Smith, popularly known as 'Father of Economics' proposed his first treatise on the subject in his scholarly work known as 'An Enquiry into Nature and Causes of Wealth of Nations'. In this book, he identified the two market forces which form a crucial aspect of the study of economics in terms of study of demand and supply forces.

## 1.3 DEFINITIONS OF ECONOMICS

Economics has been defined by various thinkers and developers of economic thought in different manners. These contributors have considered different aspects while framing these definitions. In this connection, Barbara Wotton asserted that 'Whenever there are six economists, there are seven opinions!'. However, broadly the definitions of economics are reflected in Fig. 1.1.

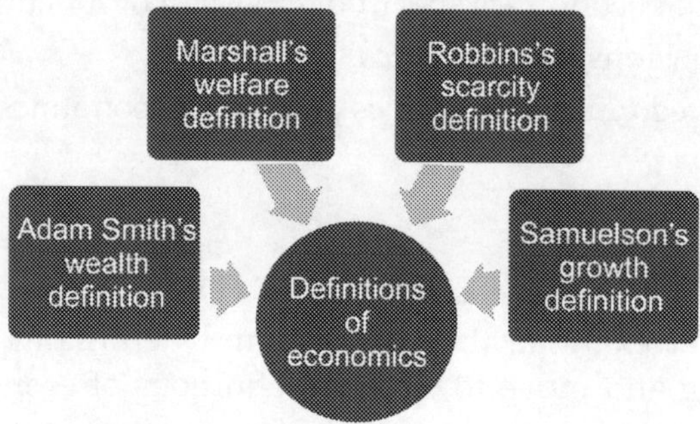


**Fig. 1.1** Definitions of Economics

### 1. Wealth Definitions: The Classical View

The wealth definition has the following characteristics:

- The definition is attributed to Adam Smith (1723- 1790), in his book 'An Inquiry into Nature and Causes of Wealth of Nations' (1776).
- The economics has been defined as the science of wealth creation.
- It was opined that each producer in the economy is not working in order to satisfy consumer but to satisfy his own interest or gain and in this, he is led by an "invisible hand" to promote societal interests though he has no real intention to promote the society's interests.

*Criticism*

The definition lays excessive emphasis on accumulation of material wealth. In an age when religious sentiments ran high, this conception of economics was interpreted as concerning only the acquisition of riches or money. However, in this regard, following points were laid:

- This definition fails to consider the major problems faced by a society or an individual. Thus, it is narrow in its approach.
- This definition considers man as an 'economic man' who is concerned with wealth-hunting. Hence, it focuses on materialistic aspects more.
- Some economists criticized it on the ground that it fails to consider the fundamental problems of scarcity and choice which are fundamental to any economic system.
- It was asserted that it fails to consider the production of non-material goods and services, such as the services of doctors, teachers, etc.

**2. Welfare Definitions: The Neoclassical View**

The welfare definition has the following characteristics:

- This definition was propounded by Alfred Marshall, a supporter of neoclassical school of economic thought.
- The definition covers the boarder perspective of human welfare and emphasized not only on man but also his welfare.
- He calls economics as a social science as it studies the behaviour and performance of human beings.
- Economics is concerned with welfare of mankind, rather than the acquisition of wealth as emphasized under classical view.
- Neoclassical school led by Prof. Alfred Marshall gave economics a respectable place among other social sciences disciplines.
- According to the definition, wealth is regarded as the source of human welfare, not an end in itself but a means to an end.

*Criticism*

Marshall's definition of economics has been criticized on the following grounds:

- Marshall has defined human welfare in terms of money. But 'welfare' is an abstract concept and is not amenable to measurement.
- According to Lionel Robbins, non-material welfare should be supplemented to material welfare (as asserted by Marshall) in order to have complete understanding of economics.
- Robbins argued that Marshall failed to explain the relationship between economic activities of human beings and human welfare. There are certain activities like production of war materials, wine that affect human welfare

in negative manner, but are a part of economic activities. It was pointed that although these activities pose a threat to human welfare but are a part of study of economics as these are economic activities.

- Marshall's definition aims at measuring human welfare in terms of money. But 'welfare' is not amenable to measurement, since 'welfare' is a subjective concept.
- Robbins asserted that Marshall's definition ignores the fundamental problem of scarcity of any economy. In order to lay his concept, Robbins gave 'scarcity definition of economics' where economics was defined in terms of allocation of scarce resources in order to satisfy unlimited human wants.

### 3. Scarcity Definition of Robbins

The next definition of economics was propounded by Lionel Robbins who formulated it on the basis of scarcity of resources. According to Robbins, neither wealth nor human welfare should be considered the subject-matter of economics. He called economics a science which studies human behaviour as a relationship between ends and scarce means which have alternative uses.

This definition talks about the following postulates:

- Economics is concerned with maximization of satisfaction.
- The wants are unlimited and are of recurring nature. If a particular want is satisfied, others emerge to take its place.
- Ends or means to satisfy wants are scarce in relation to their demands. If the resources would have been abundant, there would not have been any economic problems. Thus, scarcity of resources is the fundamental economic problem and gives rise to 'problem of choice'.
- The scarce means, in addition, have alternative uses. The use of a resource for one purpose prevents its use for any other purpose.

***Criticism***

- The theory deals with ends and means to satisfy them. However, it thoroughly ignores the study of welfare.
- Economics has been described in terms of positive science and completely ignores the normative aspect.
- The definition ignores the problems of growth and stability.
- The theory downplays the role of economics as a social science.
- The primary focus is on scarcity as a major economic issue and human issues have been ignored.

However, among all the definitions, Robbins's definition is popular as it relates to the fundamental problems of scarcity and choice which is the root of all economic problems. Thus, it is considered to be the most suitable definition of economics.

#### 4. Samuelson's Growth Definition

The main characteristics of this growth-oriented definition are as follows:

- Samuelson accepted the scarcity definition given by Robbins. He emphasized the problem of scarcity of resources in relation to unlimited wants. He also asserted that the resources are not only scarce but have alternative uses.
- Additionally, the definition highlights the study of macroeconomics by focusing on growth aspects of economy. Samuelson linked the growth aspects with the scarcity of productive resources.
- Unlike Robbins who regarded economics as a science of individual behaviour, Samuelson regards economics as a social science.
- Samuelson has linked the growth aspects with the scarcity of productive resources.
- Samuelson's definition is applicable in both barter economy and monetary economy.
- All the aspects of production, consumption and distribution have been considered.
- In order to evaluate the resources, the contemporary technique of 'cost-benefit analysis' was used.

Thus, economics is a branch of study that focuses on human behaviour as a relationship between ends and scarce means which have alternative uses.

## 1.4 ECONOMIC ISSUES

#### 1. Limited Economic Resources Require Optimization

All the economies including the affluent ones, have limited resources but their populations have unlimited wants. This leads to careful examination of decisions at individual, business corporations, and societal level. For example, an office is to be constructed. It involves decision making in the following manner:

- The land where the business would be run would be decided first.
- Next, the financial requirement to execute the purchasing decision of the office. In this step, the decisions related to opportunity costs of various project proposals are also undertaken.
- Further, the decisions related to the framework and architect of house are undertaken. These decisions are important as they define the basic look and appeal of the office.
- Next step is employment of physical and human capital so that the actual decisions can replace the virtual decisions.
- Once the office is constructed, the business operations can be executed.

It can be observed here that the office construction involved a series of actions and coordination of various factors of production. A careful examination of resources and their allocation is undertaken. The resources must be utilized carefully in order to avoid wastage of resources. This is required so that the benefits accruing from the project exceed the cost of undertaking the decisions.

The concept of optimum utilization of resources is not only applicable to the businesses; the same is applicable to the economies at large. Given the factor endowments, an economy uses the available factors in such a manner that it fetches maximum benefits. Thus, the optimum utilization of various factors is done in order to get maximum possible solutions for the economy. It is to be noted here that the employment of factors in one project puts a resource constraint in such manner that the other project would not be considered. Thus, careful examination of economic issues is to be made.

### 2. The Problem of Scarcity and Choice

The economic issue of scarcity and choice is at the heart of economics. This issue emerges as each economy is blessed with different factor endowments. The resources are thus limited in quantity and quality. An economy has to produce millions of goods and services. Thus, the problem of choice arises so that there can be optimum utilization of resources. This can be understood by taking an example, say Indian economy. In the context of Indian economy, the sectoral division and problem of choice has been explained with the help of Table 1.1.

**TABLE 1.1** Sectoral Division and Corresponding Problem of Scarcity and Choice

| Sr. No. | Sectoral Division | Problem of Scarcity and Choice |
|---|---|---|
| 1. | In primary sector | • To utilize the land for cultivation of rice or wheat.<br>• To cultivate own land or give it to tenant farmers. |
| 2. | In secondary sector | • To use land in order to construct a factory or an office.<br>• Use of land for making furniture from wood or as retail shop of outsourced furniture. |
| 3. | In tertiary sector | • To use land for coaching centre or rent it out to others.<br>• To use the land for running a computer café or rent it out to a bank to be used as a bank branch. |

Thus, the issue of scarcity and choice is imperative in every economy. Each section, segment and sector of the economy faces constraints and has to make choice among the available options to maximize the returns.

## 1.5 THREE FUNDAMENTAL ECONOMIC QUESTIONS

An economy is confronted with the problem of utilization of available resources in such a manner that maximum satisfaction flows to the people with unlimited wants.

While doing so each economy is faced with the three basic problems, which are called 'central problems of an economy'. These have been reflected in Fig. 1.2.

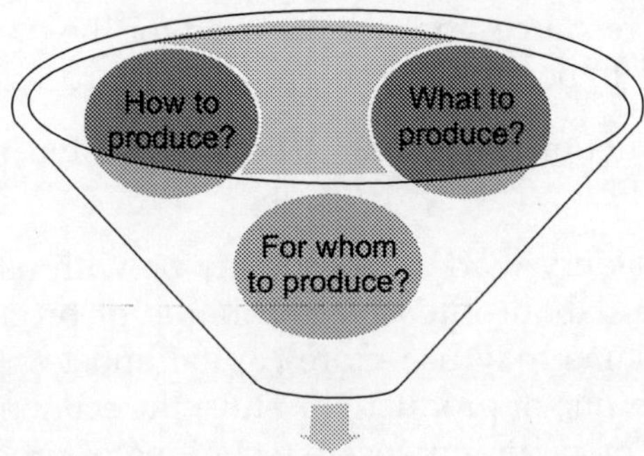


**Fig. 1.2** Three Central Problems of an Economy

In every economic system, whether capitalist, socialist or mixed economy, there are three central problems of the economy. These are 'what, how and for whom to produce'. However, the manner in which these problems are dealt with varies depending on the functioning of the economy. Each of the fundamental problems has been discussed as follows.

**1. What to Produce?**

In a market economy, the decisions related to 'what to produce?' problem are made mainly by sellers with the objective of making rational decisions with respect to the following two related questions:

- Which goods are to be produced?
  Here, an economy has to decide whether it has to produce consumer goods or capital goods; durable goods or non-durable goods, etc.
- In what quantities those goods, which the economy has decided to produce, are to be produced. Here, the decisions related to allocation of resources for the production of consumer goods and capital goods are undertaken. In other words, an economy has to decide that how much resource will be allocated to the respective quantities of consumer goods and capital goods.

Thus, here the type of goods and their quantity is decided. These decisions are vital for any economy on account of the following reasons:

- Productive resources are limited and they have to cater to unlimited wants.
- The production of one product in a larger quantity leads to withdrawal or sacrifice of resources for the production of some other products.

***For example:*** If the microwaves are in demand, then a producer should produce microwaves. In this case, what to produce decision is oriented towards the production of microwaves.

**2. How to Produce?**

This decision related to 'how to produce' relates to the following:

- The combination of resources that will be used for the production of goods and which technology is to be used in the production process.
- Technique of production including labour-intensive and capital-intensive techniques.

For instance, the embroidery work on cloth may be with use of more labour and less capital therefore, uses labour-intensive technique of production. However, the embroidery done by machine may use more capital and less manpower and thus, use capital-intensive technique of production. Thus, the economy has to make choice between labour-intensive or capital-intensive technique of production.

However, the choice between the techniques would depend on the factor-endowment and the prices of the factors of production. It is in the interest of any economy to use those techniques of production that lead to the maximum use of the relatively plentiful resources.

**3. For Whom to Produce?**

This decision is related to 'for whom to produce' relates to the following:

- It deals with the distribution of the national product among the members of the society. However, those people who have larger incomes get greater share of goods and services and those with low incomes get less of it.
- The main difficulty in distribution of national product or income is the disparity of 'equity and justice' aspect of distribution with the 'incentive' aspect.
- In case of equity and justice aspect, the distribution of national product or income should be done on the basis of equality. Each person irrespective of income level should get equal share.
- In case of incentive aspect, incentive is either destroyed or greatly diminished as a result of promoting equality; the total national output available for sharing may be so less that the living standards of all may go down.

## 1.6 NATURE AND SCOPE OF ECONOMICS

### 1.6.1 Nature of Economics

There is no universal agreement among the economists regarding the nature of economics. Some call it a science while some specify that it is an art. In the opinions of economists, if it is science then it is either positive science or normative science.

### 1. Economics as a Science

There are numerous controversial arguments among economists regarding the consideration of economics as a science or art.

Science has following features:

- It is a systematized body of knowledge.
- Based on observation and experimentation.
- Has its own principles, theories and laws.
- Is based on cause and effect relationship.
- Concepts have universal validity.

Economics qualifies for science as it fulfills the above-mentioned grounds. However, economics keeps on revising its conclusions in the light of new facts based on observations. The following arguments are in support of economics as a science:

(a) Economics is also a systematic study of knowledge and facts. All the concepts and facts related with both microeconomics and macroeconomics are systematically collected, classified and analyzed.

(b) Economics is also based on cause and effect relationship. For example, quantity demanded and price are inversely related, i.e., rise in price causes decline in quantity demanded and vice versa, keeping the effect of other variables constant.

(c) All the economic laws such as the law of demand, law of supply, law of diminishing marginal utility, etc., have universal acceptance.

(d) Theories and laws of economics are based on experiments, like, the law of diminishing marginal utility is the outcome of repeated tests and experiments conducted on a number of individuals and then it becomes a universal truth and thus is known as an economic law.

#### *Economics: Positive or Normative Science*

There is no universal consensus regarding the nature of economics as positive or normative. Some economists call it positive while others call it a normative science. Some economists like Robbins, Friedman and J.S. Mill were of the opinion that economics is a positive science. They were of the opinion that the science of economics is concerned with what is and not with what ought to be of a particular situation. On the other hand, economists like Marshall and Pigou asserted that economics is only a positive science. They opined that it also focuses on the problems of firms where the utilization of normative approach is indispensible. However, the viewpoints in favour of each have been specified in Table 1.2.

**TABLE 1.2** Economics: Positive or Normative Science

| Economics as Positive Science | Economics as Normative Science |
|---|---|
| 1. It is based on cause and effect relationship and is able to give logical clarifications. | 1. Economics is a science of human welfare and thus involves value judgments which make it normative in its approach. |
| 2. The principles, concepts and theories define the past and present of any situation. | 2. Economics involves the study of economic planning where several economists give their opinions for the successful implementation of economic plans or policies. Hence, economics comes under the preview of normative science. |

**2. Economics as an Art**

Eminent economists like Pigou and Marshall regarded economics as an art. They were of the opinion that science lays down principles while art puts these principles into practical use. Economics as an art deals with the practical application of knowledge for achieving particular goals.

For instance, the analysis of causes and effects of inflation relates to the study of science. However, to define a framework that aims at mitigation of inflation level is an art. Economics is thus, both a science and an art in this sense.

Thus, it can be concluded that economics is neither a science nor an art only. It is the blend of science as well as art as it qualifies the features of both of them.

## 1.6.2 Scope of Economics

Scope of economics relates to the area of expansion of its subject matter and its application. It defines the area of functioning of economics.

The subject matter of economics is classified under two categories:

**1. Traditional Economics:** It is studied under major five divisions. These are:

- Consumption
- Production
- Exchange
- Distribution
- Public finance

**2. Modern Economics:** Under the contemporary or modern approach, Sir Ragnar Frisch coined the two terms, viz. 'micro' means 'small' and 'macro' means 'large'. Thus, the study of economics was bifurcated under two main heads:

- **Microeconomics** refers to the study of economic problems related to individual units. These individual units may be a consumer, a producer or an industry. It involves the microscopic study of the conduct and behaviour of individual entities in order to understand the decision-making process at micro level. It is based on 'step-by-step analysis' and on the assumption of 'Ceteris Peribus' which means 'keeping the effect of other variables constant'.

  It includes the study of the following:

  - Demand analysis
  - Demand forecasting
  - Theory of consumer behaviour
  - Theory of firm
  - Supply analysis
  - Price and output decision in product market
  - Theory of production
  - Cost analysis
  - Market for factor inputs and their pricing
  - Theory of market failures

- **Macroeconomics** is the study of the economic problems of all units in an economic system. Since, it deals with the aggregates, and their performance in the economic system, it is also called 'Aggregative Economics'.

  It includes the study of the following:

  - Study of national income and related aggregates
  - Theories of income, output and employment
  - Analysis of money and banking
  - IS-LM analysis
  - Analysis of consumption, saving and investment
  - Inflation and deflation
  - Monetary and fiscal policies
  - Balance of payment and balance of trade

## 1.7 BRANCHES OF ECONOMICS

Economics is a wide discipline that deals with optimum utilization of scarce resources in order to fulfill the unlimited wants of the population of an economy. It is generally agreed that there are two branches of economics, namely microeconomics and macroeconomics. However, in reality, there are other branches also which focus on different aspects. These branches have been shown in Fig. 1.3.

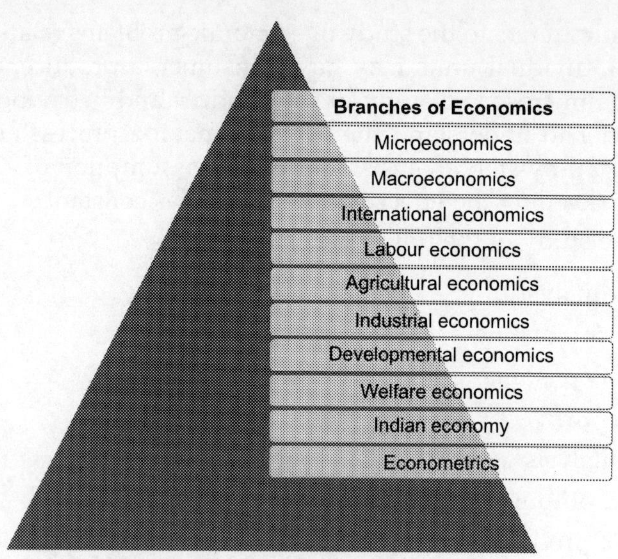


**Fig. 1.3** Branches of Economics

## 1.8 COMPARISON BETWEEN MICROECONOMICS AND MACROECONOMICS

Macroeconomics is the study of economic behaviour and conduct of all the units taken together as compared to microeconomics which involves the study of individual units. However, the main points of difference between these two have been illustrated in Table 1.3.

**TABLE 1.3** Comparison between Microeconomics and Macroeconomics

| Basis | Microeconomics | Macroeconomics |
|---|---|---|
| 1. Meaning | Involves the study of behaviour, conduct and performance of individuals. | Involves the study of behaviour, conduct and performance of economy as a whole. |
| 2. Alternative name | It is also known as Price Theory | It is also known as Income Theory or Aggregative Economics |
| 3. Focus | Individual units | Aggregates |
| 4. Assumption of Ceteris Paribus | Applicable | Not applicable |

| 5. Assumption of full employment | Assumes full employment. | Does not assume full employment. |
|---|---|---|
| 6. Subject matter of study | It deals with the interplay of market forces, determination of price, cardinal approach to utility analysis, ordinal approach to utility analysis, producer's equilibrium, study of market forms, etc. | It deals with the study of macroeconomic aggregates, national income determination, theories of employment, unemployment, general price level, inflation, deflation, economic growth, economic policies, IS-LM analysis, etc. |
| 7. Metaphor used by Prof. Boulding | Study of trees rather than forest | Study of Forest rather than Trees |
| 8. Economic view | Worm's-eye view | Bird's-eye view |
| 9. Equilibrium analysis | Equilibrium is ascertained where, Demand = Supply | Equilibrium is ascertained where, Aggregate demand = Aggregate supply |

## Summary

✓ Economics is a branch of study that focuses on human behaviour as a relationship between ends and scarce means which have alternative uses.

✓ Different propounders of economic thought have considered different aspects while framing definitions of economics. Thus, the major contributions are reflected in form of the following:

- Adam Smith's definition emphasizes that economics is the science of wealth creation where firms are not working in order to satisfy consumer but to satisfy their own interests.
- Marshall's definition defines economics as social science as it studies the behaviour and performance of human beings.
- Robbins's definition specifies economics as science which studies human behaviour as a relationship between ends and means.
- Samuelson's definition delineates that economics is the study of problem of scarcity of resources in relation to unlimited wants and resources which have alternative uses. It also highlighted the importance of macroeconomics.

✓ Each economy and underlying businesses face economic issues in terms of optimization of limited economic resources and problem of scarcity of resources and choice that would ensure maximum benefits.

✓ There are three central problems of an economy. These are:

- What to produce?
- How to produce?
- For whom to produce?

These problems are basic to every economy, hence called 'fundamental problems'.

- ✓ Economics is the blend of science as well as art. It is both a positive and a normative science. However, it is more of positive science rather than normative science.
- ✓ Economics has wide scope. It encompasses the study of two categories:
  - Traditional economics includes the study of consumption, production, exchange, distribution and public finance.
  - Modern economics includes the study of microeconomics and macroeconomics.
- ✓ Microeconomics is the study of individual units whereas macroeconomics is the study of all units taken together.
- ✓ Apart from microeconomics and microeconomics, the other branches of economics are international economics, labour economics, agricultural economics, industrial economics, developmental economics, welfare economics, Indian economy and econometrics.

## Review Questions

1. What is economics? Explain the transitions in economic literature relating to the definitions of economics.
2. Critically evaluate Robbins's Scarcity definition. Do you think Samuelson's Growth definition is an improvement over Robbins's definition? Justify your answer.
3. "Each producer in the economy is not working in order to satisfy consumer but to satisfy his own interest". Critically examine.
4. "Economics is a social science as it studies the behaviour and performance of human beings". Critically examine.
5. Delineate the underlying economic issues that are faced by each economy. Also explain the problem of optimum utilization of resources with reference to sectoral division of any economy.
6. What is positive or normative science? In your opinion, is economics positive or normative in nature? Give reasons in support of your answer.
7. What is economics? Explain the concept in the light of nature and scope of economics.
8. "Economics is the study of microeconomics and macroeconomics". Explain the statement in the light of other branches of economics.
9. "There is really no opposition between the microeconomics and macroeconomics. Both are absolutely vital. You are half educated if you understand one while being ignorant of the other". Do you agree with the statement? Justify your answer.

# 2 CHAPTER

# Applied Economics: Business Economics

**LEARNING OBJECTIVES**

By the end of this chapter, reader should be able to understand:

- ✓ The meaning and concept of business economics as an applied branch of economics.
- ✓ The nature and boundaries of operation of business economics.
- ✓ The distinction of business economics and abstract economic theory.
- ✓ The contribution and application of business economics in business practice.
- ✓ The fundamental concepts of economics that are frequently applied in contemporary businesses.

## 2.1 INTRODUCTION

The traditional economic theory essentially imbibes the study of concepts, principles, conventions and theories that provide the consolidated base of careful analysis and interpretation by the planners, policymakers and the economic analysts. It involves the study of perspectives and issues pertaining to economies and helps in understanding the economic structure of several economies. It includes the study of demand analysis, supply analysis, demand forecasting, theory of consumer behaviour, production analysis, study of market forms, etc.

In reality, the economic activities involve decision making at one stage or the other. The economist or business marketer is required to deal with various aspects related to demand, production, cost and distribution of goods or services. Here, comes the role of Business Economics as a branch of economic thought. It studies the application part of study of behaviour, structure and performance of various units of the economy. It consists of applied economics that carefully examines the theoretical frameworks contributed by the contributors of economic thought. The business economics is thus, an application oriented branch of economics as it integrates economic theory with business practice so that business decision problems may be resolved.

For instance, a manager while managing business comes across numerous situations like ascertaining demand for a product, impact of advertisement on demand, impact of price of related goods like substitute or complementary products on demand of a commodity. In order to analyze such situations, Business economics provides concepts like demand forecasting techniques for ascertaining demand, advertisement elasticity for ascertaining the impact of advertisement expenditure on demand of the commodity, cross-elasticity for estimating the impact of change in prices of substitute or complementary products on the demand of the commodity in question.

In this chapter, the readers will be able to explore the concept of business economics as an application based branch of economics. Thereafter, the nature and scope of the business economics in terms of business operations has been discussed. The chapter further proceeds with the discussion on the major differences between business economics and economics. This has been made in terms of various attributes such as concept, orientation, nature, scope, etc. The contribution of business economics in real business practice has been further discussed. In this direction, the role of decision sciences has also been elaborated. Later on, the fundamental concepts of economics that have an important role in implementation of business economics as an applied branch of economics have been discussed.

## 2.2 MEANING OF BUSINESS ECONOMICS

Business economics or managerial economics refers to a branch of economics that deals with the application of economic theories and concepts in order to analyze present and future business situations. It is a discipline that brides the gap between abstract economic theory and real business practices through careful examination of business situations. It involves the use of economic relationships in order to understand the current business situations so that the current managerial decision problems can be addressed and planning for future can be done. Since, business economics helps in solving managerial decision-making problems; it is also called managerial economics or economics for business management. It has been reflected in Fig. 2.1.

**Fig. 2.1** Components of Business Economics

## 2.3 DEFINITIONS OF BUSINESS ECONOMICS

Salvatore defined managerial economics as "the application of economic theory and tools of analysis of decision science to examine how an organization can achieve its aims or objectives most effectively".

In the words of Haynes, "Managerial economics makes use of the tools of economic analysis in clarifying problems, in organizing and evaluating information and in comparing alternative courses of action".

According to D.C Hague, managerial economics uses "the logic of economics, mathematics and statistics to provide effective ways of thinking about management decision problems".

Spencer and Siegelman defined managerial economics (or business economics) as "the integration of economic theory with business practice for the purpose of facilitating decision-making and forward planning by management."

## 2.4 NATURE OF BUSINESS ECONOMICS

The nature tends to explain the characteristics or features of business economics. These define the entire composition of Business Economics. The nature of Business Economics can be explained with the help of Fig. 2.2.

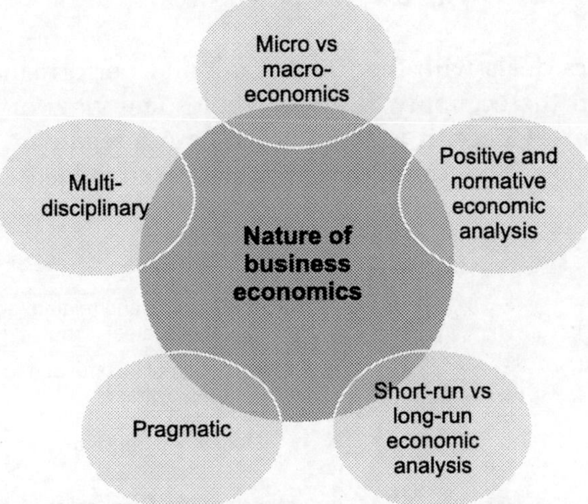


**Fig. 2.2** Nature of Business Economics

### 1. The Study of Micro- vs Macroeconomics

The subject matter of business economics involves the study of both microeconomics and macroeconomics. These branches of economics have been explained as under:

(a) **Microeconomics** deals with the study of individual units such as households, firms, industry or any individual resource owner. It focuses on individual units and gives the microscopic view of the performance of the individual economic units under consideration. It is most commonly known as the study of trees (individual units) rather than the forest (aggregate).

Figure 2.3 includes some of the topics that are considered subject matter of study of microeconomics:

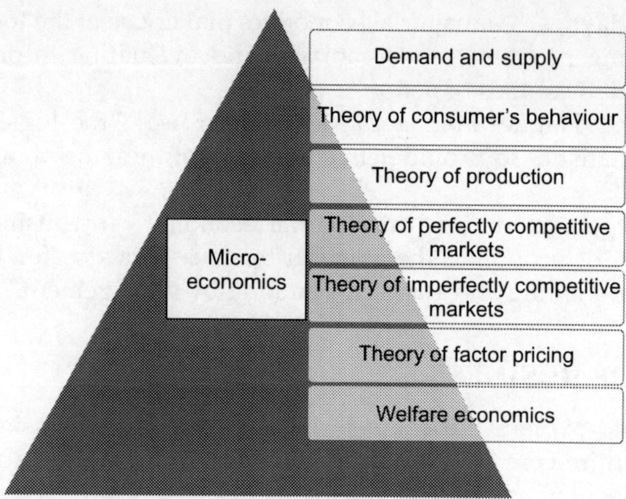


**Fig. 2.3** Microeconomics

**(b) Macroeconomics** deals with the functioning and performance of all the units or aggregates in the economy. It gives wholesome view or aggregative view of economic units. Hence, it is also known as Aggregative Economics. Figure 2.4 includes some of the topics that are considered subject matter of study of macroeconomics:

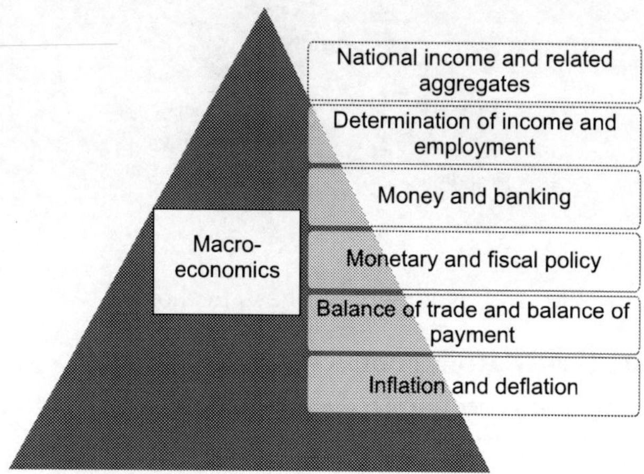


**Fig. 2.4** Macroeconomics

**2. Study of Positive and Normative Economic Analysis**

The study of business economics involves the study of two approaches of economic analysis, normative and positive economic approaches. These approaches have been explained as follows:

(a) **Positive Economics** is descriptive in nature and deals with the current or present state of affairs. It helps in explaining "What is" or "will be" of a particular situation. It throws light on the current situations or questions of fact.

*For example:*

(a) The current GDP growth rate of India for current financial year 2017-18 as estimated by Niti Aayog is 6.9-7.0%.

(b) The future projection GDP reflects that the GDP growth rate of India is likely to be 7.5% for FY 2018-19 as per the estimates of Niti Aayog.

The first example is explaining an economic fact whereas the second situation is describing a future economic situation. Thus, both the situations come in the realm of positive economics.

(b) **Normative economics** is prescriptive in nature. It deals with ethical considerations and norms of fairness of economic state of affairs. It specifies and explains "What ought to be done?" in a particular situation. It basically focuses on value judgments in order to achieve the specified goals of business.

*For Example:* Cash reserve ratio should be enhanced to mitigate the impact of inflation in Indian Economy.

It is a prescriptive statement as it prescribes what should be done in a particular economic situation.

Business economics is the blend of both normative and positive economic theories. However, it is more related to normative economic principles as it is concerned with decision-making at firm's level. In business concern, a manager faces enormous changes that he becomes more concerned with what should be done in a particular situation. Thus, a business manager follows more of normative approach as compared to the positive approach of economic analysis. Thus, unlike traditional economic theory which was more oriented towards the positive economics, business economics is more inclined towards normative economics.

**3. Study of Short-Run vs Long-Run Economic Analysis**

In order to consider the role of time in production and cost analysis, the study of business economics is done under two broader horizons of time periods, i.e., short run and long run.

(a) **Short-run period of economic analysis** refers to a time period in which firm can alter production by changing constraints or factors that are variable while other constraints or factors are fixed. These variable factors include material and labour while fixed factors include land and capital.

(b) **Long-run period of economic analysis** refers to the time period in which all constraints or factors are variable and are capable for being adjusted or modified.

**4. Pragmatic**

Business economics is pragmatic in nature as it follows the practical approach that is suitable for handling ever-changing business situations. Thus, it is more realistic and practical in its approach as compared to traditional economic theory that was more based on theoretical perspectives and considerations.

**5. Multidisciplinary**

Business economics is multidisciplinary in nature as it takes the help of decision sciences like statistics, operations research, research methodology, mathematics, psychology, etc., to analyze the conditions (internal or external) relevant to business.

## 2.5 SCOPE OF BUSINESS ECONOMICS

The "scope" of business economics is wide as its subject matter on one side includes the study of traditional economic theory whereas on the other side, due to its multidisciplinary nature it takes the help of decision sciences in order to solve and analyze the managerial decision making problem. The scope of business economics has been explained in Fig. 2.5 as follows:

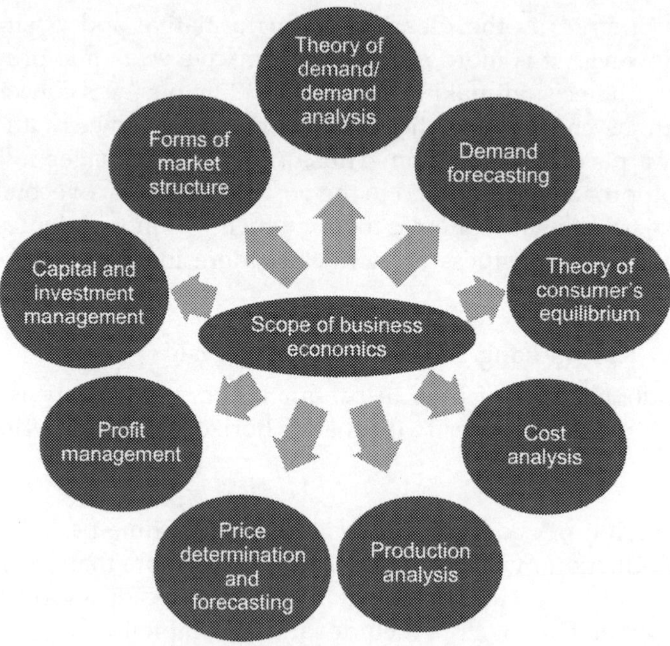


**Fig. 2.5** Scope of Business Economics

### 1. Theory of Demand/Demand Analysis

The knowledge and awareness of the demand is a crucial sphere of business decision-making. Any wrong estimate may hamper the growth and expansion perspectives of the business. The demand estimation helps a firm in understanding the following crucial questions?

- What type of commodity is being demanded by the consumer?
- What is the factor that influences the demand of the commodity, price or any other factor?
- Is there any overproduction or underproduction of the concerned product?
- The degree of responsiveness of change in demand on account of change in price or any associated factor?

The demand analysis helps in finding the answers to these questions and hence occupies a strategic place in managerial economics. Thus, business economics at the outset elaborates the economic theory related to analyses of demand for the product and facilitates the decision making at firm and industry level.

### 2. Demand Forecasting

Another subject matter of business economics is the anticipation of quantity of the commodity that the consumer is able and willing to purchase in the future. The sequence of steps that are carried out in order to predict the demand is known as demand forecasting. Thus, it facilitates business planning and occupies a strategic place in managerial economics.

### 3. Theory of Consumer's Equilibrium

The theory of consumer's equilibrium is helpful in the following manner:

- It specifies the decision-making criteria of the consumer by explaining the concept of consumer's equilibrium on the basis of marginal utility and price.
- It elucidates the allocation of his income among different baskets of commodities.
- It explains the point of satiety which helps in understanding the point when the marginal utility becomes zero and consumer stops consuming the commodity.

The knowledge of the above concepts helps the business manger in planning the sales targets more effectively and devising appropriate sales promotion strategies to market the product.

### 4. Cost Analysis

One of the important objective of business is to minimize the cost components. It is based on the notion that the reduced cost would help in elevating the level of profits. In this direction, the cost incurred in production and distribution must be ascertained and recorded.

Business economics helps in the analysis and study of elements of cost which further helps in performing business operations in an efficient manner.

### 5. Production Analysis

Another area that defines the scope of business economics is production analysis, popularly known as theory of firm. The production analysis specifies the scope of business economics in following manner:

- Production analysis includes the study of production function which establishes relationship between input and output in production process.
- It also throws light on the impact of change in one factor of production on total output (keeping other factors constant) as well as the impact when all factors are changed simultaneously.
- Production theory is also connected with cost curves by explaining the relationship between average and marginal costs. It highlights how a change in production can affect average cost and marginal cost curves.

### 6. Price Determination and Forecasting

The determination of price is an important area. Business economics is helpful in the following manner:

- The equilibrium price determination can be explained in the various forms of market such as perfect competition, monopoly, monopolistic competition, and oligopoly both in short as well as long run.
- It also helps in forecasting future prices on the basis of past trends.

### 7. Profit Management

The main aim of any business concern is to maximize quantum of profits. The profits are calculated as the difference between revenue and cost. In this direction, the study of cost and revenue curves are helpful. Business economics facilitates the study of profits by explaining the concept of profit using TR-TC approach and MR-MC approach. These approaches help in understanding the progression of revenue and cost curves and taking remedial policy measures.

### 8. Capital and Investment Management

The business economics also explains the allocation of capital in various project proposals. It is immensely helpful by contributing the concepts like:

- Time value of money–It helps in calculating the present value of future inflows.
- Analysis of efficiency of capital (MEC)
- Analysis of efficiency of investment (MEI)
- Choice of projects on the basis of comparison of MEC and the rate of interest.

### 9. Forms of Market Structure

Business economics facilities the study of forms of market structure so as to provide knowledge about the following aspects:

- The cost and revenue curves under the various market structures and their impact on equilibrium determination.
- Impact of availability of substitutes or degree of competition on prospective policies of business.
- Impact of selling homogeneous or differentiated product on the revenue curves and henceforth profits.

## 2.6 COMPARISON BETWEEN BUSINESS ECONOMICS AND ECONOMICS

Economics is the study of theoretical concepts and theories. These concepts and theories are related to demand or supply of the product, consumer decision making, supplier decisions making, breakeven analysis, profit analysis, shut down point, equilibrium determination and analysis, etc.

Business economics, on the other hand, is the application of economic theory and methodology to decision-making problems of business. It basically bridges the gap between abstract theory and real business practices and situations. Hence, is more pragmatic in its approach. However, the major points of difference between business economics and economics have been mentioned in Table 2.1.

**TABLE 2.1** Comparison between Business Economics and Economics

| Area of Difference | Economics | Business Economics |
|---|---|---|
| 1. Meaning | Deals with sets and subsets of theoretical concepts and theories. | Deals with the application of theoretical perspectives in real business practice. |
| 2. Orientation | Theoretical | Applied |
| 3. Nature | Descriptive | Perspective |
| 4. Approach | Both normative and positive but more positive in its approach. | Both normative and positive but is more normative in its approach. |
| 5. Economic branches studied | Deals with:<br>1. Microeconomics<br>2. Macroeconomics<br>3. Agricultural economics<br>4. Industrial economics<br>5. Indian economy, etc. | Deals with the study of microeconomics. |

*Contd.*

| | | |
|---|---|---|
| 6. Scope of the study | It has a wider scope as it involves the study of both household and business firms. | It has narrow scope as compared to economics as it deals with the problems related to the firms and decision-making at firm level. |
| 7. Study of distribution theories | All distribution theories are studied. These are:<br>• Theory of rent<br>• Theory of interest<br>• Theory of wages<br>• Theory of profits | Deals with the study of problems of the firms.<br>The main aim of the firms is to maximize profit. Hence, it gives more emphasis on profit theory. |
| 8. Focus | Creation of economic models on the basis of assumptions. | Construct and reconstruct economic models by making changes in the existing economic models in order to cater to the turbulences in the business. |

## 2.7 CONTRIBUTION AND APPLICATION OF BUSINESS ECONOMICS TO BUSINESS

Business is an economic activity that is mainly pursued to maximize the profits. There are other objectives also which include cost minimization, growth maximization, enhancing market share, maximization of earning per share, etc. The ways to attain all these objectives require decision-making at micro- or macro level. A business manager is required to make decisions by evaluating all the alternative courses of action and choosing the best one. Further, the business environment is affected by political, legal, and social factors which lead to turbulence in business decisions. Thus, the ever-changing business environment and growing complexity of business decisions necessitated the application of traditional economic theory into a separate branch of study, commonly known as business economics or managerial economics.

### Business Economics: An Applied Framework of Economic Knowledge

Business economics or managerial economics is a branch of study that involves the use and application of theoretical perspectives and principles of economics. Thus, it deals with the application part and addresses the managerial decision-making problem. It acts as a linking pin between economic theory and managerial policy-making in real life. It considers the theories, principles and approaches of traditional economics and uses them to take decisions in current scenario and to ensure forward planning. Thus, business economics is the application of traditional economic theory with managerial policy-making so as to arrive at present and future managerial decisions. Figure 2.6 shows business economics as an applied framework of economic knowledge.

**Fig. 2.6** Business Economics: An Applied Framework of Economic Knowledge

### Business Decisions and Related Complexities

The business manager while managing business is confronted with the decisions that may be related to analysis of current demand, analysis of future demand, determinants of demand, effect of determinants of demand on demand for the product, etc. The following are the major decisions that are a part of decision-making process on regular basis:

- The estimation of demand of the product.
- The factors affecting demand either it is price, income of the consumer, price of substitute or complementary products, taste and preferences, fashion, advertisement, etc.
- The impact on demand if there is a change in any of its determinants.
- The decision-making process of allocation of income of consumer on purchase of products.
- To increase the intensity of advertisement or to opt for any other method of sales promotion.
- The analysis and forecasting of individual and market demand.
- The relationship between input and output during production process.

### Contribution of Business Economics in Business Decision-Making

Business economics contributes to business decision-making by contributing the following concepts:

1. **Determinants of Demand:** For understanding the demand for the concerned product and factors influencing its demand (price, income of the consumer, price of related product, etc).
2. **Equilibrium Analysis:** For estimation of price at which it would be sold and the quantity that the consumers are willing and able to purchase.
3. **The Elasticity of Demand:** Defining the extent of responsiveness of change in quantity on account of change in any of the determinants of demand for the product.
4. **Theory of Consumer's Behaviour:** To understand the decision-making process on the part of consumer regarding his consumption level and pattern of his allocation of income.

5. **Advertisement Elasticity of Demand:** To understand the impact of advertisement on the demand or sales of the product.
6. **Demand Forecasting:** The analysis and forecasting of demand.
7. **Production Function:** To understand the relationship between input and output during the production process.
8. **Theory of Risk and Uncertainty:** Helpful to a business manger in analyzing the conditions of risk and uncertainty by framing various models which may predict the economic conditions.

Thus, the major contribution of business economics is its subject matter that helps in the achievement of short- and long-run objectives of business. Business economics specifies its subject matter in the form of economic concepts and theories that facilitate managerial and administrative decision-making.

**Application of Business Economics to Business Decision Making**

Figure 2.7 reflects the application of business economics to business decision-making under four main heads:

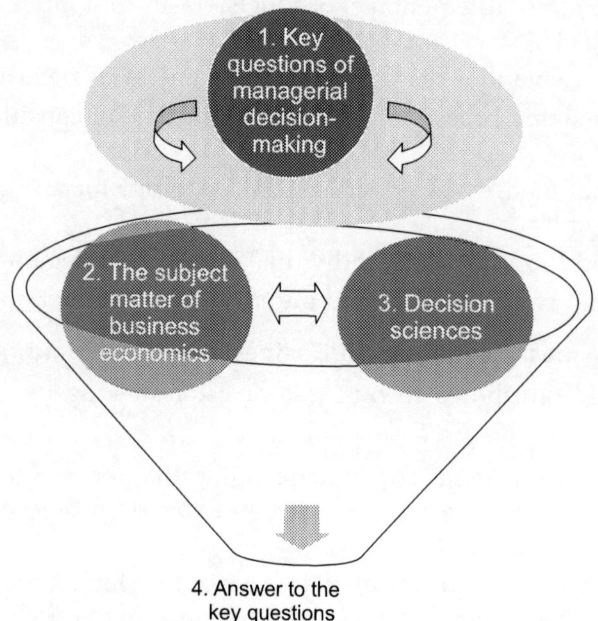


**Fig. 2.7** Application of Business Economics

**1. The Key Questions of Managerial Decision-Making**

Every business requires decision-making. These decisions may be related to production, cost, consumer's behaviour, analysis of demand or supply, forecasting of demand or sales of the product. Thus, a manager while handling business is confronted with the following questions:

- What is the anticipated demand of the product?
- What should be the price at which the commodity should be sold?
- How much is the impact of price on consumer's buying behaviour?
- How much quantity should be supplied in the market?
- Is the consumer price sensitive?
- Should there be in-house production or the commodity should be outsourced?
- What should be the price of the product?
- Does customer favour the product?
- What is the impact of change in price of substitute product on the commodity?

**2. The Subject Matter of Business Economics**

The following activities define the subject matter of business economics that help in building framework for business decisions:

- The demand analysis and forecasting
- The equilibrium analysis in perfect and imperfect commodity markets
- The concept of price elasticity of demand
- Income elasticity of demand
- Cross-elasticity of demand
- Advertisement elasticity of demand
- Analysis of consumer's behaviour
- Production analysis
- Cost structure and its analysis
- Market structure and its equilibrium analysis in short and long run

**3. Decision Sciences**

These disciplines provide tools of analysis and help in establishing its relationship with other disciplines. These are:

1. **Mathematics:** Mathematics helps in explaining economic relationships for facilitating further decision-making. The widely used mathematical concepts that explain and establish economic relationships include: functions, determinants, matrix algebra, differentials and integrals.
2. **Statistics:** Statistical tools also help in business decision-making. These tools include correlation analysis, regression analysis, and theory of probability to process and analyze business data.
3. **Accountancy:** It helps in providing data related to the costs, revenues and profits which are crucial for business decision-making.
4. **Research Methodology:** It includes the study of sampling techniques, tools of analysis, deciding the sample size, etc.

5. **Psychology:** It helps in analyzing the psychological facets related to buyer and seller. It helps in analyzing the importance of non-economic factors behind the purchase of the product.

4. **Answer to the Key Questions by Collaboration of the Subject Matter of Business Economics and Decision Sciences**

The integration of economic theory with decision sciences is done in order to address and answer the key questions of managerial decision-making. It further helps in making current plans and deciding forward or futuristic plans.

## 2.8 FUNDAMENTAL CONCEPTS OF ECONOMICS APPLIED IN BUSINESS ECONOMICS

### 2.8.1 Principle of Opportunity Cost

Economics deals with unlimited wants and limited resources that too have alternative uses. Every economy cannot produce or own all the resources. In order to produce one commodity, the economy has to sacrifice the production of another commodity that could have been produced using the available resources. Thus, there is an involvement of sacrifice that leads to emergence of concept of opportunity cost. Opportunity cost refers to the cost of the next best alternative foregone. These foregone alternatives represent opportunities. Hence, the revenue sacrificed by not availing the alternatives is called opportunity cost.

This principle can be explained with the help of the following example:

Suppose a farmer has 1 acre of land. He rather than using land for cultivation rents it to another person and in lieu of it receives rent from him. Thus, the receipt of rent had an opportunity cost. The opportunity cost in this case is the amount of revenue foregone as the farmer did not cultivate the land on his own.

Similarly, if a businessman invests Rs. 10 lakh in his own business instead of investing in mutual funds. Then the amount of revenue that he would have earned on mutual funds represents the opportunity cost.

### 2.8.2 Time Value of Money – Discounting Concept

The concept of time value of money or time perspective has an important place in the readings and discussions of Prof. Marshall, one of the major contributors to microeconomics.

This concept states that the money to be received today is more valuable as compared to the money that will be received on a future date.

**Reasons for Calculating Time Value of Money**

1. The future is unknown, incalculable and beyond the control.
2. The future involves lot of risk and uncertainty.
3. The amount can be invested and can generate interest income.

***For example:***

Mr. X lends an amount of Rs. 100 to Mr. Y for a period of two years. Then the present value of money following the time value of money would be calculated as follows:

$$PV = \frac{A}{(1 + r/100)} n$$

where,

*PV* represents present value

*A* represents amount

*r* represents discounting rate

*n* represents time period

Thus, the present value (*PV*) can be calculated as follows (assuming $r = 10\%$):

1. The present value of Rs. 100, after one year
   $PV = \text{Rs. } 100/(1+10/100)^1 = \text{Rs. } 90.91 = \text{Rs. } 91$
2. The present value of Rs. 100, after two years
   $PV = \text{Rs. } 100/(1+10/100)^2 = \text{Rs. } 82.60 = \text{Rs. } 83$

Thus, if the person receives Rs. 100 at the end of one year, in that case the real worth of that Rs. 100 is Rs. 91 after one year and the value will further decline to Rs. 83 at the end of two years.

**Importance:**

- The concept of time value of money is important in the sense that it focuses on consideration of cost and revenue decisions in consonance with the time period involved. This helps in analyzing the real worth of investment decisions that are related to future time periods.
- It helps in analyzing the cost and revenue concepts related to different investment proposals.

### 2.8.3 Marginalism

In common parlance, the concepts of marginalism and incrementalism are used synonymously. However, in economic literature, there is a difference between these concepts. Marginalism refers to one of the fundamental concepts of business economics which aim at analyzing the impact of change in units of independent variable from '*n*' to '*n* + 1' on dependent variable.

***For example:*** There are 100 farmers that are engaged in production of wheat. They are collectively able to produce 1000 quintals of wheat. Now, an additional farmer is employed to cultivate wheat which results to rise in production to 1007 quintals of wheat. Now, on account of additional farmer, there is rise in production from 1000 quintals to 1007 quintals. It means that the additional worker (independent variable) leads to addition in output of wheat (dependent variable). Thus, under marginalism, the impact of an additional variable on dependent variable is studied.

### 2.8.4 Incrementalism

In incrementalism, the impact of changes in independent variable on independent variable on dependent variable is analyzed in wholesomeness. Thus, the analysis is not confined to change of $n$ to $n + 1$, rather it takes the form of change from $n$ to $n + z$ where, $z$ is a positive number and is greater than one.

***For example:*** Let's again suppose that there are 100 farmers engaged in production of wheat and the production is 1000 quintals of wheat initially. Now, 10 additional farmers are employed that are able to collectively cultivate 1100 quintals of wheat. It can be noted here that in incrementalism, chunk of farmers cultivated and produced as a result of which the output increased from 1000 quintals to 1100 quintals. The concept of incrementalism explains that the addition of 10 workers (independent variable) increased the output from 1000 to 1100 quintals (dependent variable). Such an analysis comes under the ambit of incrementalism.

The term incremental also means additional. However, this concept studies the additions in terms of chunk or wholesome change rather than the unit changes (i.e. '$n$' to '$n + 1$' unit change). In the wake of management decision problems which are strategic in nature and economic environment which is dynamic, the incremental concept is gaining popularity. This is on account of the fact that the study of per unit changes becomes difficult on day-to-day basis. Thus, the additional changes are studied but in their wholesomeness.

***For example:*** Continuing the same example of 100 factory workers who were able to produce 300 chairs. Now, twenty more workers join and there is increase in the production of chairs from 300 chairs to 320 chairs. Thus, this change in dependent variable (production of chairs) was on account of these twenty additional workers (independent variables) who produced 20 additional units of chairs. This additional production of 20 chairs on account of contribution of these additional twenty workers explains the concept of incrementalism. It is to be noted here that more than one independent variable (twenty additional workers) were analyzed, unlike marginal analysis where only one additional worker was considered.

## Summary

- ✓ Business economics is an application based branch of economics that deals with real business practices.
- ✓ Business economics is a branch of study that bridges the gap between abstract economic theory and real business practice to facilitate business decision-making process.
- ✓ Business economics makes use of various concepts like demand forecasting, advertisement elasticity, cross-elasticity, etc., to undertake careful examination of business situations.

- ✓ Business economics is the blend of both microeconomics and macroeconomic principles. While microeconomics is concerned with the study of individual units, macroeconomics is concerned with the study of economy as a whole.
- ✓ Business economics studies both positive (descriptive) and normative (perspective) aspects of economics. It studies both the time periods, namely, short run and long run.
- ✓ The scope of business economics includes the study of demand analysis, demand forecasting, theory of consumer's equilibrium, cost analysis, production analysis and price determination and forecasting. The scope of business economics, of course, is much vast and is still expanding with the expansion of business activities.
- ✓ Every business involves certain complex and vital issues like estimation of demand of the product, factors affecting demand, decision relating to allocation of income of consumer on purchase of products, intensity of advertisement, etc. Business economics is a step in the direction of addressing these issues.
- ✓ In order to provide better solutions, business economics uses the decision sciences such as mathematics, statistics, accountancy, research methodology, psychology, etc. In this direction, certain fundamental concepts of business economics like opportunity costs, time value of money, marginalism and incrementalism have been discussed. The studies of these concepts facilitate the consolidated analysis and healthier interpretations of economic models.

## Review Questions

1. "Business economics integrates economic theory, business theory and business practice to facilitate business decision-making and forward planning by business firms". Explain.
2. Explain the relationship between business economics and traditional theory of economics.
3. Managerial economics is essentially the application of microeconomic theory of business decision making. Discuss the statement.
4. Discuss the nature and scope of business economics. Is it positive or normative economics?
5. 'Business economics uses economic models to analyze the business situations'. Elucidate.
6. 'Business economics bridges the gap between abstract theory and business practice. It uses tools of economic analysis to classify and evaluate problems'. Explain.
7. Elucidate the contribution of business economics in business decision-making.
8. Write a detailed note on the basic economic concepts used in managerial economics.

9. 'Business economics is prescriptive rather than descriptive in nature'. Comment.
10. What are the complexities involved in business decision-making process. Explain the role of business economist in solving those complexities.
11. What are the key questions that confront a business economist? What role does business economics play in solving those questions?
12. What is the subject matter of the study of business economics. What role does decision sciences play in facilitating decision-making process in the present scenario.
13. How is business economics related to other disciplines? What role the other disciplines play in taking effective decisions?
14. Discuss the importance of marginalism and incrementalism in decision-making.
15. What are the areas of difference between economics and business economics?
16. What is meant by decision sciences? Elucidate the areas of common concern that are studied under both decision sciences and business economics.
17. Write a detailed note on the fundamental economic concepts in managerial economics.
18. Are there any differences between marginal and incremental concepts? If yes, what are they?
19. What is time value of money? Why it is calculated? Explain the concept with the help of an example.
20. Write short notes on the following:
    (a) Managerial economics
    (b) Decision sciences
    (c) Opportunity cost
    (d) Time value of money
    (e) Marginalism
    (f) Incrementalism

## CASE STUDY: J.K. ELECTRONICS LTD. (MARCH, 2017)

In the wake of rise in commercial and residential demand for air conditioners around the world, the manufacturers are increasingly making an effort to make the product approachable and affordable to the customers. On one hand, the demand for residential air conditioners has increased multifold with the emergence of 'central air system'. This mechanism ensures both heating and cooling attributes. On the other hand, the commercial air conditioners are demanded feature of almost every new construction. As a result, a commodity which was considered a luxury is now seemingly a necessity. Thus, the sellers around the world are making efforts in order to increase their product efficiency by working on the components and technology. They are doing so in order to position their product in the minds of consumers and to make them product loyal. Keeping this in mind, many companies ventured into the provision of air conditioning units and systems. J.K. Electronics Ltd was one such company that ventured into the business of manufacturing the air conditioners from March 5, 2017.

The company received its first order of production of air conditioners on July 8, 2017. The order was to produce 1000 units in 3 months. The order was a major benchmark for the company as it was their first order. Mr. Ravi Kumar who was the managing director of the company, instructed the production manager regarding the timely execution of the order. The production manager started working immediately and called the meeting with the workers. After completion of meeting, he considered the attendance record and reported Mr. Ravi that "at present the company required 100 workers who were supposed to execute the order of 1000 units of air conditioners". At the time, the company had 89 workers and total production of the company stood at 890 units. The next week, the company employed one more worker and as a result, there was an addition of 20 units in current production process. In the wake of the urgent need to execute the order on time, the production manager estimated that if he employs 10 additional workers then the level of output would consolidate to 1000 units and the order would be completed on time.

## Questions

1. Analyze the above case in the context of fundamental concepts of marginalism and incrementalism.
2. Elaborate the case in terms of study of dependent and independent variables.
3. Which one of the two concepts is flexible in its approach: Marginalism and incrementalism? Give reasons in support of your answer.

3 CHAPTER

# Market Equilibrium, Risk and Profit Analysis

**LEARNING OBJECTIVES**

By the end of this chapter, reader should be able to understand:

- ✓ The meaning and concepts of market, market forces, market equilibrium and their determination.
- ✓ The concept, measurement and types of risk.
- ✓ The distinction between risk and uncertainty.
- ✓ The meaning of return and trade-off between risk and return.
- ✓ Meaning and concept of profit.
- ✓ The fundamental approaches of profit maximization.

## 3.1 INTRODUCTION

In economic analysis, the concept of equilibrium assumes a major role. It defines those areas where both the components of market, viz., producer and consumer are in a state of balance and have no tendency to alter their performance in the market system. Thus, market is a structure that is defined by the working performance and behaviour of its two elements, viz., consumer and the producer. They relate to demand and supply sides of market, respectively. Their interplay and performance determines the overall framework of the market. Thus, study of market and the corresponding analysis of its players assume a major role in economic analysis. In this direction, the present chapter discusses the concepts of market, market forces and determination of equilibrium with the help of market forces.

The chapter further proceeds with the discussion on risk analysis. The discussion on risk analysis is imperative as it helps the managerial economist in making strategic decisions. In strategic decision-making the firm is required to make decisions when it has imperfect knowledge of market conditions in the long run. The imperfections relate to the changes in economic conditions, government regulations, amendments in laws, changes in consumer's taste and preferences, changes in competitor's strategy, etc. In such cases, a rational firm needs to evaluate the economic environment. For evaluating the economic environment, reference to the concepts of risk and uncertainty are vital. Thus, in the present chapter, risk analysis has been discussed in terms of the concept, measurement and types of risk. In addition, the allied concepts like risk vs uncertainty and the risk-return trade-off have been explained.

The study and examination of profit and its analysis occupies an important role in economic decision-making. Profit is heart and soul of business operations. The business activities are oriented towards profit maximization. Thus, the study of profit analysis is requisite and necessary. Thus, the latter half of the chapter moves with the explanations pertaining to profit analysis. In profit analysis, the conceptual analysis of the profit has been done in terms of concept of profit, types and approaches of profit maximization.

## 3.2 CONCEPT OF MARKET AND MARKET FORCES

### Market

In common parlance, market refers to a place where buyers and sellers of a particular product or service interact with each other. The purpose of such an interaction is to execute a transaction for a value. The transaction is executed when both buyers and sellers are at equilibrium. In conventional markets, the market refers to the place of interaction of buyers and sellers. Both of them meet, discuss and bargain to make purchase and sale operational. However, with the advancement of e-commerce and m-commerce, the markets are no longer confined to a particular place and face-to-face interaction of both parties is also no longer a requisite to compose a market structure. However, it covers the entire range where both buyers and sellers are located. Thus, the overall framework of online orders, digital payment system and online shopping also characterize markets in contemporary era.

### The Major Players in Market

The major players behind the market forces are:

**The buyers** represent the demand side of the market. These forces are interested in executing purchase of a particular product.

**The sellers** represent the supply side of the market. These forces are interested in executing sale of a particular product.

### Market Forces

These are the forces or the powers that lead to functioning of free market mechanism. An interplay of these forces leads to determination of market equilibrium. It is the equilibrium analysis that further clarifies the price to be charged and quantity to be bought or sold at that price.

The market forces are:

1. **Forces of Demand:** Quantity demanded of the commodity that the buyers are willing and able to purchase at a price during a period of time.
2. **Forces of Supply:** Quantity supplied of the commodity that sellers are willing and able to sell at a price during a period of time.

This composition of market forces is shown in Fig. 3.1.

**Fig 3.1** Composition of Market Forces

## 3.3 THE CONCEPT OF MARKET EQUILIBRIUM

### Market Equilibrium

Equilibrium refers to the state of rest or balance. Market equilibrium refers to the state of balance between the two market forces, viz., market demand and market supply. This state of balance is ascertained at the point of intersection of market demand and market supply curve.

### Fundamental Concepts of Market Equilibrium

In order to understand market equilibrium, study of certain fundamental concepts is required. These are the concepts that facilitate the study of equilibrium analysis. These are:

1. **Equilibrium point** refers to the point of intersection or equality of market demand and market supply curve. It means the point where both buyers and sellers have come to a consent regarding the level of price and level of output.
2. **Equilibrium price** refers to the price that will be charged in the market. It is ascertained on *Y*-axis (vertical axis) and corresponds to equilibrium point.
3. **Equilibrium quantity** refers to the quantity that will be sold in the market. The quantity is ascertained on *X*-axis (horizontal axis) and corresponds to equilibrium point.

## 3.4 DETERMINATION OF EQUILIBRIUM

Figure 3.2 shows the determination of equilibrium with the help of following attributes:

- *DD* and *SS* are the demand and supply curves reflecting the consumer's side and the supplier's side respectively.
- Both the demand and supply curves intersect at *E* where demand and supply curves become equal. This has been reflected at point *E* in the diagram below where, $D = S$.
- Corresponding to point *E* on price axis (*Y*-axis), we get *OP* which is the equilibrium price.
- Vertically down towards the *X*-axis, *OQ* is determined which represents equilibrium quantity.
- The price level where demand and supply are not equal (price above or below *OP*) represents points of disequilibrium.
- At any price above *OP*, supply exceeds demand. The quantity level where quantity supplied of a product exceeds the quantity demanded is known as excess supply. This level exists above the equilibrium price (*OP*). In this case, since supply of product is more and consumers are demanding less of the product, the prices come down. This is due to the fact that availability of more products for supply as compared to the demand prompts the firms to reduce the price so that consumers are motivated to purchase more. As a result of reduction in the price level, the incentive to produce would decline and the incentive for consumers to buy would increase. Hence, the market would move back to its equilibrium.
- At any price below *OP*, demand exceeds supply. The quantity level where quantity demanded of a product exceeds the quantity supplied is known as excess demand. This level exists below the equilibrium price (OP). In this case, at low price the inducement to sell, seller's part reduces whereas, the inducement to purchase the product on buyer's part rises. But the product is scarce as compared to its demand. High demand with less supply drives the prices up, eventually equilibrium level is restored.

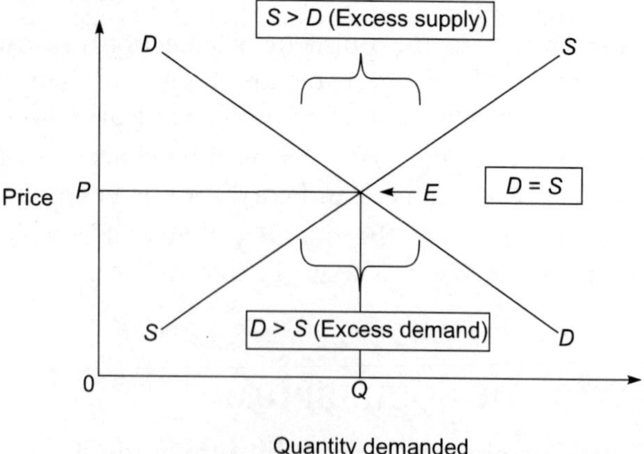


**Fig. 3.2** Determination of Equilibrium

## 3.5 CONCEPT OF RISK AND ITS MEASUREMENT

Every business involves investments at initial and later stages of business operation. These investments need to be analyzed carefully because any wrong investment made may adversely affect the functioning of the business. Thus, risk analysis occupies an important pace in business decision-making.

### Risk

Risk refers to the phenomena which reflect the occurrence of more than one outcome for a decision and the probability of its occurrence can be predicted. There are two main features of risk:

(a) Existence of more than one outcome

(b) The probability of occurrence of the event is known

For instance, if an investor is required to purchase 10,000 equity shares of XYZ company, then he is fully aware that the investment may or may not be profitable. He knows that three outcomes are involved in this investment, viz., probability of earning profits, losses or just breakeven. Thus, there is an element of risk involved in such an investment. In addition, there is surety that event will surely happen.

In economics, on the basis of risk, there are three types of investors. These are shown in Fig. 3.3.

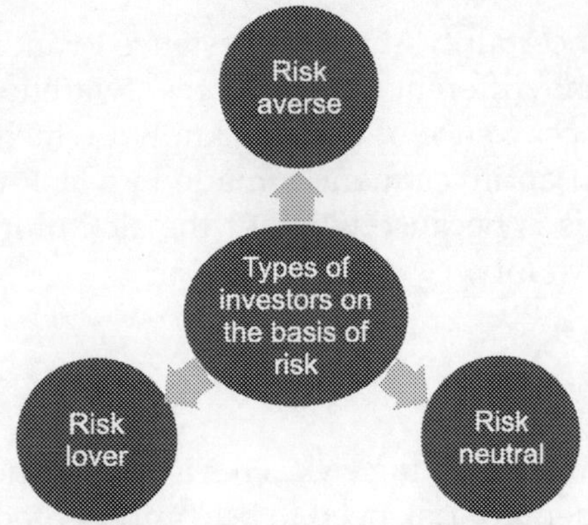


**Fig. 3.3** Types of Investors on the Basis of Risk

1. **Risk Averse:** An investor is said to be risk averse when he likes to avoid risk in any investment proposal. He is most inclined to invest in an investment proposal that fetches him fixed returns with surety of outcome.
2. **Risk Neutral:** An investor is said to be risk neutral when he is inclined to make mixed investments. He invests in risky as well as those options where investments are safe. He follows the middle path between risk taking and risk avoiding behaviour.

3. **Risk Lover:** An investor is said to be risk lover when he prefers investing in the investment proposals with higher returns. According to him, higher risk is a key to higher return. Thus, he is inclined towards the investments proposals with greater risk as they will fetch him more returns.

The risk can be measured by calculating standard deviation. Higher the standard deviation, higher would be the degree of risk and vice versa.

## 3.6 TYPES OF RISK

Risk is broadly classified under two categories:

1. **Diversifiable risk or unsystematic risk** is associated with the specific investment proposal or a number of investment proposals. It can be removed by investing in many projects.

2. **Non-diversifiable risk or systematic risk** cannot be removed through diversification or investing in many projects. It is associated with market returns and is related to macroeconomic factors such as war, recession, inflation, etc.

## 3.7 RISK VS UNCERTAINTY

In case of both risk and uncertainty, there is existence of more than one occurrence or many occurrences but the difference arises in the awareness of outcomes. In case of risk, the probability of occurrence of event is known which is unknown in case of uncertainty. For instance, if an investment is made in a sick unit that needs revival, it involves uncertainty. This is because whether the sick unit will be revived or not cannot be asserted with certainty.

## 3.8 CONCEPT OF RETURN

Return represents the reward for taking risk. This is due to the fact that the investors who are assuming supplementary risk need to be compensated. Thus, there is a trade-off between risk and return. This trade-off signifies that as the investor increases his readiness to take risk, there is a parallel rise in the probability of getting more return. It does not make sure or guarantee that the actual returns will be high. In addition, higher potential losses also can be one of the consequences of taking risk.

## 3.9 RISK AND RETURN: THE RISK-RETURN TRADE-OFF

Risk and return are two interrelated concepts. Return represents the reward for taking risk. Figure 3.4 represents the relationship between risk and return:

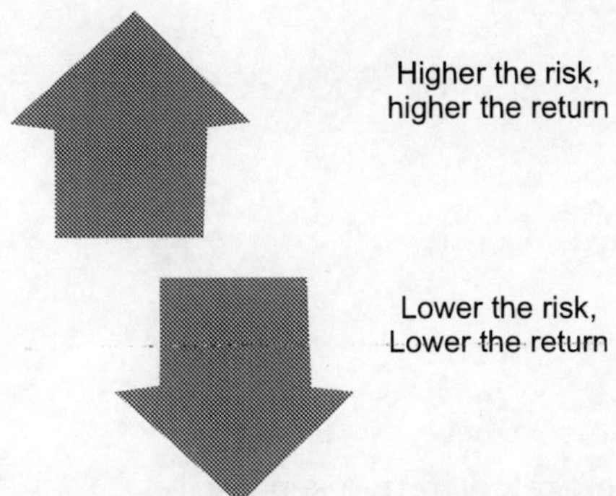


**Fig 3.4** Relationship between Risk and Return

This has been shown diagrammatically with the help of Fig. 3.5.

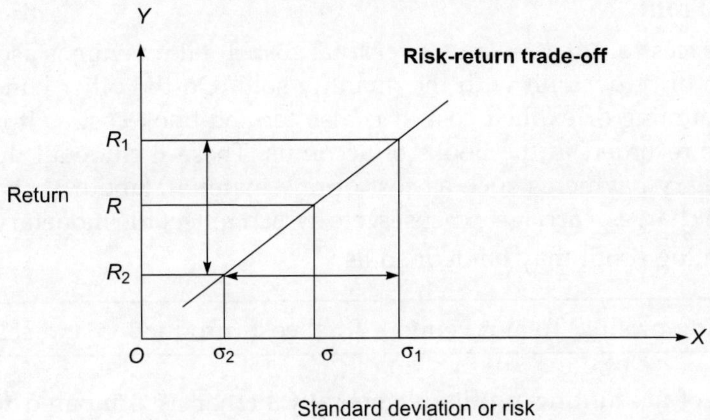


**Fig. 3.5** The Risk-Return Trade-off

The above diagram has following attributes:

- When the risk at $O\sigma$, then the returns are reflected by $OR$.
- At reduced risk $O\sigma_2$, the returns are reflected by $OR_2$.
- At higher risk $O\sigma_1$, the returns are reflected by $OR_1$.

The above relationship clarifies that risk and return are directly related with each other.

## 3.10 MEANING AND CONCEPT OF PROFIT

### Meaning of Profit

Profit is one of the most important business objectives. It is a measuring rod of the efficiency of business operations. It refers to the excess of revenue over the cost. The revenue here represents the receipts from sale of a commodity. The cost, on the other hand reflects the amount incurred in order to produce and sell the product.

Symbolically,

$$\Pi = TR - TC$$

where,

Π (pie) denotes total profits
*TR* means total revenue
*TC* means total cost

## The Concepts of Profit

The concept of profit is interpreted in two senses:

1. Accounting profit
2. Economic profit

### 1. Accounting Profit

It refers to the excess of total revenue over total cost. Total revenue is ascertained by multiplying the price per unit with the quantity sold. On the other hand, total cost reflects the accounting or explicit cost. It is also termed book cost as it includes the cost that can be recorded in the books of accounts. These include all the costs that represent monetary payments such as cost of raw material, labour cost, advertising expenses, octroi charges, carriage expenses, etc. which reflect the monetary payments.

Thus, accounting profit may be defined as:

| Accounting profit = Total revenue – Total cost (production and selling) |
|---|

The amount of accounting profits is generally higher as compared to economic profits as they consider only explicit cost and do not take into consideration implicit costs as a deduction from total revenue.

### 2. Economic Profit or Pure Profit

Economic profit refers to the excess of total revenue over the economic cost. The economic cost is the submission of explicit costs and imputed costs or implicit cost. It can be represented as:

Economic profit = Total revenue – Total economic cost

or

Economic profit = Total revenue – (Explicit costs + Imputed costs)

or

Economic profit = Total revenue – Explicit costs – Imputed costs ...(1)

but

Accounting profit = Total revenue – Explicit costs ...(2)

Substituting the value of accounting profit from equation (2) in equation (1), economic profit can be calculated as

Economic profit = Accounting profit – Imputed costs

In economics, the concept of economic profit assumes more importance as it takes into account not only the explicit or money cost but also considers imputed cost of business operations.

## 3.11 APPROACHES OF PROFIT MAXIMIZATION

The two approaches of profit maximization are as follows:

(a) *TR* and *TC* approach

(b) *MR* and *MC* approach

**(a) *TR* and *TC* approach** emphasizes the calculation of profits by considering the total revenue and cost involved in producing a particular level of output. Total revenue refers to the revenue receipts from sales of a commodity. Total cost refers to the submission of variable cost and fixed cost.

The profit therefore is defined as follows:

$$\text{Profit} = TR - TC$$

where, $TR = f(Q)$

$TC = f(Q)$

$TR$ = Total Revenue = Unit price ($P$) × Quantity ($Q$) = $PQ$

$TC$ = Total Cost = Variable Cost ($VC$) + Fixed Cost ($FC$)

**(b) *MR* and *MC* approach** considers the marginal revenue and marginal cost curves for specifying profit maximizing conditions. The marginal revenue means the revenue that is generated by producing an additional unit of output, whereas marginal cost refers to the cost involved in producing an additional unit of output. The profit maximizing conditions, using *MR-MC* approach are as follows:

(i) Necessary condition or the first-order condition

(ii) Sufficient condition or the second-order condition

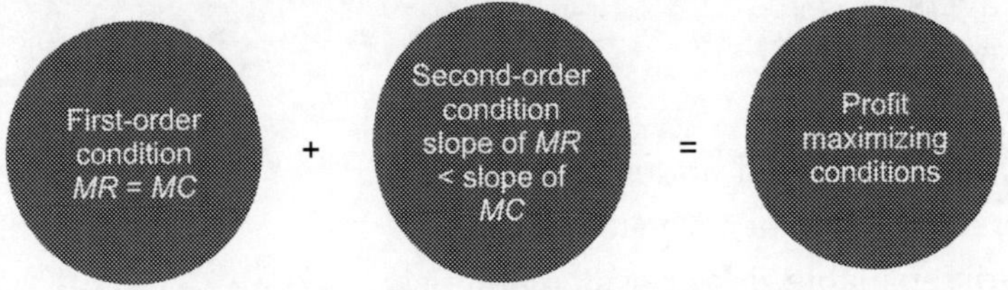


**Fig. 3.6** Profit Maximizing Conditions

Figure 3.6 specifies the profit maximizing conditions under the following heads:

**(i) The first-order condition (*or necessary*) condition**

This condition requires that at maximum profit, marginal revenue (MR) must be equal to marginal cost (*MC*). By definition, 'marginal revenue' means the additional revenue obtained from the production and sale of one additional unit of output, while 'marginal cost' refers to the additional cost incurred as a result of production of the one additional unit of output.

Thus, where $MR = MC$, profits would be maximum subject to qualification of second order condition.

**(ii) The second-order condition (*or sufficient) condition***

This condition requires the fulfilment of first order condition when *MR* is falling and *MC* is rising. It means that *MC* should cut *MR* curve from below. It can be written as

Slope of $MR$ < Slope of $MC$

It means that *MC* must have a steeper slope than *MR*.

Thus, the *MR* – *MC* approach specifies the fulfilment of both the first and second order conditions in order to maximize profits.

## Summary

- ✓ Market refers to the entire range where both buyers and sellers are located.
- ✓ These are the forces or the powers that lead to functioning of free market mechanism.
- ✓ Equilibrium refers to the state of rest or balance. Market equilibrium refers to the state of balance between the two market forces, viz., market demand and market supply.
- ✓ Risk refers to phenomena which reflect the occurrence of more than one outcome for a decision and the probability of its occurrence can be predicted.
- ✓ There are two main features of risk:
  - (a) Existence of more than one outcome
  - (b) The probability of occurrence of event is known
- ✓ There are three types of investors:
  - (a) Risk averse
  - (b) Risk neutral
  - (c) Risk lover
- ✓ Risk is broadly classified under two categories:
  - (a) Diversifiable risk or unsystematic risk
  - (b) Non-diversifiable risk or systematic risk:
- ✓ In case of both risk and uncertainty, there is more than one occurrence or many occurrences but the difference arises in awareness of the outcomes.
- ✓ The risk-return trade-off refers to the excess of revenue over the cost. The revenue here represents the receipts from sale of a commodity. The cost, on the other hand reflects the amount incurred in order to produce and sell the product.

- ✓ The concept of profit is interpreted in two senses:
  - (a) Accounting profit
  - (b) Economic profit
- ✓ The two approaches of profit maximization are:
  - (a) *TR* and *TC* approach
  - (b) *MR* and *MC* approach
- ✓ *TR-TC* approach emphasizes the calculation of profits by considering the total revenue and cost involved in producing a particular level of output.
- ✓ *MR-MC* approach considers the marginal revenue and marginal cost curves for specifying profit maximizing conditions.

## Review Questions

1. What is risk? Explain the concept of risk-return trade-off. What are the types of investors in case of risk?
2. What are the basic parameters that explain whether an investor is a risk lover or risk seeker?
3. Explain the determination of market equilibrium using the demand and supply analysis.
4. Define the following concepts:
   - (a) Equilibrium point
   - (b) Equilibrium price
   - (c) Equilibrium quantity
5. Define risk. What are the types of risk? How is risk different from uncertainty?
6. Distinguish between:
   - (a) Accounting profit and economic profit
   - (b) Risk and uncertainty.
7. Why do profits arise? Explain in context of approaches to profit maximization.
8. Explain the concept of profit maximization with the help of *TR-TC* and *MR-MC* approaches.

## CASE STUDY: KIDS REFLECTION (2017-18)

Kids Reflection is one of the retailing outlets in New Delhi that provides the kids' wear and accessories at an affordable price. The company believes in following a unique style statement and follows stringent quality standards in making the product available to the buyers. It extensively deals with kids fashion and sells assortments such as Jeans, T-shirts, formal shirts, casual shirts, pants, trousers, ethnic wear, night wears, and many more. The following figures give the reflections of supply and demand data pertaining to the company for FY 2017-18:

| Price (In Rs.) | Quantity Demanded ($Q_d$) | Quantity Supplied ($Q_s$) |
|---|---|---|
| 4.40 | 220 | 220 |
| 4.30 | 240 | 200 |
| 4.20 | 260 | 180 |
| 4.10 | 280 | 160 |
| 4.00 | 300 | 120 |

## Questions

1. What is the original equilibrium price and equilibrium quantity in the above case?
2. Suppose, the manufacturing cost declines which results in increase in supply at each price by 20 per cent. What would be the new equilibrium price and quantity?
3. Calculate the price elasticity of demand when the price changes from Rs. 4.20 to Rs. 4.10. Interpret the result.
4. Calculate the price elasticity of supply when the price changes from Rs. 4.40 to Rs. 4.10. Interpret the result.

4 CHAPTER

# Demand Analysis

**LEARNING OBJECTIVES**

By the end of this chapter, reader should be able to understand:

- ✓ The concept of demand and the factors that influence the demand for a commodity.
- ✓ The mathematical expression of relationship between demand and its determinants.
- ✓ The prevalence of law of demand and the associated factors.
- ✓ The cases where the law of demand fails to operate.
- ✓ The change in demand vs change in quantity demanded.

## 4.1 INTRODUCTION

In this chapter, we begin our analysis by focusing on the dynamics related to the consumer demand. The synthesis or the analysis of demand is imperative as the success of every business depends on its ability to satisfy its customers. According to Peter Drucker (1954), "there is only one definition of business purpose: to create a customer". Thus, the motive behind the business activities is to ensure and enhance customer satisfaction level. The reference of the word customer points towards the 'demand' dimension of the market forces. The demand analysis is required in order to understand the quantum of quantity demanded, to analyze the factors that lead to generation of demand and to predict the future demand. This chapter discusses the segments of market forces, that is, demand analysis. In the forthcoming chapter, the supply analysis and elasticity of supply have been discussed.

## 4.2 THE CONCEPT OF DEMAND

The word demand in economics literature refers to the quantity of a commodity that a consumer is willing and able to purchase at a particular price during a period of time.

Demand not only relates to the ability and willingness to purchase but also includes the ability to part with the funds at the quoted or negotiated price.

Therefore, the integration of adequate purchasing power or resources, willingness to purchase and the readiness to spend money create a framework for demand. It may be represented in Fig. 4.1 in the following manner:

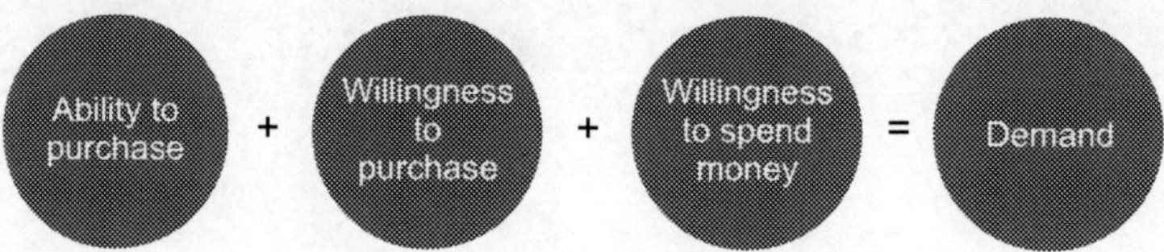


**Fig. 4.1** Composition of Demand

It is worth noting that if a person is willing as well as desirous of purchasing a commodity but is reluctant to spend his money, then it will not constitute demand.

***Example:*** A person wants to purchase a car. He has adequate funds and is also desirous to purchase the car but if he is reluctant to spend his money for the purchase of the car, it will not constitute demand. On the other hand, if the person is willing to spend money, it will be called demand.

In addition to the above, any statement related to demand for a commodity in which price or the time period is absent fails to define demand and is meaningless. For instance, a statement like 'demand for 50,000 air conditioners is of no use and is vague. Thus, if we say that a consumer is willing to purchase 2 litres of milk per day at a price of Rs. 41 per litre then 2 litres of milk will be called quantity demanded as it has all the three requisites of demand, namely, price, quantity and time. Hence, it is an economically relevant statement.

## Definitions of Demand

In the words of Miller, "Demand is the willingness and ability of consumers to purchase a commodity at a given price over a particular period of time".

According to Vera Anstey, "The demand for a particular good is the amount that will be purchased at a given price at a given time".

## Demand Schedule

Demand Schedule is a tabular representation of various combinations between price and quantity demanded (ceteris paribus). It reflects quantities of a commodity that will be demanded at various levels of price, during a given period of time.

Demand schedule is of two types:

1. Individual demand schedule
2. Market demand schedule

## Individual Demand

Individual demand schedule refers to a tabular representation of various quantities of a commodity corresponding to each price level that a consumer is willing to purchase during a given period of time. This has been shown in Table. 4.1.

**TABLE 4.1** Individual Demand Schedule

| Price (Rs.) | Quantity Demanded of Commodity X (units) |
|---|---|
| 1 | 30 |
| 2 | 25 |
| 3 | 20 |
| 4 | 15 |
| 5 | 10 |

## Market Demand

Market demand schedule refers to a tabular statement showing various quantities of a commodity that all the consumers are willing to purchase at various levels of price, during a given period of time. It can be obtained by "horizontally adding" the demand curves of the individual consumers at each and every level of price.

Market demand schedule is expressed as: $D_m = D_A + D_B + \ldots$

where, $D_m$ is the market supply and $D_A + D_B + \ldots$ are the individual demands of consumer *A*, consumer *B* and so on.

**TABLE 4.2** Market Demand Schedule

| | Individual Demand Units | | | Market Demand (units) |
|---|---|---|---|---|
| Price (Rs.) $P_x$ | $D_A$ | $D_B$ | $D_C$ | $(D_A + D_B + D_C)$ |
| 1 | 30 | 37 | 100 | 167 |
| 2 | 25 | 34 | 90 | 149 |
| 3 | 20 | 31 | 80 | 131 |
| 4 | 15 | 28 | 70 | 113 |
| 5 | 10 | 25 | 60 | 95 |

Table 4.2 reflects that market demand can be calculated by adding up the individual demand of consumer *A*, *B* and *C*. It can be clearly seen that market demand is 167 units at a price of Rs. 1 per unit. Further, the market demand is 149 units, 131 units and 113 units at a price of Rs. 2, 3, and 4 per unit, respectively. It clearly indicates that market demand is inversely related to the level of prices. The more the level of prices, the lesser each consumer is willing to purchase.

## Demand Curve

A demand curve is the diagrammatic representation of various combinations of price and quantity demanded. It exhibits the economic relationship between price and quantity demanded. It shows how much consumers are willing and able to consume at each price. However, the demand curve assumes that the effect of other factors will remain constant. The other factors include change in income of the consumer, price of related commodities, taste and preferences, season, etc.

The outcome is a relationship reflected in the form of a curve or line which shows various price-Qs pairs. That point shows the amount of the good that consumers would choose to purchase at that price.

## 4.3 DETERMINANTS OF DEMAND (FACTORS AFFECTING DEMAND)

The determinants of demand reflect the factors that cause emergence of demand for a commodity. These factors influence purchase decisions and generate the demand of the commodity. These factors have been bifurcated as price as the major factor and factors other than price as other factors. These other factors include income of the consumer, price of related commodity, taste and preferences, season, fashion, advertisement, population, consumer credit facility, etc. These determinants are shown in Fig. 4.2 as follows:

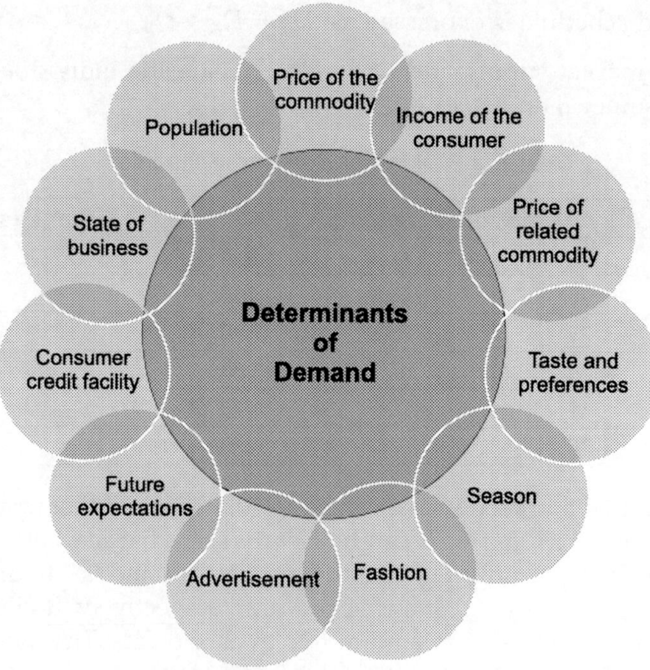


**Fig. 4.2** Determinants of Demand

1. **Price of the Commodity:** The price of the commodity in question is a major factor that influences the demand for a commodity in long run and the only factor in short run. There prevails an inverse relationship between price and quantity demanded. It means that at higher price, the consumers buy less of the commodity and more of the commodity is purchased at lower price, ceteris peribus.

   The Latin word 'ceteris peribus' means keeping the effect of variables except price as constant. These other variables include income of the consumers, prices of the related goods, consumer's taste and preference, season, fashion, number of consumers, etc.

   It may be written as:

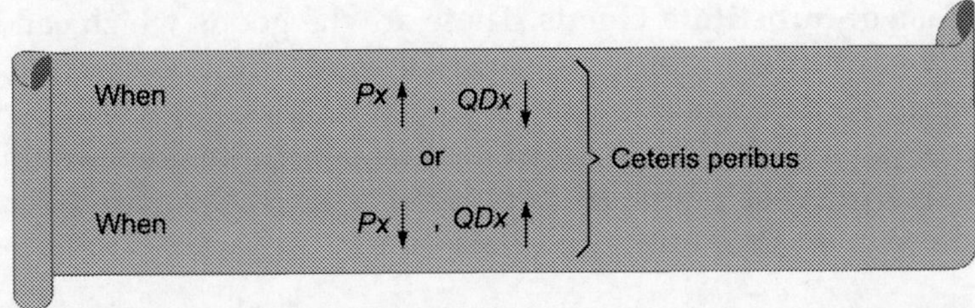


2. **Income of the Consumer:** The level and size of income of the consumers influences the demand for a commodity to a large extent. In common parlance, a direct relationship exists between income and demand for a commodity. However, this involves the study under the following heads:

   (a) **The Case of Normal Goods:** There prevails a direct relationship between income of the consumer and demand for normal goods. In other words, if the level of income of the consumer is high, he has more funds to be spent on purchase of various commodities, hence the demand will be more and vice versa. It may be written as:

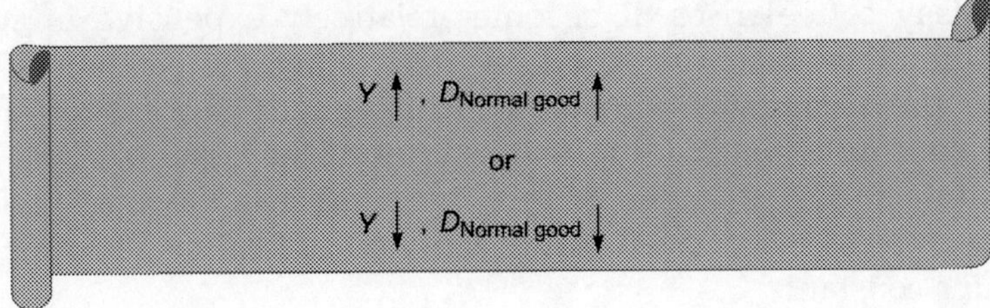


   (b) **The Case of Inferior Goods**: In case of inferior goods, an inverse relationship prevails between income of the consumer and demand for inferior goods. In other words, if the level of income of the consumer is high, he has more funds to be spent on purchase of various commodities, therefore he will be utilizing those funds for the purchase of a normal good, as a result of which the demand for inferior goods will decline and vice versa. It may be written as:

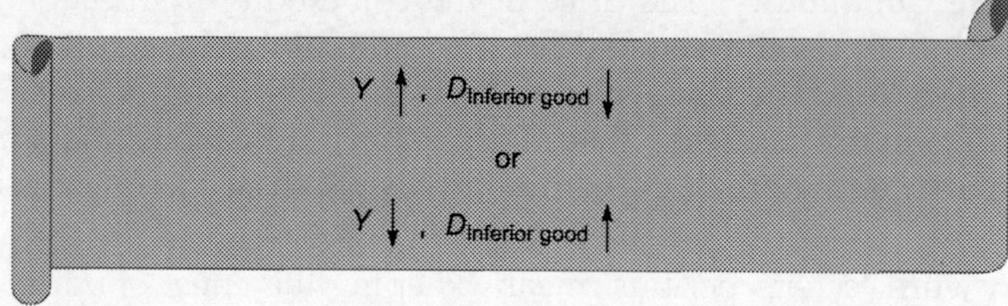


3. **Prices of Related Goods:** Another determinant that affects the demand for a commodity includes prices of related goods. The study of related goods is done under two heads:

   **(a) The Case of Substitute Goods:** These are the goods which can be used in place of each other in order to satisfy a want. In case of substitute goods, there exists a direct relationship between the price of one substitute good and the quantity or demand for the other substitute good. In other words, when the price of one substitute good rises, the demand for the other substitute good rises and vice versa.

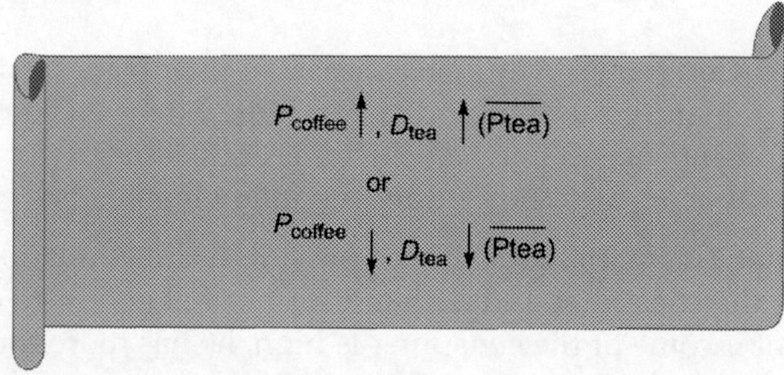


This is on account of the reason that when the price of one substitute good (say coffee) rises, it becomes relatively expensive in comparison with the other substitute good (say tea). Now, the customers who were earlier purchasing the commodity (coffee) start purchasing more of the other substitute commodity (tea) as a result the customer base of second substitute good (tea) expands. This expanded customer base pushes up the demand for the second substitute commodity (tea) even through its price remains constant.

More examples of substitute goods include:

| | | |
|---|---|---|
| Coca-cola and Pepsi | Car and public transport | Bananas and apples |
| Burger King and McDonald's burgers | Colgate and Sensodyne | Radio and gramophone. |

(b) **The Case of Complementary Goods:** These are the jointly demanded goods which are used together. In case of such interrelated goods, there is an inverse relationship between the price of one complementary good and the quantity or demand for the other complementary good. In other words, when the price of one complementary good increases, the demand for the other complementary good reduces and vice versa.

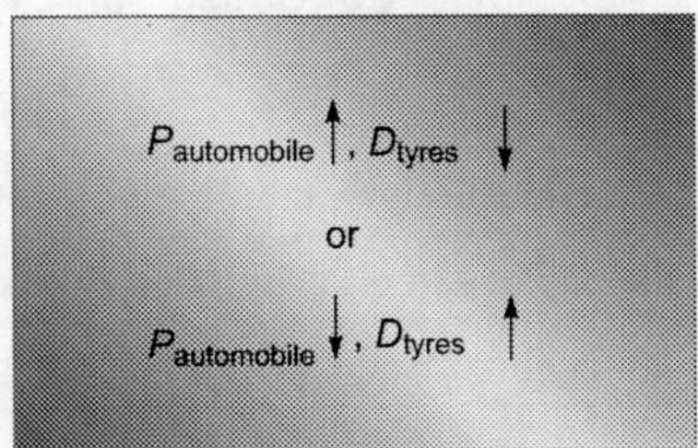


It is clearly evident that if price of automobile goes up, demand for tyres will decline. This is on account of decline in demand of automobile. Hence, the rise in price of automobile not only reduces its demand, but also the demand of jointly demanded product, i.e., tyres.

More examples of complementary goods have been mentioned in Table 4.3.

**TABLE 4.3** Examples of Complementary Goods

| | | |
|---|---|---|
| Automobile and fuel | Pen and ink | Ball pen and refill |
| Printer and cartridge | Cart and horse | Shoes and polish |
| Pencils and erasers | Torch and battery | Mobile phones and sim cards |

4. **Tastes and Preferences of the Buyer:** Consumer's taste and preference also play a vital role in determining demand for a commodity. The taste and preference to a large extent depend on the customs, values, beliefs, lifestyle, age, gender and habits of the people. Any change in taste and preference in favour of the commodity is likely to induce the demand for a commodity. However, a change in taste and preference against the commodity is likely to reduce the demand for that commodity. This has been reflected in Table 4.4.

**TABLE 4.4** Change in Taste and Preference

| Favour of commodity | Against the commodity |
|---|---|
| ↓ | ↓ |
| More demand | Reduced demand |

5. **Seasons Prevailing at the Time of Purchase:** Season and weather conditions also affect the demand for a commodity. If the seasonal changes and weather conditions are in favour of a commodity, then demand is likely to be high and vice versa. Table 4.5 reflects some demanded commodities pertaining to a particular season.

**TABLE 4.5** Impact of Season on Demand

| Season | Demanded Commodity |
|---|---|
| Summer | Air conditioners, coolers, fan, cold drinks |
| Winter | Coats, sweaters, pullovers, quilts, blankets |
| Rainy | Umbrella, raincoats |

6. **Fashion:** Fashion is another factor that determines the demand for a commodity as it acts as a basis for modification in terms of addition or reduction in the current consumption behaviour. If the customers presume that an article is an 'article of fashion', then the demand goes up for such articles.

   For example, a particular apparel worn by a leading actor or actress becomes an article of fashion as it is considered a 'mod' good which helps in creating favourable impression on others as a result the demand goes up for such an article.

7. **Advertisement and Sales Promotion:** Advertisement and sales promotion expenses are the expenses that are incurred in order to stimulate the demand of a product. The purpose of incurring such expenses is to create awareness among the consumers and positioning the product in the minds of the consumers.

   The advertisement and sales promotion expenses are directly related with demand for the product. This is on account of the reason that more the advertisement, more is the awareness, more is the likelihood of generation of demand, vice versa.

8. **Future Expectations**: Any expectation regarding the future prices is likely to influence the demand for a commodity. Any future expectation leading to rise in price of a particular commodity raises the demand of the commodity, although there was no reduction in current prices. In the same manner, if consumers anticipate the fall in price, as a result the consumers purchase less so that more units of the commodity can be purchased later at reduced prices.

9. **Consumer Credit Facility:** The size of credit facility available to the consumer by banks and financial institutions also affects the demand for a commodity. There prevails a direct relationship between size of credit facility and quantum of demand. The attributes of consumer credit facility is studied under the following heads:

Easy availability of credit: More is the demand for the commodity.
Greater size of credit: More is the demand for the commodity.
Difficulty in access to credit: Less is the demand for the commodity.
Smaller size of credit: Less is the demand for the commodity.

10. **State of Business:** The degree and extent of wellness of condition of business also influences the demand for a commodity. In case of economic boom, the demand is likely to be more while in case of an economy facing depression or recession, the demand is likely to be negatively affected.
11. **Population of the Country:** The population of a country reflects the number of mouths to be fed, which in turn, determines the mass consumption. Keeping the effect of other factors as constant, the larger the population, the larger the demand for a commodity and vice versa. Hence, with an expansion in population, the demand will be more as the increasing number of consumers demand more products. Therefore, the size of population also determines demand for a commodity.

## 4.4 DEMAND FUNCTION

The demand for a commodity depends on the factors that affect demand. These factors include price of the commodity, income of the consumer, price of related commodity, taste and preferences, season, fashion, etc. All these factors are known as independent variables. Since, with change in each variable, the value of demand changes, therefore demand is known as dependent variable. All these variables when framed in the form of a functional relationship with demand, then it leads to formation of demand function.

Thus, demand function refers to the statement of factors affecting demand in terms of mathematical symbols. Therefore, demand functions exhibit the functional relationship between demand (dependent variable) and factors affecting demand (independent variables). The functional relationship has been shown as:

$$D_x = f(P_x, Y, P_y, T, S, F, A, P, U)$$

In the above equation,

$D_x$ = Demanded for commodity $x$
$P_x$ = Price of the commodity $x$
$Y$ = Consumer's income
$P_y$ = Price of related good $y$
$T$ = Tastes and preferences of consumer
$S$ = Seasonal conditions
$F$ = Fashion
$A$ = Advertisement
$P$ = Population
$U$ = Any other factor affecting demand for a commodity such as state of business, consumer credit facility, etc.

## 4.5 THE LAW OF DEMAND

The law of demand exhibits the relationship between quantity demanded (dependent variable) and price of the commodity (independent variable). It is to be noted here that the demand for a commodity is a function of price variable and other variables except price. The variables other than price are income of the consumer, price of related commodity, taste and preferences, etc. When the effect of all these variables is held constant and only the relationship between price and quantity demanded is studied, it becomes the subject matter of law of demand.

It can be represented in the form of equation as:

$$D_x = \overset{\frown}{f(P_x}, \overline{Y}, \overline{P_R}, \overline{T}, \overline{S}, \overline{U})$$

where,

$D_x$ means price of the commodity $x$, $Y$ means income of the consumer

$P_R$ means price of related goods, $T$ means taste and preferences,

$U$ means other factors that affect demand for a product

### 4.5.1 Meaning of Law of Demand

The law of demand states that there is an *inverse relationship* between price and quantity demanded of a commodity. It means that when price of the commodity reduces, the quantity demanded rises and on the other side, if the price of the commodity rises, the quantity demanded falls, ceteris peribus. It can be represented as:

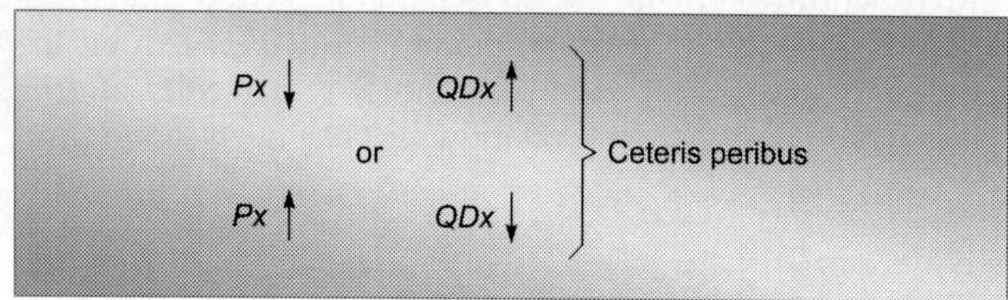


The law holds good under the condition of "ceteris peribus". The Latin words 'ceteris peribus' means that other things remain constant and do not influence demand during the study of the law. These "other things" include the determinants of demand other than price, viz., consumers' income, price of the substitutes and complements, taste and preferences of the consumer, etc.

This supposition of keeping the effect of other variables constant is only applicable in short run. In the long run, all these variables are subject to change. The law of demand, therefore, holds only in the short run.

### 4.5.2 Assumptions of the Law

The assumptions of the law relates to the supposition of other things remaining same. Thus, the assumptions of law are:

1. The income of the consumer remains same.
2. There is no change in the price of substitutes and complementary goods.
3. Taste and preferences do not change.
4. There is no change in weather condition.
5. No amount is spent on advertisement and sales promotional activity.
6. There is no change in the size of the population.

### 4.5.3 Operation of the Law

The operation of the law of demand can be explained with the help demand schedule and reflection of demand curve. Thus, the inverse relationship between price and quantity demanded can be explained with the help of the following:

**(a) Demand Schedule**

The demand schedule reflects the tabular representation of the relationship between price and quantity demanded. It shows the inverse relationship between these variables and gives information of various quantities demanded at its respective price. A hypothetical demand schedule is as follows:

**TABLE 4.6** Demand Schedule

| Price of Apple (Rs. per kg) | Quantity Demanded of Apples (kg) |
|---|---|
| 5 | 1 |
| 4 | 2 |
| 3 | 3 |
| 2 | 4 |
| 1 | 5 |

The above table shows that the consumer demands more of a commodity at lower price. It is clear that when the price of the apple was Rs. 5 per kg, he demands only one apple but at low price Rs. 4 per kg, the consumer demanded 2 apples and so on.

**(b) Demand Curve**

Demand curve shows the diagrammatic representation of the relationship between price and quantity demanded. The demand schedule plotted graphically is known as demand curve. In a graph, price of a product is represented on $y$-axis and quantity demanded is represented on $x$-axis.

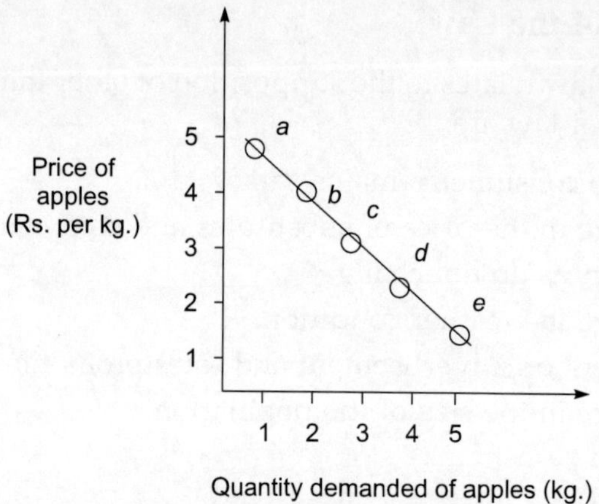


**Fig. 4.3** Demand Curve

Corresponding to the demand schedule, the quantity demanded of apples has been taken on *x*-axis, whereas price in terms of Rs. per kg. has been taken on the *y*-axis.

The consumer purchases one apple when the price is Rs. 5 per kg, which is reflected by combination "*a*". At a lower price of Rs. 4 per kg, the consumer purchases more (two) units of apples shown by combination "*b*". Thereafter, the subsequent quantities are purchased at lower price as reflected by combination "*c*" and combination "*d*". Thus, finally consumer purchases 5 apples when the price reduces to Rs. 1 per kg., reflected by combination "*e*". Thus, joining combination "*a*", "*b*", "*c*", "*d*" and "*e*", we get demand curve. It is to be noted here that the demand curve is downward sloping from left to right.

### 4.5.4 Reasons of Operation of Law of Demand (Why Demand Curve Slopes Downward from Left to Right)

The demand curve slopes left downward to right establishing an inverse price demand relationship. It means, when quantity demanded increases with a fall in price and reduces with a rise in price. The factors contribute to the inverse relationship between quantity demanded and price has been explained as under.

**1. Law of Diminishing Marginal Utility (DMU)**

The law of DMU is one of the basis of operation of law of demand. The law states that as a consumer goes on consuming more and more units of the commodity, the additional satisfaction derived from the consumption of an additional unit of the commodity goes on declining. Thus, the additional consumption of the commodity reduces the level of satisfaction of the consumer, and then he is ready to buy more units of the commodity only at lower price. Thus, the law of DMU gives the justification of operation of the law of demand.

This law can be explained by a simple example. Suppose, a student after completing college reaches home. The student is hungry. His mother serves him *paranthas*. The first *parantha* gives him immense pleasure and has great utility for him. Then the student consumes the second *parantha*, the utility derived this time will be less than that of the first one. It is on account of the fact that now his hunger has been satisfied by the first parantha to some extent. If he further consumes third *parantha* then utility of this *parantha* will be even lesser than that of second and so on. If this student would be further forced to eat more, it leads to disutility causing total utility to decline. A point will come when the consumer will say "no more of this commodity". This is the point where the utility with the consumption of every successive unit till it drops down to zero. This is the "point of satiety". At that point, the marginal utility will become negative. Therefore, the additional units of the commodity would be consumed at lower price.

### 2. Substitution Effect

Another major factor leading to operation of law of demand is the substitution effect. It refers to the phenomenon associated with the price of related goods. It means that the consumer prefers comparatively less expensive goods than the expensive ones. In other words, it refers to the substitution of one commodity by the consumer, when the price of another commodity rises. It is said to occur when the price of one commodity rises, then the demand for its rival commodity rises, even though the prices of the rival commodity remain same. Thus, the substitution effect is of two types:

- Positive/favourable substitution effect: rise in demand due to fall in price
- Negative/unfavourable substitution effect: fall in demand due to rise in price

Both the above cases lead to operation of law of demand.

For instance, tea and coffee are the substitute goods. If the price of tea goes down, the consumers may substitute tea for coffee, although price of coffee remains the same. This is on account of the reason that the consumers always prefer relatively cheaper goods than the expensive ones. Thus, on account of favourable substitution effect the consumers tend to purchase more of tea. The reverse case will be there if the price of tea goes up. It may be written as:

$P_{tea}\uparrow, Q_{tea}\downarrow; D_{coffee}\uparrow$

(Even though $P_{coffee}$ remaining same) and vice versa

### 3. Income Effect

Income effect is another factor responsible for downward sloping shape demand curve. In this case the main point which requires attention is that here the real income is being considered and not the nominal income. The real income of a consumer is measured in terms of goods and services purchased by the consumer. It is irrespective of rise or fall in consumer's nominal income.

Income effect refers to the phenomenon which is characterized by rise in the demand for a commodity on account of increase in real income of the consumer. As the real income of the consumer increases, the consumer can now purchase more of the commodity whose price has fallen. It can be explained with the help of Fig 4.4.

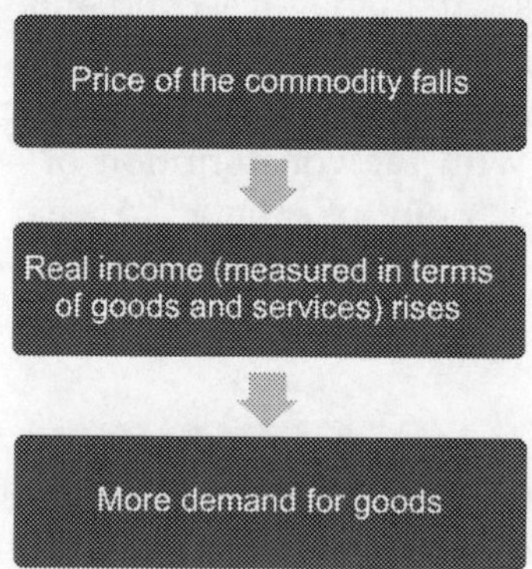


**Fig. 4.4** Income Effect

Table 4.7 illustrates the income effect with the help of an example.

**TABLE 4.7** Explanation of Income Effect

| Price of Apple (Per Kg.) | Income of Consumer (p.m.) | Quantity of Apple (kg.) |
|---|---|---|
| Rs. 100 | Rs. 20000 | 1 |
| Rs. 80 | Rs. 20000 | More than one kg. |

As the price of one kg apples fall from Rs 100 per kg to Rs. 80 per kg, the real income of the consumer goes up, even though the nominal income of the consumer remains same (Rs. 20000 p.m.). Real income is measured in terms of goods and services. It means that there is now rise in consumer's income by Rs. 20. In this case, the consumer can buy more than before or can buy some other commodity with his increased real income.

**4. Change in Number of Consumers /New Consumers**

When the price of commodity falls, the consumers who were not consuming that commodity start consuming it. As a result, this new customer base pushes up the demand for the commodity.

**5. Several Uses of a Commodity**

There are some commodities which can be put to more than one use which is also one of the reasons of downward sloping shape of the demand curve. When the price of such commodities rises, their use is restricted to most urgent purposes, as a result of which there is decline in demand which leads to inverse relationship between price and commodity demanded. On the other side, if there is decline in price of such commodities then such commodities can be put to more uses, leading to a rise in demand.

***For example:*** Electricity and milk are the commodities which can be put to more than one use. For instance, electricity can be used for cooking, heating, lighting, cooling and so on. Similarly, milk can be used for preparing curd, sweets, cheese, custard, tea, coffee, etc. At higher prices, these commodities may not be used by for all the purposes to which they can be put and their consumption may be restricted to most urgent purposes. But if the price of any of these commodities falls, people may expand the usage of the product to other uses also. Thus, the demand for the commodities with several uses rises at lower price and vice versa. It can be written in the form of Fig. 4.5.

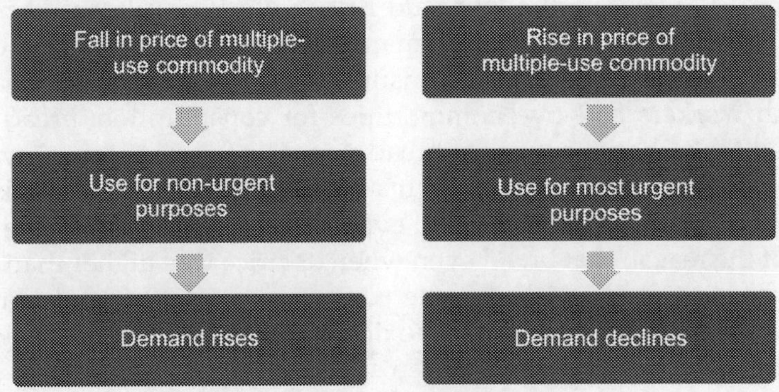


**Fig. 4.5** Several Uses of a Commodity

### 4.5.5 Exceptions to the Law of Demand

The law of demand establishes an inverse relationship between price and quantity demanded.

There are cases where the law of demand does not hold good. These are the cases where more will be demanded at a higher price and less at a lower price. Thus, there are exceptional cases which establish a direct relationship between price and quantity demanded. The exceptional cases where the law of demand fails to operate are as follows:

(i) **Conspicuous Goods:** This exception is associated with the doctrine propounded by Sir Thorsten Veblen. They are also known as Veblen goods and prestige goods. These are the articles of distinction which are purchased by the rich and affluent. Rich people associate their prestige with the price of the commodity. Higher the price of a product, higher is the prestige of the consumer. These goods are not considered affordable by common man and again demanded on account of their high price. These goods lose their ostentation when their price falls. The decline in their price is associated with the deterioration in quality and reduction in inherent value. Thus, the law of demand does not hold in case of Veblen goods.

*For example:* Diamonds, platinum jewellery, expensive cars, branded watches, precious stones, antique pieces, etc.

**(ii) Giffen Goods:** Another exception of low of demand is associated with the name of Sir Robert Giffen. These are the goods which are considered of low quality by the consumers but occupy a substantial place in consumer's budget. A rise in their prices may not lead rise in quantity demanded as the consumers to shift their demand for a superior commodity.

The concept of Giffen goods finds its origin in the doctrine of Giffen's paradox, which refers to a situation which should not be true but ultimately turns out to be true. This paradoxical situation relates back to 19th century when Sir Robert Giffen, a Scottish statistician and economist, observed that when the price of bread increased, the low paid British workers purchased more bread. This was contrary to the low of demand as when the prices of a commodity were rising; the consumers were consuming more of bread. He analyzed that the British workers had two commodities for consumption, bread and meat. He noticed that when the price of bread was rising, price of meat was rising at a tremendous rate as compared to bread. In that situation, the British workers had no option but to consume bread even when its price was rising. This is on account of the reason that bread even when its price was higher than before was still the cheapest food article, people consumed more of it and not less when its price went up. This led to a paradoxical situation of the direct price-demand relationship which is known as Giffen's Paradox.

Goods which exhibit direct price-demand relationship are called 'Giffen goods'. Examples of such goods are coarse grains like maize, bajra, low quality rice and wheat, etc.

**(iii) Future Expectations about Prices/Speculative Effect:** it refers to the future expectations regarding the price. If consumers observe a rising trend in price of a commodity, and expect further rise, they start buying larger quantities of the commodity, even though the price may not rise in future. Similarly, when the price of a commodity falls leading a further expectation of fall in price, the consumers may defer their current purchase with the view of purchasing when the price will actually fall.

An interesting observation in this case is that the law of demand is not invalidated in real sense as the relationship between price and quantity remains unaffected whereas the demand is affected on account of factors other than price i.e. future expectations regarding the prices which were earlier kept constant.

*For example:* A rise in price of onion may lead to further rise in demand. The consumers start presuming that the prices will rise further and purchase more of the commodity even though the price may remain same.

**(iv) Fear of Shortage:** Another factor leading to a direct relation between price and quantity demanded is the fear of shortage of the commodity in question. If the consumers fear the shortage of a particular commodity, it may lead to 'panic buying' leading to 'hoarding' and 'stockpiling'. As a result they may end up buying more of the commodity even at higher price. This is contrary to the law of demand. It may happen in case of anticipation of war, actual war situation, draught and famines, floods, riots, etc.

*For example:* The demand for goods like sugar, wheat, salt, kerosene may rise on event of an anticipated enemy attack and the consumers are ready to pay any price for the commodity.

**(v) Ignorance Effect:** It refers to a phenomenon which involves purchase of the commodity at enhanced price by the consumers. This is on account of the reason that the consumer may be ignorant of the prevailing price of the commodity and thus pays a higher price. In such a situation, the law will not be valid.

*For example:* Mr. X visits a local market in order to purchase cauliflower. He is ignorant of the price of product and pays the amount quoted by the vegetable seller which was even higher after the bargain. Thus, Mr. X ends up paying higher price on account of his ignorance. In such a situation, the law of demand will be invalidated as he may purchase more of the commodity at a higher price.

**(vi) Change in Other Factors:** The law of demand may also fail if there is any significant change in factors other than price. These factors include change in income of the consumer, price of the related commodities, weather conditions, fashion, etc. In such cases, the inverse relationship between demand and price may not hold good.

## 4.6 MOVEMENT ALONG DEMAND CURVE VS SHIFT IN DEMAND CURVE (CHANGE IN QUANTITY DEMANDED VS CHANGE IN DEMAND)

As explained above, demand for a commodity is a function of price of the commodity, income of the consumer, price of related commodity, taste and preferences, season, fashion, etc. If we group these factors, then two subgroups can be made. The first subgroup is related to price of the commodity in question and the second is related to factors other than price (including income of the consumer, price of related commodity, taste and preferences, season, fashion, etc.). Thus, all the factors in ceteris peribus category are a part of the second subgroup. On this basis, there are following changes in demand:

1. Movement along the same demand curve (change in quantity demanded).
2. Shift in demand curve (change in demand)

The change in demand has been explained with the help of Fig. 4.6.

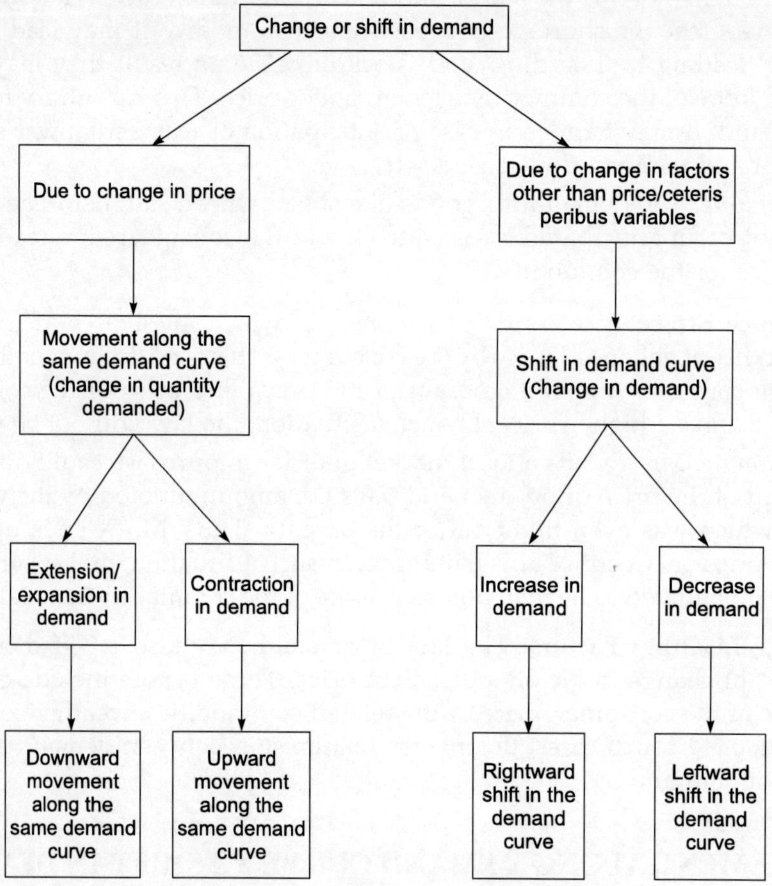


**Fig. 4.6** Change or Shift in Demand

## 1. Movement along the Same Demand Curve (Change in Quantity Demanded)

### *Meaning*

Other things being equal, if the price of the commodity in question changes, it induces a change in the quantity demanded, movement is said to occur along the same demand curve. It is also called change in quantity demanded of the commodity. Now, this movement can either be upward or downward which further forms the basis of its classification.

### *Types*

The movement along the demand curve is divided under two heads:

1. Extension/expansion of demand (downward movement)
2. Contraction of demand (upward movement)

**Extension/expansion of demand:** It refers to rise in quantity demanded due to fall in the price of the commodity, effect of other factors except price remaining constant. The concept of extension in demand has been shown with the help of Fig. 4.7.

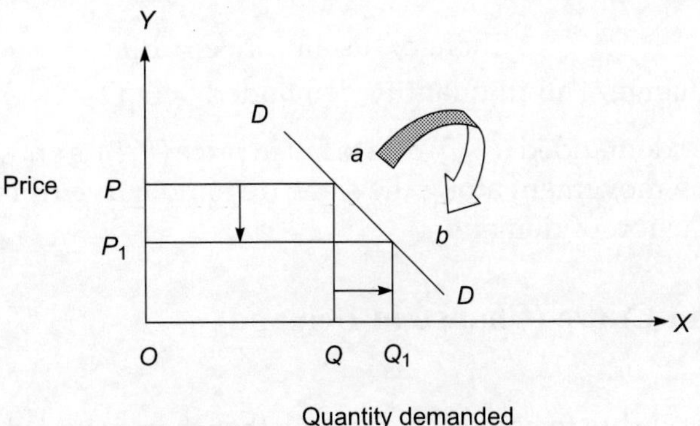


**Fig. 4.7** Expansion of Demand

$$\text{Initial price} = OP, \text{ Initial quantity} = OQ$$
$$\text{New price} = OP_1, \text{ New quantity} = OQ_1$$

Now,

$$\text{Change/Fall in price} = PP_1$$
$$\text{Change/rise in quantity demanded} = QQ_1$$

The rise in quantity demanded ($QQ_1$) due to fall in price ($PP_1$) is known as extension/ expansion of demand. Thus, the movement along the same demand curve from point *a* to point *b* is known as expansion of demand.

**Contraction of Demand:** It refers to fall in quantity demanded due to rise in the price of the product, effect of other factors except price remaining constant. The concept of contraction in demand has been shown with the help of Fig. 4.8.

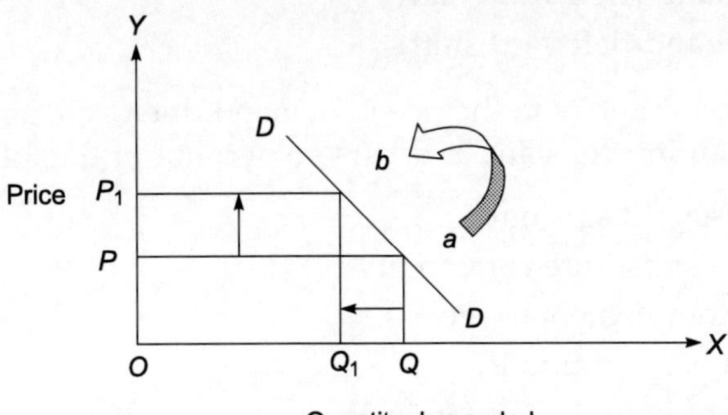


**Fig. 4.8** Contraction of Demand

$$\text{Initial price} = OP, \text{ Initial quantity} = OQ$$
$$\text{New price} = OP_1, \text{ New quantity} = OQ_1$$

Now,

$$\text{Change/Rise in price} = P_1P$$
$$\text{Change/Fall in quantity demanded} = Q_1Q$$

The fall in quantity demanded ($Q_1Q$) due to fall in price ($P_1P$) is known as contraction of demand. Thus, the movement along the same demand curve from point $a$ to point $b$ is known as contraction of demand.

## 2. Shift in Demand Curve (Change in Demand)

### *Meaning*

The change in demand due to change in factors other than price is known as shift in the demand curve. It is also called change in demand of the commodity. Apart from price, the demand for a commodity also depends on other factors like income of the consumer, price of related goods, population, taste and preference of consumers, etc. Keeping price constant, the change in demand on account of change in any of the factors other than the price is called shift in demand. Graphically, if there is a change in any one of the factors which were held constant in drawing demand curve causes the shift in the entire demand curve. It is to be noted here that in this case, there is a shift in position of demand curve from its original position to a new position and thus a new demand curve is obtained at the same price. These positional changes and a new demand curve can either be rightwards or leftwards which further forms the basis of its classification.

### *Types*

The shift in demand curve is divided under two heads:

1. Increase in demand (rightward shift)
2. Decrease in demand (leftward shift)

**1. Increase in demand:** It refers to the rise in demand due to change in factors other than price, price remaining constant. It occurs on account of the following factors:

(a) increase in household's income,
(b) rise in price of a substitute commodity
(c) fall in price of complementary goods,
(d) favourable weather conditions,
(e) increase in size of household's family,
(f) favourable change in consumer's taste, etc.

The concept of increase in demand has been shown with the help of Fig. 4.9.

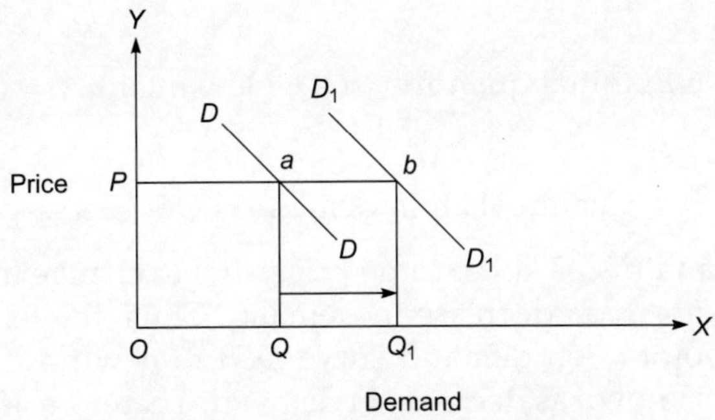


**Fig. 4.9** Increase in Demand

Price = $OP$, Initial quantity = $OQ$, New quantity = $OQ_1$

Now,

$$\text{Change/Rise in demand} = QQ_1$$

The rise in demand ($QQ_1$) at the same price, due to change in any of the factors affecting demand is known as increase in demand. Thus, the rightward shift of the demand curve from point *a* (on demand curve *DD*) to new position as point *b* (on demand curve $D_1D_1$) is known as increase in demand. Therefore, if more quantity $OQ_1$ is demanded at the same price ($OP$) or same quantity $OQ$ is demanded at price higher price than $OP$, increase in demand is said to exist.

**2. Decrease in demand:** It refers to fall or decline in demand due to change in factors other than price, price remaining constant. It occurs on account of the following factors:

(a) fall in household's income,
(b) fall in price of a substitute commodity,
(c) rise in price of complementary goods,
(d) unfavourable weather conditions,
(e) fall in size of household's family,
(f) unfavourable change in consumer's taste, etc.

The concept of decrease in demand has been shown with the help of Fig. 4.10.

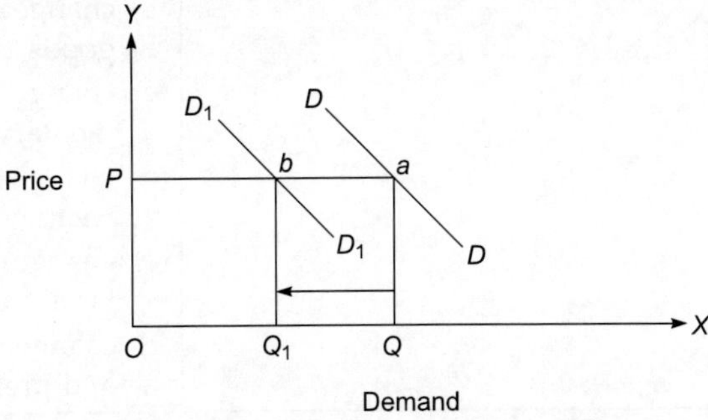


**Fig. 4.10** Decrease in Demand

Here,

$$\text{Price} = OP, \text{ Initial quantity} = OQ, \text{ New quantity} = OQ_1$$

Now,

$$\text{Change/Fall in demand} = QQ_1$$

The decline in demand ($OQ_1$) at the same price, due to change in any other factors affecting demand is known as decrease in demand. Thus, the leftward shift of the demand curve from point *a* (on demand curve *DD*) to new position as point *b* (on demand curve $D_1D_1$) is known as decrease in demand. Therefore, if less quantity $OQ_1$ is demanded at the same price (*OP*) or same quantity *OQ* is demanded at a price lower than *OP*, decrease in demand is said to exist.

On the basis of the foregoing discussion, we may now analyze the difference between the two types of changes in demand, viz., movement along the demand curve and shift in demand curve (Table 4.8).

**TABLE 4.8** Movement Along the Demand vs Shift in Demand

| Basis of Difference/ Parameters | Movement along the Demand | Shift in Demand Curve |
|---|---|---|
| 1. Meaning | It refers to an economic phenomenon which reflects the change in the quantity demanded due to change in price, other factors affecting price remaining constant. | It refers to an economic phenomenon which reflects the change in demand due to change in factors other than price, keeping price constant. |
| 2. Alternative name | Change in quantity demanded | Change in demand |
| 3. Causal variable/ variables | It is caused by change in price of a commodity | It is caused by change in factors other than price. These factors include:<br>(a) change in consumer's income,<br>(b) change in price of substitute goods,<br>(c) change in price of complementary goods,<br>(d) change in season and weather conditions,<br>(e) change in size of consumer's family, and<br>(f) change in consumer's taste and preferences. |

*Contd.*

| | | |
|---|---|---|
| 4. Constant considerations | Factors other than price are kept constant | Price is kept constant. |
| 5. Types | It is of two types:<br>(a) extension/expansion in demand<br>(b) contraction in demand | It is of two types:<br>(a) increase in demand, and<br>(b) decrease in demand. |
| 6. Direction of change | It refers to upward movement (in case of contraction in demand) or downward movement (in case of expansion in demand) along the same demand curve. | It refers to rightward shift (in case of increase in demand) or leftward shift (in case of decrease in demand) of original demand curve. |
| 7. Price considerations | It refers to change in quantity demanded due to change in price. | It refers to change in demand at the same price, i.e., with no change in price. |
| 8. Graphic representation | 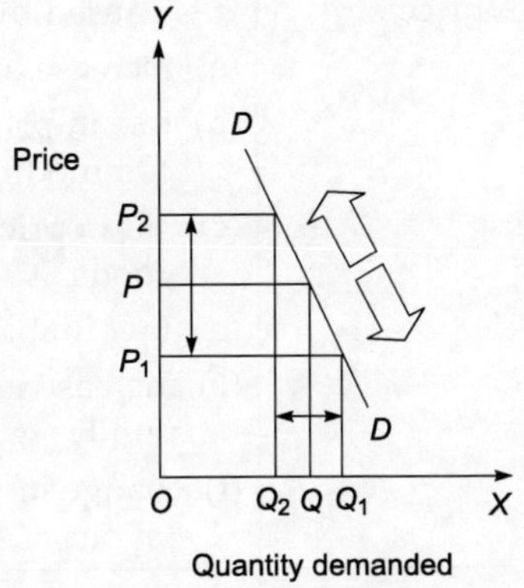 **Fig. 4.11** Movement along the Demand<br><br>**Explanation:**<br>Original demand curve = *DD*<br>Initial price = *OP*<br>Initial quantity = *OQ* units.<br>**Extension in demand:**<br>As a result of reduction in price of the commodity from *OP* to $OP_1$, there is a rise in quantity demanded from *OQ* to $OQ_1$.<br>**Contraction in demand:**<br>As a result of rise in price of the commodity from *OP* to $OP_2$, there is a decline in quantity demanded from *OQ* to $OQ_2$. | 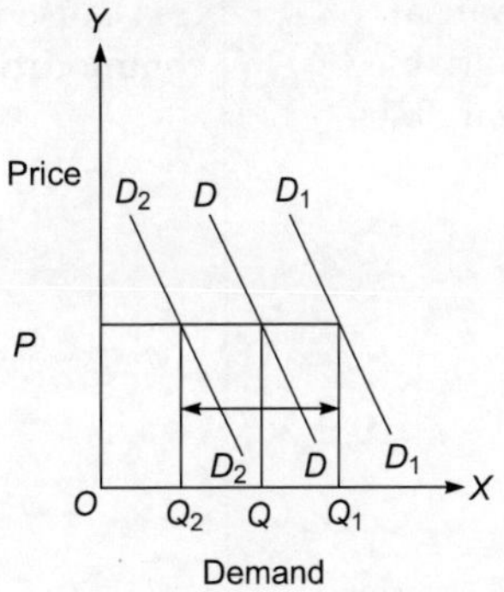 **Fig. 4.12** Shift in Demand Curve<br><br>**Explanation:**<br>Original demand curve = *DD*<br>Initial price = *OP*<br>Initial quantity = *OQ* units.<br>**Increase in demand:**<br>As a result of rise in income of the consumer, price being constant, there is a rise in demand from *OQ* to $OQ_1$.<br>**Decrease in demand:**<br>As a result of fall in income of the consumer, price being constant, there is a decline in demand for the commodity from *OQ* to $OQ_2$. |

On the basis of above explanation, let us understand the difference between expansion vs increase in demand and contraction vs decrease in demand.

## A. Difference between Extension in Demand and Increase in Demand

**TABLE 4.9** Extension in Demand vs Increase in Demand

<table>
<tr><th>Basis of Difference/ Parameters</th><th>Extension in Demand</th><th>Increase in Demand</th></tr>
<tr><td>1. Meaning</td><td>Other things remaining same, a rise in quantity demanded on account of fall in price is known as extension in demand.</td><td>Price remaining same, a rise in demand on account of other than the price of the commodity is known as increase in demand.</td></tr>
<tr><td>2. Broader concept</td><td>It is part of movement along the same demand curve.</td><td>It is part of shift of the demand curve.</td></tr>
<tr><td>3. Causal variable/ variables</td><td>It is caused by fall in price of a commodity.</td><td>It is caused by:<br>(a) increase in consumer's income,<br>(b) rise in price of substitute commodity,<br>(c) fall in price of complementary goods,<br>(d) favourable weather conditions,<br>(e) increase in size of consumer's family, and<br>(f) change in consumer's taste in favour of the commodity.</td></tr>
<tr><td>4. Constant considerations</td><td>Factors other than price are kept constant</td><td>Price is kept constant.</td></tr>
<tr><td>5. Direction of change</td><td>It refers to downward movement along the same demand curve.</td><td>It refers to rightward shift of the demand curve from its original position.</td></tr>
<tr><td>6. Price considerations</td><td>It involves change in quantity demanded due to change in price.</td><td>It involves change in demand at the same price, i.e., with no change in price.</td></tr>
<tr><td>7. Demand Schedule.</td><td>Expansion in demand with the help of demand schedule.<br><table><tr><th>$P_x$</th><th>$Q_x$</th></tr><tr><td>4</td><td>1</td></tr><tr><td>3</td><td>2</td></tr><tr><td>2</td><td>3</td></tr><tr><td>1</td><td>4</td></tr></table></td><td>Increase in demand with the help of demand schedule.<br><table><tr><th>$P_x$</th><th>$Q_x$</th></tr><tr><td>4</td><td>1</td></tr><tr><td>4</td><td>2</td></tr><tr><td>4</td><td>3</td></tr><tr><td>4</td><td>4</td></tr></table></td></tr>
</table>

*Contd.*

| | | |
|---|---|---|
| 8. Graphic representation | 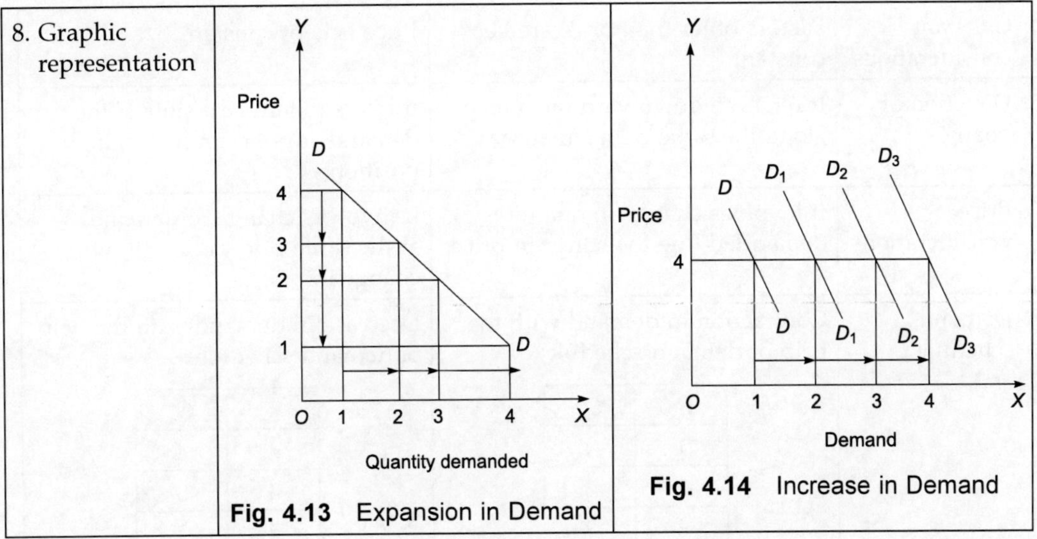 | |



**Fig. 4.13** Expansion in Demand

**Fig. 4.14** Increase in Demand

## B. Difference between Contraction in Demand and Decrease in Demand

**TABLE 4.10** Contraction in Demand Vs Decrease in Demand

| Basis of Difference/ Parameters | Contraction in Demand | Decrease in Demand |
|---|---|---|
| 1. Meaning | Other things remaining same, when a rise in price leads to fall in quantity demanded, it is known as contraction in demand. | Price remaining same, when there is fall in demand on account of factors other than the price of the commodity, it is known as increase in demand. |
| 2. Broader concept | It is part of movement along the same demand curve. | It is part of shift of the demand curve. |
| 3. Causal variable/ variables | It is caused by rise in price of a commodity. | It is caused by:<br>(a) decrease in consumer's income,<br>(b) fall in price of substitute commodity,<br>(c) rise in price of complementary goods,<br>(d) unfavourable weather conditions,<br>(e) reduction in size of consumer's family, and<br>(f) change in consumer's taste (against the commodity). |

*Contd.*

<table>
<tr><td>4. Constant considerations</td><td>Factors other than price are kept constant.</td><td>Price is kept constant.</td></tr>
<tr><td>5. Direction of change</td><td>It refers to downward movement along the same demand curve.</td><td>It refers to leftward shift of the demand curve from its original position.</td></tr>
<tr><td>6. Price considerations</td><td>It involves change in quantity demanded due to change in price.</td><td>It involves change in demand at the same price, i.e., with no change in price.</td></tr>
<tr><td>7. Demand schedule</td><td>Contraction in demand with the help of demand schedule.
<table>
<tr><th>$P_x$</th><th>$Q_x$</th></tr>
<tr><td>1</td><td>4</td></tr>
<tr><td>2</td><td>3</td></tr>
<tr><td>3</td><td>2</td></tr>
<tr><td>4</td><td>1</td></tr>
</table></td><td>Decrease in demand with the help of demand schedule.
<table>
<tr><th>$P_x$</th><th>$Q_x$</th></tr>
<tr><td>4</td><td>4</td></tr>
<tr><td>4</td><td>3</td></tr>
<tr><td>4</td><td>2</td></tr>
<tr><td>4</td><td>1</td></tr>
</table></td></tr>
<tr><td>8. Graphic representation</td><td> 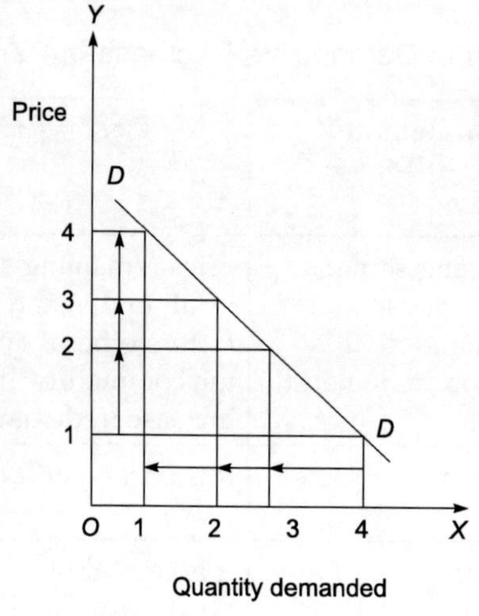Y<br>Price<br>D<br>4<br>3<br>2<br>1<br>D<br>O 1 2 3 4 X<br>Quantity demanded<br>**Fig. 4.15** Contraction In Demand</td><td>Y<br>Price<br>D<br>$D_2$ $D_1$<br>$D_3$<br>4<br>$D_3$ $D_2$ $D_1$ D<br>O 1 2 3 4 X<br>Demand 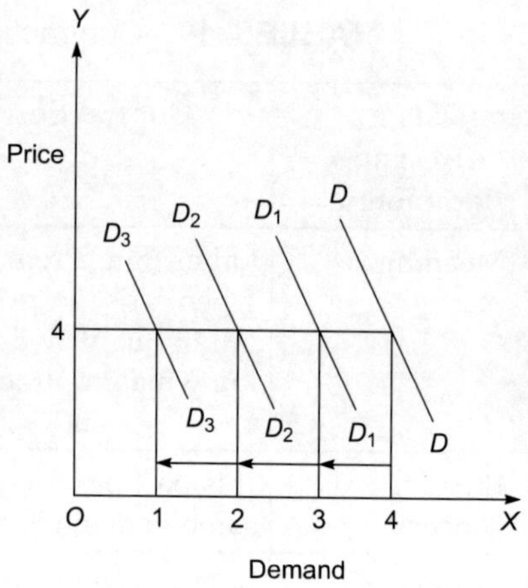<br>**Fig. 4.16** Decrease in Demand</td></tr>
</table>

## Implication

It is imperative for a business manager to know the price-quantity relationship and the factors that cause shifts in the demand function (or curve). Though price is an important variable, however, in certain cases, other determinants like income, taste, fashion, and business activity have a strong bearing in demand for products. Thus, in certain cases, changes in other factors or shifts in demand curve rather than movement along the demand curve is of greater implication to the managerial decision-making in the firm.

## Summary

✓ Demand refers to the phenomenon that reflects the quantity of a commodity that the consumer is able and willing to purchase. In addition, the customer should have willingness to part with the funds.

✓ The economically relevant statement defining demand must include the following:
  - Price of the commodity
  - Time period

✓ In order to qualify for demand, the following attributes must be present:
  - ability to purchase,
  - willingness to purchase,
  - willingness to part with the funds,
  - prevalence of a particular price, and
  - a time horizon in which the commodity is demanded.

✓ The factors that influence the demand for a commodity are as follows:
  - Price of the commodity
  - Income of the consumer
  - Price of related commodity
  - Taste and preferences
  - Season
  - Fashion
  - Advertisement
  - Future expectations
  - Consumer credit facility
  - State of business
  - Population

✓ Demand schedule is a tabular representation of various combinations of price and quantity demanded (ceteris paribus).

✓ Market demand schedule refers to a tabular representation of various quantities of a commodity corresponding to each price level that each consumer is willing to purchase during a given period of time.

✓ A supply curve is the diagrammatic representation of various combinations of price and quantity demanded, ceteris paribus.

✓ Demand function exhibit the functional relationship between demand (dependent variable) and factors affecting demand (independent variables).

✓ The law of demand defines an *inverse relationship* between price and quantity demanded of a commodity. It means that when price of the commodity reduces, the quantity demanded rises and on the other side, if the price of the commodity rises, the quantity demanded falls, ceteris peribus.

✓ The latin words 'ceteris peribus' mean that other things remain constant and do not influence demand during the study of the law. These "other things" include the determinants of demand other than price, viz., consumers' income, price of the substitutes and complements, taste and preferences of the consumer, etc.

✓ The factors contribute to the inverse relationship between quantity demanded and price are:
  - Law of diminishing marginal utility
  - Substitution effect
  - Income effect
  - Change in the number of consumers/new consumers
  - Several uses of a commodity

- There are exceptional cases which establish a direct relationship between price and the quantity demanded. These are the cases where the law of demand fails to operate:
  - Conspicuous goods
  - Giffen goods
  - Future expectations about price/speculative effect
  - Fear of shortage
  - Ignorance effect
  - Significant change in other factors

✓ Change in demand occurs in two ways:
  - Movement along the same demand curve
  - Shift in the demand curve

✓ Movement along the same demand curve is also called change in the quantity demanded of the commodity. It occurs due to change in price of the commodity.
  It is of two types:
  Expansion or extension in demand – Downward movement along the demand curve
  Contraction in demand – Upward movement along the demand curve

✓ Shift in demand curve is also called change in demand of the commodity. It occurs due to change in factors other than price such as income of the consumer, price of related commodities, taste and preferences, etc.
  It is of two types:
  Increase in demand – Rightward shift of the demand curve
  Decrease in demand – Leftward shift of the demand curve

## Review Questions

1. Define demand. Explain the factors that influence the demand of a commodity.
2. What is law of demand? Will a beggar desiring to purchase Maruti car constitute demand? State the factors determining the law of demand and exceptions to it.
3. To what extent do you think that price is the most important determinant of demand?
4. Elucidate the differences between:
   - Extension of demand and increase in demand.
   - Contraction of demand and decrease in demand.
5. Explain the concept of demand with the help of demand schedule. Also explain the determinants of demand.
6. Distinguish between 'extension of demand', and increase in demand' and 'contraction in demand' and 'decrease in demand'. Explain the factors which bring about change in demand.
7. Why demand curve slopes downward from left to right? What are the exceptions to this rule?
8. Explain the situations in which there prevails a direct relationship between price and quantity demanded?
9. Explain demand schedule, demand curve and demand function. Derive demand curve from demand schedule: $Q = 60 - 20P$.
10. From the demand function $Qd = 2000 - 30P$ and supply function $Qs = 20P$, find:
    - Equilibrium price
    - Equilibrium quantity
    - Gap between demand and supply at $P =$ Rs. 20 and $P =$ Rs. 50
11. Explain with the help of diagrams the effect of the following changes on the demand of a commodity:
    - A fall in the price of complementary goods
    - A fall in the price of substitute goods.
12. Distinguish between change in demand and change in quantity demanded. Use diagrams.
13. Write short notes on:
    - Difference between movement along demand curve and shift in demand curve.
    - Expansion in demand and decrease in demand

## CASE STUDY 1: EDIFICE AMBITIONS (APRIL 2019)

Mr. Anjanya is the managing director of Edifice Ambitions, which is one of the largest real estate developers in India with more than 60 years of experience in the realty sector. The company is part of the Anjanya International Investment Group (AIIG). The company follows a holistic approach and deals with all stages of real estate development. These include land searching, selection, acquisition, action plan execution, construction of units, décor and marketing of housing units. The company has a good reputation in market and generates its revenues from both sales and rentals of its units. The prime focus of the company is excellence in construction and provision of product at an affordable price. The management is a mix of people from diverse backgrounds like construction, architecture and interior designing. The company has successfully completed many projects and fourteen business models are still in pipeline. The company's total income reached US$ 1.25 billion in FY18 and it wants to pitch for US$ 2 billion during FY20.

On April 2019, Mr. Anjanya considered the company's sales figures. He was perturbed that the business that was doing well for past 60 years is now witnessing decline in sales by 25 per cent at the end of Q1 of FY2019. He was of the view that "the market conditions have been favourable for our business over the last years and the properties were either sold or rented at a fast pace. With the generated profits either further investments or reinvestment has been made. This is able to create a multiplier effect for business. In case, the funds were falling short, then the company resorted to borrowings but paid loans on time". Now, the most disturbing fact is 25 per cent decline in sales and 28 per cent decline in market share over Q1 of FY2019. This was an alarming signal for the company as it required immediate execution of action plans and the company is also considering the matter seriously in the wake of the crisis situation.

### Questions

1. What is your opinion regarding the probable reason for 25 per cent decline in sales of Edifice Ambitions?
2. How sensitive the demand for house property is in relation to pricing quotation of the company?
3. How the demand for house property is likely to react as a result of increase in income of the buyers?
4. What can be the future implications of 25 per cent decline in sales for Edifice Ambitions?
5. What would be the probable reaction of demand for house property if there is reduction in apartment rentals?
6. Do you think that demand for house property would be affected if there is a change in social tastes in such a manner that consumers think that buying a house is no more related to acquisition of status symbol commodity?

## CASE STUDY 2: TRANSITIONS IN MR. MYRAN'S CONSUMPTION PATTERN (2011-17)

Mr. Myran was a factory worker engaged in production in Company A in year 2011. He was working in factory A where he was earning Rs. 8000 per month for rendering his services. After the day's work, his consumption pattern revealed the consumption of commodities such as jawar, bajra, etc. He continued his services in factory A. Finally after six years, his salary reached the bench mark of Rs. 16,000 p.m. He decided to change his consumption pattern to the purchase of rice and wheat. His mindset was that now he can afford rice and wheat on account of increase in his income.

### Questions

1. Analyze the above case in light of study of normal and inferior goods.
2. In light of above case what role does income play in case of demand for jawar/bajra.
3. What will be the shape of income demand curve in case of the following:
   (a) Bajra
   (b) Rice
4. Also show the diagrammatic representation of income demand curve of the commodities mentioned in question number 3.

## CASE STUDY 3: MR. WITTYNUTS (2013)

Mr. Wittynuts was exporter of peanuts and was running this business since 2013. He was a miser and was in habit of accumulating money. He used to spend money only for most urgent purposes. He always wanted to purchase diamond-set vintage watch which was supported by his budget as well. He used to discuss the matter with his friends and family members. He had a strong desire to purchase the diamond watch. But at time of actual purchase, he always used to defer the purchase of the watch. His wish to purchase the watch was not supported by his willingness to spend money.

### Questions

1. Do you think Mr. Wittynuts's desire to purchase diamond-set vintage watch will constitute demand? Give reasons in support of your answer.
2. Analyze the above case in light of applicability or non-applicability of law of demand in case of goods of conspicuous consumption such as possessing a diamond watch.
3. What would be the shape of demand curve in case where the commodity represents goods of conspicuous consumption?

# 5 CHAPTER

# Price Elasticity of Demand

**LEARNING OBJECTIVES**

After going through this chapter, reader would be able to understand:

- ✓ The meaning and concept of elasticity of demand.
- ✓ Factors that influence price elasticity of demand.
- ✓ Meaning and definitions of price elasticity of demand.
- ✓ Coefficient of price elasticity of demand.
- ✓ The methods through which the coefficients of price elasticity of demand are calculated.

## 5.1 INTRODUCTION

In chapter 4, the law of demand was explained that established an inverse relationship between price and quantity demanded, keeping the effect of other variables affecting demand constant. The law of demand merely explained the direction of change as a result of rise or fall in the prices of the commodities. It reflected that when prices reduce, the quantity demanded is likely to be more and when prices rise, the quantity demanded is likely to be less. This happens when other factors apart from price like income of the consumer, price of related commodities, taste and preferences, advertisement expenditure are not amenable to change throughout price-quantity demanded (*P-Q*) analysis. However, the magnitude or quantum of change is unanswered in case of law of demand.

In the present chapter, we introduce the concept of elasticity of demand. This concept explains the extent of relationship between price and quantity demanded in terms of degrees of elasticity of demand. In the further discussion, the concept of elasticity has been discussed in terms of main determinant of demand, that is, price. Thus, the chapter proceeds with the discussion on meaning and explanation of concept and factors that influence the price elasticity of demand. These factors have been examined in terms of nature of the commodity, availability of substitutes, number of uses, postponement of the use, joint demand, price level, income level, etc.

In the latter half of chapter, the methods of measurement or estimation of elasticity of demand in terms of percentage method, total expenditure method, point method and arc method have been explained.

## 5.2 MEANING OF ELASTICITY OF DEMAND

The concept of elasticity of demand was propounded by Prof. Alfred Marshall in his book 'Principles of Economics' published in 1890. The term elasticity of demand refers to 'degree or extent of responsiveness of demand on account of change in the level of price'.

As we have studied, the demand function specifies the relationship between demand and its determinants. The major determinants are price of the commodity, income of the consumer, price of related goods, advertisement expenditure, future expectation regarding price, etc. The concept of elasticity of demand is thus, related with the extent of change in quantity demanded on account of changes in the determinants of demand in the following manner:

(a) Price of the commodity – Price elasticity of demand
(b) Income of the consumer – Income elasticity of demand
(c) Price of related goods – Cross elasticity of demand
(d) Advertisement expenditure – Advertisement elasticity of demand

## 5.3 MEANING AND DEFINITIONS OF PRICE ELASTICITY OF DEMAND

### 5.3.1 Meaning

Price elasticity of demand (*Ed*) refers to the degree of responsiveness of quantity demanded of a commodity on account of changes in its price. Price elasticity of demand represents the ratio of percentage change in the quantity demanded to the percentage change in the price of the commodity in question.

### 5.3.2 Definitions

The popular definitions propounded by different economists are as under:

According to Prof. Alfred Marshall, "Elasticity of demand may be defined as the percentage change in quantity demanded to the percentage change in price."

In the words of Prof. J.M. Keynes: "The elasticity of demand is a measure of the relative change in quantity to a relative change in price."

Prof. Dominick Salvatore however, explained that "The elasticity of demand measures the responsiveness in quantity demanded of a commodity to changes in each of the forces that determine demand."

### 5.3.3 Coefficient of Price Elasticity of Demand

The coefficient of price elasticity of demand (*Ed* or *Ep*) can be expressed as under:

$$Ed/Ep = \frac{\text{Percentage change in quantity demanded}}{\text{Percentage change in price}}$$

$$Ed/Ep = \frac{\Delta Q * P}{\Delta P\ Q}$$

where,

$Ed/Ep$ = Coefficient of price elasticity of demand

$\Delta Q$ = Change in quantity demanded

$\Delta P$ = Change in price

$P$ = Original price

$Q$ = Original quantity demanded

***Note:*** The coefficient of *Ed* has negative value on account of inverse relationship between price and quantity demanded.

## 5.4 DETERMINANTS OF ELASTICITY OF PRICE/FACTORS DETERMINING PRICE ELASTICITY OF DEMAND

There are a numbers of factors that determine elasticity of demand. Some of these factors have been explained in Fig. 5.1.

**1. Nature of the Commodity**

On the basis of nature, the commodities can be divided into three broad categories, viz., luxury, necessity, and comfort commodities. The influence of each on elasticity of demand has been defined in Table 5.1.

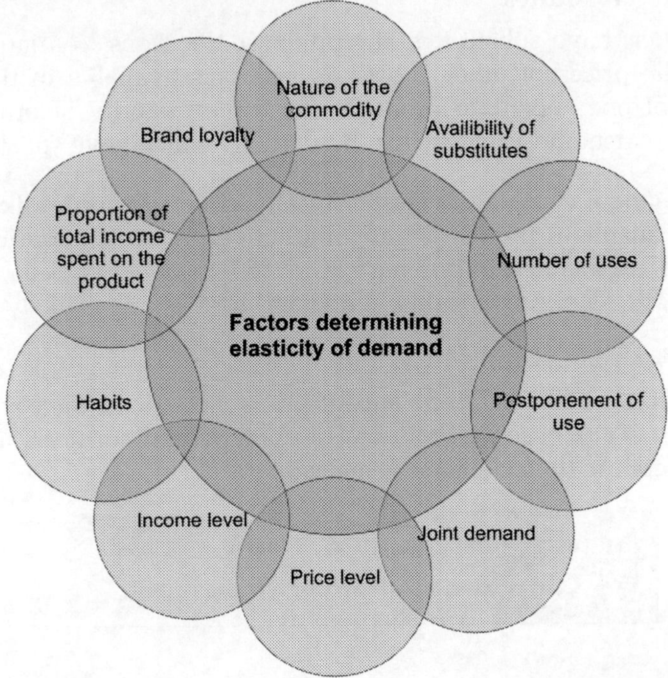


**Fig. 5.1** Factors Determining Elasticity of Demand

**TABLE 5.1** Influence of Nature of Commodity on Elasticity of Demand

| Nature of the Commodity | Luxury Commodities | Necessary Commodities | Comfort Commodities |
|---|---|---|---|
| Degree of *Ed* | Relatively elastic | Less than elastic or inelastic | • More elastic demand than necessities<br>• Less elastic than luxuries |
| Reason | Consumers are highly influenced by the prices. Thus, a small change in price leads to more than proportionate change in quantity demanded. | The price changes do not affect demand much as they are purchased in required amount at any price.<br>Hence, price changes do not affect the demand much. | • Less urgent than necessity commodities<br>• More urgent than luxury commodities. |
| Examples: | Cars, ornaments, expensive decoration items | Salt, sugar, life saving drugs | Tasteful and nutritious foods, a well furnished house |

**2. Availability of Substitutes**

The study of availability of substitutes can be done under the following heads:

**(a) Products with Substitutes**

In case the products have substitutes, the purchase decisions to a large extent are determined by the prices of other substitute products available in the market. A change in price of one substitute product affects the quantity of other substitute product. Therefore, demand is elastic for those goods which have substitutes.

***For example:*** Demand for Colgate is elastic since its close substitutes like Pepsodent, Sensodyne are available in the market at competitive prices. If the price of Colgate rises, then people are inclined to purchase more of Pepsodent or Sensodyne or any other brand of toothpaste. As a result, the demand for Colgate is likely to fall.

**(b) Products with no Substitutes**

The demand for commodities with no substitutes is inelastic as the consumer is left with no option but to purchase the product. For example: salt, turmeric and milk have no substitutes, therefore their demand is inelastic.

**Products with Substitutes: Elastic**
**Products with no Substitutes: Inelastic**

Table 5.2 shows the influence of availability of substitutes on elasticity of demand.

**TABLE 5.2** Influence of Availability of Substitutes on Elasticity of Demand

| Availability of Substitutes | Products with Substitutes | Products with no Substitutes |
|---|---|---|
| Degree of *Ed* | Elastic | Inelastic |
| Reason | A change in price of one substitute product affects the quantity of other substitute product. | The consumer is left with no option but to purchase the product. |
| Examples: | Toothpastes, toothbrushes, fruits, modes of transport. | Salt, turmeric and milk |

### 3. Number of Uses

The number of uses or range of usage of a commodity also influences elasticity of demand of the product. The study of number of uses can be done under the following heads:

#### (a) Multi-use Commodities

There are certain products which can be called multi-use commodities as they can be put to several uses. A change in their price causes more than the proportionate change in demand for such a commodity. Therefore, the demand for such a commodity generally increases more than the proportionate decrease in its price. On the contrary, as the price of a multi-use commodity increases, people contract their consumption and confine it to most urgent purposes. The demand for these commodities is thus, more than elastic.

For instance, milk is one such commodity which may be converted into curd, paneer, sweets, preparing tea, cheese, ghee and buttermilk. The demand for milk will therefore be more than elastic. Another example is electricity which can be used for lighting, cooking, heating and for industrial purpose. Therefore, demand for electricity also has more than elastic demand.

#### (b) Single-use Commodities

These are the commodities which can be put to use for a specific purpose. A change in their price causes less than proportionate change in demand for such a commodity. The demand for such a commodity is generally less than the proportionate change in its price. The demand for these commodities is thus, less than elastic.

**For instance,** turmeric is a single use product and has less than elastic demand.

**Multi-use Commodities: Elastic**
**Single-use Commodities: Inelastic**

## 5.5 METHODS OF MEASUREMENT OF ELASTICITY OF DEMAND

There are several methods of measurement of elasticity of demand. However, the most popular ones are shown in Fig. 5.2.

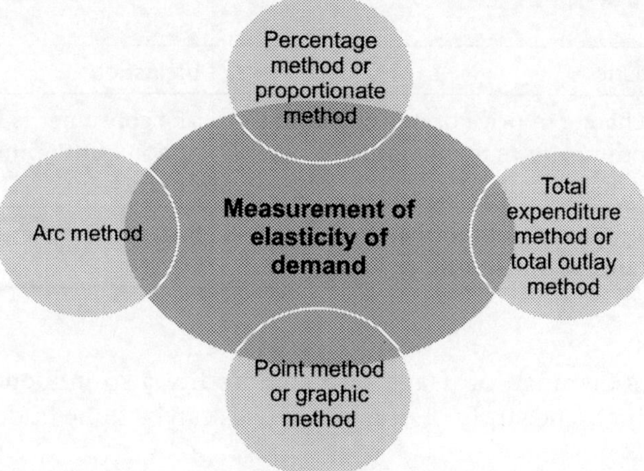


**Fig. 5.2** Measurement of Elasticity of Demand

### 5.5.1 Percentage Method or Proportionate Method

#### *5.5.1.1 Concept*

Price elasticity of demand refers to the degree of responsiveness or extent of sensitiveness of quantity demanded of a commodity due to change in its price.

#### *5.5.1.2 Coefficient of Price Elasticity of Demand*

The coefficient of elasticity of demand can be calculated by considering the ratio of percentage or relative change in quantity demanded to percentage change in its price.

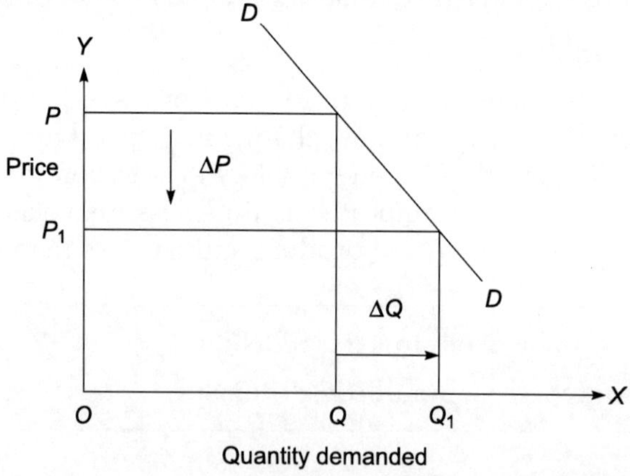


**Fig. 5.3** Price and Quantity Demanded Relationship

The absolute value of coefficient of *Ed* ranges from zero to infinity ($0 < Ed > \infty$). In addition, the coefficient of price elasticity has a negative value, because of the inverse relationship between price and quantity demanded. It is usually symbolized by *Ep* or Greek letter eta ($\eta$). Thus, we have

$$Ed/Ep/\eta = \frac{\text{Percentage change in quantity demanded}}{\text{Percentage change in price}}$$

It measures the elasticity by applying the mathematical concepts, hence it is known as mathematical method. It is also known as the ratio method, and arithmetic method.

### 5.5.1.3 Derivation

$$Ed/Ep/\eta = \frac{\text{Percentage change in quantity demanded}}{\text{Percentage change in price}}$$

$$= \frac{\dfrac{\text{Change in quantity demanded}}{\text{Original quantity demanded}} \times 100}{\dfrac{\text{Change in price}}{\text{Original price}} \times 100}$$

$$= \frac{\dfrac{\text{New quantity} - \text{Original quantity}}{\text{Original quantity}}}{\dfrac{\text{New price} - \text{Original price}}{\text{Original price}}}$$

Symbolically, it can be written

$$Ed = \frac{\dfrac{Q_2 - Q_1}{Q_1}}{\dfrac{P_2 - P_1}{P_1}}$$

In general terms,

$$= \frac{\dfrac{\Delta Q}{Q}}{\dfrac{\Delta P}{P}}$$

$$= \frac{\Delta Q}{\Delta P} \times \frac{P}{Q}$$

By rearranging terms,

$$Ed = \frac{\Delta Q}{\Delta P} \times \frac{P}{Q}$$

Here,

$\Delta Q$ = Change in quantity demanded

$Q$ = Original quantity demanded

$\Delta P$ = Change in price

$P$ = Original price

The symbol $\Delta$ means the change.

As such, price elasticity of demand is a pure number, that is, it has no units of measurement attached to it. This allows meaningful comparison between the price elasticity of demand of different commodities.

***For example:*** At Rs. 46 per unit, the demand for a commodity is 30 units. If the price increases from Rs. 46 to Rs. 50 per unit, the demand decreases from 30 units to 15 units. The price elasticity of demand is:

$$Ed/Ep/\eta = -\frac{\Delta Q}{\Delta P} \times \frac{P}{Q}$$

$$Ed = -\frac{\Delta Q}{\Delta P} \times \frac{P}{Q}$$

Here,

$Q_1$ = 30 units, $Q_2$ = 15 units, $\Delta Q$ = 15 units – 30 units = –15 units

$P_1$ = Rs. 46, $P_2$ = Rs. 50, $\Delta P$ = Rs. 50 – Rs. 46 = Rs. 4

$$Ed = -\frac{15}{4} \times \frac{46}{30}$$

$$Ed = 5.75$$

### 5.5.1.4 *Degrees of Price Elasticity*

Since the value of coefficient of elasticity of demand lies between zero and infinity. The value of the coefficient varies according to the type of the commodity. Some commodities have elastic demand while others have inelastic demand. The coefficients of elasticity of demand assume the values, viz., zero, less than one, equal to one, greater than one and infinity. This is shown in Fig. 5.4.

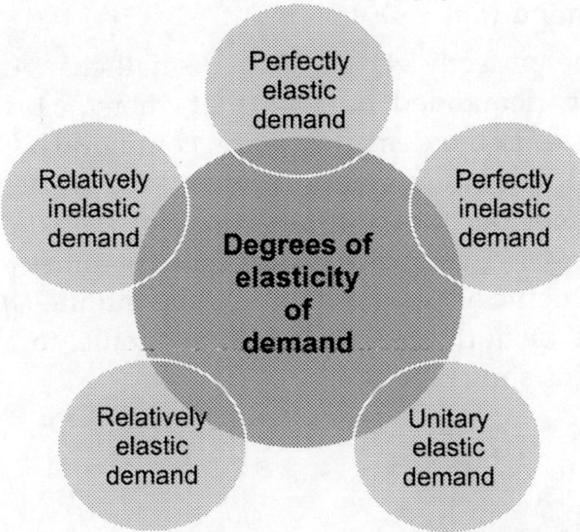


**Fig. 5.4** Degrees of Elasticity of Demand

The attributes of these five degrees of elasticity of demand have been shown in Table 5.3:

**TABLE 5.3** Degrees of Elasticity of Demand

| Degree or Type of *Ed* | Explanation | Coefficient of *Ed* | Shape of Demand Curve |
|---|---|---|---|
| Perfectly elastic demand | When a fall in price leads to infinite increase in quantity demanded and a small rise leads to zero demand for the commodity. | $Ep = \infty$ | Horizontal straight line parallel to *X*-axis |
| Perfectly inelastic demand | Quantity demanded does not change when price changes. | $Ep = 0$ | Vertical straight line parallel to *Y*-axis |
| Unitary elastic demand | Equal and proportionate changes in price and quantity. | $Ep = 1$ | Rectangular hyperbola |
| Relatively elastic demand | Quantity demanded changes by a larger percentage than percentage change in price. | $Ep > 1$ | Flatter downward sloping curve |
| Relatively inelastic demand | Quantity demanded changes by a smaller percentage change in price. | $Ep < 1$ | Steeper downward sloping curve |

These specific degrees of elasticity of demand have been explained as under:

**1. Perfectly Elastic Demand ($Ep = \infty$)**

The demand is said to be perfectly elastic when a small change in price leads to an infinite change in quantity demanded. It means that when the price of the commodity falls, it leads to infinite rise in the demand for the commodity. On the other hand, if there is slight rise in the price of the commodity, then quantity demanded falls to zero. It means that the consumer purchases infinite units of the commodity at the same prevailing price. Any further rise in price induces the customer to buy nothing of the commodity. Hence, the coefficient of elasticity will be infinite ($\eta = \infty$) and the shape of the demand curve will be horizontal straight line parallel to *X*-axis. The graph for perfectly elastic demand is shown below:

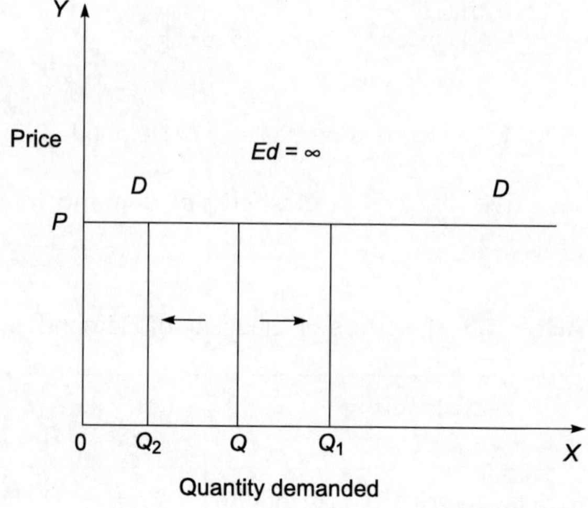


**Fig. 5.5** Perfectly Elastic Demand

Figure 5.5 reflects that at the ruling price *OP*, the demand is infinite. A minimal rise in price leads to reduction in quantity demanded to zero. Whereas, the reduction in price leads to expansion in quantity demanded to an infinite level. Thus, the consumer can purchase any quantity at the prevailing price. Products with perfectly elastic demand do not exist in reality as it is not possible that a minute change in price leads to stockpiling up to infinite level. Thus, it is a fictitious degree of elasticity of demand.

**2. Perfectly Inelastic Demand ($Ep = 0$)**

Perfectly inelastic demand curves are those in which quantity demanded is totally unresponsive to changes in price. Under the perfectly inelastic demand, there is absolutely no change in the quantity demanded even if there is rise or decline in the price. It means that the quantity is fixed and independent of changes in the price. The coefficient of elasticity of demand in this case is equal to zero ($\eta = 0$) and the shape of the demand curve will be a vertical straight line parallel to *Y*-axis. The graph for perfectly inelastic demand is shown below:

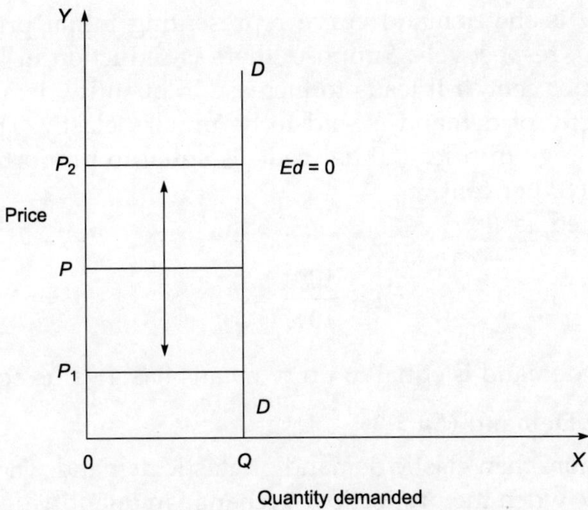


**Fig. 5.6** Perfectly Inelastic Demand

In Figure 5.6, the initial price is *OP* at which *OQ* units are demanded. Now, suppose there is reduction in price from *OP* to $OP_1$, the quantity demanded remains intact. Similarly, if the price rises from *OP* to $OP_2$ , the demand still remains the same. It means that the quantity demanded is unaffected by rise (from *OP* to $OP_2$) or fall ($OP$ to $OP_1$) in prices. This is another form of degree of elasticity of demand, which is fictitious in nature and is far from reality.

**3. Unitary Elastic Demand ($Ep = 1$)**

The demand is said to be unitary elastic when a proportionate change in the price level leads to equal and proportionate change in quantity demanded. The value of coefficient of elasticity of demand in this case is equal to one ($Ep = 1$). This demand curve is called rectangular hyperbola.

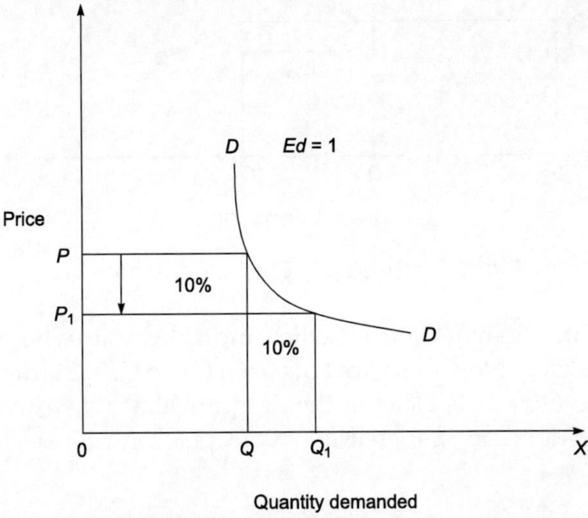


**Fig. 5.7** Unitary Elastic Demand

In Figure 5.7, *DD* is the demand curve representing initial price and quantity levels at *OP* and *OQ*, respectively. Suppose, there is reduction in level of prices of a commodity by 10 per cent, if it leads to increase in quantity demanded by 10 per cent, then the elasticity of demand is said to be unitary elastic. This is because of the proportionate change in price (10 per cent) is equal to proportionate change in quantity demanded (10 per cent).

It can be represented as:

$$Ep = \frac{10\%}{10\%} = 1$$

Thus, elasticity of demand is equal to unity means has a value equal to one.

**4. Relatively Elastic Demand (*Ep* > 1)**

It is also known as more than elastic demand or elastic demand. The demand is said to be relatively elastic when the proportionate change in quantity demanded is more than proportionate change in price.

***For example:*** When a 10 per cent change in price causes more than 10 per cent say 28 percent change in quantity demanded. In such a case, the elasticity of demand is said to be relatively elastic. This is shown in Fig. 5.8.

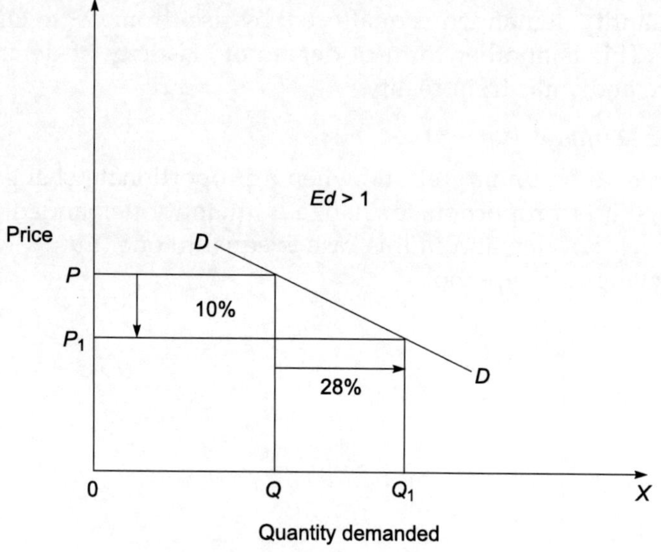


**Fig. 5.8** Relatively Elastic Demand

In Fig. 5.8, *DD* is the demand curve which indicates that when price is *OP*, the quantity demanded is $OQ_1$. Now the price falls from *OP* to $OP_1$, the quantity demanded increases from *OQ* to $OQ_1$. It is clear in the diagram that when the price fell by 10 percent, the quantity demanded increased by 28 per cent. Since the proportionate change in quantity demanded (28%) is more than percentage the change in price (10%), therefore the demand is said to be relatively elastic.

Symbolically,

$$Ep = \frac{28\%}{10\%} = 2.8 \text{ (which is >1)}$$

**5. Relatively Inelastic Demand (*Ep* < 1)**

It is also known as less than elastic demand or inelastic demand. Under the relatively inelastic demand a given percentage change in price leads to less than percentage change in quantity demanded. Thus, the percentage change in price is more as compared to percentage change in the quantity demanded.

***For example:*** If as a result of reduction in price of a commodity by 10 per cent, there is change in quantity demanded by less than 10 per cent( say 8 per cent), the demand is said to be less than unitary elastic. Demand is said to be less than one as shown in Fig. 5.9.

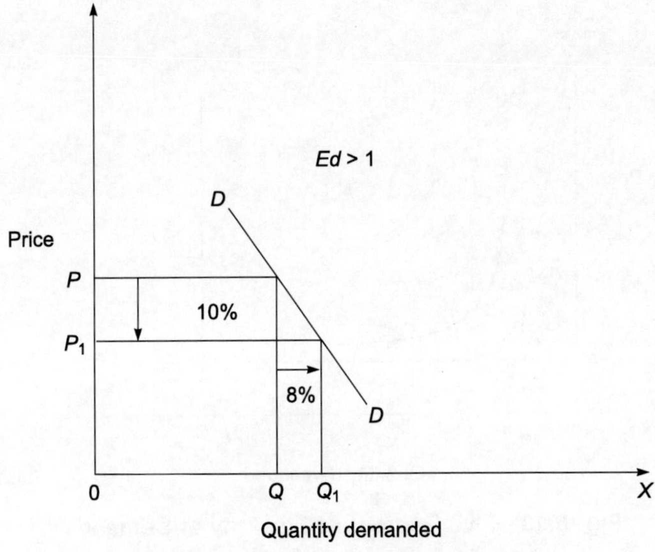


**Fig. 5.9** Relatively Inelastic Demand

In the above figure, *DD* is the demand curve representing initial price and quantity levels at *OP* and *OQ* respectively. Suppose, there is reduction in level of price of a commodity by 10 per cent, if it leads to increase in quantity demanded by less than 10 percent (say 8 per cent), then the elasticity of demand is said to be less than unitary elastic. This is because of the proportionate change in price (10 per cent) leads to less than proportionate change in quantity demanded (8 per cent).

It can be shown as:

$$Ep = \frac{8\%}{10\%} = 0.8 \text{ (which is <1)}$$

All the five degrees of elasticity of demand have been shown in Figure 5.10 as a composite diagram. The quantity demanded has been taken on *X*-axis and price has been considered on *Y*-axis. These have been shown as:

where,

1. *AB* — Perfectly elastic demand ($Ep = \infty$)
2. *CD* — Perfectly inelastic demand ($Ep = 0$)
3. *EF* — Unitary elastic demand ($Ep = 1$)
4. *GH* — Relatively elastic demand ($Ep > 1$)
5. *GI* — Relatively in elastic demand ($Ep < 1$)

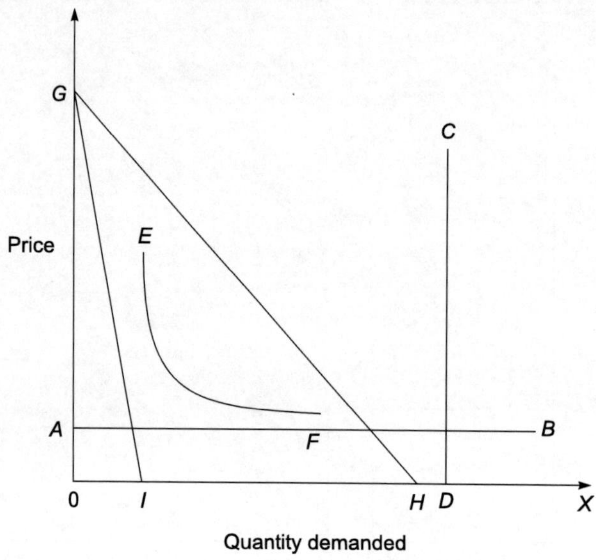


**Fig. 5.10** Five Degrees of Elasticity of Demand

## 5.5.2 Total Expenditure Method or Total Outlay Method

This method was propounded by Dr. Marshall to measure the price elasticity of demand by considering the total amount of money spent on purchasing a product. In this method, the coefficient of elasticity of demand is calculated by considering the changes in the prices and the subsequent effect on the total expenditure made on purchase of different quantities of the commodities. It is to be noted here that by total outlay method, we can know only whether price elasticity is equal to one, greater than one or less than one. The exact coefficient of price elasticity of demand cannot be determined.

Under this method, total expenditure has been defined as:

**Total expenditure/Total outlay = Price per unit × Quantity demanded.**

There is possibility of three types of elasticity under this method.

### 1. Greater than Unity (*Ed* >1)

If there prevails an inverse relationship between price and total expenditure, the demand is said to be more than unitary elastic or elastic. In other words, when as a result of fall in price of the commodity (quantity demanded increases), the total expenditure increases or with a rise in price of the commodity (quantity demanded falls), the total expenditure falls, in that case price elasticity of demand is greater than one.

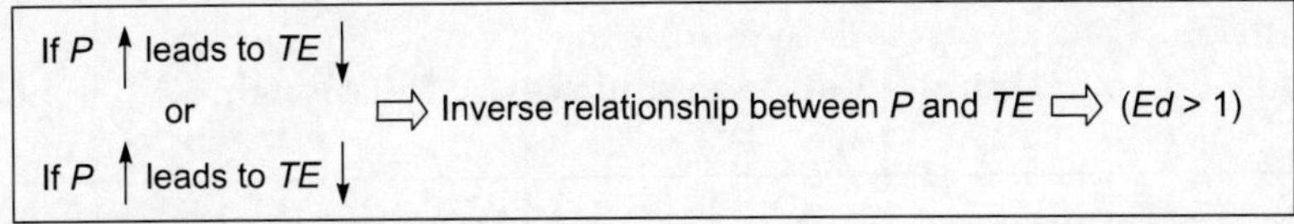


### 2. Equal to Unity (*Ed* = 1)

If as a result of change in the price, the total expenditure remains unaffected, the demand in such a case is said to be unitary elastic and assumes value equal to one. In other words, if with a rise in price (quantity demanded falls) or fall in the price (quantity demanded increases), the total expenditure remains the same, the demand will be unitary elastic, i.e., (*Ed* = 1).

If *P* ↓ leads to $\overline{TE}$

or ⇨ Constant relationship between *P* and *TE* ⇨ (*Ed* = 1)

If *P* ↑ leads to $\overline{TE}$

### 3. Less than Unity (*Ed* < 1)

If there prevails a direct relationship between price and total expenditure, the demand is said to be less than unitary elastic or inelastic. In other words, with a fall in price (quantity demanded rises), the total expenditure also falls, and with a rise in price (demand falls) the total expenditure also rises, price elasticity of demand is less than one i.e. (*Ed* < 1).

If *P* ↓ leads to *TE* ↓

or ⇨ Direct relationship between *P* and *TE* ⇨ (*Ed* < 1)

If *P* ↑ leads to *TE* ↑

Tables 5.4 and 5.5 make the concept clear.

**TABLE 5.4** Total Expenditure Possibilities

| Variables | Total Expenditure Possibilities | | |
|---|---|---|---|
| **Changes in Price** | **Total Expenditure Falls** | **Total Expenditure Remains Same** | **Total Expenditure Rises** |
| Fall in price | *Ed* < 1 | *Ed* = 1 | *Ed* > 1 |
| Rise in price | *Ed* > 1 | *Ed* = 1 | *Ed* < 1 |

It can be further understood with the help of following schedule:

**TABLE 5.5** Total Expenditure Schedule

| Price per unit | Quantity Sold | Total Expenditure | Symbolic Representation | Type of Relationship | Price Elasticity of Demand |
|---|---|---|---|---|---|
| 1 | 10 | 10 | If $P\uparrow$ leads to $TE\uparrow$ OR If $P\downarrow$ leads to $TE\downarrow$ | Direct relationship between price & total expenditure | *Ed* < 1 |
| 2 | 9 | 18 | | | |
| 3 | 8 | 24 | | | |
| 4 | 7 | 28 | | | |
| 5 | 6 | 30 | If $P\downarrow$ OR $P\uparrow$, $\overline{TE}$ | Constant relationship between price & total expenditure | *Ed* = 1 |
| 6 | 5 | 30 | | | |
| 7 | 4 | 28 | If $P\uparrow$ leads to $TE\downarrow$ OR If $P\downarrow$ leads to $TE\uparrow$ | Inverse relationship between price & total expenditure | *Ed* > 1 |
| 8 | 3 | 21 | | | |
| 9 | 2 | 18 | | | |
| 10 | 1 | 10 | | | |

Explanation of three possibilities under expenditure method is as under:

**1. More Elastic Demand**

When price is Rs. 7 per unit, the consumer demands 4 units and therefore, total expenditure becomes Rs. 28. Now, there is rise in price from Rs. 7 per unit to Rs. 10 per unit, the quantity demanded thus, reduces from 4 units to 1 unit. Correspondingly, the total expenditure reduces from Rs. 28 to Rs. 10. Therefore; here an inverse relationship prevails between price (rise from 7 per unit to Rs. 10 per unit) and total expenditure (from Rs. 28 to Rs. 10). Thus, it is clear that with the rise in price, the total expenditure reduces and vice versa.

So elasticity of demand is greater than one or *Ed* > 1.

**2. Unitary Elastic Demand**

If price is Rs. 5 per unit, at that price 6 units are being demanded, then total outlay comes to Rs. 30. Now, price increases to Rs. 6 per unit, as a result, the quantity demanded reduces to 5 units but the total expenditure remains the same, i.e., Rs. 30. Thus, it is clear that with the rise in price (Rs 5 per unit to Rs. 6 per unit), the total expenditure remains the same (Rs. 30) and vice versa. The elasticity of demand in this case is equal to one or is unitary elastic.

**3. Less Elastic Demand**

If price is Re. 1 per unit, then the quantity demanded is 10 units. As there is gradual rise in price (from Re. 1 per unit to Rs. 4 per unit), there is increase in total expenditure (from Rs. 10 to Rs. 18). Thus, there prevails direct relationship between price and total expenditure. Thus, in this case, the price elasticity of demand is less than unity.

Diagrammatic representation of the three possibilities are shown in Fig. 5.11.

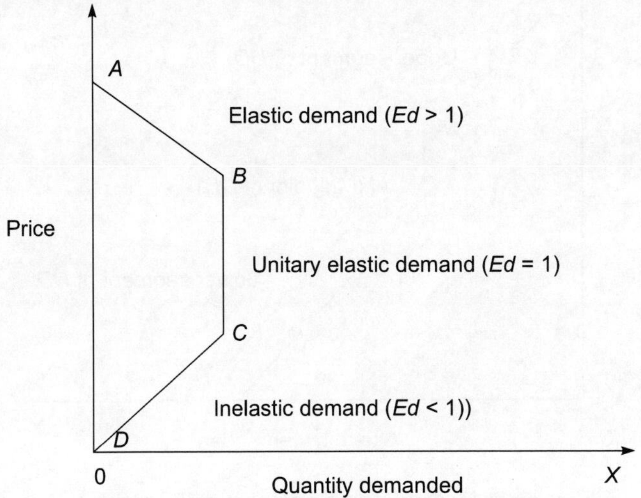


**Fig. 5.11** Elasticity under Expenditure Method

where,

$AB$ = More elastic demand or elastic demand ($Ed > 1$)

$BC$ = Unitary elastic demand ($Ed = 1$)

$CD$ = Less elastic demand or inelastic demand ($Ed < 1$)

$ABCD$ = Total expenditure curve

## 5.5.3 Point Method or Graphic Method

This method of measurement of elasticity of demand was given by Prof. Alfred Marshall. This is a method of measurement of elasticity of demand in case of linear or straight line curves. In this method, the price elasticity is measured at a specific point on a linear demand curve. It is for this reason it is known as 'point method' of measurement of elasticity of demand. Since, the demand curve is used in order to ascertain elasticity; therefore, it is also known as geometrical method.

According to Prof. Marshall, the elasticity at a point on demand curve is calculated as per the following formula:

$$Ed = \frac{\text{Lower segment (portion) of demand curve}}{\text{Upper segment (portion) of demand curve}}$$

It has been shown in Figure 5.12.

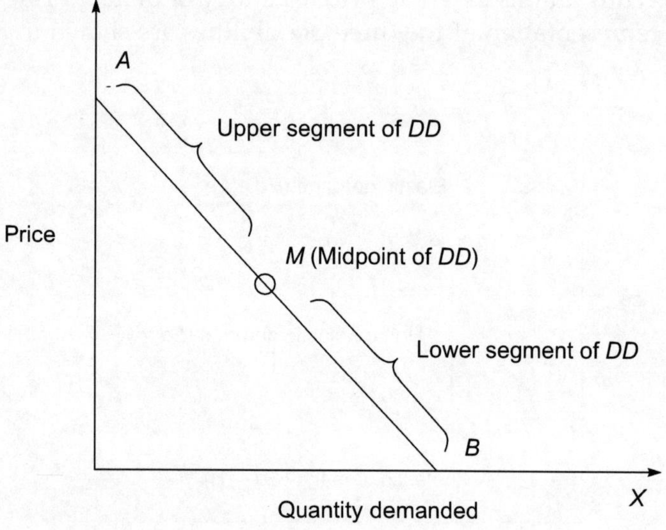


**Fig. 5.12** Point Method and Segments of Demand Curve

where,

$M$ = Midpoint of demand curve

$MB$ = Lower segment (portion) of demand curve

$AM$ = Upper segment (portion) of demand curve

Now, after considering the upper and lower segments, different points on the demand curve with the help of the Fig. 5.13 are given below:

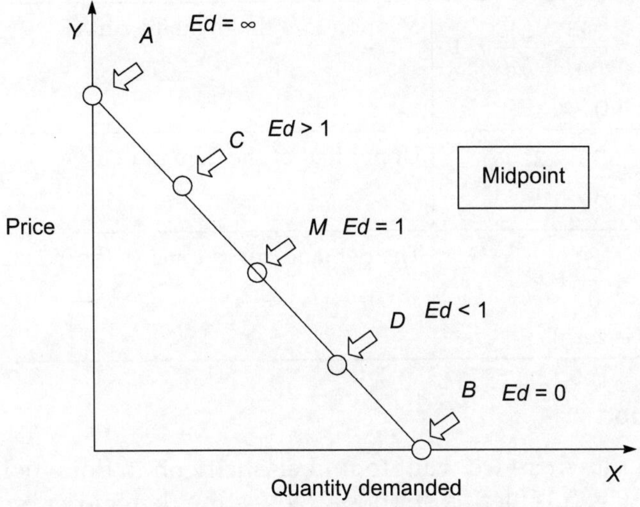


**Fig. 5.13** Point Method and Elasticity of Demand Curve

In Fig. 5.13, *AB* is a linear demand curve. *M* reflects the mid-point on the linear demand curve. It is the point which divides the demand curve in two equal segments (portions), viz., lower segment (*MB*) and upper segment (*AM*). Now, in order to ascertain the elasticity of demand at any point on linear demand curve, the lower segment from that point is kept in the numerator and the upper segment is considered a part of the denominator.

Thus, considering the formula of elasticity of demand, we have

$$Ed = \frac{\text{Lower segment (portion) of demand curve}}{\text{Upper segment (portion) of demand curve}}$$

The calculation of different coefficients of elasticity of demand is shown in Table 5.6.

**Table 5.6** Coefficients of Elasticity of Demand

| Calculation of Coefficients of *Ed* | Position of Point of Reference | Coefficients of *Ed* |
|---|---|---|
| (a) *Ed* (at point *B*) = $\frac{0}{AB} = 0$ (upper segment is zero) | The demand curve touches the *X*-axis | $Ed = 0$ |
| (b) *Ed* (at point *D*) = $\frac{DB}{AD} = \frac{1}{3} = < 1$ | Lower half of the demand curve | $Ed < 1$ |

*Contd.*

| | | |
|---|---|---|
| (c) $Ed$ (at point $M$) = $\frac{MB}{AM} = \frac{MB}{MB} = 1$<br>($M$ is the midpoint) | Midpoint on the demand curve | $Ed = 1$ |
| (d) $Ed$ (at point $C$) = $\frac{CB}{AC} = \frac{3}{1} = 3 > 1$ | Upper half of the demand curve | $Ed > 1$ |
| (e) $Ed$ (at point $A$) = $\frac{AB}{0} = \infty$<br>(lower segment is zero) | The demand curve touches the $Y$-axis | $Ed = \infty$ |

### 5.5.4 Arc Method

This method is useful where we want to find elasticity on to finite points lying close to one another. In Fig. 5.14, let us suppose, $DD_1$ is the demand curve and we want to find elasticity of demand at arc $AB$. For this purpose, we consider the average of original and new quantities as well as original and new prices.

Let $P_1$ = Original price
$P_2$ = New price
$Q_1$ = Original quantity
$Q_2$ = New quantity

This is represented in the following figure:

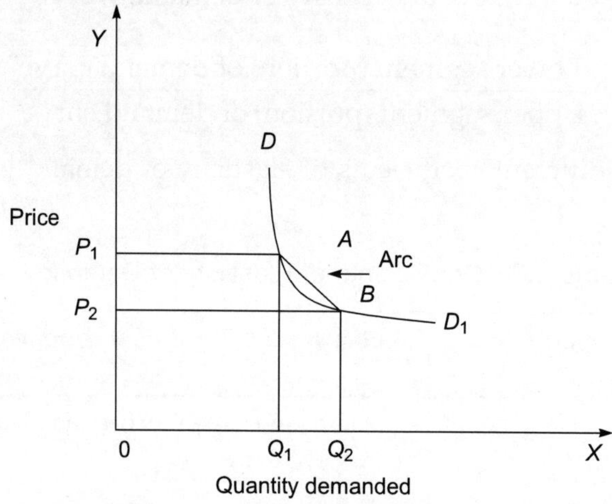


**Fig. 5.14** Arc Method for Measurement of Elasticity of Demand

Average price and quantity may be written as:

$$\text{Average price} = \frac{P_1 + P_2}{2}$$

$$\text{Average price} = \frac{Q_1 + Q_2}{2}$$

Now, the coefficient of elasticity using arc method can be calculated as:

$$Ed \text{ (along } AB) = \frac{\dfrac{\text{Change in quantity}}{\text{Average quantity}}}{\dfrac{\text{Change in price}}{\text{Average price}}}$$

$$Ed \text{ (along } AB) = \frac{\dfrac{Q_2 - Q_1}{Q_1 + Q_2/2}}{\dfrac{P_2 - P_1}{P_1 + P_2/2}}$$

$$Ed \text{ (along } AB) = \frac{\dfrac{Q_2 - Q_1}{Q_1 + Q_2}}{\dfrac{P_2 - P_1}{P_1 + P_2}}$$

By rearranging terms:

$$Ed \text{ (along } AB) = \frac{Q_2 - Q_1}{Q_1 + Q_2} \times \frac{P_1 - P_2}{P_2 + P_1}$$

Thus, using arc method, the coefficient of elasticity is as follows:

$$Ed \text{ (along } AB) = \frac{\text{Difference in quantity}}{\text{Sum of quantity}} \times \frac{\text{Sum of prices}}{\text{Difference in prices}}$$

## Summary

- ✓ The concept of elasticity of demand was propounded by Prof. Alfred Marshall in his book 'Principles of Economics' published in 1890.
- ✓ The price elasticity of demand refers to the degree or extent of responsiveness of demand on account of change in the level of price.
- ✓ The concept of elasticity has been further defined in terms of determinants of demand function. The influence of each factor on quantity demanded or demand is linked with relative concept of elasticity of demand as follows:
  - Price of the commodity – Price elasticity of demand
  - Income of the consumer – Income elasticity of demand
  - Price of related goods – Cross elasticity of demand
  - Advertisement expenditure – Advertisement elasticity of demand

✓ The factors that determine elasticity of demand are:

- Nature of the commodity
- Availability of substitutes
- Number of uses
- Postponement of use
- Joint demand
- Price level
- Income level
- Habits
- Proportion of total income spent on the product
- Brand loyalty

✓ Coefficient of price elasticity has a negative value, because of the existence of inverse relationship between price and quantity demanded.

✓ There are four methods of measurement of elasticity of demand:

- Percentage method or proportionate method
- Expenditure method or total outlay method
- Point method or graphic method
- Arc method

✓ There are five degrees of price elasticity of demand:

- Perfectly elastic demand – demand curve is a horizontal straight line parallel to *X*-axis
- Perfectly inelastic demand – demand curve is a vertical straight line parallel to *Y*-axis
- Unitary elastic demand – demand curve is a rectangular hyperbola
- Relatively elastic demand – demand curve is a flatter downward sloping curve
- Relatively inelastic demand – demand curve is a steeper downward sloping curve.

## Review Questions

1. Define price elasticity of demand. What are the factors that determine price elasticity of demand?
2. What are the various methods of measurement of price elasticity of demand?
3. What is price elasticity of demand? Explain the concept with the help of proportionate method and point method.
4. What is the price elasticity of demand? Explain the concept with the help of total outlay method and arc method.

5. What is meant by price elasticity of demand? What are its various degrees?
6. Explain the concept of price elasticity of demand in the context of the following values:
   (a) Infinity
   (b) Zero
   (c) Equal to one
   (d) More than one
   (e) Less than one
7. Explain the types of price elasticity of demand under expenditure method.
8. Explain the calculation of elasticity of demand under the following situations:
   (a) When demand curve is linear
   (b) When demand curve is curvilinear
9. Explain the concept of price elasticity using graphic method and arc method.
10. Write short notes on:
   (a) Percentage method or proportionate method
   (b) Total expenditure method or total outlay method
   (c) Point method or graphic method
   (d) Arc method

## CASE STUDY: ESTIMATION OF OWN PRICE ELASTICITY OF DEMAND FOR FOOD COMMODITIES IN INDIA (2011)

| Food | Own Price Elasticity of Demand |
|---|---|
| Cereals | −0.031 |
| Pulses | −0.635 |
| Vegetables and fruits | −0.917 |
| Milk | −1.035 |
| Edible oil | −0.377 |
| Sugar | −0.010 |
| Other food commodities | −1.259 |

*Source*: Kumar P., Kumar A., Parappurathu S. and Raju S.S. (2011). Estimation of Demand Elasticity for Food Commodities in India (permission duly received). Retrieved from https://www.researchgate.net/publication/227365120_Estimation_of_Demand_Elasticity_for_Food_Commodities_in_India/link/02e7e51c3c97e3d74d000000/download on September 22, 2019.

It is explicit from the above table that the price elasticities of demand calculated for all the food commodities on the basis of commodity's own price is negative in all cases. The negative exhibits the inverse relationship between quantity demanded of the commodity and its price.

However, further analysis reflects that other food commodities such as meat, fish and eggs have highly elastic demand (1.26). This is followed by milk (1.03). This means that 1 per cent increase in price leads to reduction in quantity demanded by 1.26 per cent in case of other food commodities and by 1.03 per cent in case of milk. It shows that the demand is more than unitary elastic and is highly responsive in case of commodities (meat, fish and eggs) and milk. However, in case of commodities such as vegetable and fruits, the coefficient of elasticity is –0.917 which is on the borderline. This is followed by pulses (–0.635) and edible oils (–0.377). Here, the value of coefficient of own price elasticity of demand is less than one indicating that one per cent increase in commodity's own price leads to less than proportionate increase in expenditure on these commodities. The least value of price elasticity of demand exists in case of sugar (–0.010) which indicates that the consumer is very less responsive to purchase of sugar. It also indicates that one per cent increase in sugar's own price leads to very small rise in expenditure on this commodity.

# 6 CHAPTER

# Elasticities of Demand other than Price

**LEARNING OBJECTIVES**

After going through this chapter, reader would be able to understand:

- ✓ The meaning and concept of income elasticity of demand
- ✓ The meaning and concept of cross elasticity of demand
- ✓ The meaning and concept of advertising elasticity of demand

## 6.1 INTRODUCTION

Chapter 4 explained the inverse relationship between price and quantity demanded for the product. The entire analysis assumed the constancy of other factors except price. These other factors include income of the consumer, price of related goods, advertisement expenditure, season, fashion, etc. Now, we work on these factors and ascertain their impact on demand for the product. The previous chapter (chapter 5) elaborated the discussion on price elasticity of demand. The impact of change in price on the quantity demanded of the same product was studied. In the present chapter, we begin our analysis with the concept of elasticity of demand in terms of other factors that determine the demand for the product. Elasticity of demand in terms of other factors determining demand is one of the important aspects of study of business or managerial economics.

In demand function, consumer's income is one of the factors that influences demand for a commodity. Unlike the negative price-demand relationship, generally a positive relationship exists between demand for a commodity and income of the consumer. But an exception to this rule is also exists, i.e., in case of inferior goods when income-elasticity of demand is negative because of negative substitution effect. Thus, when the degree of sensitivity of demand as dependent variable is ascertained in relation to change in income as an independent variable is known as income elasticity of demand. The initial explanations relate to the preparation of income demand curves establishing relationships between income of the consumer and demand for the product.

Price of related goods like substitute goods and complementary goods also affect demand for commodity to a great extent. When the measure of response of change in demand is considered a result of change in price of concerned commodity, it is called price elasticity. However, when effect on the quantity of one commodity is studied as a result of change in price of its related commodity, then the phenomenon studied is cross elasticity of demand. The chapter further proceeds with the impact of change in level of price of related goods on the demand for the product.

In the contemporary scenario, most of the firms spend considerable amounts of money on advertisement and other sales promotional activities in order to position the product in the minds of the customers. The purpose is to promote its sales and thereby generating revenue and maximizing profits. The present chapter deals with the study of impact of change in advertising or other promotional expenses on the demand or sales. It is defined as ratio of proportionate change in demand for a commodity to the proportionate change in advertisement expenditure. Thus, the quantum of rise or decline in demand in terms of change in advertisement expenditure is studied in the present chapter.

## 6.2 INCOME ELASTICITY OF DEMAND

### 6.2.1 Meaning

Income elasticity of demand refers to the degree of responsiveness or extent of response of change in demand for a product on account of changes in consumer's income. In simple words, income elasticity of demand is the ratio of percentage change in demand to the percentage change in consumer's own income level. Income elasticity of demand is, thus, a measure of the relative change in quantity purchased of a product in response to a relative change in income of the consumer.

### 6.2.2 Coefficient of Income Elasticity of Demand

The coefficient of income elasticity of demand can be expressed as under:

$$Ye = \frac{\text{Percentage change in demand}}{\text{Percentage change in income of the consumer}}$$

Thus, we have

$$Ye = \frac{\Delta Q}{\Delta Y} \times \frac{Y}{Q}$$

where,

$Ye$ = Coefficient of income elasticity of demand
$\Delta Q$ = Change in demand
$\Delta Y$ = Change in income
$Y$ = Original income of the consumer
$Q$ = Original demand

### 6.2.3 Derivation

$$Ye = \frac{\text{Percentage change in demand}}{\text{Percentage change in income}}$$

$$= \frac{\dfrac{\text{Change in demand}}{\text{Original demand}} \times 100}{\dfrac{\text{Change in income}}{\text{Original income}} \times 100}$$

$$= \frac{\dfrac{\text{New quantity} - \text{Original quantity}}{\text{Original quantity}}}{\dfrac{\text{New income} - \text{Original income}}{\text{Original income}}}$$

Symbolically, it can be written as

$$Ed = \frac{\dfrac{Q_2 - Q_1}{Q_1}}{\dfrac{Y_2 - Y_1}{Y_1}}$$

In general terms,

$$= \frac{\dfrac{\Delta Q}{Q}}{\dfrac{\Delta Y}{Y}}$$

$$= \frac{\Delta Q}{\Delta Y} \times \frac{P}{Q}$$

By rearranging terms,

$$\boxed{Ed = \frac{\Delta Q}{\Delta Y} \times \frac{Y}{Q}}$$

Here,

$\Delta Q$ = Change in demand
$Q$ = Original demand
$\Delta P$ = Change in income
$P$ = Original income

The symbol $\Delta$ means the change.

### 6.2.4 Degrees/Types of Income Elasticity of Demand

**1. Positive Income Elasticity of Demand (Case of Normal Goods)**

Income elasticity of demand is said to be positive when there is a direct relationship between demand for goods and services and consumer's income. Income elasticity of demand is positive in case of normal goods as their demand increases as a result of increase in the income of the consumer and vice versa.

Symbolically,

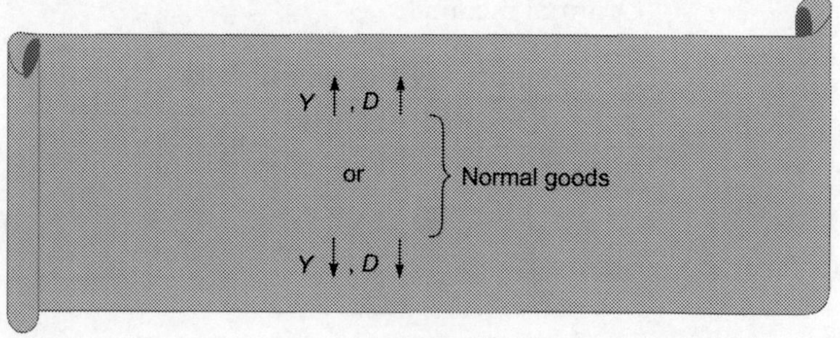


The diagrammatic representation of positive income elasticity of demand is as follows:

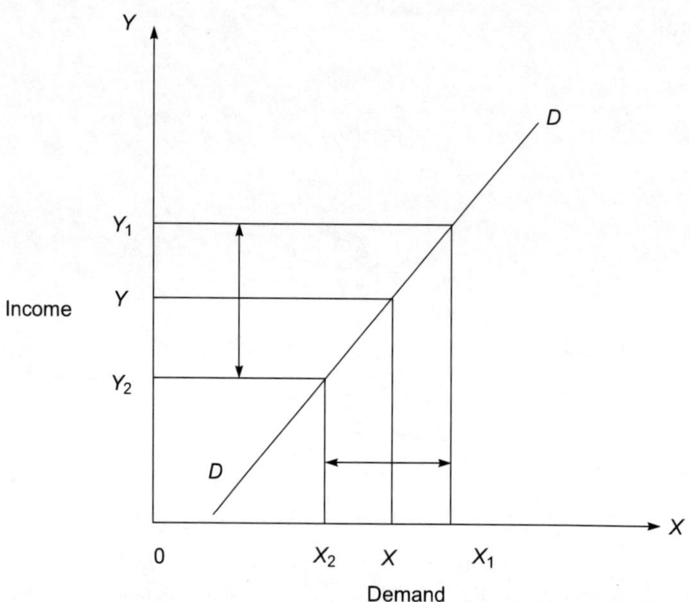


**Fig. 6.1** Positive Income Demand Curve

In Fig. 6.1, units of commodity have been measured on *X*-axis and income of the consumer on *Y*-axis. Let the initial income be *OY* and at that price *OX* units of a commodity are demanded. Now with an increase in income of consumer from *OY* to $OY_1$, the demand increases from $OX$ to $OX_1$ and with decrease in income, the demand also falls. Thus, a positive income-demand relationship is reflected by *DD*. *DD* is the positively sloped income demand curve. It slopes upwards from left to right indicating that increase in income is accompanied by increase in demand of goods and services and vice versa.

*Example:* Rice and wheat are normal goods.

There are three cases under positive income elasticity of demand:

**(a) Income Elasticity is Greater than One (*Ye* > 1)**

Income elasticity is said to be more than elastic when the proportionate change in income leads to more than proportionate change in demand.

***For example:*** If there is change in income of consumer by 10% and it leads to 18% change in demand for the commodity, income demand is said to be more than unitary elastic and the value of its coefficient is greater than one or unity. This occurs in case of luxury goods.

Income elasticity > 1 when

$$Ye = \frac{18\%}{10\%} = 1.8 \text{ which is greater than one}$$

**(b) Income Elasticity is Unity (*Ye* = 1)**

Income elasticity is unitary elastic when the proportionate change in income is equal and proportionate to the change in demand for the commodity.

***For example:*** If there is change in income of consumer by 10% and it leads to 10% change in demand, income demand is said to be unitary elastic. This occurs in case of comfort goods.

Income elasticity = 1 when

$$Ye = \frac{10\%}{10\%} = 1 \text{ or unity}$$

**(c) Income Elasticity is Less than One (*Ye* < 1)**

Income elasticity is said to be less than elastic when the proportionate change in income leads to less than proportionate change in demand. In that case, the income elasticity of demand is less than one or unity and the value of its coefficient is less than one or unity.

***For example:*** If there is change in income of consumer by 10% and it leads to 4% change in demand, income demand is said to be less than unitary elastic. This occurs in case of necessity goods.

Income elasticity <1 when

$$Ye = \frac{4\%}{10\%} = 0.4 \text{ which is less than one}$$

## 2. Negative Income Elasticity of Demand (Case of Inferior Goods)

Income elasticity of demand is said to be negative when there is an inverse relationship between demand for goods and services and consumer's income. It means that if there is rise in demand on account of fall in the income of the consumer and fall in demand due to rise in income of the consumer, there is negative income elasticity of demand.

Income elasticity of demand is negative in case of inferior goods. This is due to the reason that as a result of rise in income of the consumer, consumers start purchasing more of a superior commodities (normal goods). Due to this, there is decline in demand for an inferior commodity.

Symbolically,

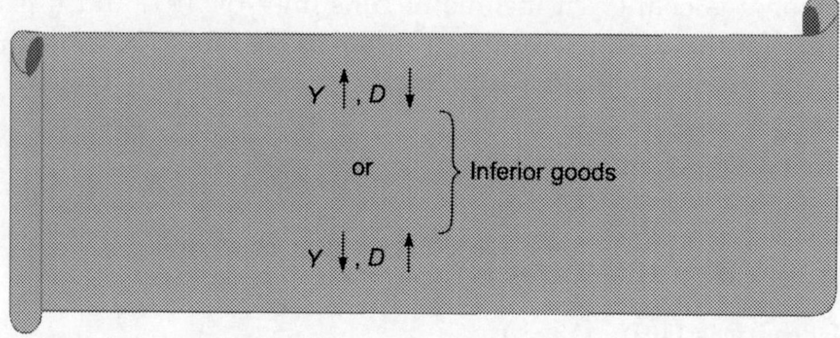


The diagrammatic representation of positive income elasticity of demand is as follows:

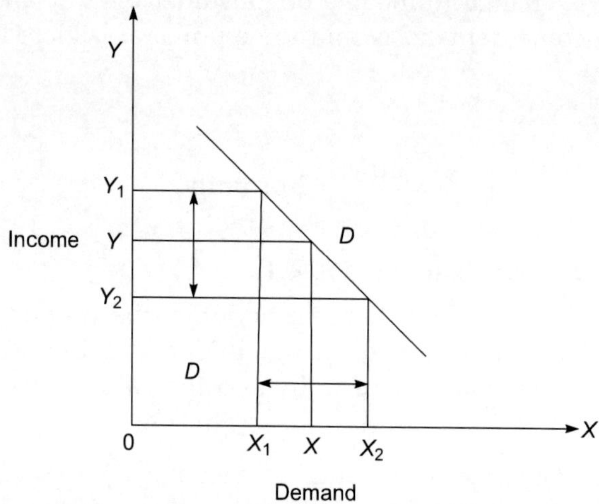


**Fig. 6.2** Negative Income Demand Curve

In Fig. 6.2, when income of the consumer is $OY$, demand for goods and services is $OX$. Now as the income of consumer rises from $OY$ to $OY_1$, then the demanded falls $OX$ to $OX_1$. Conversely, if the consumer's income falls from $OY$ to $OY_2$, the demand rises from $OX$ to $OX_2$. $DD$ is the negative income elasticity of demand. Thus, a negative income demand relationship exists which is reflected by negatively sloped $DD$. $DD$ is negatively sloped indicating inverse relationship between demand and income of the consumer.

***For example:*** Bajra and Ragi are inferior commodities against normal goods like rice and wheat.

Jaggery is an inferior commodity against sugar.

Tonned milk is considered an inferior commodity against full cream milk.

**3. Zero Income Elasticity of Demand**

Zero income elasticity of demand is said to exist when a change in income induces no change in demand for a commodity. In other words, increase or decrease in income has no impact on the demand of goods and services. In this case, the commodity lies between a necessity and an inferior commodity.

Symbolically,

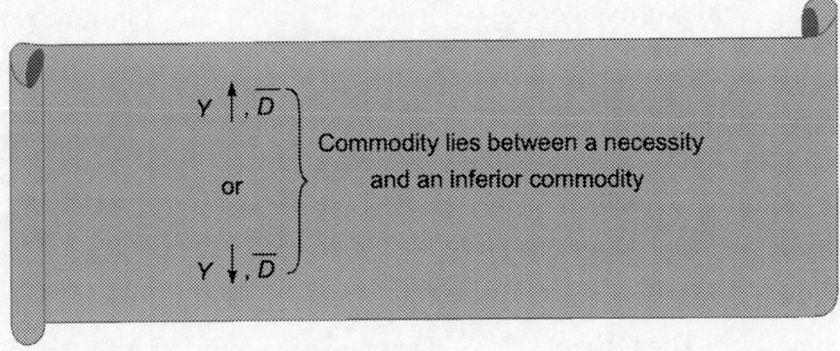


The diagrammatic representation of zero income elasticity of demand is as follows:

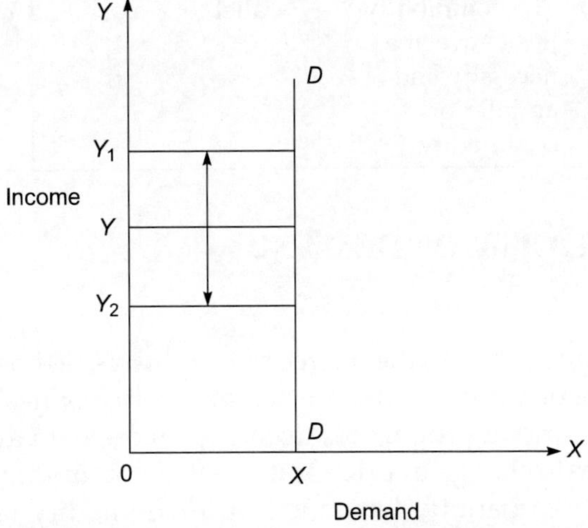


**Fig. 6.3** Zero Income Demand Curve

In Fig. 6.3, the initial income of the consumer is $OY$ at which $OX$ units are demanded. Now, income increases to $OY_1$, demand remains unchanged at $OX$. Even after reduction in income to $OY_2$, the demand remains constant at $OX$. It is thus, clear that a rise or fall in income of the consumer does not affect the demand for the commodity.

A comprehensive view of explanation of degrees of income elasticity of demand is shown in Table 6.1.

**TABLE 6.1** Explanation of Degrees of Income Elasticity of Demand

| Degree of Income Elasticity of Demand | Type of Commodity | Income Demand Curve | Value/Range of Coefficient of Income Elasticity of Demand |
|---|---|---|---|
| **1.** Positive income elasticity of demand | 1. The case of normal goods | Upward sloping from left to right | $0 < Ye < 1$ |
| | (a) Normal goods: luxury goods | | Income elasticity is greater than one ($Ye > 1$) |
| | (b) Normal Goods: comfort goods | | Income elasticity is unity ($Ye = 1$). |
| | (c) Normal Goods: necessity goods | | Income elasticity less than one ($Ye < 1$) |
| **2.** Negative income elasticity of demand | 2. The Case of inferior goods | Downward sloping from left to right | $Ye < 0$ |
| **3.** Zero income elasticity of demand | 3. The commodity lies between a necessity and an inferior commodity | Parallel to $Y$-axis | $Ye = 0$ |

## 6.3 CROSS ELASTICITY OF DEMAND

### 6.3.1 Meaning

Cross elasticity of demand refers to the degree of responsiveness or extent of response of change in demand of one product due to change in price of its related commodity. It is represented as the ratio of proportionate change in the demand of commodity $X$ to the given proportionate change in price of its related commodity, $Y$. It is a measure of relative change in the quantity demanded of a commodity (say commodity $X$) due to a change in the price of its substitute or complementary commodity (say commodity $Y$). Generally speaking, the concept of cross elasticity of demand arises in case of substitutes and complements.

### 6.3.2 Coefficient of Cross Elasticity of Demand

The coefficient of cross elasticity of demand can be expressed as under:

$$Ye = \frac{\text{Percentage change in demand for commodity, } X}{\text{Percentage change in price for commodity, } Y}$$

Thus, we have

$$\boxed{Ce = \frac{\Delta Q(X)}{\Delta P(Y)} \times \frac{P(Y)}{Q(X)}}$$

where,

$$\begin{aligned}
\Delta Q(X) &= \text{Change in demand of commodity X} \\
\Delta P(Y) &= \text{Change in price of commodity } Y \\
Q(X) &= \text{Original demand of commodity X} \\
P(Y) &= \text{Original price of commodity } Y
\end{aligned}$$

### 6.3.3 Derivation

$$C_e = \frac{\text{Percentage change in demand for commodity } X}{\text{Percentage change in price for commodity } Y}$$

$$= \frac{\dfrac{\text{Change in demand for commodity X}}{\text{Original in demand of commodity X}} \times 100}{\dfrac{\text{Change in price of commodity } Y}{\text{Original price of commodity } Y} \times 100}$$

$$= \frac{\dfrac{\text{New demand (commodity X)} - \text{Original demand (commodity X)}}{\text{Original demand (commodity X)}}}{\dfrac{\text{New price (commodity } Y) - \text{Original price (commodity } Y)}{\text{Original price (commodity } Y)}}$$

Symbolically, it can be written

$$C_e = \frac{\dfrac{Q_2(\text{commodity X}) - Q_1(\text{commodity } X)}{Q_1(\text{commodity X})}}{\dfrac{P_2(\text{commodity } Y) - P_1(\text{commodity } Y)}{P_1(\text{commodity } Y)}}$$

In general terms,

$$= \frac{\frac{\Delta Q(\text{commodity } X)}{Q(\text{commodity } X)}}{\frac{\Delta P(\text{commodity } Y)}{P(\text{commodity } Y)}}$$

$$= \frac{\Delta Q(\text{commodity } X)}{\Delta P(\text{commodity } Y)} \times \frac{P(\text{commodity } Y)}{Q(\text{commodity } X)}$$

By rearranging terms,

$$\boxed{Ce = \frac{\Delta Q(X)}{\Delta P(Y)} \times \frac{P(Y)}{Q(X)}}$$

where,

$\Delta Q(X)$ = Change in demand of commodity $X$
$\Delta P(Y)$ = Change in price of commodity $Y$
$Q(X)$ = Original demand of commodity $X$
$P(Y)$ = Original price of commodity $Y$

The symbol $\Delta$ means the change.

### 6.3.4 Degrees/Types of Cross Elasticity of Demand

**1. Positive Cross Elasticity of Demand (Case of Substitute Goods)**

The cross elasticity is said to be positive when there is a direct relationship between price of one commodity and the quantity of the other. In other words, an increase in the price of one commodity (say commodity $Y$) leads to an increase in the demand of another commodity (say commodity X) and vice versa. This is on account of substitution effect that the consumer starts purchasing more of a substitute product when the price of the another substitute product rises. It happens when goods are substitutes of each other. In this case, the cross demand curve is upward sloping from left to right.

Symbolically,

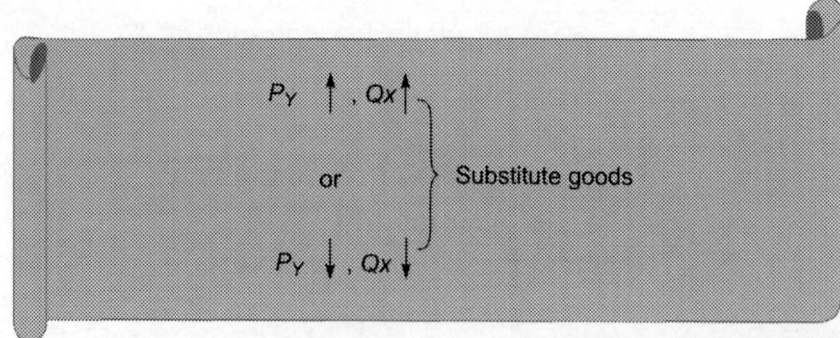

The diagrammatic representation of positive cross elasticity of demand is shown in Fig. 6.4 as follows:

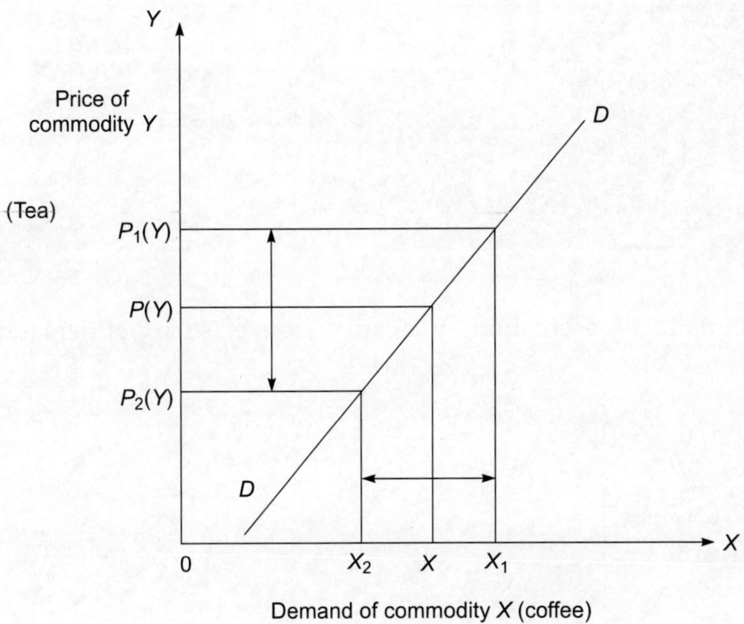


**Fig. 6.4** Positive Cross Elasticity of Demand

In Fig. 6.4, *DD* is the cross demand curve. Here, quantity of commodity, *X*, i.e., coffee has been measured on X-axis and price of commodity *Y* (tea) on *Y*-axis. Now, when there is an increase in the price of tea, demand for coffee will increase. It is to be noted here that the demand for coffee has risen because of prices of its substitute product, not because of its own price. Suppose the initial price of tea is $OP(Y)$ and quantity of coffee is OX. Now, if there is rise in the price of tea from $OP(Y)$ to $OP_1(Y)$, then there is rise in demand for the coffee from $OX$ to $OX_1$. Thus, cross elasticity of demand is positive in case of substitute goods.

**2. Negative Cross Elasticity of Demand (Case of Complementary Goods)**

The cross elasticity is said to be negative when an inverse relationship is between price of one commodity and the quantity of the other. It means that if an increase in the price of one commodity (say commodity *Y*) leads to a decrease in the demand of another commodity (say commodity *X*) and vice versa, then in that case the cross elasticity of demand is negative. This is due to the fact that both the products are jointly demanded and used together to satisfy a given need. Thus, it happens in case of complementary goods. In this case, the cross demand curve is downward sloping from left to right.

Symbolically,

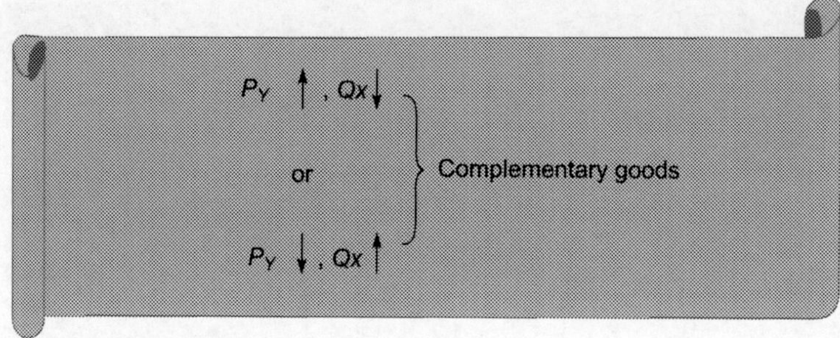


The diagrammatic representation of negative cross elasticity of demand is shown in Fig. 6.5.

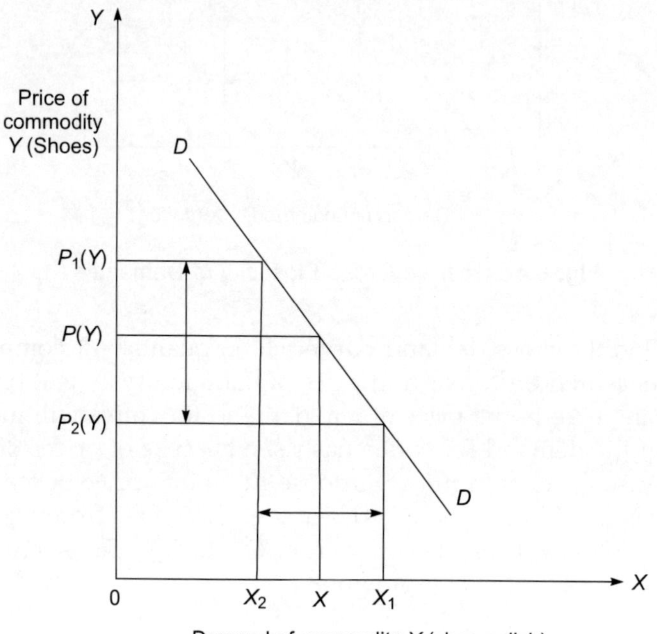


**Fig. 6.5** Positive Cross Elasticity of Demand

In Fig. 6.5, quantity of commodity $X$ (shoe polish) has been measured on $X$-axis while price of commodity $Y$ (shoes) has been measured on $Y$-axis. $DD$ is the cross demand curve. Now, suppose, there is rise in the price of shoes from $OP(Y)$ to $OP_1(Y)$, as a result there is decline in demand for the commodity from $OX$ to $OX_2$, and vice versa. This is due to the fact that these products are jointly demanded products and a rise in price of one will lead to decline in demand of another. Therefore, cross elasticity of demand in case of complementary products is negative.

### 3. Zero Cross Elasticity of Demand

Cross elasticity of demand is zero when two goods are not related to each other. It means that the price of one commodity does not affect the demand for another commodity. Thus, a rise or fall in price of one commodity will not affect the demand for another commodity. Therefore, in this case, the price and quantity relationships of both the products are independent of each other. This happens in case of unrelated goods. In this case, the cross demand curve is parallel to the *Y*-axis.

Symbolically,

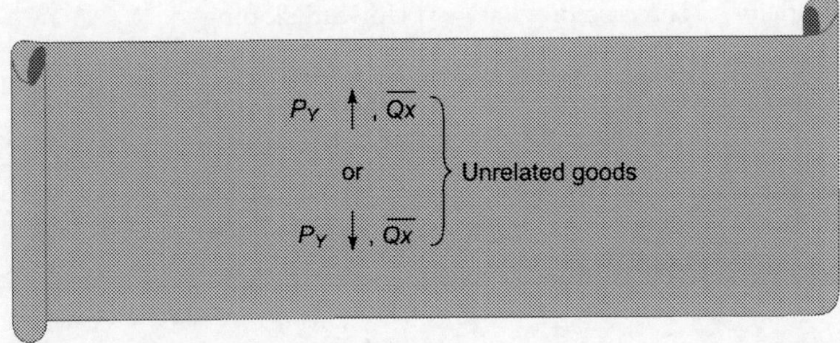


The diagrammatic representation of zero cross elasticity of demand is shown in Fig. 6.6.

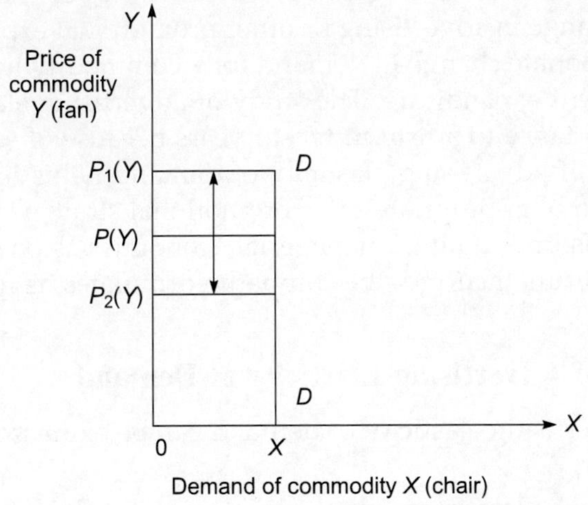


**Fig. 6.6** Zero Cross Elasticity of Demand

In Fig. 6.6, a rise in price of fan from $OP(Y)$ to $OP_1(Y)$ or fall from $OP(Y)$ to $OP_2(Y)$, does not affect the demand of commodity *X*, i.e., chair. It means that the consumer is purchasing the same units of chair irrespective of price of fan. Thus, increase or fall in price of fan does not affect the demand of chair. Thus, cross elasticity of demand is zero.

The comprehensive view of explanation of degrees of cross elasticity of demand is shown in Table 6.2.

**TABLE 6.2** Explanation of Degrees of Cross Elasticity of Demand

| Degree of Cross Elasticity of Demand | Type of Commodity | Cross Demand Curve | Value/Range of Coefficient of Cross Elasticity of Demand |
|---|---|---|---|
| Positive cross elasticity of demand | The case of substitute goods | Upward sloping from left to right | $Ce > 0$ |
| Negative cross elasticity of demand | The case of complementary goods | Downward sloping from left to right | $Ce < 0$ |
| Zero cross elasticity of demand | The case of unrelated goods | Parallel to $Y$-axis | $Ce = 0$ |

## 6.4 ADVERTISING OR PROMOTIONAL ELASTICITY OF DEMAND

### 6.4.1 Meaning

Advertising elasticity refers to the degree of responsiveness of change in demand or sales on account of change in advertising or other promotional expenses. It is defined as the ratio of proportionate change in demand for a commodity to the proportionate change in advertisement expenditure. The study of advertising elasticity of demand is of paramount importance to a firm in recent years because of severe competition. An in-depth analysis of advertising elasticity of demand helps in determination of prices and formulation of appropriate sales promotional strategy. Thus, the study of advertising elasticity is important in managerial economics as on the basis of actual advertisement expenditure incurred, the company formulates its future action plans.

### 6.4.2 Coefficient of Advertising Elasticity of Demand

The coefficient of advertising elasticity of demand can be expressed as under:

$$A_e = \frac{\text{Percentage change in demand/sales}}{\text{Percentage change in advertisemnt expenditure}}$$

Thus, we have,

$$Ed = \frac{\Delta Q}{\Delta A} \times \frac{A}{Q}$$

where,

$\Delta Q$ = Change in demand of the product
$Q$ = Original demand of the product
$\Delta A$ = Change in advertisement expenditure
$A$ = Original advertisement expenditure incurred

### 6.4.3 Derivation

$$A_e = \frac{\text{Percentage change in demand or sales}}{\text{Percentage change in advertisement expenditure}}$$

$$= \frac{\dfrac{\text{Change in demand or sales}}{\text{Change in demand or sales}} \times 100}{\dfrac{\text{Change in advertisement expenditure}}{\text{Original advertisement expenditure}} \times 100}$$

$$= \frac{\dfrac{\text{New demand (or sales) – Original demand (or sales)}}{\text{Change in demand (or sales)}}}{\dfrac{\text{New advertisement expenditure – Original advertisement expenditure}}{\text{Original advertisement expend diture}}}$$

Symbolically it can be written as,

$$Ae = \frac{\dfrac{Q_2 - Q_1}{Q_1}}{\dfrac{A_2 - A_1}{A_1}}$$

In general terms,

$$= \frac{\dfrac{\Delta Q}{Q}}{\dfrac{\Delta A}{A}}$$

$$= \frac{\Delta Q}{\Delta A} \times \frac{A}{Q}$$

By rearranging terms,

$$\boxed{Ae = \frac{\Delta Q}{\Delta A} \times \frac{A}{Q}}$$

where,

$\Delta Q$ = Change in demand of the product
$Q$ = Original demand of the product
$\Delta A$ = Change in advertisement expenditure
$P$ = Original advertisement expenditure incurred

The symbol Δ means the change.

The concept of advertising elasticity of demand can be understood with the help of a company's hypothetical advertisement expenditure and sales record. Suppose, the company spends Rs. 8000 in the month of February in 2019. The sales record reflects that the sales figure stood at 1,00,000 units in that month. The company decided to see the impact of advertisement expenditure on the sales of the product. As a result, it enhances the amount that is spent on advertisement to Rs. 10,000 in the next month. The new sales figure was ascertained at 1,50,000 units. In order to find out the impact of advertisement expenditure on the sales of the product, the managerial economist resorts to advertising elasticity of demand and pens down the following figures:

Original sales = 1,00,000 units, Original advertisement expenditure = 8000
New sales = 1,50,000 units, New advertisement expenditure = 10000

The calculation of advertising elasticity of demand is as follows:

$$Ae = \frac{\Delta Q}{\Delta A} \times \frac{A}{Q}$$

$$Ae = \frac{50,000}{2000} \times \frac{8000}{1,00,000} = 2, \text{ which is greater than 1}$$

It implies that the demand for the product that the company sells is more than elastic. It clearly reveals that the demand for the company's product is highly responsive to the advertisement expenditure incurred by the company. This is an important information for managerial economist that the customers are greatly influenced by the advertisement expenditure the company incurs. Thus, the company should work on its advertisement and promotional strategies in order to promote the sales of its products.

## Summary

✓ Apart from price elasticity of demand, there are other elasticities of demand. These elasticities are related to the factors other than price in demand function. These are:

- Income elasticity of demand
- Cross elasticity of demand
- Advertising elasticity of demand

- ✓ Income elasticity of demand means the degree of responsiveness or extent of response of change in demand for a product on account of changes in consumer's income.
- ✓ There are three degrees of income elasticity of demand, namely:
  - Positive income elasticity of demand: Occurs in case of normal goods. In such case, the income demand curve is upward sloping from left to right. It is further divided in three sub-degrees:
    - (a) Income elasticity is greater than one ($Ye > 1$): This occurs in case of luxury goods.
    - (b) Income elasticity is unity ($Ye = 1$): This occurs in case of comfort goods.
    - (c) Income elasticity is less than one ($Ye < 1$): This occurs in case of necessity goods.
  - Negative income elasticity of demand: Occurs in case of inferior goods. In such case, the income demand curve is downward sloping from left to right.
  - Zero income elasticity of demand: The commodity lies between a necessity and an inferior commodity. In such case, the income demand curve is parallel to *Y*-axis
- ✓ Cross elasticity of demand refers to the degree of responsiveness or extent of response of change in demand of one product due to changes in price of its related commodity.
- ✓ There are three degrees of cross elasticity of demand, namely:
  - Positive cross elasticity of demand: Occurs in case of substitute goods.
  - Negative cross elasticity of demand: Occurs in case of complementary goods.
  - Zero cross elasticity of demand: Occurs in case of unrelated goods.
- ✓ Advertising elasticity refers to the degree of responsiveness of change in demand or sales on account of change in advertising or other promotional expenses. An in-depth analysis of advertising elasticity of demand helps in determination of prices and formulation of appropriate sales promotional strategy.

## Review Questions

1. What is income elasticity of demand? Elucidate the various degrees of income elasticity of demand.
2. Explain the concept of income elasticity of demand under the following cases:
   (a) When commodity is a normal product
   (b) When commodity is an inferior product

3. Show the derivation of coefficient of income elasticity of demand. Also explain the degrees of income elasticity of demand.
4. Define cross elasticity of demand. Explain its various degrees.
5. Cross elasticity tells the relationship between the price of the commodity and its demand. Comment.
6. Explain the concept of cross elasticity of demand
   (a) In case of substitute goods
   (b) In case of complementary goods
7. Derive the coefficient of cross elasticity of demand. Also explain its degrees.
8. Cross elasticity of demand is not same for all consumer goods. Explain the statement.
9. Write short notes on:
   (a) Cross elasticity of demand
   (b) Advertisement elasticity of demand
10. Explain the concept of promotional elasticity of demand? What is the use of this concept in managerial decision-making?
11. Advertisement elasticity of demand helps in formulation of appropriate sales promotional strategy. Explain the statement.
12. How can the effectiveness of an advertisement campaign be determined? Explain in light of advertisement elasticity of demand.

## CASE STUDY: ESTIMATION OF INCOME ELASTICITY OF DEMAND FOR FOOD COMMODITIES IN INDIA (2011)

In this case, the food demand behaviour has been explained by taking into consideration the income elasticity of demand with respect to major food commodities in India. The major food commodities included in the present analysis are: cereals, pulses, fruits and vegetables, milk, edible oils, sugar and other food commodities such as meat, fish and eggs. For the purpose of the study, the sample households were categorized into four expenditure/income groups. These were; very poor, moderately poor, non-poor lower and non-poor higher (Table 1).

The 'very poor' class comprised households which have income level below 75 per cent of the poverty line (PL), between 75 per cent of PL to PL were defined as 'moderately poor', between PL and 150 per cent of PL were grouped as 'Non-poor lower' (middle income group) and households having per capita income above 150 per cent of PL were categorized as 'Non-poor higher' (high income group).The values of income elasticities of food groups are presented in Table 1 given below:

**TABLE 1** Estimation of Income Elasticity of Demand for Food Commodities in India (2011)

| Food | Very Poor | Moderately Poor | Non-Poor Lower | Non-Poor Higher | Income Elasticity of Demand |
|---|---|---|---|---|---|
| (1) | (2) | (3) | (4) | (5) | (6) |
| Cereals | 0.514 | 0.424 | 0.312 | –0.006 | 0.187 |
| Pulses | 0.993 | 0.895 | 0.793 | 0.580 | 0.716 |
| Vegetable and fruits | 0.759 | 0.785 | 0.811 | 0.839 | 0.817 |
| Milk | 2.342 | 2.018 | 1.773 | 1.556 | 1.640 |
| Edible oil | 0.935 | 0.876 | 0.817 | 0.695 | 0.772 |
| Sugar | 1.052 | 1.007 | 0.968 | 0.898 | 0.942 |
| Other food commodities | 0.840 | 0.872 | 0.895 | 0.894 | 0.887 |

*Source*: Kumar P., Kumar A., Parappurathu S. and Raju S.S. (2011). Estimation of Demand Elasticity for Food Commodities in India (permission duly received). Retrieved from https://www.researchgate.net/publication/227365120_Estimation_of_Demand_Elasticity_for_Food_Commodities_in_India/link/02e7e51c3c97e3d74d000000/download on September 22, 2019.

The above table reveals that income elasticities of food commodities in India are positive (refer col. 6). It means that the demand for these commodities will increase with increase in household income. However, the overall income elasticity has highest value in case of milk (1.64). It means that one per cent increase in consumer's income leads to 1.64 per cent increase in expenditure on milk. Thus, it is more than unitary elastic and is highly responsive to rise in income of the consumer. This is followed by sugar (0.94) which is on the borderline. Thereafter, the vegetables & fruits (0.82), edible oils (0.77), pulses (0.72) are in pipeline. In these cases, the value of coefficient of income elasticity of demand is less than one indicating that one per cent increase in consumer's income leads to less than proportionate increase in expenditure on these commodities. The least value of income elasticity exists in case of cereals (0.19) which indicates that the consumer is reluctant to spend his increased amount of income on purchase of cereals. It clearly reflects that the consumer's spending is more inclined towards the purchase of milk and least towards the purchase of cereals.

Col. 2 - col. 5 clearly reveal that the coefficients of income elasticities are much higher for poor households than for comparatively richer households. It is to be noted here that the demand for milk is highly responsive to change in income in case of both rich and poor. It is clearly evident from the above table that demand for milk is highly responsive to change in income of consumers. However, the poor are more responsive to act as a result of rise in income as compared to rich. It is to be noted here that the demand for cereals is negative (–0.006) as shown in column 5. The negative sign here reflects that one per cent change in income causes 0.006 per cent reduction in the expenditure on cereals in case of rich households who consider the product an inferior one. However, considering the case of cereals, in case of very poor, moderately poor and non-poor lower, the coefficient of income elasticity of demand is positive but is less than elastic. Thus, this income group considers the same product a normal commodity (necessity).

# 7 CHAPTER

# Supply Analysis

**LEARNING OBJECTIVES**

After going through this chapter, reader would be able to understand:

- ✓ Concept and the factors that influence the supply of a commodity.
- ✓ The mathematical expression of relationship between supply and its determinants.
- ✓ The prevalence of law of supply and the associated factors.
- ✓ The cases where the law of supply fails to operate.
- ✓ The change in supply vs change in quantity supplied.

## 7.1 INTRODUCTION

In chapter 4, demand as one of the important dimensions of market forces was discussed. It reflected the ability and willingness to buy and willingness to part with the funds at a specific price during a period of time. In this chapter, the analysis of another dimension of market forces would be conducted. Thus, this chapter discusses the supply side of market forces. The chapter focuses on the conceptual framework and the factors that influence the supply. The components of supply function have also been discussed. The operations of law of supply and associated dynamics in market economy have also been discussed. Additionally, the concepts that cause changes in supply in terms of price of the commodity, price of other goods, prices of factors of production, technology, taxes, subsidies, and expected prices have also been discussed and elaborated in the present chapter.

## 7.2 CONCEPT OF SUPPLY

Supply is one of the components of the market forces. It represents the willingness and ability of potential or existing sellers to produce and sell a product or service. It refers to the quantities of a product that producers will make available for sale in the market at series of possible prices during a specific period. Thus, there will be a quantity corresponding to each level of price in a period of time. In general, producers are inclined to sell their product or service for a price that covers the cost to produce an additional unit of the product and their markup.

Therefore, the integration of willingness to sell and ability to sell together create a framework for supply analysis. It has been represented in Fig. 7.1 as follows:

**Fig 7.1** Concept of Supply

It is to be noted here that the supply analysis is conducted with reference to time period and always considers the price dimensions.

***For example:*** A producer wants to sell chairs. He is able and willing to sell them but this will constitute supply only and only when it is at a price and during a period of time. Thus, to say that the seller sells 100 chairs is economically an irrelevant statement as it fails to consider the time and price element. The rectified statement is "a seller sells 100 chairs in a month at Rs 600 per chair". This is an economically significant statement.

## Definitions of Supply

According to Gillespie, "Supply reflects what producers are willing and able to produce at each and every price".

In the words of Lipsey and Chrystal "the amount of a product that the firms are able and willing to offer for sale is called quantity supplied".

## Supply Schedule

Supply schedule is a tabular representation of various combinations of price and quantity supplied (ceteris paribus). It reflects quantities of a commodity that will be supplied at various levels of price, during a given period of time.

Supply schedule is of two types:

1. Individual supply schedule
2. Market supply schedule

## Individual Supply Schedule

Individual supply schedule refers to a tabular representation of various quantities of a commodity corresponding to each price level that each producer is willing to sell during a given period of time. The individual supply schedule is given in Table 7.1 below:

**TABLE 7.1** Individual Supply Schedule

| Price (per Packet of Biscuits in Rs.) | Quantity Supplied of Biscuits (units) |
|---|---|
| 10 | 1 |
| 20 | 2 |
| 30 | 3 |
| 40 | 4 |
| 50 | 5 |

It is evident from the above table that when price per packet of biscuits is rising from Rs. 10 to Rs. 20 per packet, the seller is willing to supply more of the commodity from 1 packet to 2 packets and so on.

## Market Supply Schedule

Market supply schedule refers to a tabular representation of various quantities of a commodity corresponding to each price level that each producer is willing to sell during a given period of time. It is derived from individual supply in exactly the same way that market demand is derived from individual demand. It is ascertained by "horizontally adding individual supply curves". The supply curves of the individual producers at each and every level of price are added to obtain market supply curve.

It is represented as:

$$S_m = S_A + S_B + S_C + \dots + S_N$$

where

$S_m$ is the market supply
$S_A$ is individual supply of supplier $A$
$S_B$ is individual supply of supplier $B$
$S_C$ is individual supply of supplier C and so on.

## Market Supply Schedule

**TABLE 7.2** Market Supply Schedule

| $P_x$ (Rs.) | Individual Supply (units) | | | Market Supply (units) $\{S_A + S_B + S_C\}$ |
|---|---|---|---|---|
| | $S_A$ | $S_B$ | $S_C$ | |
| 10 | 1 | 2 | 3 | 1 + 2 + 3 = 6 |
| 20 | 2 | 4 | 6 | 2 + 4 + 6 = 12 |
| 30 | 3 | 6 | 9 | 3 + 6 + 9 = 18 |
| 40 | 4 | 8 | 12 | 4 + 8 + 12 = 24 |

Table 7.2 reflects that market supply can be calculated by adding up the individual supply of supplier *A*, *B* and *C*. It can be clearly seen that market supply is 6 units at a price of Rs. 10 per unit. Further, the market supply is 12 units, 18 units and 24 units at a price of Rs. 20, 30 and 40 per unit, respectively. It clearly indicates that market demand is directly related the level of prices. The more the level of prices, the more each seller is inclined to sell in market.

### Supply Curve

A supply curve is the diagrammatic representation of various combinations of price and quantity supplied, ceteris paribus. It exhibits the economic relationship between price and quantity supplied. It shows how much producers are willing and able to produce at each price. However, the supply curve assumes that the effect of other factors will remain constant. The other factors include change in the cost of production, capacity expansion, climatic conditions, technological changes, etc.

The outcome is a relationship reflected in form of a curve or line which shows various price-Qs pairs. That point shows the amount of the product that sellers would choose to sell at that price.

## 7.3 DETERMINANTS OF SUPPLY (FACTORS AFFECTING SUPPLY)

The determinants of supply reflect the factors that cause changes in supply. These are the factors that induce the sale decisions of the seller and result in generation or changes in the supply of the commodity. Figure 7.2 reflects the determinants of supply. Let's consider how changes in each of these determinants affect supply.

### 1. Price of the Given Commodity

Price is the most important factor that determines the supply of a commodity. In common parlance, price of a commodity and its supply are directly related. It means that as a result of rise in price, the quantity supplied of the given commodity also rises and vice versa. It happens as the supply represents producer's perspective in the sense that when prices rise, there are greater chances of getting higher revenue and hence more profits. Thus, the probability of getting higher price induces the firm to offer more for sale in the market.

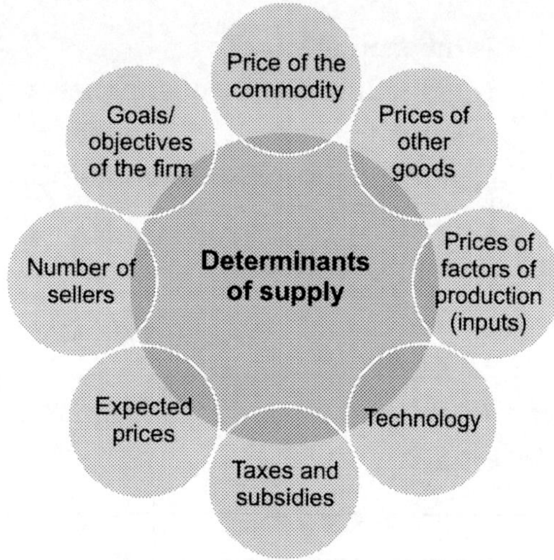


**Fig. 7.2** Determinants of Supply

The relationship between supply and price can be expressed as:

$$\text{Supply} = f\text{ (Price)}$$

It may be written as:

$$S = f(P)$$

Thus, there is a direct relationship between price and quantity supplied, keeping the effect of other variables affecting supply as constant.

It may be written as:

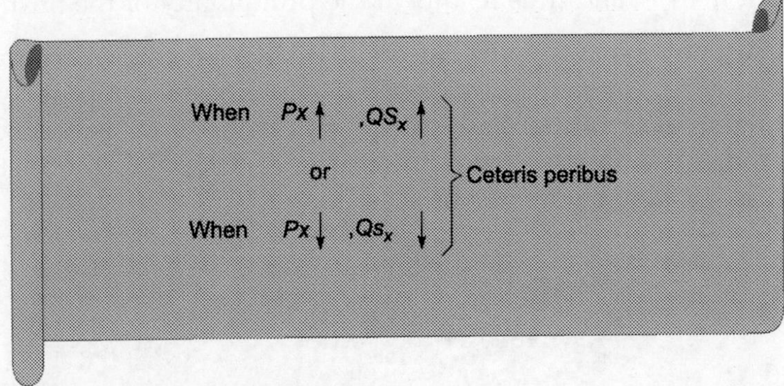


**2. Prices of Other Goods**

Prices of other commodities also affect the quantity supplied of a commodity to a great extent. This is due to the reason that a rise in the prices of other goods makes them more profitable to sell. Thus, the producer becomes more inclined to produce the commodity whose prices have risen as it will fetch more revenue to the seller as compared to the given commodity. As a result, the firm allocates its limited resources from production of the given commodity to production of other goods whose prices have risen.

***For example:*** A rise in the price of other product (say, wheat) will induce the farmer to produce wheat in place of the given commodity (say, rice). This is because it gives him more revenue and thus more profit. It may be written as:

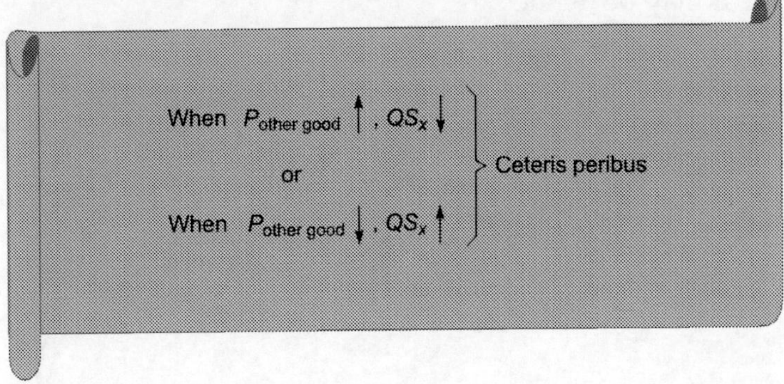

**3. Prices of Factors of Production (inputs)**

A rise in price factors of production leads to rise in cost of inputs. As a result there are cost overruns in the form of higher cost of production. Higher cost of production adversely affects the profits. As a result, seller tends to reduce the supply of the commodity.

On the other hand, decrease in amount payable to factors of production or inputs, increases the supply. This is on account of fall in the cost of production which leads to increased profit margin and thus results in the profitability of the business.

***For example:*** A carpenter may require inputs like land, labour, wood, tools, etc. to make wooden furniture. A rise in price of one or more of these inputs will increase the cost of production of furniture. Thus, the profit margin of the seller reduces with rise in cost of production, thus he tends to reduce the supply of product when the prices of inputs rise. It may be defined as:

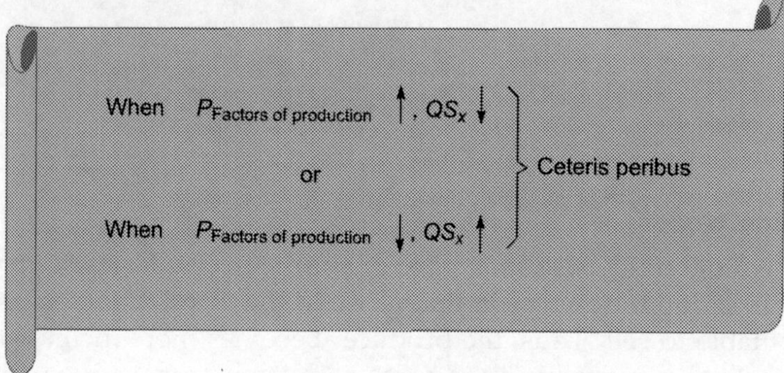


**4. Technology**

As a result of technological improvement (say advanced techniques of production, better tools and equipment for production), the firms are able to produce units of output with fewer resources. The use of less resources lowers production costs. Lower production cost increases the profitability of the business which induces the supply of the commodity. It may be defined as:

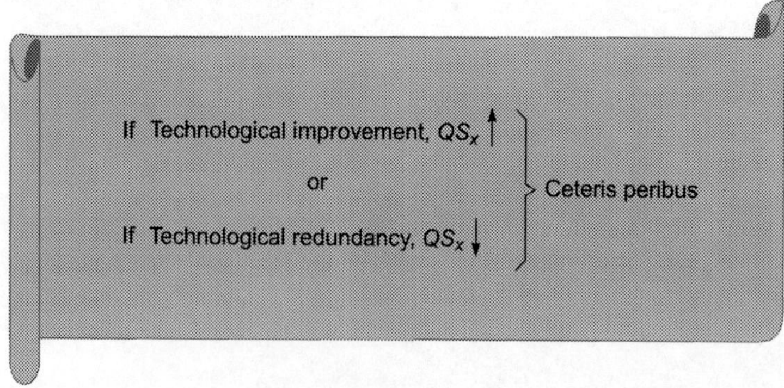

### 5. Taxes and Subsidies

Taxes and subsidies also influence the supply of commodities. Payment of taxes tends to increase the production cost and reduce profit margins. On the contrary, subsidies lower the producers' costs and tend to increase supply. It may be defined as:

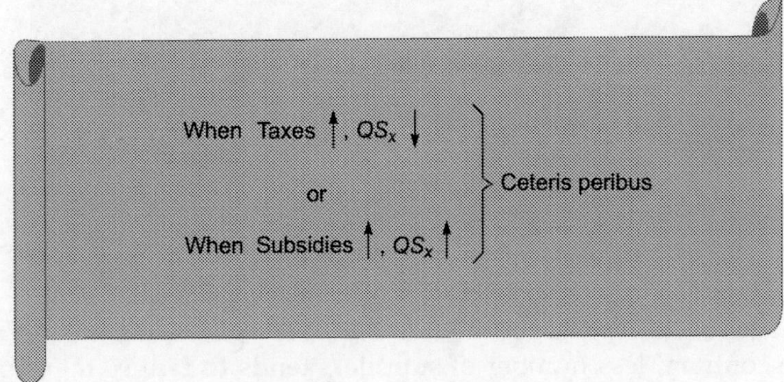


The impact of taxes and subsidies on the quantity supplied is shown in Fig. 7.3.

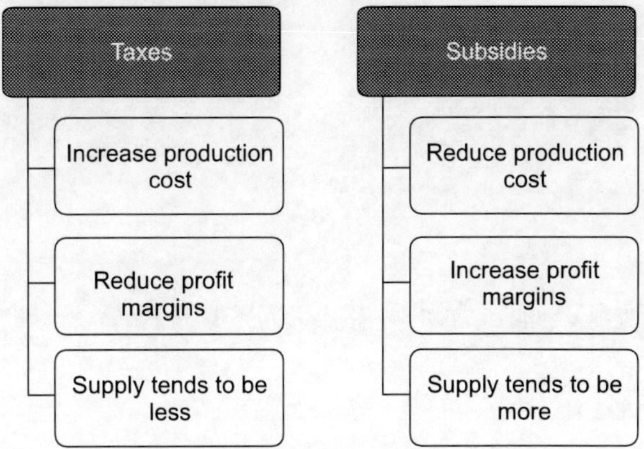


**Fig. 7.3** Impact of Taxes and Subsidies on Quantity Supplied

### 6. Expected Prices

Expectations about the rise in future price of a product may affect producer's current willingness to supply a product. If the seller anticipates that the price of the commodity will rise, he may withhold some of their current supplies with the intention of selling it at higher price in future. As a result, the current supply of the product will decline. However, in certain manufacturing industries, like ice creams, air conditioners, woollens, anticipation of price rise would lead to employment of more workers or to expand their production facilities, which leads to rise in current supplies. It may be defined as:

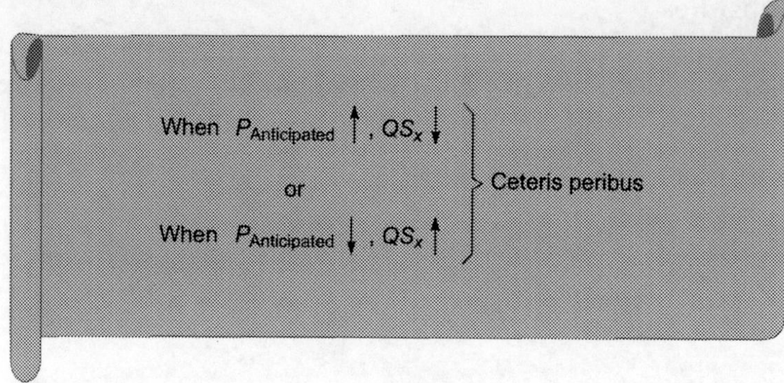


**7. Number of Sellers**

Other things being equal, the larger the number of suppliers, the greater the market supply. On the contrary, less number of suppliers tends to reduce the supplies. This is evident from the fact that as more firms enter an industry, the supply curve shifts to the right. This indicates rise in the quantity supplied. However, if the firms leave industry, supply curve shifts to the left indicating reduction in market supply. It may be defined as:

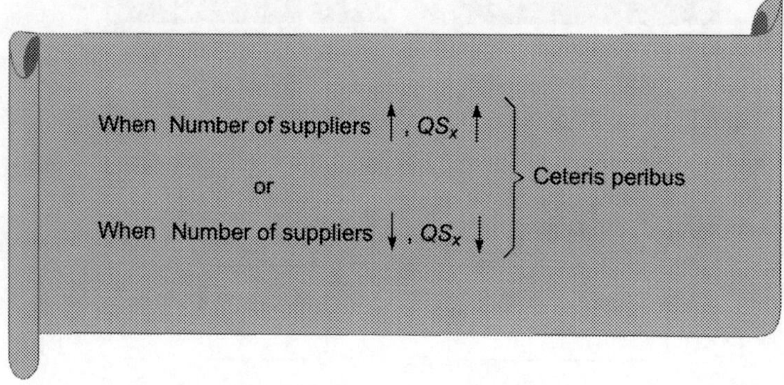


**8. Goals/Objectives of the Firm**

Apart from profit maximization, a firm may pursue other objectives like sales maximization, growth maximization, maximization of market share, creating brand image, etc. If the main objective of the business is to pursue any of these objectives, in such a case firms are willing to supply more even at the prices, which do not maximize their profits. Thus, supply tends to be more. But in case the firm opts for profit maximization motive, then it may sell less in present period with the motive of gaining higher profit at a certain price.

It may be defined as:

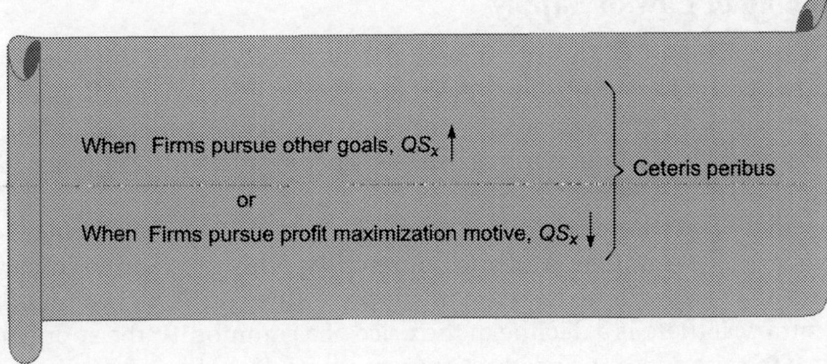


## 7.4 SUPPLY FUNCTION

The supply for a commodity depends on the factors that affect supply. These factors include price of the commodity, price of related goods, price of factors of production, state of technology, taxation policy, expected price, number of sellers, etc. All these factors are known as independent variables. Since, with change in each variable, the value of supply changes, therefore supply is known as a dependent variable. All these variables when framed in the form of a functional relationship with supply, lead to formation of supply function.

Thus, supply function refers to the statement of factors affecting supply in terms of mathematical symbols. Therefore, supply function exhibits the functional relationship between supply (dependent variable) and factors affecting supply (independent variables).

The supply function can be expressed as:

$$S_x = f(P_x, P_R, P_F, S_T, T, E_P, N_S, G, U)$$

where,

$S_x$ = Supply of the commodity $x$
$P_x$ = Price of the commodity $x$
$P_R$ = Price of related goods
$P_F$ = Price of factors of production
$S_T$ = State of technology
$T$ = Taxation policy
$E_P$ = Expected price
$N_S$ = Number of sellers
$G$ = Goals of the firm
$U$ = Any other factor apart from above-mentioned factors that influences supply

## 7.5 LAW OF SUPPLY

### 7.5.1 Meaning of Law of Supply

The law of supply refers to the fundamental law of economics that expresses the relationship between the supply and price of a commodity. According to the law of supply, there is a direct relationship between the price of a commodity and its supply, ceteris peribus. 'Ceteris peribus' means 'keeping the effect of other variables as constant'.

It specifies that when there is a rise in price of a commodity, the producers would prefer to increase the production of the commodity with the motive to earn more profit. As a result, there will be increase in supply of the concerned commodity.

On the contrary, if there is a decline in the price of a commodity, the supplier would tend to reduce the supply of the product for some time. He will do so in order to take the advantage of selling the commodity when the price of the commodity will rise in future. It can be represented as:

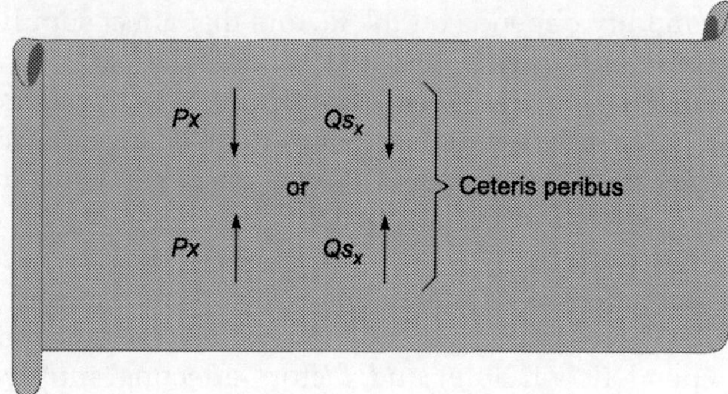


### 7.5.2 Assumptions of Law of Supply

The main assumptions of the law relate to what we call 'ceteris paribus'. Thus, the assumptions of the law are as follows:

1. There is no change in the price of other goods
2. State of technology remains unchanged
3. Prices of factors of production remain the same
4. There is no change in the taxation policy
5. Goals of the producer remain the same

### 7.5.3 Operation of the Law

The operation of law of supply can be explained with the help of supply schedule and reflection of supply curve. Thus, the direct relationship between price and quantity demanded can be explained with the help of the following:

### (a) Supply Schedule

The supply schedule is the tabular representation of the relationship between price and quantity supplied. It shows the direct relationship between *P* and *Qs* and gives information of various quantities supplied at its respective price. A hypothetical supply schedule is as follows:

Table 7.3 shows that the producer supplies more of a commodity at higher price. It is clear that when the price of the apple was Rs. 100 per kg, he supplies only one kg apples but at higher price Rs. 200 per kg, the consumer demanded 2 kg apples. Finally, at the price of Rs. 500 per kg the seller supplies 5 kg apples.

**TABLE 7.3** Supply Schedule: Explanation to Law of Supply

| Price of Apples (Rs. per kg) | Quantity Supplied of Apples (kg) |
|---|---|
| 100 | 1 |
| 200 | 2 |
| 300 | 3 |
| 400 | 4 |
| 500 | 5 |

### (b) Supply Curve

Supply curve is the diagrammatic representation of relationship between price and quantity supplied. In other words, the supply schedule plotted graphically is known as supply curve. Corresponding to the supply schedule, the quantity demanded of apples has been taken on X-axis, whereas price in terms of Rs per kg has been taken on the *Y*-axis.

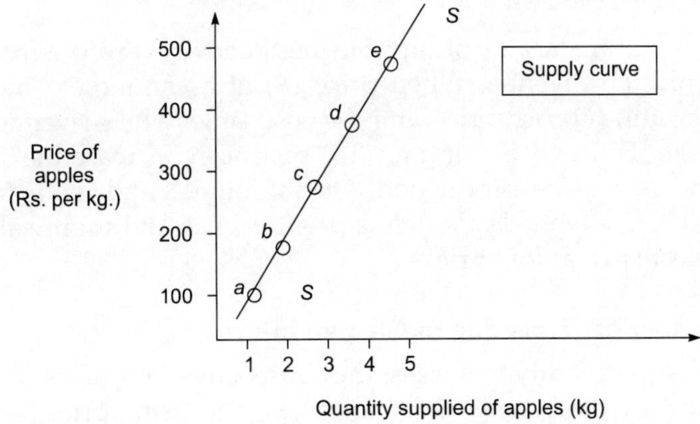


**Fig 7.4** Supply Curve: Explanation to Law of Supply

Figure 7.4 shows that the producer sells one apple when the price is Rs. 100 per kg, which is reflected by combination '*a*'. At a higher price of Rs. 200 per kg, the seller sells more (two) units of apples shown by combination '*b*'. Thereafter, the subsequent quantities are sold at higher price as reflected by combinations '*c*' and '*d*'. Finally, the consumer purchases 5 apples when the price level is Rs. 500 per kg., reflected by combination '*e*'. Thus, joining combination '*a*', '*b*', '*c*', '*d*' and '*e*', we get supply curve. It is to be noted here that the supply curve is upward sloping from left to right.

### 7.5.4 Reasons of Operation of Law of Supply (Why Supply Curve Slopes Upwards from Left to Right)

The supply curve slopes upwards from left to right establishing a direct relationship between price and quantity supplied, ceteris peribus. The factors contributing to the direct relationship between quantity supplied and price are shown in Fig. 7.5.

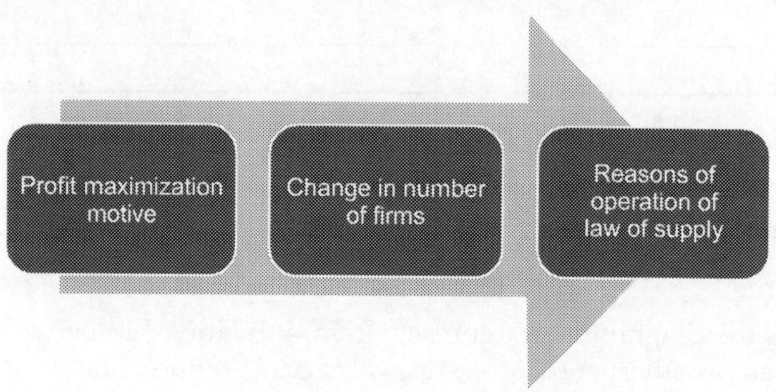


**Fig 7.5** Reasons of Operation of Law of Supply

#### 1. Profit Maximization Motive

Maximum profit is the main aim of any business activity. Profit is ascertained by deducting cost from the revenue. When price (*P*) of a commodity increases, total revenue (*R* = *P* per unit **Q*) rises. Keeping the cost same, when revenue rises, profit (*P* = *R* – C) also rise. Thus, with rising profits, producers increase the supply of the commodity by increasing the production. On the other hand, with fall in prices, revenue falls. Reduced revenue leads to less profit. Hence, the supply also decreases as profit margin decreases at low prices.

#### 2. Change in Number of Firms due to Change in Price

When the price of a commodity increases, the prospective producers try to enter the market in order to take the benefit of rising prices. The rising prices lead to higher revenue and thereby a higher profit. Thus, they raise market supply.

However, as a result of decline in the prices, the firms either stop the production or reduce the sales of their product. This leads to reduction in the supply of the given commodity as the number of firms in the market decreases.

### 7.5.5 Exceptions to the Law of Supply

These are the cases that are contrary to the law of supply. In other words, these are the cases where the positive relationship between quantity supplied and price may not hold true. These exceptional cases are reflected in Fig. 7.6.

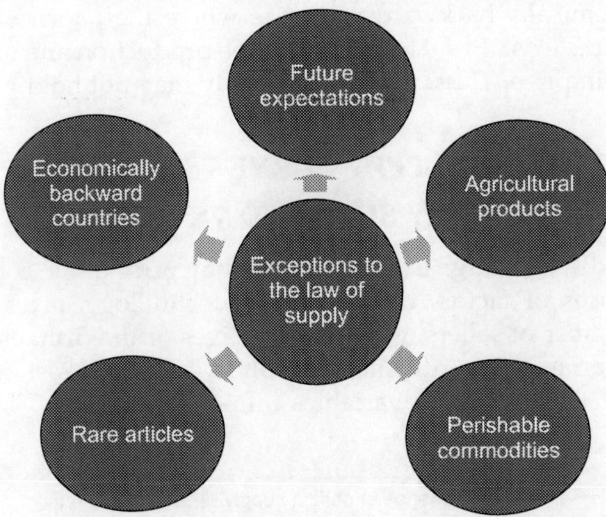


**Fig. 7.6** Exceptions to the Law of Supply

**1. Future Expectations**

These are the anticipations regarding the future rise or fall in the price. In such a case, if the producers anticipate fall in price of their commodity in future, then in order to avoid the future loss of profit, they will be willing to sell more even at reduced price. However, if they expect that the price will rise in the future, they would not supply the whole quantity of the product or reduce the supply of the commodity. They do so in order to supply the commodity later at a high price. Thus, future expectations represent one of the exceptions of law of supply.

**2. Agricultural Products**

In case of agricultural products, the law of supply does not hold good. This is on account of the reason that their supply is a function of season or climatic conditions. If there is a change in these conditions, it automatically affects the supply of the commodity. Thus, in case of adverse or unfavourable weather conditions, their supply cannot be increased, even at higher prices.

**3. Perishable Commodities**

In case of perishable commodities like vegetables, fruits, etc., sellers are not in a position to hold them for long. Thus, they tend to supply more of the commodity, despite the declining prices. The law of supply fails to operate in such cases.

**4. Rare Articles**

In case of rare collections or precious articles, the supply cannot be increased, even if their prices are increased. Thus, the law of supply may not hold good in such cases.

**5. Economically Backward Countries**

These are the economically backward countries where the paucity and non-proper utilization of resources exist. In such economies the production and supply cannot be increased with rise in price. Thus, the law of supply may not hold good.

## 7.6 MOVEMENT ALONG SUPPLY CURVE VS SHIFT IN SUPPLY CURVE (CHANGE IN QUANTITY SUPPLIED VS CHANGE IN SUPPLY)

Supply of a commodity to a large extent is affected by price of the commodity, prices of other goods, prices of factors of production, technology, taxes and subsidies, expected prices, number of sellers, goals or objectives of the firm, etc. Among these factors, the major variable that influences supply is price and rest of them together come under the category of 'other variables influencing supply'. These have been shown in Fig. 7.7.

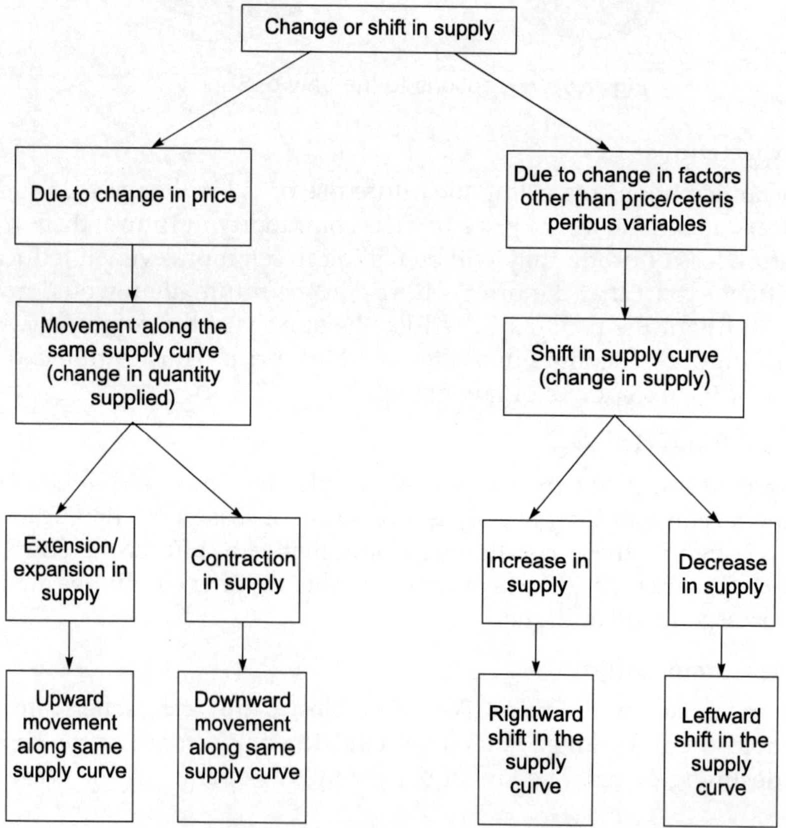


**Fig. 7.7** Change or Shift in Supply

On this basis, there are following changes in supply:

1. Movement along the same supply curve (change in quantity supplied)
2. Shift in supply curve (change in supply)

## 1. Movement along the Same Supply Curve (Change in Quantity Supplied)

### *Meaning*

Other things being equal, a change in the price of the commodity induces changes in the quantity supplied, movement is said to occur along the same supply curve. It is also called change in quantity supplied of the commodity. Now, this movement can either be upward or downward which further forms the basis of its classification.

### *Types*

The movement along the supply curve is divided under two heads:

1. Extension/expansion of supply (upward movement)
2. Contraction of supply (downward movement)

#### (a) Extension/Expansion of Supply

Extension of supply refers to the rise in quantity supplied on account of rise in the price of the commodity, effect of other factors remaining constant. This has been shown in Fig. 7.8.

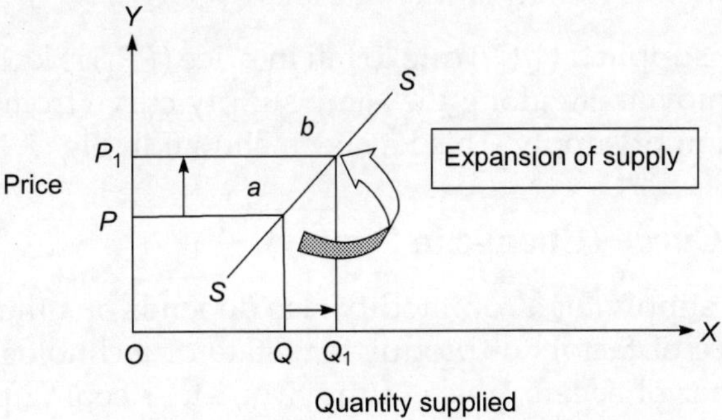


**Fig. 7.8** Extension/Expansion of Supply

Initial price = $OP$, Initial quantity = $OQ$

New price = $OP_1$, New quantity = $OQ_1$

Now,

Change/Rise in price = $PP_1$

Change/Rise in quantity supplied = $QQ_1$

The rise in quantity supplied ($QQ_1$) due to rise in price ($PP_1$) is known as extension/ expansion of demand. Thus, the movement along the same supply curve from point *a* to point *b* is known as expansion of supply.

### (b) Contraction of Supply

It refers to fall in quantity supplied due to fall in the price of the good, effect of other factors remaining constant.

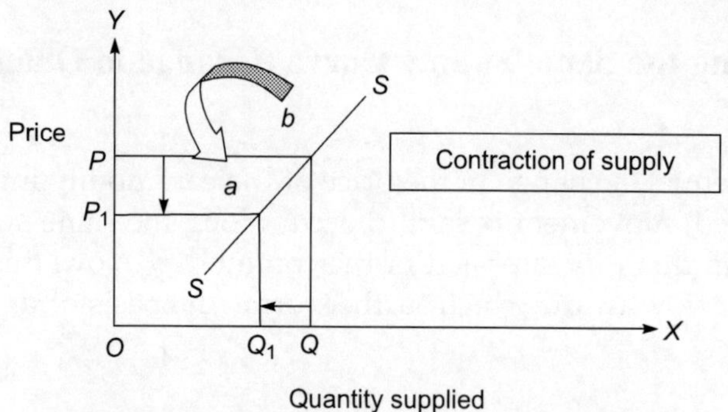


**Fig. 7.9** Extension/Expansion of Supply

$$\text{Initial price} = OP, \text{ Initial quantity} = OQ$$

$$\text{New price} = OP_1, \text{ New quantity} = OQ_1$$

Now,

$$\text{Change/Fall in price} = PP_1$$

$$\text{Change/Fall in quantity supplied} = QQ_1$$

The fall in quantity supplied ($QQ_1$) due to fall in price ($PP_1$) is known as contraction of supply. Thus, the movement along the same supply curve from point *b* to point *a* is known as contraction of supply. This has been shown in Fig. 7.9.

## 2. Shift in Supply Curve (Change in Supply)

Apart from price, the supply for a commodity also depends on other factors like price of related goods, price of factors of production, state of technology, taxation policy, expected price, number of sellers, goals of the firm, etc. Keeping price constant, the change in supply on account of change in any of the factors other than the price is called shift in supply.

### *Meaning*

The change in the position of supply curve on account of change in factors other than price like change in costs of labour or raw material is known as shift in the supply curve. It is also called change in supply of the commodity.

### *Types*

The shift in demand curve is divided under two heads:

(a) Increase in supply (rightward shift)
(b) Decrease in supply (leftward shift)

**(a) Increase in Supply:** It refers to rise in supply due to change in factors other than price, price remaining constant. It occurs on account of following factors:

- **Decrease in Costs of Production:** Reduced cost of production in terms of lower wages, lower raw material costs, etc., gives an incentive to producer to produce and sell more at each price.
- **Capacity Expansion:** Expansion in capacity like building a new plant, machinery and factory may also result in enhanced supplies.
- **Related Commodity:** Easy availability or increase in supply of related goods also leads to rise in supply.
- **Climatic Conditions:** Change in weather conditions in favour of the commodity also leads to rise in supply.
- **Technological Advancements:** Improvements in technology helps in reducing costs of production and distribution. It also inspires the sellers to supply more.
- **Low Rate of Taxes:** Lower direct taxes reduce the cost of goods, as a result the producers tend to supply more.
- **Government Subsidies:** Increase in government subsidies also reduces the cost of goods, thus sellers are inclined to supply more.

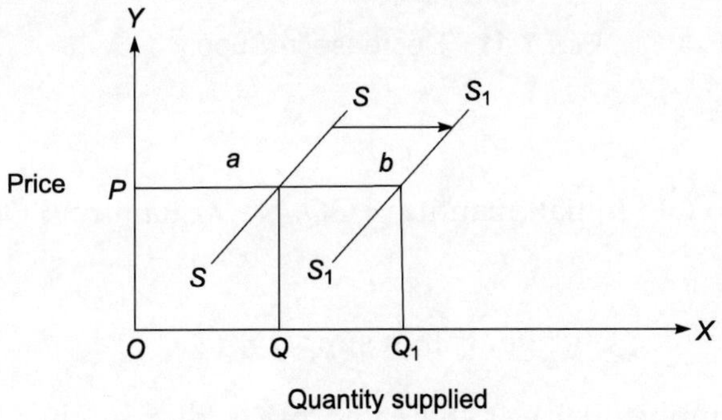


**Fig. 7.10** Increase in Supply

Price = $OP$, Initial quantity = $OQ$, New quantity = $OQ_1$

Now,

Change/Rise in supply = $QQ_1$

The rise in supply ($QQ_1$) at the same price, due to change in any of the factors affecting supply is known as increase in supply. Thus, the rightward shift of the supply curve from point *a* (on supply curve *SS*) to new position as point *b* (on supply curve $S_1S_1$) is known as increase in supply. Therefore, if more quantity ($OQ_1$) is supplied at the same price (*OP*), increase in supply is said to exist. This has been shown in Fig. 7.10.

### (b) Decrease in Supply

It refers to fall or decline in supply due to change in factors other than price, price remaining constant. It occurs on account of the following factors:

- Increase in costs of production
- Change in climatic conditions against the commodity
- Technological redundancy
- High rate of taxes

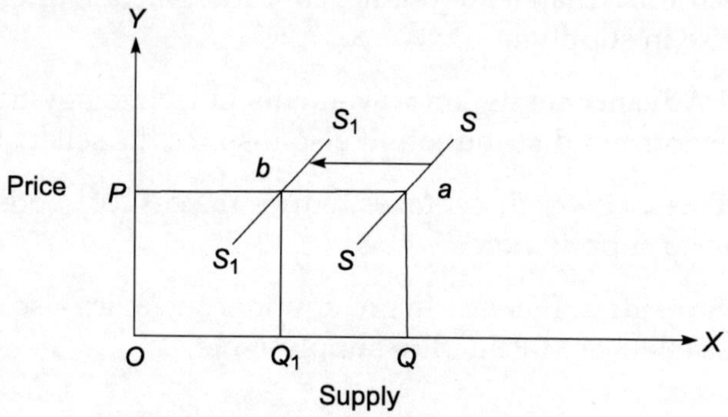


**Fig. 7.11** Decrease in Supply

Here,

Price = *OP*, Initial quantity = *OQ*, New quantity = $QQ_1$

Now,

Change/Fall in supply = $QQ_1$

The decline in supply ($QQ_1$) at the same price, due to change in any of the factors affecting demand is known as decrease in supply. Thus, the leftward shift of the supply curve from point a (on supply curve *SS*) to new position as point *b* (on supply curve $S_1SI$) is known as decrease in supply. Therefore, if less quantity ($QQ_1$) is supplied at the same price (*OP*) decrease in supply is said to exist. This has been shown in Fig. 7.11.

Movement along the supply curve and shift in supply curve have been shown in Table 7.4.

**TABLE 7.4** Movement along the Supply Curve vs Shift in Supply Curve

| Basis of Difference/ Parameters | Movement Along the Supply | Shift in Supply Curve |
|---|---|---|
| 1. Meaning | It refers to an economic phenomenon which reflects the change in quantity supplied on account of change in price, other factors affecting supply remaining constant. | It refers to an economic phenomenon which reflects the change in supply due to change in factors other than price, keeping price constant. |
| 2. Alternative name | Change in quantity supplied | Change in supply |
| 3. Causal variable/ variables | It is caused by change in price of a commodity | It is caused by change in factors other than price. |
| 4. Constant considerations | Factors other than price are kept constant | Price is kept constant. |
| 5. Types | It is of two types: (a) Extension/expansion in supply (b) Contraction in supply | It is of two types: (a) Increase in supply (b) Decrease in supply |
| 6. Direction of change | It refers to leftward movement (in case of contraction in supply) or rightward movement (in case of expansion in supply) along the same demand curve | It refers to outward shift (in case of increase in demand) or inward shift in case of decrease in demand) of original demand curve. |
| 7. Price considerations | It refers to change in quantity demanded due to change in price. | It refers to change in demand at the same price, i.e., with no change in price. |
| 8. Graphic representation | 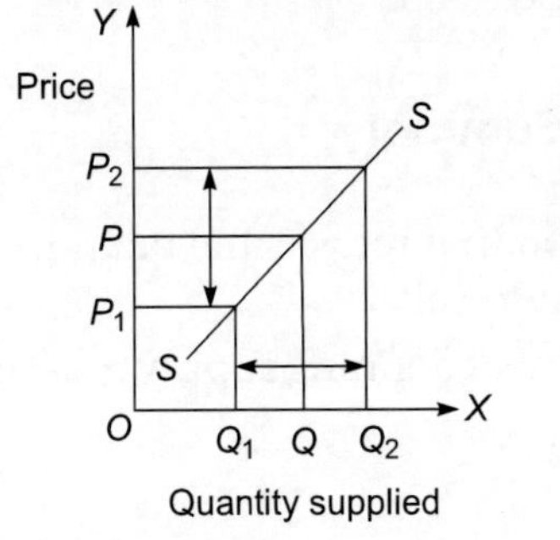 Y; Price; S; $P_2$; P; $P_1$; S; O; X; $Q_1$ Q $Q_2$; Quantity supplied; **Fig. 7.12** Movement Along the Supply | 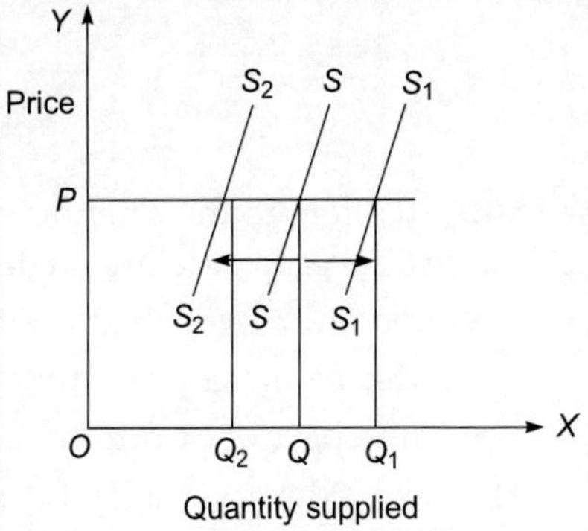 Y; Price; $S_2$ S $S_1$; P; $S_2$ S $S_1$; O; X; $Q_2$ Q $Q_1$; Quantity supplied; **Fig. 7.13** Shift in Supply Curve |

*Contd.*

| | | |
|---|---|---|
| | **Explanation**<br>Original supply curve = $SS$<br>Initial price = $OP$,<br>Initial quantity = $OQ$ units. | **Explanation**<br>Original supply curve = $SS$<br>Initial price = $OP$,<br>Initial quantity = $OQ$ units. |
| | **Expansion in Supply**<br>As a result of rise in price of the commodity from $OP$ to $OP_2$, there is a rise in quantity supplied from $OQ$ to $OQ_2$. | **Increase in Supply**<br>As a result of reduction in cost of production, price being constant, there is a rise in supply from $OQ$ to $OQ_1$. |
| | **Contraction in Supply**<br>As a result of reduction in price of the commodity from $OP$ to $OP_1$, there is a rise in quantity supplied from $OQ$ to $OQ_1$. | **Decrease in Supply**<br>As a result of increase in cost of production, price being constant, there is a decline in supply for the commodity from $OQ$ to $OQ_2$. |

## Implication

A business manager while maintaining strategic production decisions takes into consideration both demand and supply decisions. The demand decisions are important as they reflect the purchase decisions or probability of purchase of a product by the prospective and the existing buyers. On the other side, supply analysis is important as it reflects the price at which the commodity would be sold. This, in turn, reflects the likely revenue as revenue is calculated using price per unit and units sold. This further reflects the profitability of a business firm, subject to cost considerations. Thus, it is imperative for a business manager to know the price-quantity relationship and the factors that cause the shifts in the supply function (or curve). Though price is an important variable, however in certain cases, other determinants also dominate. These factors are price of other goods, prices of factors of production, technology, taxes, subsidies, and expected prices, etc. Thus, in certain cases, changes in other factors or shifts in supply curve overpower the supply dynamics and have greater impact on managerial decision-making in the firm.

### Summary

- ✓ Supply refers to the phenomenon that reflects the quantity of a commodity that the producer is able and willing to sell.
- ✓ The economically relevant statement defining supply must include the following:
    - Price of the commodity
    - Time period duration
- ✓ Thus, in order to qualify for supply, the following attributes must be present:
    - Ability to sell
    - Willingness to sell

  - Prevalence of a particular price
  - A time horizon in which the commodity is demanded
- ✓ Supply schedule is a tabular representation of various combinations of price and quantity supplied (ceteris paribus).
- ✓ Market supply schedule refers to a tabular representation of various quantities of a commodity corresponding to each price level that each producer is willing to sell during a given period of time.
- ✓ A supply curve is the diagrammatic representation of various combinations of price and quantity supplied, ceteris paribus.
- ✓ The factors that influence the demand for a commodity are:
  - Price of the commodity
  - Prices of other goods
  - Prices of factors of production (inputs)
  - Technology
  - Taxes and subsidies
  - Expected prices
  - Number of sellers
  - Goals/objectives of the firm
- ✓ Supply function exhibits the functional relationship between supply (dependent variable) and factors affecting supply (independent variables).
- ✓ The law of supply defines a *direct relationship* between price and quantity supplied of a commodity. It means that when price of the commodity reduces, the quantity supplied reduces and on the other side, if the price of the commodity rises, the quantity supplied rises, ceteris peribus.
- ✓ The Latin words 'ceteris peribus' means that other things remain constant and do not influence supply during the study of the law. These "other things" include the determinants of supply other than price, viz., prices of other goods, prices of factors of production (inputs), technology, taxes and subsidies.
- ✓ The factors contribute to the direct relationship between quantity supplied and price are:
  - Profit maximization motive
  - Change in number of firms
- ✓ There are the exceptional cases which establish a direct relationship between price and quantity supplied. These are the cases where the law of supply fails to operate:
  - Future expectations
  - Agricultural products
  - Perishable commodities
  - Rare articles
  - Economically backward countries

✓ Change in supply occurs in two ways:
    - Movement along the same supply curve
    - Shift in the supply curve

✓ Movement along the same supply curve is also called change in the quantity supplied of the commodity. It occurs due to change in price of the commodity. It is of two types:

✓ Expansion or extension in supply – upward movement along the supply curve

✓ Contraction in supply – downward movement along the supply curve.

✓ Shift in supply curve is also called change in supply of the commodity. It occurs due to change in factors other than price such as change in costs of production, change in climatic conditions against the commodity, technological redundancy, high rate of taxes, etc.
It is of two types:

✓ Increase in supply – rightward shift of the supply curve

✓ Decrease in supply – leftward shift of the supply curve

## Review Questions

1. What is supply? Explain the determinants of supply of the commodity.
2. What is law of supply? Explain the reasons of operation of the law. Are there any exceptions to the law?
3. Elucidate the concept of law of supply with assumptions. Also throw light on the determinants of law of supply.
4. Distinguish between:
    - Extension of supply and increase in supply.
    - Contraction of supply and decrease in supply.
5. Explain the operation of law of supply with the help of supply schedule. Also explain the determinants of the law.
6. 'Supply curve slopes downward from left to right'. Explain the statement. What are the exceptional cases in this regard?
7. Explain the situations in which there prevails an inverse relationship between price and quantity supplied?
8. Distinguish between change in supply and change in quantity supplied. Use diagrams.
9. Distinguish between movement along supply curve and shift in supply curve.
10. Write short notes on:
    - Supply function
    - Contraction in supply and increase in supply
    - Expansion in supply and decrease in supply

## CASE STUDY: FREQUENT SPIKES IN ONION PRICES IN INDIA (OCTOBER, 2019)

Onions in India have been witnessing an upswing in their prices on a regular basis for quite a long time. The saga of price spike in onions is as old as three decades. Way back in 1980, in an unprecedented manner onions went beyond the reach of the common man; the price hike revisited the country again after a decade in 1998 and again in 2010. Within a span of three years, the price of onions skyrocketed to an all-time high of about Rs. 150/kg in some major cities of the country in 2013. Two years later during the month of August 2015, onion prices soared again. This year too, onions have become dearer, leaving the consumers teary-eyed. The wholesale price of onion in Asia's largest onion market, Lasalgaon in Maharashtra, increased to almost Rs. 40/kg, while the retail price soared to about Rs. 60/kg in metropolitan cities.

Drought in year 2018, delayed monsoon followed by excessive rain in major growing regions of Maharashtra and Karnataka, has been cited as the main reason for the price hike. Every time onion price hikes revisit the country, economists and policy-makers debate as to what triggers the periodic upswing. Some have emphatically pointed out that the price spikes can be attributed to a large extent to fragmented supply chain.

While some others invariably hold the supply constraint as the causal factor for the price hike along with a complex interplay of several factors such as rising consumption, drought and flood induced crop failures in major growing regions, poor infrastructure and inefficient storage facilities. What is the real truth? Onion a staple diet for majority of the people in India. They consume approximately 15 million tonnes of onion per year, and shelling out Rs. 80-100 to buy a kg of onion will definitely pinch the common man. This begs the question: How can a culinary ingredient witness such a steep hike in a few months? Besides blaming the inadequate storage and transportation facilities and improper distribution system, policy-makers invariably point out that such a stupendous price hike is only due to supply-demand constraints.

How can supply be held responsible for the price hike when data from the Ministry of Agriculture clearly show that the production of onion has surged from 2.5 million tonnes in 1980-81 to 22.43 million tonnes in 2016-17? Erratic monsoon can at the most lead to a 5-10 per cent shortfall in supply, but nowhere severe enough to warrant a quadrupling of prices within a span of few weeks. The data analysis at National Horticulture Research and Development Foundation (NHRDF) reveals that supply has nothing to do with the abnormal price rise. The Consortium of Indian Farmers Association (CIFA) and a study by Competition Commission of India (CCI) have pointed out that cartelisation and traders are jacking up the prices.

*Source*: Narayanamoorthy A. and Alli P. (2019), "Why the frequent spikes in onion prices?": Hindu Business line, Published on October 14, 2019 retrieved from https://www.thehindubusinessline.com/opinion/why-the-frequent-spikes-in-onion-prices/article29682736.ece on October 25, 2019.

## Questions

1. What according to you is the causal factor leading to reduction in the supply of onions in India?
2. What role does 'hoarding dynamics' play role in elevating prices of onions in India?
3. Show the changes in supply curve of onions when 'hoarding dynamics' comes into picture?
4. What would be the impact of the following on the supply curve for onions:
   (a) An indirect tax is of a fixed amount is placed on producer.
   (b) An indirect tax is imposed as a fixed percentage of prices.
   (c) The government provides subsidies to producers so that they are able to produce at reduced price.
5. Do you think that onion price hike has benefitted farmers? Give reasons in support of your answer.
6. Discuss the role played by middlemen in extracting profits out of the entire transaction.
7. What do you think would be the consequence of onion crop destroyed on account of flood on the business of small restaurant owners?
8. Through light on the policy considerations that will help in seeking long run solutions to evade the problem.

8 CHAPTER

# Elasticity of Supply

**LEARNING OBJECTIVES**

After going through this chapter, reader would be able to understand:

- ✓ Concept of elasticity of supply
- ✓ The factors determining elasticity of supply
- ✓ The degrees of elasticity of supply

## 8.1 INTRODUCTION

In chapter 7 we studied the supply dynamics and law of supply. The law of supply specifies that if price goes up, supply will increase and vice versa. It merely indicates the direction of change. However, it fails to specify the magnitude of change of supply as a result of change in the price of the commodity. Thus, the law of supply fails to answer that "by how much supply will rise in response to an increase in price?" The answer to this is provided by the concept of elasticity of supply. In this chapter, the focus is on the elasticity of supply. It also includes the study of meaning and concept of elasticity of supply, the factors determining elasticity of supply and the degrees of elasticity of supply.

## 8.2 CONCEPT OF ELASTICITY OF SUPPLY

### Meaning

Elasticity of supply (*Es*) refers to the degree of responsiveness of quantity supplied of a commodity on account of a change in its price. It is also defined as the ratio of percentage change in quantity supplied to percentage change in price. It reflects the magnitude of change of quantity supplied on account of change in price of the commodity.

## Definition

Lipsey and Chrystal defined price elasticity of supply as "percentage change is quantity supplied divided by the percentage change in price that brought it about".

## Coefficient of Price Elasticity of Supply

The coefficient of elasticity of supply can be calculated by considering the ratio of percentage or relative change in quantity supplied to percentage change in its price. This is shown in Fig. 8.1.

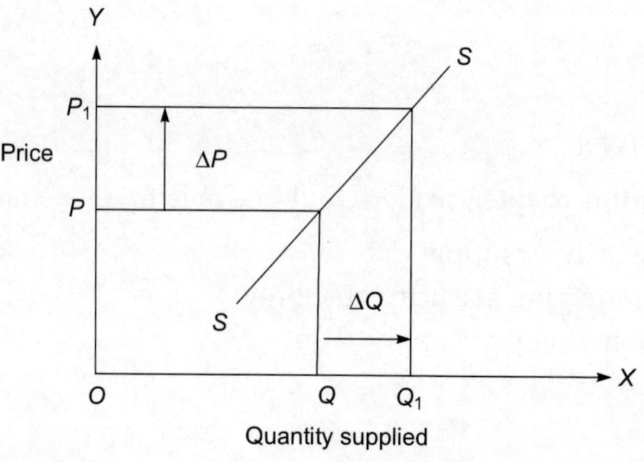


**Fig. 8.1** Coefficient of Price Elasticity of Supply

The absolute value of coefficient of *Ed* ranges from zero to infinity ($0 < Ed > \infty$). In addition, the coefficient of elasticity of supply has a positive value, because of the direct relationship between price and quantity supplied. The coefficient of elasticity of supply (*Es*) can be expressed as under:

$$Es = \frac{\text{Percentage change in quntity supplied}}{\text{Percentage change in price}}$$

$$Es = \frac{\Delta Qs}{\Delta P} \times \frac{P}{Qs}$$

where,

$Es$ = Coefficient of elasticity of supply
$\Delta Qs$ = Change in quantity supplied
$\Delta P$ = Change in price
$P$ = Original price
$Qs$ = Original quantity supplied

## Derivation

$$Es = \frac{\text{Percentage change in quntity supplied}}{\text{Percentage change in price}}$$

$$= \frac{\dfrac{\text{Change in quantity supplied}}{\text{Original quantity supplied}} \times 100}{\dfrac{\text{Change in price}}{\text{Original price}} \times 100}$$

$$= \frac{\dfrac{\text{New quantity} - \text{Original quantity}}{\text{Original quantity}}}{\dfrac{\text{New price} - \text{Original price}}{\text{Original price}}}$$

Symbolically, it can be written as

$$Es = \frac{\dfrac{Q_2 - Q_1}{Q_1}}{\dfrac{P_2 - P_1}{P_1}}$$

In general terms,

$$= \frac{\dfrac{\Delta Q}{Q}}{\dfrac{\Delta P}{P}}$$

$$= \frac{\Delta Q}{\Delta P} \times \frac{P}{Q}$$

By rearranging terms,

$$\boxed{Es = \frac{\Delta Q}{\Delta P} \times \frac{P}{Q}}$$

Here,

$\Delta Q$ = Change in quantity supplied
$Q$ = Original quantity
$\Delta P$ = Change in price
$P$ = Original price

The symbol $\Delta$ it means the change.

***For Example:*** At Rs. 80 per unit, the supply for a commodity is 30 units. If the price increases to Rs. 86 per unit, the supply increases to 35 units. The price elasticity of supply is:

$$Es = \frac{\Delta Q_S}{\Delta P} \times \frac{P}{Q_S}$$

Here,

$Q_1$ = 30 units, $Q_2$ = 35 units, $\Delta Q$ = 35 units – 30 units = 5 units

$P_1$ = Rs. 80, $P_2$ = Rs. 86, $\Delta P$ = Rs. 86 – Rs. 80 = Rs. 6

$$Es = \frac{5}{6} \times \frac{80}{30}$$

$$Es = 2.22$$

## 8.3 DETERMINANTS OF ELASTICITY OF SUPPLY/FACTORS INFLUENCING SUPPLY ELASTICITY

In this section, the factors that determine elasticity of supply are discussed. Some of these factors have been explained in Fig. 8.2.

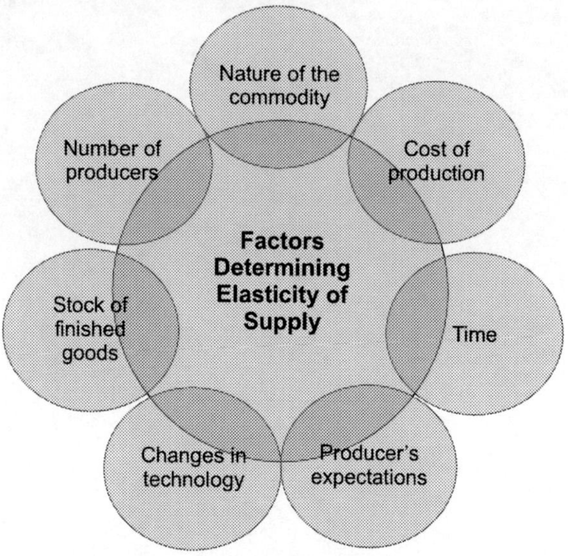


**Fig. 8.2** Factors Determining Elasticity of Supply

### 1. Nature of the Commodity

On the basis of nature, the commodities can be divided into two broad categories, viz., perishable commodities or durable commodity. The influence of each on elasticity of supply has been defined in Table 8.1.

TABLE 8.1 Nature of the Commodity

| Nature of the Commodity | Non-durable and Perishable Goods | Durable Commodity |
|---|---|---|
| Degree of *Es* | Less than elastic or inelastic | More than elastic or elastic |
| Reason | The goods have short lifespan. Their supply is not affected by changes in their price. Therefore, as a result of rise in price, the producer is not inclined to increase supply because it is either non-durable or perishable in nature. | The goods have long lifespan and hence price changes affect the demand significantly. Therefore, a rise in price leads to increase in supply in considerable manner and vice versa. |

### 2. Cost of Production

This concept is studied in consonance with the rate of rise or decline in the level of prices. The degree here varies on the basis whether the price rise leads to increase in per unit cost of production at a faster rate or at a slower rate. Thus, as far as cost of production is concerned, there are following cases as reflected in Table 8.2.

TABLE 8.2 Cost of Production

| Cost of Production | Price rise leads to increase in per unit cost of production at a faster rate | Price rise leads to increase in per unit cost of production at a slower rate |
|---|---|---|
| Degree of *Es* | Less than elastic or inelastic | More than elastic or elastic |
| Reason | In order to increase supply, the employment of resources is imperative, which involves raising the prices of these resources. As their prices rise, cost of production goes up. So seller tends to supply lesser commodity when the cost to produce the commodity is enhancing and hence supply becomes relatively inelastic. | In this case, as the prices of factors of production that are required to produce the commodity rise but at slower rate. So the seller tends to supply more of commodity as compared to a situation when the prices of factors of production are rising rapidly. Thus, supply becomes relatively elastic or more than elastic. |

### 3. Time

Time is also one of the major variables that influences the elasticity of supply. The study of time period is done in Table 8.3.

**TABLE 8.3** Time

| Time Period | Short Run | Long Run |
|---|---|---|
| Degree of *Ed* | Less than elastic or inelastic | More than elastic or elastic |
| Reason | In short run, the time period is too short to shift resources among products as a result the supply is not much responsive and hence is inelastic. | In long run, it is easy to shift resources among products as a result of the supply is responsive to change in their relative prices and hence is elastic. |

### 4. Producers' Expectations

The producers expectations regarding the rise and decline in the prices may also affect the supply. It may be understood with help of Table 8.4.

**TABLE 8.4** Producers' Expectations

| Producers' Expectations | Price of a commodity will rise in the future | Price of a commodity will decline in the future |
|---|---|---|
| Degree of *Ed* | Less than elastic or inelastic | More than elastic or elastic |
| Reason | If producers expect that price of a commodity will rise in the future, they will reduce the supply. This is because they would like to sell the commodity only when the prices will rise in future. As a result, the supply will be inelastic and non-responsive to change in the level of price. | If they expect the price will decline in the future, they will increase the supply. Consequently, the supply will become elastic and more responsive to changes in price. |

### 5. Changes in Technology

The intensity and extent of improvement also impacts the price elasticity of supply. This may be understood as follows (refer Table 8.5):

**TABLE 8.5** Changes in Technology

| Technology | Improvement | Redundant |
|---|---|---|
| Degree of *Ed* | More than elastic or elastic | Less than elastic or inelastic |
| Reason | Technological advancement or improvement leads to improved products with better features. This inspires the sellers to increase the supplies in the market. Hence, the supply is likely to be more than elastic or elastic. | The industries with redundant technology or no technological improvement find it challenging to sell their products in contemporary turbulent business environment. Hence, the elasticity of their supplies tends to be less than elastic or inelastic. |

### 6. Stock of Finished Goods

The stock of finished goods also affects the elasticity of supply. It can be understood with help of Table 8.6 in the following manner.

**TABLE 8.6** Stock of Finished Goods

| Stock of Finished Goods | High | Low |
|---|---|---|
| Degree of *Ed* | More than elastic or elastic | Less than elastic or inelastic |
| Reason | High stock/inventory leads to quick replenishment as and when required. Thus, when the prices rise, these high stock companies are in a position to easily supply more of their product. Thus, the price elasticity of supply would be elastic. | The industries which are low on stock/inventory are not in a position to quickly replenish the stock as a result of price rise. Thus, the elasticity of supply would be inelastic. |

### 7. Number of Producers

The number of produces also determines the degree of elasticity of supply. It can be understood with the help of Table 8.7.

**TABLE 8.7** Number of Producers

| Number of Producers | More | Less |
|---|---|---|
| Degree of *Ed* | More than elastic or elastic | Less than elastic or inelastic |
| Reason | More the number of producers, more it is possible to raise the supply in response to change in the prices. Thus, the supply tends to be more elastic. | Less the number of producers, less is the possibility of raising the supply in response to change in the prices. Thus, the supply tends to be less elastic. |

## 8.4 DEGREES OF ELASTICITY OF SUPPLY

Like demand analysis, the concept of supply also has certain degrees that tend to quantify its impact. Some commodities have elastic supply while others have inelastic supply. On this basis, the coefficient of elasticity of supply has also been categorized under five broad categories, viz., perfectly elastic, perfectly inelastic, unitary elastic, relatively elastic and relatively inelastic. Corresponding to the degrees the value of coefficient of elasticity of supply varies between zero and infinity.

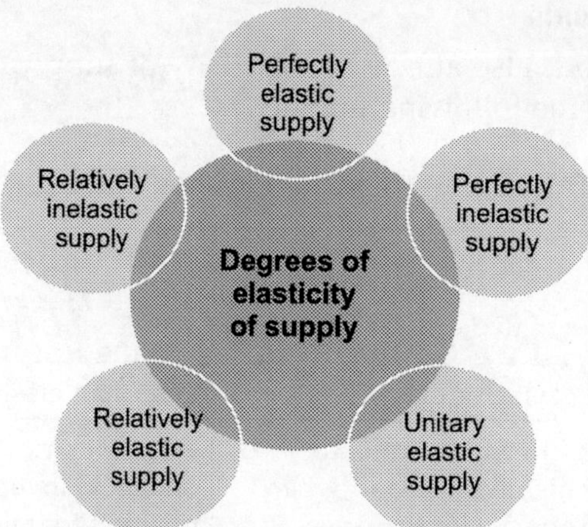


**Fig. 8.3** Degrees of Elasticity of Supply

The coefficient of elasticity of supply is categorized under five broad categories, viz., zero, less than one, equal to one, greater than one and infinity. These coefficients are shown in Fig. 8.3.

The attributes of these five degrees of elasticity of supply have been shown in Table 8.8.

**TABLE 8.8** Degrees of Elasticity of Supply

| Degree or Type of *Es* | Explanation | Coefficient of *Ed* | Shape of Supply Curve |
|---|---|---|---|
| Perfectly elastic supply | When a rise in price leads to an infinite increase in quantity supplied and a small fall leads to zero supply for the commodity. | $Es = \infty$ | Horizontal straight line parallel to X-axis. |
| Perfectly inelastic supply | Quantity supplied does not change when price changes. | $Es = 0$ | Vertical straight line parallel to Y-axis |
| Unitary elastic supply | Equal and proportionate changes in price and quantity. | $Es = 1$ | Rectangular hyperbola |
| Relatively elastic supply | Quantity supplied changes by a larger percentage than percentage change in price. | $Es > 1$ | Flatter upward sloping curve |
| Relatively inelastic supply | Quantity supplied changes by a smaller percentage change in price. | $Es < 1$ | Steeper upward sloping curve |

These specific degrees of elasticity of supply have been explained as under.

**1. Perfectly Elastic Supply (*ES* = ∞)**

Supply is perfectly elastic when a minimal rise in price leads to an infinite increase in the quantity supplied and a small fall in price leads to quantity supplied as zero. It means that the producer sells infinite units of the commodity at the same prevailing price. Any further rise in price induces the supplier to sell nothing of the commodity. In such a case, the numerical value of elasticity of supply reaches up to infinity. This type of elasticity however does not exist in reality. In such a case, the supply curve is drawn parallel to the X-axis or the horizontal axis.

The graph for perfectly elastic supply is shown below:

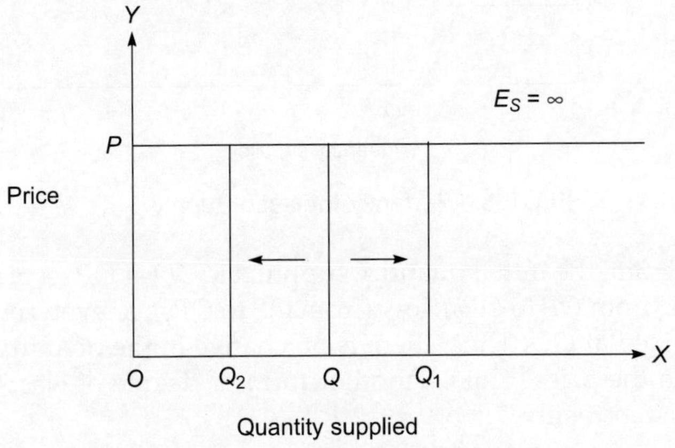


**Fig. 8.4** Perfectly Elastic Supply

In Fig. 8.4, the unlimited quantity is being offered for sale at *OP* price. If price slightly drops down below *OP*, the quantity supplied would fall to zero. Whereas, a small rise in price would lead to expansion in the quantity supplied to an infinite level. Thus, the producer can sell any quantity at the prevailing price. The cases of products with perfectly elastic supply do not exist in reality as it is not possible that a minute rise in price leads to stock replenishment to an infinite level. Thus, it is a fictitious degree of elasticity of supply.

**2. Perfectly Inelastic Supply ($E_S = 0$)**

This is an extreme case where whatever the price of the commodity, high, low or zero, there is no impact on the quantity supplied. It remains unaffected at *OQ* level of output. In such a case, the supply curve is drawn parallel to the *Y*-axis or the vertical axis.

This case does not exist in product market. However, such possibility is studied in labour market in relation with the supply of land as factor of production from the viewpoint of a country. The graph for perfectly inelastic supply is shown in Fig. 8.5.

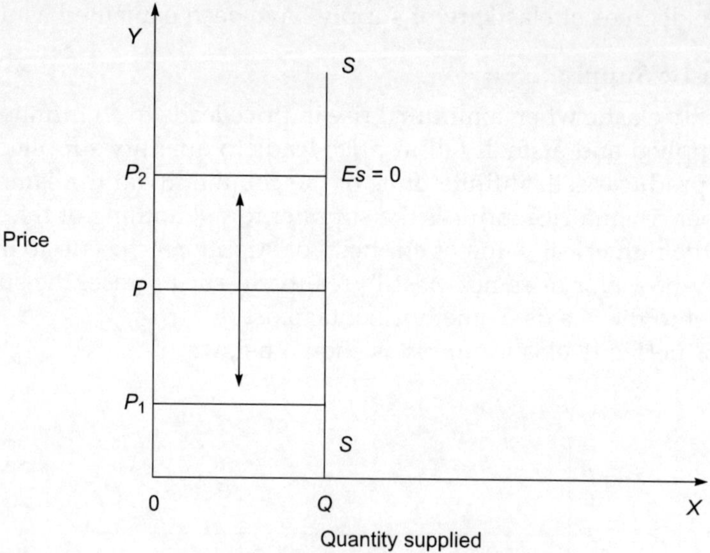


**Fig. 8.5** Perfectly Inelastic Supply

In the above diagram, the initial quantity supplied is *OQ* at *OP* level of prices. If the price becomes high (from *OP* to $OP_2$), low (from *OP* to $OP_1$), or even zero, the quantity supplied remains fixed at *OQ*. Thus, there is no change in the quantity supplied as a result of changes in the price. This is another form of degree of elasticity of supply, which does not exist in reality.

**3. Unitary Elastic ($E_S$ = 1)**

Supply is said to be unitary elastic when the proportionate change in price leads to equal and proportionate change in the quantity supplied. In such a case, the numerical value of $E_s$ will be equal to one. It is to be noted here that if price and quantity supplied change by the same magnitude, then we have unit elasticity of supply. The value of coefficient of elasticity of supply in this case is equal to one (*Es* = 1). The curve diagrammatically would be reflected by a straight line supply curve passing through the origin. The graph for unitary elastic supply is shown in Fig. 8.6.

In Fig. 8.6, *SS* is the supply curve which indicates that when price is *OP*, the quantity supplied is *OQ*. Now the price rises from *OP* to $OP_1$, the quantity supplied increases from *OQ* to $OQ_1$. It is clear in the diagram that when the prices rose 10 per cent, the quantity supplied increased by same proportion, that is, 10 percent. Since the proportionate changes in quantity supplied (10%) are equal to the percentage change in price (10%), therefore the supply is said to be unitary elastic.

It can be represented as:

$$Es = \frac{10\%}{10\%} = 1$$

Thus, elasticity of supply is equal to unity means it has a value equal to one.

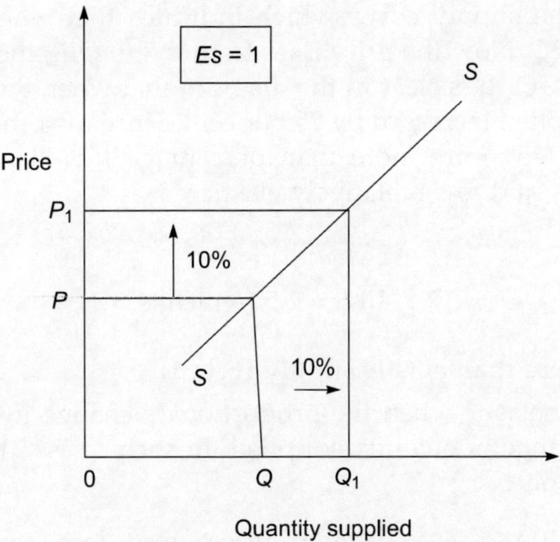


**Fig. 8.6** Unitary Elastic Supply

**4. Elastic Supply/More than Elastic Supply (*ES* > 1)**

Supply is said to be elastic when the proportionate change in price leads to more than proportionate change in the quantity supplied. In such a case, the numerical value of $E_s$ will be greater than one but less than infinity.

***For example:*** When a 10 per cent change in price causes more than 10 per cent say 25 per cent change in the quantity supplied. In such a case, the elasticity of supply is said to be relatively elastic.

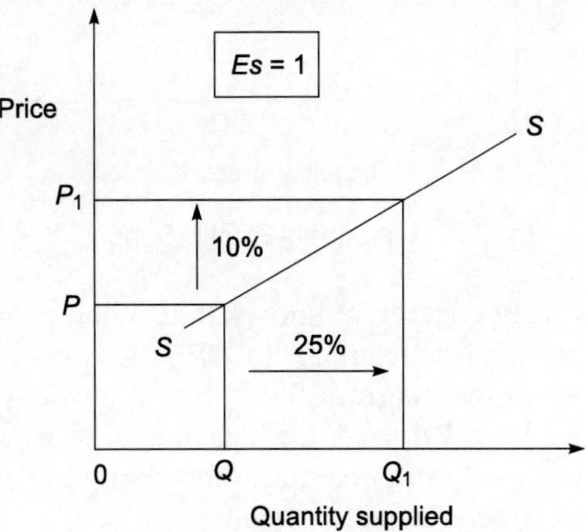


**Fig. 8.7** More than Elastic Supply

In Fig. 8.7, *SS* is the supply curve which indicates that when price is *OP*, the quantity supplied is *OQ*. Now the price rises from *OP* to $OP_1$, the quantity supplied increases from *OQ* to $OQ_1$ It is clear in the diagram that when the prices rose 10 per cent, the quantity supplied increased by 25 per cent. Since the proportionate changes in quantity supplied (25%) are more than percentage the change in price (10%), therefore the supply is said to be relatively elastic.

Symbolically,

$$Es = 25\%/10\% = 2.5 \text{ (which is > 1)}$$

**5. Inelastic Supply/Less than elastic supply ($E_S$ < 1)**

Supply is said to be inelastic when the proportionate change in price leads to less than proportionate change in quantity supplied. In such a case, the numerical value of $E_s$ will be less than one.

***For example:*** when a 10 per cent change in price causes less than 10 per cent say 4 percent change in the quantity supplied. In such a case, the elasticity of supply is said to be relatively inelastic.

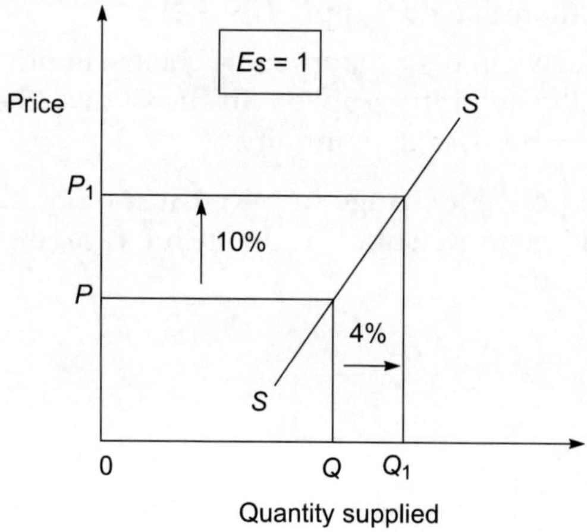


**Fig. 8.8** Less than Elastic Supply

In Fig. 8.8, *SS* is the supply curve that shows that when price is *OP* the quantity supplied is *OQ*, now the price rises from *OP* to $OP_1$, the quantity supplied increases from *OQ* to $OQ_1$. It is clear in the diagram that when the prices rose 10 per cent, the quantity supplied increased by 4 per cent. Since the proportionate changes in the quantity supplied (4%) are less than percentage the change in price (10%), therefore the supply is said to be relatively inelastic.

Symbolically,

$$Es = 4\%/10\% = 0.4 \text{ (which is < 1)}$$

## Summary

- ✓ Elasticity of supply refers to the degree of responsiveness of the quantity supplied of a commodity on account of a change in its price.
- ✓ The factors that determine elasticity of supply are:
  - Nature of the commodity
  - Cost of production
  - Time
  - Producer's expectations
  - Changes in technology
  - Stock of finished goods
  - Number of producers
- ✓ The coefficient of elasticity of supply can be calculated by considering the ratio of percentage or relative change in quantity supplied to percentage change in its price.
- ✓ There are five degrees of price elasticity of supply:
  - Perfectly elastic supply – Supply curve is a horizontal straight line parallel to X-axis
  - Perfectly inelastic supply – Supply curve is a vertical straight line parallel to Y-axis
  - Unitary elastic supply – Supply curve is upward sloping from left to right
  - Relatively elastic supply – Supply curve is upward sloping flatter curve moving from left to right
  - Relatively inelastic supply – Supply curve is upward sloping steeper curve moving from left to right

## Review Questions

1. Define the concept of elasticity of supply. What are the factors that determine elasticity of supply?
2. What is the elasticity of supply? Explain the degrees of elasticity of supply?
3. Explain the concept of elasticity of supply in the context of the following values:
   (a) Infinity
   (b) Zero
   (c) Equal to one
   (d) More than one
   (e) Less than one

4. Show the derivation of coefficient of elasticity of supply. Also explain the degrees of elasticity of supply.
5. Explain how the following factors influence the elasticity of supply:
   (a) Cost of production
   (b) Nature of the commodity
   (c) Time
   (d) Stock of finished goods
   (e) Number of producers
6. Explain how producer's expectations and changes in technology influence the magnitude of supply under supply analysis?

## CASE STUDY 1: SUPPLY OF GOLD IN INDIA (2017)

India is one of the largest consumers and importers of gold in the world. The decision to invest in gold is on account of its high resale value, demonstration effect, rising affluent middle class, a hedge against inflation and a safe haven for black money. Moreover, intergenerational transfer of gold as a symbol of love and affection is also rampant due to its high store of value. In addition, gold is considered to be auspicious and is therefore significant in festivals like Akshaytritiya and Dhanteras.

India imports about 800-1000 tonnes of gold every year and is the second highest component of the import's bill after crude oil. The average demand of gold per year in India is 900 tonnes, whereas the domestic production is 100 tonnes which leads to dependence on imports. More than 20,000 thousand tonnes of gold is lying idle with Indian households, institutions and temple trust which is not being utilized properly.

In the last few years, gold imports have been rising significantly. India is the largest consumer of gold in the world, accounting for around 25 per cent in the year 2015. Thus, India accounts for more than a quarter of global gold imports despite being the contributor of less than 2 per cent in the global trade.

The percentage contribution of gold imports was nearly 30 per cent in the trade deficit of India between 2009–10 and 2012–13. In the year 2013, high gold imports were one of the reasons of pushing up India's current account deficit. Faced with such a situation, the Government hiked import duty to a record 10% and also imposed high excise duties. As a result, the imports fell but this had a limited impact.

Towards the second quarter of 2013, the government took another action of banning the import of gold coins and imposing tight restrictions on gold bullion imports. At that time government took a major step by linking the imports with the level of exports by adopting "80:20" rule. The 80:20 rule stipulated that 20% of all gold imported must be exported before further imports can be made. The new regulations resulted temporarily decline in imports of gold but again the physical demand for gold mounted from 17 per cent in quarter ended march 2015 to nearly 25 per cent by the quarter ended June 2015. Thus, the imports of gold lead to outflow of foreign currency and mounting current account deficit.

A quick glance at the demand and supply of gold in India and amount of gold imported to India paints a stark picture.

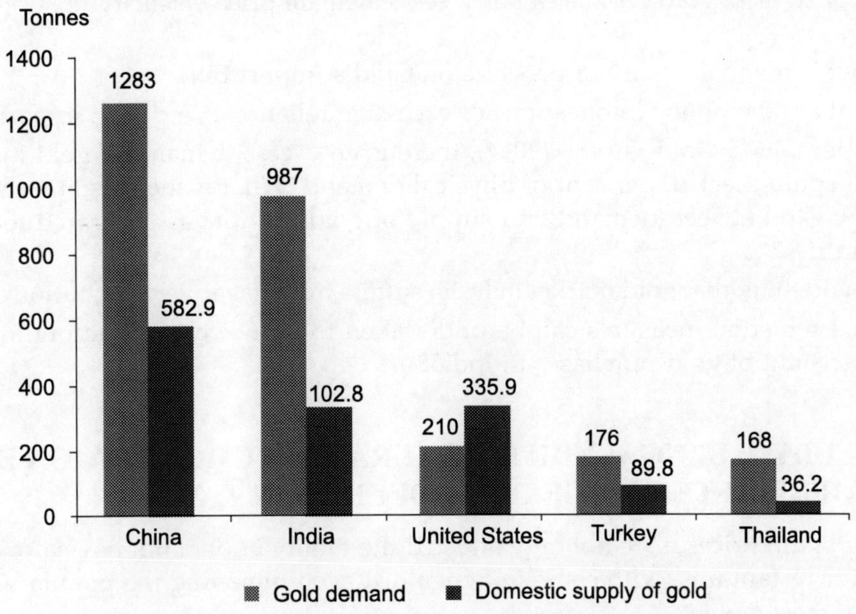


*Source*: Gold Fields Mineral Services (GFMS) Survey (2014)

**Fig. 1** Demand and Domestic Supply

Looking at the top five countries (Figure 1.1), India is the only country whose prime sources of gold supply (mine and old scrap) would meet barely 10 per cent of physical demand.

*Source*

(a) Murria P. (2017). Yellow Metal Goes Monetized: Dynamics and Challenges. ITIHAS - The Journal of Indian Management. Vol. 7. Issue 3. pp. 38-43.

(b) FICCI- World Gold Council Report (2014) retrieved from https://www.gjc.org.in/pdf/Why_India_Needs_a_Gold_Policy.pdf retrieved on October 27, 2019.

## Questions

1. Do you think that supply of gold is price elastic or not? Give reasons in support of your answer.
2. In your opinion what determines the supply of gold in India?
3. Prepare supply function of gold on the basis of factors explained in the above case.
4. Show the diagrammatic representation of supply curve of gold.

5. Suppose, you are a jeweller. At an average price of gold of $ 45, the quantity supplied is 10 gold necklaces per week. If the price increases to $ 48, the quantity supplied is 12 gold necklaces per week, calculate price elasticity of supply for gold.
6. What is the main cause of pressure on Gold's Import Bill?
7. What are the policy implications of excessive reliance of India on imports?
8. As per GFMS Gold Survey (2014), there is an excess demand of gold in India as it could meet 10 per cent of physical demand. What is the reason for such a huge gap between demand and supply of gold in India as compared to other countries?
9. Do you think that gold market in India suffers from negative substitution effect?
10. What remedial measures can be undertaken to reduce current account deficit on account of gold purchases in India?

## CASE STUDY 2: BENGALURU RESTAURANTS REMOVE ONION DOSA FROM MENU AFTER PRICE HIKE (DECEMBER 1, 2019)

The rising onion prices have not only affected the family budget but have also made it worse for restaurants, with some in Bengaluru even removing the popular Onion Dosa from their menus.

Due to the unprecedented hike in onion prices, most affected are the low and mid-level eateries which have to walk a thin line between serving delicacies and keeping the prices affordable for their patrons.

Customers said that the reduction in usage has also taken a toll on the taste of the food served at their favourite outlets. "They have reduced the usage of onions in the hotels while some eateries and canteens have completely stopped serving them. The removal of onions has also affected the taste of food in our favourite eateries," Laxman, a customer at a local eatery, said.

Another young customer, Rohan, a student of Class 9 said that the taste of food has taken a hit due to the reduced usage of onions and urged the government to take steps to reduce the price.

Gunawati, a customer at a local eatery, said that the government should help the farmers and formulate policies which will ensure such situations do not emerge in the future.

"Onions are selling close to Rs 100 per kg in Bengaluru. The government should take note of this and help the farmers at the initial level to ensure such situations never arise in the future," she said.

*Source*: *India Today* (December 1, 2019) retrieved from https://www.indiatoday.in/trending-news/story/bengaluru-restaurants-remove-onion-dosa-from-menu-after-price-hike-1624070-2019-12-01 on December 1, 2019.

## Questions

1. Why the serving of onion dosa by Bengaluru restaurants got impacted on account of onion price hike?
2. Do you think that supply of dosa is price sensitive to onion prices? Give reasons in support of your answer?
3. What role can government play to help farmers who are dealing with onions?
4. Show the diagrammatic representation of effect of onion price hike on supply curve of onion dosa.

# 9 CHAPTER

# Demand Forecasting

**LEARNING OBJECTIVES**

After going through this chapter, reader would be able to understand:

- ✓ The meaning of demand forecasting.
- ✓ The need and aim behind forecasting demand.
- ✓ The methods of anticipating demand for the existing products.
- ✓ The methods of anticipating demand for new products.

## 9.1 INTRODUCTION

Chapter 4 dealt with the dynamics related to the demand and focused on demand analysis. In this chapter, we will focus on the forecasting aspect of demand. Demand forecasting is an important tool in the hands of economic and business analyst. It is an attempt to peep into the future and thereby predict it. Now, the future is uncertain and unpredictable. Thus, these forecasts may or may not represent the correct anticipation of the facts. Still forecasting assumes importance as it helps in overcoming the problem of over- and underproduction which have their respective repercussions. In case there is overproduction, the cost overruns in the form of requirement of land for accommodating excess inventory, the need for an extra supervisor, payment of electricity bill, etc. On the other hand, underproduction may lead to inability to meet excess demand, customer dissonance, loss of customer loyalty as there is every possibility of the substitution of the product by another product. Thus, the forecasted data provides a benchmark for future decision-making pertaining to demand. These decision-making areas include production planning, execution of purchase decisions, pricing policy, sales forecasting, estimating short- and long-run financial requirements, regulating business efficiently.

Now, these predictions may be done for future for an already established product or a product that is a newcomer and is yet to establish itself in the market. For already established product, survey and statistical methods are opted. In case of new product since the consumers are unaware of the attributes of the product, evolutionary approach, growth curve approach, vicarious approach, etc., are followed. However, among both the cases, it is more difficult to forecast demand for a new product as compared to forecasting demand for an already existing product.

So, to have a comprehensive view of the concept of demand forecasting, the present chapter initially talks about the meaning of demand forecasting and its requirement. Thereafter, the methods of anticipating demand for already existing products and new methods have been discussed.

## 9.2 MEANING OF DEMAND FORECASTING

Forecasting refers to the act of predicting or anticipating any future course of action. When the concept of forecasting is applied to demand analysis, then it is known as demand forecasting. Demand forecasting refers to the well organised process of predicting or anticipating the future demand of a particular product or service. In demand forecasting, the business economist takes an initiative to peep into the future and thereby anticipate the quantity of a commodity that can be demanded by the prospective or the existing consumers. Since, it is mere prediction of future demand; it may be correct or incorrect. For instance, the forecast for a quarter's demand may reflect that the demand for a particular commodity would be of 10,000 units, however the actual demand may be more or less than the forecasted demand. Still the concept of demand forecasting occupies an important place in contemporary business environment as it helps in mitigating the risk level and reduces uncertainty associated with the turbulent business environment.

## 9.3 NEED AND OBJECTIVES OF DEMAND FORECASTING

### 9.3.1 Need

Demand forecasting is mainly required as it helps in avoiding the hassles associated with the under- or overproduction of the product. In both the cases, the company has to face the repercussions.

**Case 1: Underproduction of the Commodity (Forecasted demand < Actual Demand)**

Considering the previous case where the quarterly forecasted demand for a particular commodity is of 10,000 units. But, the actual demand turns out to be 16,000 units. Here, the forecast turned out to be false. Hence, there is a shortage or underproduction of 6000 units. This has the following repercussions for the company:

1. It creates a negative impact on company's image. The buyers assume that the company is dealing with the product but does not supply product on time.

2. The existing as well as new consumers may switch to the other seller who is able to fulfil their demand. So, there is a probability of losing the customers in such a case.

**Case 2: Overproduction of the Commodity (Forecasted demand > Actual demand)**

Considering the previous case, where the quarterly forecasted demand for a particular commodity is 10,000 units. But, the actual demand turns out to be 6000 units. Here, again the forecast turned out to be false. Hence, there is an excess or overproduction of 4000 units. This has the following repercussions for the company:

1. Additional cost to accommodate the excess stock.
2. Payment of supervisor's salary.
3. In case of perishable commodity, the cost of preservatives.

All these costs may lead to the cost overruns. Thus, demand forecasting assumes much significance.

### 9.3.2 Objectives

- To anticipate production and sales of a product. This helps in fixing of production and sales targets for an enterprise.
- To prepare a systematic policy of inventory management by eliminating the problem of underproduction or overproduction.
- To analyse financial requirements of the organisation and plan for capital budgeting requirements.
- To determine suitable pricing policy.
- To decide the expansion and diversification policies of the existing unit.

## 9.4 METHODS OF DEMAND FORECASTING

The study of demand forecasting is done under the following heads.

### 9.4.1 Demand Forecasting for Already Existing or Established Products

The demand forecasting for already existing products is undertaken with the help of methods that have been bifurcated under:

1. Survey methods,
2. Statistical methods (Fig. 9.1)

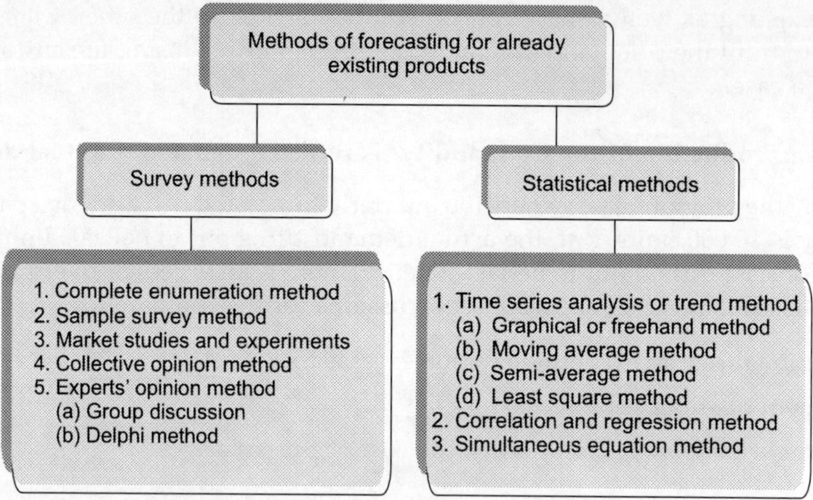


**Fig. 9.1** Methods of Forecasting for Already Existing Products

## 1. Survey Methods

In survey methods the volume of production is anticipated by conducting an extensive survey of the future purchase plans of potential buyers. In this method, opinions of experts, sales force or consumers are elicited by asking them a set of questions and inferences drawn on the basis of the response. These methods are:

### (a) Complete Enumeration Method

This method has the following attributes:

- In this method, all the units (consumers) of population (particular area or region) are approached.
- Future or probable demand is calculated on the basis of responses elicited during survey.
- The person conducting the survey is known as enumerator and the people whose responses are sought are called respondents. The set of questions is presented in form of a questionnaire.
- The enumerator asks the questions regarding the future plan of prospective buyers regarding purchasing the product in question.
- This method is most appropriate where the customers are concentrated in a small region or locality. In case consumers are widely dispersed, this method involves huge cost in terms of both time and money.
- For instance, forecast for time period $t$ may be calculated as

  $F_t$ = Demand reported by respondent $t_1$ + Demand reported by respondent $t_2$ + Demand reported by respondent $t_3$ + … + Demand reported by respondent $t_n$

It may be written as

$$F_t = D_1 + D_2 + D_3 + \ldots D_n$$

**(b) Sample Survey Method**

This method has the following attributes:

- In this method, some selected units (consumers) from the entire population are approached and questioned.
- It is based on the assumption that the selected sample is representative of the entire population.
- These prospective customers may be approached directly (direct interview method) or may be approached though mail (mailed questionnaire method).
- The responses elicited become the basis of forecasted demand.
- This method is most effective where the chosen sample represents the entire population.
- For the effectiveness of the results, it should be supplemented with the quantitative methods of demand forecasting.

**(c) Market Studies and Experiments**

This method has the following attributes:

- At first, some representative areas (three or four cities) having similar features are selected.
- These respondents are similar in terms of population, income levels, living standards, cultural and social background, occupational distribution, choices and preferences of consumers.
- Market experiments are conducted by changing controlled variables in the demand function such as by changing price, advertisement expenditure, and other controllable variables under the assumption that other things remain the same.
- After such changes, the consequent changes in the demand over a period of time (a week, a fortnight, or month) are recorded.
- On the basis of data collected, elasticity coefficients are computed and assessed to predict the future demand for the product.

**(d) Collective Opinion Method/Sales Force Opinion Method/ Sales Force Polling Method**

This method has the following attributes:

- In this method, the demand forecasts are based on the opinions and intuition of salesmen or sales force. Thus, this method relies on human judgment or the decisions made by sales personnel.
- This method is based on the assumption that sales people are closest to the customers. They are fully aware of the likes or dislikes of the customers. Hence, their opinion is most valuable while forecasting demand.

- Thus, on the basis of collective opinion of sales persons, the subjective opinions are converted into quantitative forecasts.
- Thus, finally the executive in charge takes decision from all the opinions.
- It is a cost-effective method as no additional cost is incurred on collection of data. However, there is a possibility of personal bias (optimism or pessimism) of salespersons.

**(e) Experts' Opinion Method**

It is conducted in two ways:

**(i) Group Discussion**

- In this method, the panel of experts is called and made to sit together.
- The decisions are taken with the help of brainstorming sessions or by structured discussions.
- The demand is forecasted on the basis of decisions of majority of the experts.

**(ii) Reasoned Opinion Method/Delphi Method**

- This method is also known as Delphi method.
- In this method, demand is estimated on the basis of opinions of expert corporate executives.
- In this method, each expert is provided with the relevant information along with forecasts of other experts.
- The experts are not influenced by others.
- They may revise estimates in the light of forecasts made by other experts.
- This process is repeated until the experts come to a consensus regarding the forecasted figures of demand.
- This technique is extremely useful where the product is absolutely new to market. Its efficiency is proved in case of anticipation of demand and supply of electricity, demand and supply of accommodation, etc.
- However, its major drawback is that the loss of confidential information of the company as the experts are external to the organisation.

**2. Statistical Methods**

In economics, business and commerce, it is important to estimate the values for future. For example, an economist may be interested in knowing the future population for planning and policymaking. Similarly, a businessman may be interested in knowing sales for future month, quarter or a year. For making such estimates, past information is used.

Now, the analysis of past data requires the use of certain statistical methods. These methods involve the use of statistical tools and techniques for forecasting the future demand of the product. They make projections on the basis of past data. These are based on the assumption that future would be a representative of past patterns. They are based on the ideology that the factors that were dominant in past would be dominant in future as well. These methods are:

**1. Time Series Analysis or Trend Method**

- Time series forecasting is a precise statistical version of quantitative techniques that uses past figures to predict future results. The statistical data related to past is known as time series and the corresponding analysis is called time series analysis.
- Thus, time series is a set of observations taken at specified times, usually (but not always) at equal intervals. Thus, a set of data depending on time (which may be a week, a quarter, a month, or a year) is called time series.
- It tries to ascertain the movement of dependent variable with the time, time here is an independent variable.
- In context of forecast, the relationship between dependent variable and time as independent variable is studied and thus, accordingly forecasts are made.
- However, it suffers from the major drawbacks that it assumes the past will act as benchmark for future. It does not take into account the effect of other variables that may be important determinants but it assumes them as constant.
- For example,
  - The annual production of cement in India over past 20 years.
  - Hourly temperature recorded by meteorological office in a city.

  It can be done using the following methods:

**(a) Graphical or Freehand Method**

- This method shows the graphical representation of the relationship between sales or demand and time. The time here is always a long period.
- This method gives reflection of series of past data as growing (upward sloping), constant or as declining (downward sloping) over a period of time.
- In this method, the time period is taken on *X*-axis and the corresponding sales or demand figure on *Y*-axis. Then for each year, the combinations of sales/demand and time period are ascertained on a graph. They are then joined to see the trend. It means that a free hand curve passing through most of the plotted combinations is drawn.
- To draw the line, equal number of points on each side of line are left out.
- The line so obtained gives the direction of trend. This method is extremely useful in forecasting demand for cement, jute, readymade garments, etc.

Suppose the data related to sales figures of *ABC* Company is as follows and we want to forecast demand in the form of the following figures:

**TABLE 9.1** Graphical or Freehand Method

| Year | Sales (Rs. in Crores) |
|---|---|
| 2011 | 62 |
| 2012 | 64 |
| 2013 | 65 |
| 2014 | 63.5 |
| 2015 | 67 |
| 2016 | 64.5 |
| 2017 | 69 |
| 2018 | 67 |

On the basis of Table 9.1, we can draw the trend line *AB* which has been drawn as free hand curve passing through the various points representing actual sale values (Fig. 9.2).

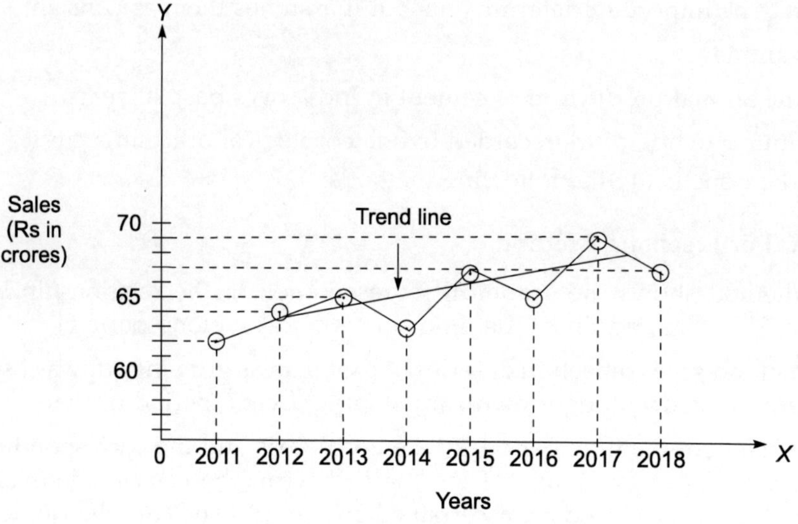


**Fig. 9.2** Freehand Method of Trend Analysis

### (b) Moving Average Method

- In this method, a series of moving averages of specific order is calculated. This is done from the initial year of the given series.
- An average for a specific number of years for the given time period or time interval is calculated and this average is then placed against the midpoint of time interval.

- Then the process is repeated by omitting the first year figure and considering the figure of next year. This is done till the end of the series.
- The moving average (simple) for a given time period is calculated as:

$$F_t = \frac{A_{t-1} + A_{t-2} + \ldots + A_{t-n}}{N}$$

where,

$F_t$ = Forecast for the future period
$A_{t-1}$ = Actual occurrence in the past one period ($t$ – 1 period)
$A_{t-2}$ = Actual occurrence in the past two periods ($t$ – 2 periods)
$A_{t-3}$ = Actual occurrence in the past three periods ($t$ – 3 periods)
$A_{t-n}$ = Actual occurrence in $t - n$ periods ago.
$n$ = Number of periods to be averaged

Suppose, a company wants to anticipate monthly demand then using moving average method, it is calculated as follows:

**TABLE 9.2** Moving Average Method

| Month | Actual Demand | Forecast Based on Simple Moving Average |
|---|---|---|
| 1 | $d_1$ | — |
| 2 | $d_2$ | — |
| 3 | $d_3$ | — |
| 4 | $d_4$ | $\frac{d_1 + d_2 + d_3}{3}$ (forecast for month 4) |
| 5 | $d_5$ | $\frac{d_2 + d_3 + d_4}{3}$ (forecast for month 5) |
| 6 | $d_6$ | $\frac{d_3 + d_4 + d_5}{3}$ (forecast for month 6) |
| 7 | $d_7$ | $\frac{d_4 + d_5 + d_6}{3}$ (forecast for month 7) |
| 8 | $d_8$ | $\frac{d_5 + d_6 + d_7}{3}$ (forecast for month 8) |

Suppose, a company deals in selling of readymade garments. It wants to anticipate demand considering moving average method for 3 months. The data pertaining to 8 months is shown as under:

**TABLE 9.3** Illustration: Moving Average Method

| Month | Sales (Rs. in lakhs) | Months | Sales (Rs. in lakhs) |
|---|---|---|---|
| 1 | 9 | 6 | 10 |
| 2 | 10 | 7 | 11 |
| 3 | 10 | 8 | 13 |
| 4 | 11 | 9 | – |
| 5 | 12 | | |

On the basis of Table 9.3, three months moving average can be calculated. The forecasted sales figures using moving average method have been shown in Table 9.4 in the following manner:

**TABLE 9.4** Illustration (Solution): Moving Average Method

| Month | Sales (Rs. in lakhs) | Three-Months Moving Average |
|---|---|---|
| 1 | 9 | – |
| 2 | 10 | – |
| 3 | 10 | – |
| 4 | 11 | (9 + 10 + 10)/3 = 9.67 |
| 5 | 12 | (10 + 10 + 11)/3 = 10.33 |
| 6 | 10 | (10 + 11 + 12)/3 = 11 |
| 7 | 11 | (11 + 12 + 10)/3 = 11 |
| 8 | 13 | (12 + 10 + 11)/3 = 11 |
| 9 | – | (10 + 11 + 13)/3 = 11.33 |

The analysis of Table 9.4 is as follows:

4th month: Actual sales Rs 11 lakh, Forecasted sales: Rs. 9.67 lakh
5th month: Actual sales Rs 12 lakh, Forecasted sales: Rs. 10.33 lakh
6th Month: Actual sales Rs 10 lakh, Forecasted sales: Rs. 11 lakh
7th Month: Actual sales Rs 11 lakh, Forecasted sales: Rs. 11 lakh
8th Month: Actual sales Rs 13 lakh, Forecasted sales: Rs. 11 lakh
9th month: Forecasted sales: Rs. 11.33 lakh

**(c) Semi-Averages Method**

- In this method, the time series data are divided into two equal groups. The first group consists of the first half periods (years) and the second group consists of the remaining periods.
- An average for each part is then calculated. These averages are then plotted on graph against the midpoints of time intervals covered by respective two parts.
- The line joining the two points gives the required trend line.

It can be understood with the help of following example:

An aluminium company wants to anticipate the trend of production. It furnishes the following information for this purpose:

**TABLE 9.5** Illustration: Semi-Averages Method

| Year | Production (Rs. in lakh tonnes) |
|---|---|
| 2013 | 90 |
| 2014 | 96 |
| 2015 | 84 |
| 2016 | 88 |
| 2017 | 96 |
| 2018 | 107 |

On the basis of Table 9.5, production figures using semi-averages method can be calculated. The forecasted sales figures have been shown in the following manner:

The average production of aluminum for first three years = (90 + 96 + 84)/3 = 90 lakh tones

The average production of aluminum for last three years = (88 + 96 + 107)/3 = 97 lakh tones

Thus, using semi-averages method we get two points which are plotted against the respective middle years, that is, 2014 (middle year for the first three years, 2013 to 2015) and 2017 (middle year for the last three years, 2016 to 2018).

Figure 9.3 shows the trend line when the number of years is even. In case the number of years is odd, then we omit the middle year for dividing the data in two parts.

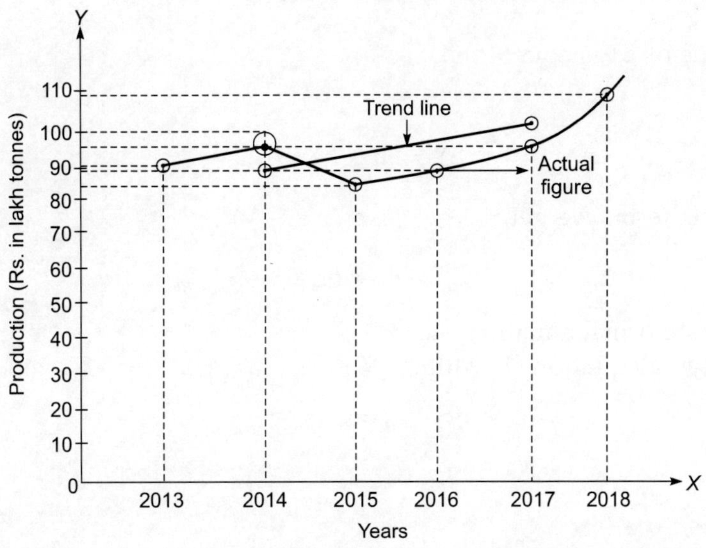


**Fig. 9.3** Semi-Averages Method

### (d) Least Square Method/Method of Least Squares

- This is the most widely used method to determine trends. In this method, we try to fit a straight line to the given data. The line is known as 'line of best fit'.
- This line of best fit tries to minimize the sum of the squares of deviation between the observed and the fitted values of the data. This can be understood as follows:

Suppose, $Y$ denotes the demand and $X$ the time period during which the commodity is being sold. Then the linear relationship between $Y$ and $X$ as per the method of least squares is as follows:

$$Y = a + bX \qquad \ldots(1)$$

where,

$a$ = Intercept

$b$ = Slope that shows the impact of the independent variable

$X$ = Independent variable

$Y$ = Dependent variable

Now the value of $a$ and $b$ can be ascertained using the past information about both the variables, that is, $X$ and $Y$. This is done through normal equations. The procedure to obtain the normal equations is as follows:

Taking $\Sigma$ on both sides of the equation:

$$\Sigma Y = \Sigma a + \Sigma bX$$

Now, since $a$ and $b$ are constants, the above equation becomes:

$$\Sigma Y = a\Sigma 1 + b\Sigma X$$

Now the value of $\Sigma 1$ is equal to $n$

Therefore,

$$\Sigma Y = an + b\Sigma X$$

By rearranging terms we get,

$$\Sigma Y = na + b\Sigma X \qquad \ldots(2)$$

This is the first normal equation.

Now multiplying equation (1) with $X$

$$XY = aX + bX^2$$

Now again taking Σ, we get

$$\Sigma XY = a\Sigma X + b\Sigma X^2$$

This gives us the second normal equation.
Thus, finally the normal equations are:

$$\Sigma Y = na + b\Sigma X$$

$$\Sigma XY = a\Sigma X + b\Sigma X^2$$

These are then solved to ascertain the values of *a* and *b*. After substituting these values the required equation of straight line trend can be ascertained. From this equation, we can find the trend values.

Suppose, a company wants to determine the trend values using a straight line which best fits its data. The company's data reflects the following figures:

**TABLE 9.6** Illustration: Method of Least Squares

| **Year** | 2014 | 2015 | 2016 | 2017 | 2018 |
|---|---|---|---|---|---|
| **Sales (Rs. in Lakhs)** | 35 | 56 | 79 | 80 | 40 |

Now the trend value for all the years can be calculated as follows:
We have line of best fit as follows:

$$Y = a + bX$$

**TABLE 9.7** Illustration (Solution): Method of Least Squares

| **Year** | **Sales (Rs. in lakhs) (*Y*)** | ***X*** | ***X*²** | ***XY*** |
|---|---|---|---|---|
| 2014 | 35 | –2 | 4 | –70 |
| 2015 | 56 | –1 | 1 | –56 |
| 2016 | 79 | 0 | 0 | 0 |
| 2017 | 80 | 1 | 1 | 80 |
| 2018 | 40 | 2 | 4 | 80 |
| | $\Sigma Y = 290$ | $\Sigma X = 0$ | $\Sigma X^2 = 10$ | $\Sigma XY = 34$ |

The normal equations are as follows:

$$\Sigma Y = na + b\Sigma X$$
$$\Sigma XY = a\Sigma X + b\Sigma X^2$$
$$290 = 5a + b(0)$$
$$a = 290/5 = 58$$
$$34 = a(0) + b(10)$$
$$b = 34/10 = 3.4$$

Substituting the values of $a$ and $b$ in equation $Y = a + bX$ is as follows:

$$\boxed{Y = 58 + 3.4X}$$

Now the trend values of each year are as follows:

**TABLE 9.8** Calculation of Trend Values using Method of Least Squares

| Year | $X$ | Trend values for line of best fit $Y = 58 + 3.4X$ |
|---|---|---|
| 2014 | –2 | $Y = 58 + 3.4(-2) = 51.2$ |
| 2015 | –1 | $Y = 58 + 3.4(-1) = 54.6$ |
| 2016 | 0 | $Y = 58 + 3.4(0) = 58$ |
| 2017 | 1 | $Y = 58 + 3.4(1) = 61.4$ |
| 2018 | 2 | $Y = 58 + 3.4(2) = 64.8$ |

Now if we want to anticipate demand for year 2019, it may be done as follows:

$$Y\text{ (sales for year 2019)} = 58 + 3.4(3) = 68.2 \text{ lakhs}$$

### 2. Regression and Correlation

The regression and correlation analysis are also called the econometric model building. These methods integrate economic theory with statistics as a decision science. These have been explained as under:

#### (a) Correlation

- Correlation is a statistical measure for finding the strength of association between two variables. The association here means the tendency of two variables to move together. It is denoted by $r$ and its value lies between –1 and 1.
- Two variables are said to be correlated when the changes on one variable leads to changes in another variable.
- The changes may be in the same direction such as one variable rising and other also rising or one variable falling and other variable also falling. In such a case, the correction is positive.

- The changes may be in opposite direction such as one variable rising and the other falling or one variable falling and the other rising. In such a case, the correction is negative.
- If there is no change in the second variable on account of change in one variable then variables are called uncorrected.
- The sign of the coefficient of correlation shows the direction of association. The magnitude of coefficient shows the strength of association.

**Interpretation of Value of *r* (Correlation Coefficient)**

1. The interpretation of correlation coefficient, $r = 0.9$ is as follows:
   The relationship between variables is positive and there is a strong association among two variables.
2. The interpretation of correlation coefficient, $r = -0.4$ is as follows:
   The relationship between variables is negative and there is a weak association among two variables.
3. A correlation near to zero shows absence of linear alliance among the variables.

The examples of correlation analysis are as follows:

- The study of relationship between the population and income inequality
- Number of working hours of employee and change in sales.
- Number of teachers in a college and the performance of students.

**(b) Regression**

- Regression (linear) means the average relationship between two variables.
- Of these variables one variable is called an independent variable or explained variable and the other is called dependent variable or explaining variable.
- It is denoted by *byx* or *bxy*.
- If there are two or more independent variables, then the regression is called multiple regression.

***For example:*** If we consider sales as dependent variable and income of consumer as an independent variable, then we conduct regression analysis to analyze the future trend.

**3. Simultaneous Equations Method**

- This method is based on the assumption that every variable influences every other variable in an economic environment.
- This method recognises the interdependence among variables.
- A typical simultaneous equation model may comprise two sets of variables:

- **Endogenous variables:** The variables whose values are included in the model as dependent variables.
- **Exogenous variables:** The variables whose values are given from outside the model.

### 9.4.2 Demand Forecasting for New Products

Forecasting the demand for a new product is a challenging task. It is more challenging than forecasting demand for already existing product. This is due to the following reasons:

1. The customers are not aware of pros and cons of the product.
2. The product is not positioned in the minds of the consumers. Thus, it is difficult to anticipate the number of consumers that will actually buy the product.
3. There is complete absence of the historical data which can act as benchmark for forecasts.
4. Consumer's taste and preferences are difficult to predict.

Thus, it is difficult to forecast the demand for new products.

Prof. Joel Dean has suggested the following methods for forecasting demand of new products (Fig. 9.4):

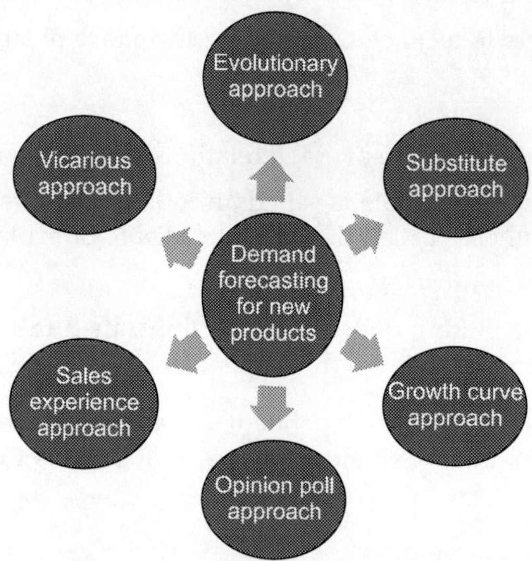


**Fig. 9.4** Methods of Demand Forecasting for New Products

These methods have been explained as under:

### 1. Evolutionary Approach

In this method, demand forecasting is done by identifying the demand of the old product. It is assumed that the forecasted demand figure of a new product is a function of demand of old product of similar nature or attributes.

***For example:*** The demand for old model of car may be taken into consideration while forecasting the demand for a new model because the latter is an improvement of the former.

Similarly, the demand for LCD TVs may be taken into consideration while forecasting the demand for a LED TVs.

### 2. Substitute Approach

This method is used where the product that is coming in market will be a substitute to the product that already exists in the market. Thus, the demand for a new product is analyzed as a substitute for the existing goods or service.

- The demand for a cell phone may be anticipated on the basis of its substitute that is land line phone.
- The demand for a scooty may be anticipated on the basis of its substitute, that is, scooter.
- The demand for air conditioner on the basis of coolers.

Demand for mop, may be anticipated on the basis of demand for floor cloth.

### 3. Growth Curve Approach

In this method, the growth rate of demand of an existing product for forecasting the growth rate of demand of a new product.

Suppose, Johnsons Baby Soap is considered safe by most of the new mothers. Suppose, a company wants to launch a baby soap product, then it is imperative on its part to consider the average sales of Johnsons Baby Soap. This is required as it will give an idea regarding the acceptability of company's product by the new mothers as customers.

Similarly, a bike manufacturing company while introducing a new model of bike will study the level of demand for the existing models of bikes.

### 4. Opinion Poll Approach

Under this method, the potential buyers are approached directly and are informed about the product.

Their responses are elicited though survey in which their responses are captured and recorded.

Thus, in such a case, direct interview method is used.

Suppose, a biscuit manufacturing firm wants to ascertain the demand of its new product then the sales representatives can directly approach the prospective consumers, give them free sample packets and can ascertain the responses regarding the future demand of the product.

**5. Sales Experience Approach**

In this method, the new product is offered for sale in a sample market generally, big marketing centers, and the demand is anticipated on the basis of customers' response.

***For example:*** A detergent is offered for sale in Big Bazaars or MORE outlet and the demand is anticipated accordingly.

**6. Vicarious Approach**

In this method the demand for a new product is predicted on the basis of responses of specialized and informed dealers who have good knowledge of market and consumer preferences and demand is anticipated accordingly.

The above methods are not mutually exclusive. It is desirable to use a combination of two or more methods in order to get better results.

## Summary

✓ Demand forecasting refers to the well organised process of predicting or anticipating the future demand of a particular product or service.

✓ Demand forecasting is mainly required as it helps in avoiding the hassles associated with the under- or overproduction of the product.

✓ It is done in two cases:
- For already established product
- For a new product

✓ The demand forecasting for already existing products is undertaken with the help of methods that have been bifurcated under:

(a) Survey methods
(b) Statistical methods

✓ The survey methods of predicting demand for already established products include further include the following methods:
- Complete enumeration method
- Sample survey method
- Market studies and experiments
- Collective opinion method
- Experts' opinion method
  (a) Group discussion
  (b) Delphi method

✓ Statistical methods of predicting demand for already established products further include the following methods:
- Time series analysis or trend method
  (a) Graphical or freehand method
  (b) Moving average method

   (c) Semi averages method
   (d) Least squares method
- Correlation and regression method
- Simultaneous equation method

✓ Demand forecasting for new products includes the following methods:
- Evolutionary approach
- Substitute approach
- Growth curve approach
- Opinion poll approach
- Sales experience approach
- Vicarious approach

## Review Questions

1. What is demand forecasting? Elaborate the methods of forecasting demand for an already established product?
2. Define demand forecasting. Elaborate the methods of forecasting demand for a new product.
3. Explain the need and objectives of demand forecasting. As a business analyst how will you predict the future demand of a new product that would be launched after four months?
4. What are the probable consequences if a large-scale firm provides its product in the market without anticipating the future demand?
5. 'Demand forecasting is an essential tool in the hands of an economic analyst'. Explain the statement with the help of appropriate examples.
6. Elucidate the trend projection methods of demand forecasting.
7. 'Elasticity of demand and demand forecasting are the two main pillars of economic analysis'. Explain the statement.
8. Write short notes on the following methods of demand forecasting:
   (a) Freehand method
   (b) Correlation and regression
   (c) Sample survey method
   (d) Market studies and experiments
   (e) Delphi method
9. As a business economist, how would you apply the survey method if you are predicting demand for an existing product line?
10. What are the various statistical methods that a business economist may use to predict demand for a product?

11. A company's data reflects the following figures:

| Year | 2016 | 2017 | 2018 | 2019 | 2020 |
|---|---|---|---|---|---|
| Sales (Rs. in crores) | 68 | 72 | 65 | 78 | 90 |

Show the predicted sales for year 2021, 2022, 2023 and 2024 using the method of least squares.

12. A cement company wants to anticipate the trend of production. It furnishes the following information for this purpose:

| Week | Production (Rs. in lakh tonnes) |
|---|---|
| 1 | 59 |
| 2 | 57 |
| 3 | 62 |
| 4 | 64 |
| 5 | 67 |
| 6 | 73 |
| 7 | 79 |
| 8 | 82 |
| 9 | 84 |
| 10 | 90 |
| 11 | – |

Anticipate the production for 11$^{th}$ week using 5 months moving average method of demand forecasting.

## CASE STUDY 1: DEMAND FORECASTING OF GLISTEN (PRODUCT) AT GLISTENING SKIN COMPANY LTD. (2019)

Glistening Skin Company Ltd., a leading company located in India, was dealing in personal care products like body wash, body cream, face wash and the like for past ten years. Five years back, it started a cosmetic soap venture known as 'Glisten' which was composed of natural ingredients. The soap had aesthetic appeal and was specially designed to cater to beauty requirements such as cleansing, moisturizing, and revitalizing. The product could be found in 5000 retail outlets, departmental stores and pharmacists. It had qualified all quality tests and was found fit for toddlers as well. The brand was leaving no stone unturned to enhance the market share in India.

After encountering the severe fluctuations in the profits, the company decided to forecast the future demand of 'Glisten' with precision and care for Q2 2019. In this regard, the shareholders made following suggestions:

- Mr. Farma, suggested to visit the representative region/ area and approach a group of people and get an idea regarding the customer preferences and thereby forecast the demand for the soap.
- Mr. Ronis opined that "it is better to consult sales representatives who are selling in their representative zones for that matter".
- Mr. Manik asserted that "the best method is to get opinions of experts in this regard. He further stated that they should be requested to explain their view-point along with the justification in support of their suggestion".
- Ms. Nishna negated all the suggestions and said that "all we need to do is fitting a trend line to the past data and anticipate the demand for the soap".

## Questions

1. Explain the concept of demand forecasting in the light of above case.
2. 'Forecasts may or may not be correct'. Then why do we need to spend time, money and effort on demand or sales forecasting?
3. Throw light on the methods of demand forecasting explained in the above-mentioned case?
4. If you were the managing director of the company, which method of demand forecasting would you consider and why?
5. Elucidate any four methods of demand forecasting apart from methods mentioned above.

## CASE STUDY 2: CHERHORIZON (2015)

In 2015, Cherhorizon started the production of wooden chairs. In the month of May 2015, it was estimated that the sales would be of 6 lakh units. However, the consumer's perspective revealed that the company is delivering a superb quality product which has good quality. The actual demand was 10 lakh units. However, 6 months later, the company anticipated that the demand would be 8 lakh units. However, the actual demand stood at 5.5 lakh units.

## Questions

1. Explain the above case in the context of demand forecasting.
2. Why at all there is a need to forecast demand?
3. What impact does a wrong forecast has on the company's revenue position.
4. What are the economic implications of 'excess demand' or 'excess supply'?

# 10 CHAPTER

# Theory of Consumer Behaviour: Cardinal Utility Analysis

**LEARNING OBJECTIVES**

After going through this chapter, reader would be able to understand:

- ✓ The concept of utility and cardinal approach to analysis of consumer's behaviour.
- ✓ The underlying assumptions that lay foundations for cardinal utility analysis.
- ✓ The fundamental laws under which cardinal utility analysis is undertaken.
- ✓ The equilibrium determination in one and two commodity case.
- ✓ The critical analysis of cardinal utility analysis.

## 10.1 INTRODUCTION

In economics, consumer is considered an important entity as it relates to one of the segments of market forces, i.e., the demand segment. Given the basic economic problems of unlimited wants with limited resources, the consumer seeks to maximize his level of satisfaction. This is the axiom of utility maximization. In order to achieve this objective, the consumer allocates his available resources like money income on purchase of different goods and services in such a manner that he derives maximum satisfaction. In this direction, theory of consumer behaviour explains the various approaches that help in determination of consumer's equilibrium in such a manner that the consumer derives maximum satisfaction. In economic theory, three approaches have been used to explain consumer behaviour. These are:

1. Cardinal utility analysis (Marshall's utility analysis)
2. Ordinal utility analysis (Hicksian utility analysis)
3. Revealed preference theory of demand (Prof. Samuelson's utility analysis)

## 10.2 MEANING OF UTILITY

Utility refers to a psychological phenomenon involving satisfaction of the wants of consumer. It is the satisfying power of a commodity. Anything that is expected to satisfy the consumer is said to possess utility. Utility is not only connected with the consumption but also the possession and usage of the product or service. Thus, anything that gives pleasure and satisfaction to consumer is said to possess utility.

***For example:*** The consumption of opium is not considered good for health in its raw form but if a consumer derives satisfaction from the consumption of the commodity, it is said to possess utility.

### Features of Utility

The concept of utility has the following features (Fig. 10.1):

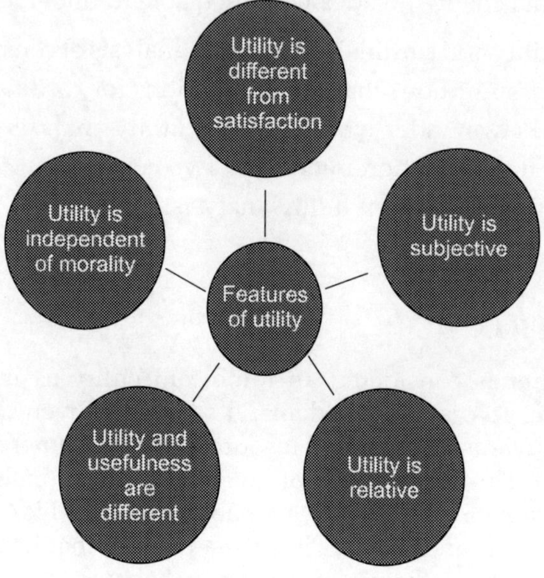


**Fig. 10.1** Features of Utility

1. **Utility is Different from Satisfaction**

   Utility is the expected satisfaction, i.e., what we expect to get from the commodity, however, satisfaction is what we actually get from the commodity.

   ***For example:*** A person is tempted to consume ice cream in that case, the commodity has not been consumed but the consumer is willing to pay for it, it is said to have utility. But if the consumer actually consumes it and feels happy after consumption, it is said to satisfy consumer.

2. **Utility is Subjective**

   It means that utility differs from one person to another, that is, the same product or service may have different utility to different persons.

   ***For example:*** Cigarette smoking has utility for a smoker but for a non-smoker, it has no utility.

3. **Utility is Relative**

   It differs from one place to another and also varies at different points of time.

   ***For example:*** Woollen coats and sweaters have utility in winters and not in summers.

4. **Utility and Usefulness are Different**

   Utility and usefulness are altogether different concepts. A commodity which has utility may or may not be useful.

   ***For example:*** Use of spurious drugs and developing drug addiction is not useful. However, if that drug is capable enough of satisfying the wants of an addict then it has utility for him.

5. **Utility is Independent of Morality**

   Utility has got nothing to do with morality, moral values and ethics. It is ethically neutral.

   ***For example:*** The consumption of any form of liquor may not be appropriate from moral point of view, but as these are able to satisfy the need of drunkards, it is said to have utility.

## 10.3 CARDINAL APPROACH TO UTILITY ANALYSIS

The theory of utility was developed by classical economists such as H. H. Gossen, Leon Walras, Jeremy Bentham, Carl Menger and W.S. Jevons. However, it was systematically developed, explained and elaborated by neoclassical economist, Prof. Alfred Marshall, a British economist. Therefore, the approach is popularly known as Marshallian Utility Analysis. This is approach to the theory of consumer behaviour is based upon the concept of utility. It considers utility as a measureable and quantifiable concept.

Cardinal utility analysis postulates that utility can be expressed quantitatively. It means that it is possible on the part of consumer to measure utility like height and weight and gives specific numbers to it. A psychological unit of measuring utility was used called 'Util'. The way money is measured in terms of rupees or paisa, the same manner, 'utils' was used as a measuring rod for defining utility. The problem that was encountered was the subjective nature of utility as it differed from one person to another. Hence, Marshall suggested the measurement of utility in terms of monetary units.

### Concept of Utility

The concept of utility is expressed in three senses:

1. **Initial utility** refers to the utility derived from consumption of the first unit of the commodity.

2. **Total utility** refers to the sum total of utilities derived by a consumer from consumption of various units of goods and services. It is the sum of the marginal utilities associated with the consumption of successive units. Suppose, the consumer consumes three units of a particular commodity, say Commodity X, at one time. The utility derived from each unit is 100 utils, 120 utils and 80 utils, then total utility from Commodity X ($TU_x$) would be 300 utils.

   Thus, *TU* can be expressed as:

$$TU_n = MU_1 + MU_2 + \dots MU_n$$
$$= \Sigma MU$$

   where,

   $TU$ = Total utility
   $MU_1$ = Marginal utility derived from consumption of the first unit of Commodity X
   $MU_2$ = Marginal utility derived from consumption of the second unit of Commodity X
   $MU_n$ = Marginal utility derived from consumption of the nth unit of Commodity X

3. **Marginal utility** is defined as the addition to the utility or change in total utility as a result of consumption of one additional unit of the commodity. It may be expressed as:

$$MU = TU_n - TU_{n-1}$$

   where,

   $MU_n$ = marginal utility of nth unity.
   $TU_n$ = Total utility of '*n*' units.
   $TU_{n-1}$ = Total utility of ($n$ – 1) units.

   Marginal utility can also be defined as addition in total utility ($\Delta TU$), as a result of increase in commodity by small amount ($\Delta Q$).

$$MU = \frac{\Delta TU}{\Delta Q}$$

   where,

   $MU$ = Marginal utility
   $\Delta TU$ = Change in total utility
   $\Delta Q$ = Change in quantity

## Types of Marginal Utility

(a) **Positive Marginal Utility:** The marginal utility is said to be positive when the consumption of additional units of commodity leads to increase in total utility.

**(b) Zero Marginal Utility:** The marginal utility is said to be zero when the consumption of additional units of commodity leads to no change in total utility.

**(c) Negative Marginal Utility:** The marginal utility is said to be negative when the consumption of additional units of commodity leads to decline in total utility.

## Relationship between Total Utility and Marginal Utility

Relationship between total utility and marginal utility is as follows:

- When *MU* is positive, *TU* increases.
- When *MU* is zero, *TU* is maximum (point of satiety)
- When *MU* is negative, *TU* decreases.

The relationship between *TU* and *MU* is reflected in Table 10.1.

**TABLE 10.1** Relationship between Total Utility and Marginal Utility

| Quantity of Commodity *X* | $TU_x$ | $MU_x$ | Description |
|---|---|---|---|
| 1 | 8 | 8 | Initial utility |
| 2 | 14 | 6 | Positive utility |
| 3 | 18 | 4 | |
| 4 | 20 | 2 | |
| 5 | 20 | 0 | Zero utility |
| 6 | 18 | –2 | Negative utility |
| 7 | 16 | –4 | |

The diagrammatic representation of *TU* and *MU* is shown in Fig. 10.2.
It shows:

(a) As a consumer consumes more and more units of a commodity, the marginal utility derived from each successive unit goes on diminishing. Therefore, *MU* is always falling. But, total utility increases at diminishing rate, reaches maximum and then eventually falls.

(b) When marginal utility is falling but positive, the total utility goes on increasing but at diminishing rate.

(c) When marginal utility is zero, vertically upwards, total utility will attain its maximum. The point where *MU* becomes zero is known as point of satiety.

(d) When marginal utility is falling and negative, the total utility declines in absolute terms.

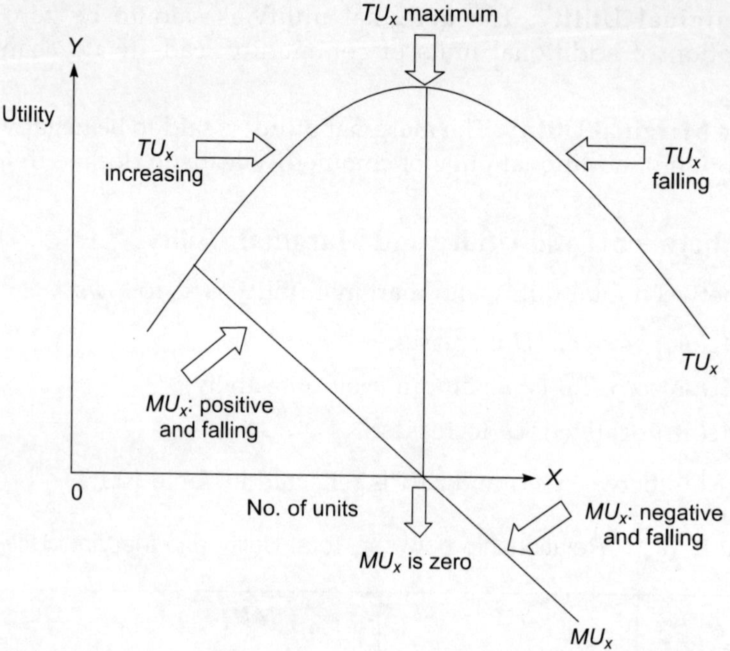


**Fig. 10.2** Relationship between Total Utility and Marginal Utility

## 10.4 ASSUMPTIONS OF CARDINAL UTILITY ANALYSIS

The cardinal utility analysis is based on the following assumptions:

- Rationality
- Utility is cardinally measurable
- Constant *MU*
- Diminishing marginal utility
- Independence of utility
- Utility is additive
- No change in personal, social and mental conditions of consumer
- Constancy of price of the commodity

**Fig. 10.3** Assumptions of Cardinal Utility Analysis

1. **Rationality:** In the cardinal utility analysis, it is assumed that the consumer is a rational decision maker. He aims at the maximization of his utility subject to the constraint imposed by his given or limited income.
2. **Utility is cardinally measurable:** The law assumes that utility is a cardinally measurable and quantifiable concept. The utility derives from consumption of one unit of commodity is equal to the money which a consumer is prepared to pay for it

$$1 \text{ util} = 1 \text{ unit of money.}$$

3. **Constant marginal utility of money:** The analysis further assumes that marginal utility of money remains constant irrespective of the level of a consumer's income. This assumption is essential and unavoidable as the theory used 'money' as the measure of utility. If the measuring rod is not kept constant, then correct analysis is not be possible. Thus, it is assumed in the theory that the marginal utility of money based for purchasing goods remains constant.
4. **Diminishing marginal utility:** This assumption states that the consumption of additional units of commodity in a given time period leads to reduction in utility levels.
5. **Independence of utility:** Utilities derived from consumption of different commodities are independent of one another. Here, cardinalists assume that the utility derived from consumption of a product depends upon the quantity purchased of that good alone and is not related to the quantity consumed of other goods.
6. **Utility is additive:** The cardinal school also believed that the utility derived from consumption of various goods and services by a consumer are independent and therefore can be added together to obtain the total utility. Thus, total utility obtained from n items can be expressed as:

$$U_n = U_1(X_1) + U_2(X_2) + U_3(X_3) + \dots + U_n(X_n)$$

   The above-mentioned equation represents the utility function which the consumer aims to maximize.
7. **No change in personal, social & mental condition of consumer:** Throughout the analysis it is assumed that the income, tastes, fashions & habits should not change..
8. **Constancy of price of the commodity:** As the successive units of the commodity are consumed, the price should remain same. It means that price should not influence the purchase decisions of the consumer.

## 10.5 LAWS OF CARDINAL UTILITY ANALYSIS

The development of cardinal utility analysis is attributed to the efforts of Prof. Alfred Marshall.

The study of cardinal utility Analysis has been explained with the help of two fundamental laws. These are:

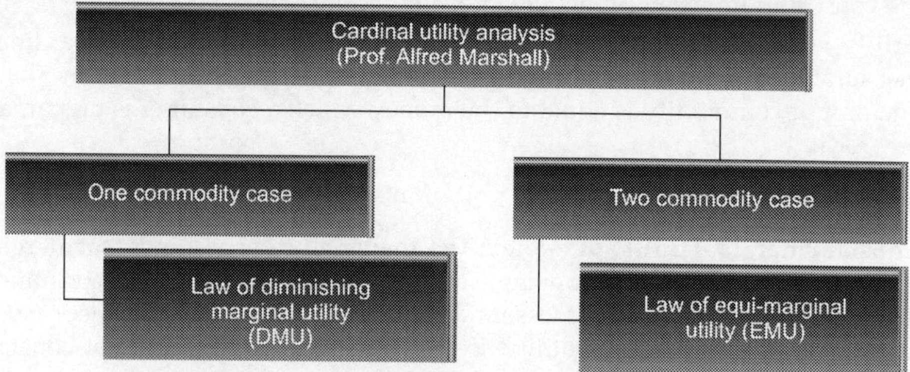


**Fig. 10.4** The Laws of Cardinal Utility Analysis

These laws, namely, law of diminishing marginal utility and law of equi-marginal utility have been explained below.

## 10.5.1 Law of Diminishing Marginal Utility (DMU)

### The Law

This is one of the fundamental laws of utility analysis and is of practical applicability. It is universally applicable as it is a part of our daily life. It is also called Gosssen's first law. According to the law of diminishing marginal utility," As a consumer goes on consuming more and more units of the commodity, the additional satisfaction derived from consumption of an additional unit of the commodity goes on diminishing. A point comes when consumer says "no more of the commodity". This is the point when *MU* becomes zero. It is called the 'point of satiety'. If any further units of commodity are served to him then it may turn 'utility' to 'disutility' as *MU* becomes negative.

### Assumptions

Law of diminishing marginal utility inherits some of the assumptions from cardinal utility analysis and adds some more to them. The law is based on the following assumptions:

1. **Rationality:** The consumer is a rational decision maker and always aims at the maximization of his utility subject to his limited income.
2. **Utility is Cardinally Measurable:** The law assumes that the utility is measurable in cardinal numbers. 'Utils' is the measuring rod for measurement of utility.
3. **Constant Marginal Utility of Money:** The analysis assumes that marginal utility of money remains constant irrespective of level of a consumer's income.

4. **Diminishing Marginal Utility:** This assumption states that the consumption of additional units of commodity in a given time period leads to reduction in utility levels and further consumption of the commodity may turn utility to disutility.

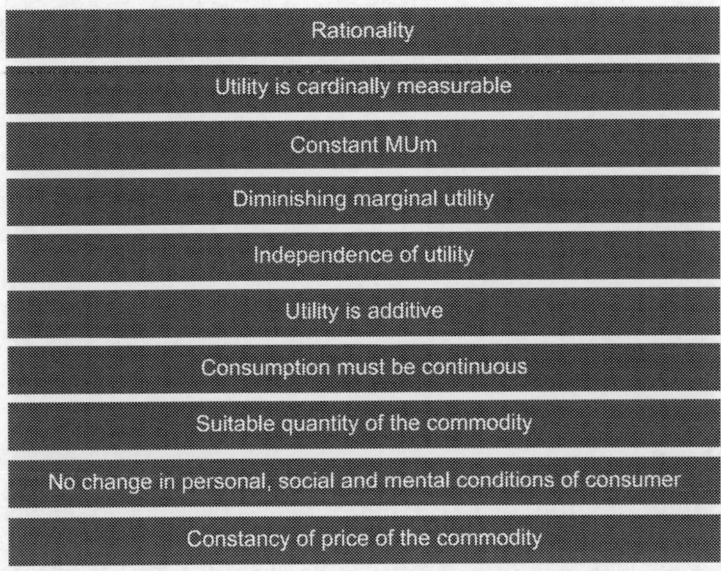


**Fig. 10.5** Assumptions of Law of Diminishing Marginal Utility

5. **Independence of Utility:** Utilities derived from consumption of different commodities are independent of one another. Thus, the utility derived from consumption of a product depends on the quantity purchased of that good alone and is not related to the quantity consumed of other goods.

6. **Utility is Additive:** The cardinal school also believed that the utility derived from consumption of various goods and services consumed by a consumer can be added together to obtain the total utility.

7. **Consumption must be Continuous:** There should be no time lag between the consumption of successive units of the commodity. If one unit of the commodity is consumed in the morning and the second in the evening, then the law may not hold good. Thus, if there is a discontinuity in the consumption, the intensity of want gets revived.

   *For example:* If the consumer takes one glass of water in the morning and the second glass in the afternoon, the marginal utility of the second glass may be more.

8. **Suitable Quantity of the Commodity:** For the applicability of the law, it is required that suitable units of the commodity should be consumed. The units consumed should not be too small as marginal utility instead of falling may increase up to a few units as the consumer consumes only a small unit as initial commodity. Similarly, if the earlier unit consumed is large and the successive units smaller, then the analysis becomes redundant as the initial large unit and the successive smaller units will make the analysis untenable.

   *For example:* If a bigger chapatti is consumed after a chapati which is too small in size then the chapatti that is eaten after consuming a small sized chapatti may give greater utility to a hungry person.
9. **No Change in Personal, Social & Mental Conditions of Consumer:** Throughout the analysis it is assumed that the income, tastes, fashions & habits should not change. Thus, any change in these variables can make the law inoperative.
10. **Constancy of Price of the Commodity:** As the successive units of the commodity are consumed, the price should remain same. It means that price should not influence the purchase decisions of the consumer.

## Explanation of the Law

Suppose, a person is very thirsty and requires a glass of water to quench his thirst. He goes to a shop to buy a glass of water. He consumes the first glass of water which gives him immense pleasure and has great utility for him. The person is even now thirsty, he takes the second glass of water. But this glass of water provided him utility that is lower than the previous glass. This is on account of the fact that the intensity of his thirst has now been blunted to a great extent. If he drinks the third glass of water, the utility of the third glass will be less than that of the second and so on. The successive consumption of the commodity will lead to decline in *MU* to zero. This is the point of satiety. It is the position of consumer's equilibrium. If the consumer is forced further to take even a single glass of water, it leads to disutility leading to decline in total utility. The marginal utility at this point will become negative. A rational consumer will have to stop consumption of water even if the availability of product is free.

**TABLE 10.2** Utility Schedule

| Glasses of Water | Total Utility (Utils) | Marginal Utility (Utils) |
|---|---|---|
| 1 | 6 | 6 |
| 2 | 10 | 4 |
| 3 | 12 | 2 |
| 4 | 12 | 0 |
| 5 | 10 | –2 |

It can be observed from Table 10.2 that the consumption of the first glass of water gave the consumer 6 utils of utility. Till three glasses of water the marginal utility is declining but positive. The consumption of fourth glass of water makes *MU* to zero (point of satiety). This is the point where *TU* is maximum. Further provision of fifth glass of water turned *MU* to negative and *TU* to decline in absolute terms.

## Exceptions of Law of Diminishing Marginal Utility

There are some exceptions to the law of diminishing marginal utility as shown in Fig. 10.6.

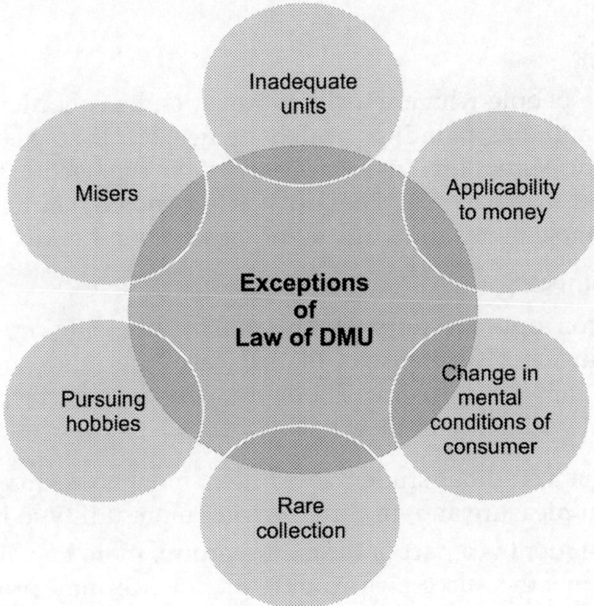


**Fig. 10.6** Exceptions of Law of Diminishing Marginal Utility

1. **Inadequate Units**

   The law fails to operate when the inadequate or inappropriate units are consumed by the consumer. This happens when there is heterogeneity in sizes of the units of the product.

   For instance, if the initial units of a commodity either too small or too large as compared to the successive units of the commodity, then the marginal utility from the additional units may be more or less than the initial commodity.

2. **Applicability to Money**

   In the law, it has been assumed that $MU_m$ remains constant. However, in reality, the more units of money a person has, the greater is the desire for holding cash. When applied to the social system, the marginal utility of money declines with richness but never falls to zero. Thus, in reality, $MU_m$ is not constant.

3. **Change in Mental Conditions of Consumer**

   For the applicability of the law it was assumed that there should be no change in mental conditions of the consumer. However, there are certain people who consume liquor, opium, drugs, or any other spurious products. In their case, after consumption of these commodities, it is presumed that they lose their control over mind and are unable to take correct decision regarding the utility derived from consumption of each successive unit of the commodity. There is every possibility that the successive units may lead to more and more utility. However, this is truer only for initial units consumed. A stage comes when these consumers too start consuming less and less and eventually end up in stopping their consumption.

4. **Rare Collection**

   There are some people who are inclined towards the collection of old postage stamps, coins, antiques, paintings, wall hangings, etc. In such a case, successive possession of the commodity gives more and more satisfaction to the consumer. Thus, *MU* rather than declining goes up. It is to be noted here that if the collector collects the homogeneous units again and again then the *MU* may not rise.

5. **Pursuing Hobbies**

   In case a person opts for pursuing his hobby like singing, playing guitar, dancing, reading, net surfing, etc. In that case, the more they pursue their passion, more they get pleasure. Therefore, *MU* goes on increasing with the acquisition and pursuance of their hobby.

   ***For example:*** For a studious student, reading of more books may give him more knowledge and pleasure and, in turn, provide more utility to him.

   Similarly, if a student is a part of dramatics group, more he will practice, more he will learn and the successive rounds of practice may provide him more satisfaction.

6. **Misers:** Miser means a person who is in habit of accumulating money. He becomes happy and happier with the successive accumulation of more and more units of wealth. In this case, the law fails to operate as *MU* rises with greater and successive accumulations.

   In nutshell, for the applicability of the law of diminishing utility, it is required that the assumptions should be strictly followed and other factors remain constant.

## Importance of Law of Diminishing Marginal Utility

The points highlighting the importance of study of law of DMU are reflected in Fig. 10.7.

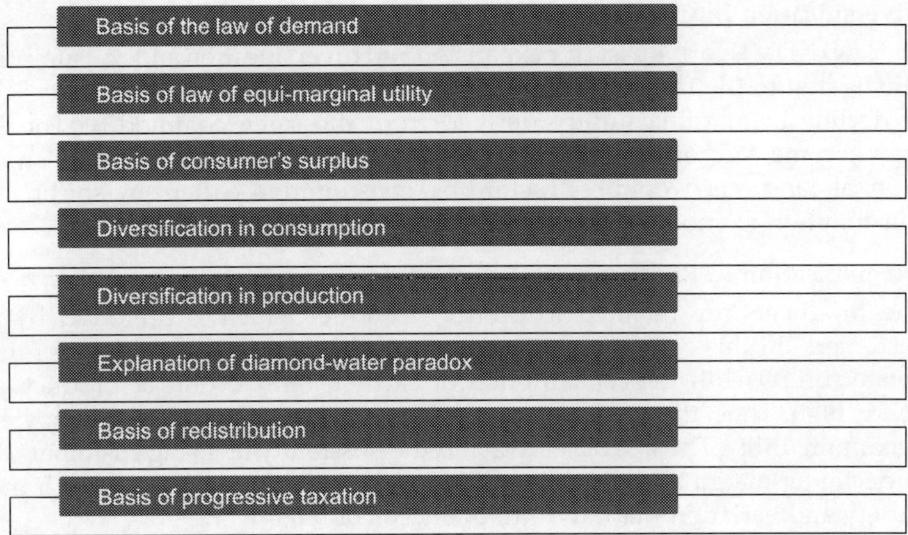


**Fig. 10.7** Importance of Law of Diminishing Marginal Utility

1. **Basis of the Law of Demand**

   The law of DMU is one of the factors that influences the law of demand. Under DMU, consumption of each successive units of the commodity leads to a decline in the utility levels. Now, the consumer is so much satisfied with the consumption of each unit of the commodity that he is ready to have more unit of the commodity only and only when its price falls.

2. **Basis of Law of Equi-marginal Utility**

   In the law of equi-marginal utility, the consumer allocates his resources in such a manner that he gets maximum satisfaction, given his money income and the prices of goods & services. The law of DMU is applicable in one commodity case, when such an analysis is expanded over more than one commodity, the law of EMU is studied. Thus, the law of diminishing marginal utility lays the foundation stone of formulation of EMU.

3. **Basis of Consumer's Surplus**

   Consumer's surplus refers to the difference between the price that the consumer is willing to pay and the price that the consumer actually pays. Thus, if the price that the consumer actually pays for the product is lesser and lesser then the price he is willing to pay, then the consumer's surplus would be more. On the basis of the law of DMU, actual price paid for the initial units will be more as they have more utility and the actual payment or successive units will be less as they have low utility levels. Thus, by influencing the actual prices of the commodities, the law of DMU influences consumer's surplus.

**4. Diversification in Consumption**

The law of DMU forms basis for expansion and diversification and consumption. This is due to the fact that continuous consumption of one commodity leads to decline in marginal utility derived from the same commodity. The *MU* may become zero or even negative. Here, comes the turning point where the rational consumer would restructure his consumption pattern by shifting the consumption to another commodity.

**5. Diversification in Production**

The producers are inclined to produce product which is preferred by the customers. In this regard, the consumers prefer a product which gives them greater utility with the consumption of each successive unit of product, i.e., *MU* is high. Thus, the producers also prefer producing a product which yields maximum utility. Thus, in order to avoid the possibility of losing customers due to declining marginal utility, the producers bring in new products with more variety and variation that can fulfil the needs of the buyer.

**6. Explanation of Diamond–Water Paradox (Value in Use vs Value in Exchange)**

The law of DMU gives a breakthrough in providing the solution to Adam Smith's diamond-water paradox. The paradox states that there are certain commodities like water which are needed for human survival, yet their value is low. On the other hand, the other commodities like diamond which are not needed for survival but are expensive.

The law of DMU explains that the price of the commodity is influenced by marginal utility. Since water is available in abundance, its marginal utility is low or even zero. Therefore it has a low price. On the other hand, diamond is scarce commodity and therefore has higher marginal utility. Thus, it has higher price. Thus, the law of DMU has played an important role in explaining the diamond-water paradox by paradox of relating prices with *MU* of the commodity. It also helped in explaining the difference between value in use and value in exchange. The law of DMU clarified that commodity having more value in use has low price like water and air while those having more value in exchange command high price.

**7. Basis of Redistribution**

The law of DMU forms an important basis for redistribution of income. The concept of redistribution of income considers two sections of the society, viz., the rich and the poor. In case of the rich, the MU of money is less as they already have abundance of funds. However, in case of the poor, since they lack funds, the MU of money is high. Thus, in order to promote welfare of the society, wealth should be distributed in such a manner that those who have less *MU* of money, i.e., the rich should get lesser income and those who have more *MU* of money, i.e., the poor should get more income.

8. **Basis of Progressive Taxation**

   Progressive taxation system refers to that system of taxation under which a person is taxed in accordance with his income. In this system of taxation, the rate of tax increases as the income of person increases. Since, *MU* of money for the rich is less, therefore they should be taxed high and the *MU* of money for the poor is more, therefore proper care must be exercised in framing any taxation policy for them. Thus, the law of DMU has played an important role by connecting *MU* with the taxation.

**Criticism of Law of Diminishing Marginal Utility**

1. In reality, measurement of utility in cardinal numbers is not possible.
2. Marginal utility cannot be estimated in all conditions.
3. The law assumes marginal utility of money as constant. However, in reality this may not be the case.
4. To assume that the utility derived from each commodity is independent is not tenable as every commodity is not an independent commodity.
5. The law is applicable only in case of divisible commodities like chapatti, fruits, and vegetables. The law thus, fails to apply in case of indivisible commodities like bottle, fan, notebook, etc.
6. For the applicability of the law, it is assumed that there should be no change in the tastes, habits, fashion, income, price levels, etc. However, in real life, all of them are amenable to change.

## 10.5.2 Law of Equi-Marginal Utility (EMU)

**The Law**

This law was coined by H.H. Gossen and hence it is also known as Gossen's second law. This law was further refined by Prof. Alfred Marshall. The law of equi-marginal utility is an extension of the law of diminishing marginal utility to two or more than two commodities. The law of equi-marginal utility is also known as law of substitution, law of maximum satisfaction and law of indifference.

The law of equi-marginal utility explains that the consumer has a basket of goods and services to consume. Given the limited resources (income) and the prices of the commodity, the consumer allocates these resources in such a manner that he may get maximum satisfaction. According to the law, the satisfaction of a consumer is maximized where he makes expenditure on goods in such a way that marginal utility derived from the last rupee spent on each commodity is equal. In this law, the prices of various goods have been related with their utility levels by equating the marginal utility-price ratio of various goods. Thus, the law is also known as proportionality rule. Suppose, there are two commodities, $X$ and $Y$, the proportionality rule sets the conditions of consumer's equilibrium as:

$$\frac{MU_x}{P_x} = \frac{MU_y}{P_y}$$

In reality, there are more than two commodities; therefore, the above condition will become:

$$\frac{MU_x}{P_x} = \frac{MU_y}{P_y} = MU_m$$

where,

$MU_x$ = Marginal utility derived from consumption of commodity $X$

$P_x$ = Price of commodity $X$

$MU_y$ = Marginal utility derived from consumption of commodity $Y$

$MU_y$ = Price of commodity $Y$

$MU_m$ = Marginal utility derived from units of money

## Assumptions of Law of Equi-Marginal Utility

The main assumptions of the law of equi-marginal utility are as follows:

1. The consumer is a rational decision maker in purchase of goods.
2. Utility is cardinally measurable and is a quantifiable concept.
3. The consumer has limited money which is to be spent on purchase of various commodities.
4. The marginal utilities derived from different commodities are independent of each other.
5. Marginal utility of money is constant.

## Explanation of the Law

Suppose, a consumer consumes two commodities, viz., $X$ and $Y$. Though he can consume even more commodities but for the sake of simplicity of explanation, it has been assumed that he is currently consuming only two commodities. Let us further assume that the consumer's income is Rs. 10. It means that the consumer has Rs. 10 to be allocated on the purchase of two commodities. Now, according to the law of equi-marginal utility, his allocation will be done in such a manner that *MU* of last rupee spent on both the commodities is equal. Let us assume that the price of one unit of each commodity is Rs. 1. Then, the consumer will spend money in such a manner that each unit of the commodity gives him highest utility. Thus, his spending pattern will reflect the following (Table 10.3):

**TABLE 10.3** Law of Equi-Marginal Utility

| Units of Commodities (*X* and *Y*) | MU of Commodity *X* ($MU_x$) | MU of Last Rupee Spent on Commodity $X = MU_x/P_x$ | MU of Commodity $Y(MU_y)$ | MU of Last Rupee Spent on Commodity $Y = MU_y/P_y$ |
|---|---|---|---|---|
| 1 | 20 | 20/1 = 20 (1) | 18 | 18/1 = 18(2) |
| 2 | 18 | 18/1 = 18(3) | 16 | 16/1 = 16(4) |
| 3 | 16 | 16/1 = 16(5) | 14 | 14/1 = 14(6) |
| 4 | 14 | 14/1 = 14(7) | 12 | 12/1 = 12(8) |
| 5 | 12 | 12/1 = 12(9) | 10 | 10/1 = 10(10) |
| 6 | 10 | 10/1 = 10 | 8 | 8/1 = 8 |
| 7 | 8 | 8/1 = 8 | 6 | 6/1 = 6 |
| 8 | 6 | 6/1 = 6 | 4 | 4/1 = 4 |

Table 10.3 shows that the consumer has income amounting to Rs. 10, then he will be allocating his income in such a manner that he gets the maximum utility. The allocation of income would be as follows:

First rupee – Commodity *X*
Second rupee – Commodity *Y*
Third rupee – Commodity *X*
Fourth rupee – Commodity *Y*
Fifth rupee – Commodity *X*
Sixth rupee – Commodity *Y*
Seventh rupee – Commodity *X*
Eighth rupee – Commodity *Y*
Ninth rupee – Commodity *X*
Tenth rupee – Commodity *Y*

The above arrangement yields maximum satisfaction in the following manner:

Total utility of 5 units of commodity *X* would be 20 + 18 + 16 + 14 + 12 = 80

Total utility of 5 units of commodity *Y* would be 18 + 16 + 14 + 12 + 10 = 70

Total utility from both goods is *TU* (commodity *X*) + *TU* (commodity *Y*) which is equal to 80 + 70 = 150.

## Limitations of the Law of Equi-Marginal Utility

1. The law assumes that the consumer is a rational decision maker and allocates his income in such a manner that he gets maximum satisfaction from the bundle

of various goods that are available to him for consumption. However, the consumer is not always rational in his approach as he at times spends money in abrupt and random manner. Thus, in that case applicability of the law is not tenable.

2. Another assumption of law states that utility is a cardinally measureable and quantifiable concept. However, utility is a subjective concept and differs from one person to another. Different consumers may give different cardinal numbers for utility for the same commodity. Hence, the applicability of law becomes doubtful.
3. The assumption of independent utilities is not applicable in reality on account of existence of substitutes and complementary commodities. Thus, the utility derived from one commodity cannot have independent existence.
4. The marginal utility of money is assumed to be constant in the analysis. However, *MU* of money can never be constant. This is on account of the reason that as the quantity of money with the consumer reduces; the consumer gets additional satisfaction from receipt of more units of money. Thus, *MU* in that case will rise and will not remain constant.

## 10.6 DETERMINATION OF CONSUMERS EQUILIBRIUM UNDER CARDINAL UTILITY ANALYSIS

Consumer's equilibrium refers to the situation of balance or stability. It arises when the consumer derives maximum satisfaction given his money income and prices of the commodities. It is a state where the consumer has no tendency to change his way of existing expenditure. This is due to his current allocation of income. The consumer's equilibrium under cardinal analysis is studied under the following cases:

### 1. One Commodity Case/Consumer's Equilibrium in Case of Single Commodity

The cardinal approach explains the consumer's equilibrium in case of a single commodity with the help of law of DMU. Thus, the assumptions of the law of DMU are used to explain consumer's equilibrium in case of a single commodity.

#### Assumptions of Equilibrium Analysis

(a) The consumer is a rational decision maker and aims at maximization of satisfaction.

(b) Utility is cardinally a measurable concept.

(c) Utility is independent and additive.

(d) Marginal utility of money is constant.

(e) Income of consumer remains same.

(f) There is no change in taste and preferences.

### Explanation of Consumer's Equilibrium

In a single commodity case, the equilibrium is attained when the commodity purchased by the consumer gives him maximum satisfaction. The consumer's equilibrium is dependent on the following two factors:

(a) Price of the commodity

(b) Marginal utility from each successive unit of the commodity

The consumer's equilibrium according to cardinal utility analysis is attained where marginal utility derived from the commodity becomes equal to price paid for the commodity.

### Condition of Equilibrium

The consumer who is consuming a single commodity (say, commodity *X*) will be at equilibrium when *MU* becomes equal to its price.

Symbolically,

$$MU_{\text{Commodity X}} = \text{Price}_{\text{Commodity X}}$$

$$MU_x = P_x$$

### Conditions of Disequilibrium ($MU_x \neq P_x$)

Any deviation from the equilibrium is known as disequilibrium. In case of single commodity case, the disequilibrium arises in following cases.

**(a) If $MU_X > P_x$**

In this case, the marginal utility derived from the product is much greater than the price paid for the commodity. It means that the consumer is getting benefitted as the benefit derived is greater than the cost. In such case, the consumer will increase the consumption of the commodity. As a result, *MU* falls because of operation of the law of diminishing marginal utility. *MU* will continue to fall till the equality between *MU* and price is attained.

**(b) If $MU_X < P_x$**

In this case, the consumer is not at equilibrium as the price paid for the commodity is more than the satisfaction it provides. Thus, the consumer will reduce consumption of the commodity to increase the marginal utility level. He will do so till *MU* becomes equal to price.

For instance, a consumer is buying commodity *X* and the price of each unit of commodity *X* is Rs. 10, then consumer's equilibrium can be ascertained in a single commodity case can be explained with the help of the following schedule (Table 10.4).

**TABLE 10.4** Consumer's Equilibrium: In Case of Single Commodity

| $Q_x$ (units) | $P_x$ (Rs.) | $MU_x$ (Utils) | $MU_x$ (Rs.) (1 Util = Re. 1) | Difference $MU_x$ (Rs.) and $P_x$ (Rs.) | $MU_x$ vs $P_x$ | Conclusion |
|---|---|---|---|---|---|---|
| 1 | 10 | 18 | 18 | 18 – 10 = 8 | $MU_X > P_x$ | Consumer will increase the consumption of the commodity |
| 2 | 10 | 14 | 14 | 14 – 10 = 4 | | |
| 3 | 10 | 10 | 10 | 10 – 10 = 0 | $MU_X = P_x$ | Consumer's equilibrium attained |
| 4 | 10 | 6 | 6 | 6 – 10 = –4 | $MU_X < P_x$ | Consumer will decrease the consumption of the commodity |
| 5 | 10 | 2 | 2 | 2 – 10 = –8 | | |
| 6 | 10 | –2 | –2 | –2 – 10 = –12 | | |

## Diagrammatic Representation

In Fig. 10.8, $MU_x$ curve slopes downwards from left to right. This is due to the operation of the law of DMU which reflects that each successive consumption of commodity $X$ leads to decline in marginal utility of the commodity. The price ($P_x$) has been reflected as horizontal and straight as it has been fixed at Rs. 10 per unit. The analysis assumes that 1 util of utility = Re. 1 of money. This has been done as in order to precede with the analysis the measuring rods must be comparable.

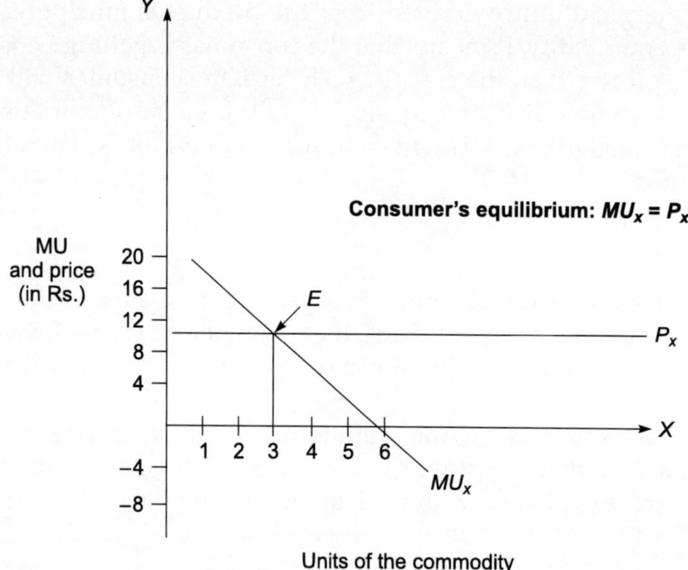


**Fig. 10.8** Consumer's Equilibrium: In Case of Single Commodity

The condition of consumer's equilibrium in case the consumer is consuming a single commodity is that $MU_X$ becomes equal to its price. Thus, from the given schedule and diagram, it is clear that the consumer will be at equilibrium at point $E$, where he consumes 3 units of commodity $X$, because at point $E$, $MU_X = P_X =$ Rs. 10. In this case, following conditions of disequilibrium are worth noting:

(i) He will not consume 4 units of commodity $X$ as $MU_X$ at 4 units (Rs. 6) < Price paid (Rs. 10).

(ii) Similarly, he will not consume 2 units of $X$ as $MU_X$ at 2 units (Rs. 14) > Price paid (Rs. 10).

So, it can be concluded that a consumer in consumption of single commodity (say, $X$) will be at equilibrium when marginal utility from the commodity ($MU_X$) is equal to the price paid for the commodity ($P_X$).

### 10.6.1 Two Commodities Case/Consumer's Equilibrium in Case of Two Commodities

In reality, the consumer does not consume a single commodity. Rather, he consumes multiple commodities. In this regard, the cardinal approach explains the consumer's equilibrium in case with the help of law of equi-marginal Utility.

**Assumptions of Equilibrium Analysis**

(a) The consumer is a rational decision maker aims at maximization of satisfaction.

(b) Utility is a cardinally measurable concept.

(c) Utility is independent and additive.

(d) Marginal utility of money is constant.

(e) Income of consumer remains same.

(f) There is no change in taste and preferences.

**Explanation of Consumer's Equilibrium**

The law of equi-marginal utility states that the consumer with the given money income will allocate his money between the goods in such a manner that the utility derived from the last rupee spent on each good is equal. According to the law of equi-marginal utility, there are two necessary components to attain consumer's equilibrium in case of two commodities:

(a) Marginal utility ($MU$) of the last rupee spent on each commodity is same

(b) $MU$ falls as consumption increases

**Condition of Equilibrium**

According to Prof. Marshall, the consumer is said to be in equilibrium when:

$$MU_X/P_X = MU_Y/P_Y = MU_M$$

where,

$MU_X$ = Marginal utility derived from consumption of commodity $X$

$P_X$ = Price of commodity $X$

$MU_Y$ = Marginal utility derived from consumption of commodity $Y$

$P_Y$ = Price of commodity $Y$

$MU_M$ = Marginal utility of money

**Conditions of Disequilibrium ($MU_X/P_X$ is not Equal to $MU_Y/P_Y$)**

1. **$MU_X/P_X > MU_Y/P_Y$**

   In this case, the marginal utility of the last rupee spent on commodity $X$ is more than commodity $Y$. Thus, the consumer will prefer and consume more of commodity $X$ and less of commodity $Y$. This will result in decline in $MU_X$ and rise in $MU_Y$. The consumer will continue to buy more of $X$ till the proportion between $MU$ and price of commodities become equal. It can be represented as:

$$MU_X/P_X = MU_Y/P_Y$$

2. **$MU_X/P_X < MU_Y/P_Y$**

   In this case, the marginal utility of the last rupee spent on commodity $Y$ is more than that of commodity $X$. Thus, the consumer will prefer and consume more of commodity $Y$ and less of commodity $X$. This will result in decline in $MU_Y$ and rise in $MU_X$. The consumer will continue to buy more of $Y$ till the proportion between $MU$ and price of commodities is equal. It may be represented as:

$$MU_X/P_X = MU_Y/P_Y$$

Suppose, the consumer consumes two commodities, $X$ and $Y$. Two commodities have been assumed for the sake of simplicity of explanation. However in reality, the consumer consumes more than two commodities. Now, the consumer with the given money income and prices of the goods allocates the income in such a manner that the marginal rupee spent on each commodity is equal. It means that for attaining consumer's equilibrium the following condition must be satisfied:

$$MU_X/P_X = MU_Y/P_Y$$

For instance, a consumer is buying two commodities, viz., $X$ and $Y$. The consumer's equilibrium can be ascertained in a single commodity case can be explained with the help of Table 10.5.

**TABLE 10.5** Consumer's Equilibrium: In Case of Two Commodities (Initial Schedule)

| Units of Commodities, X and Y | $MU_X$ | $MU_Y$ |
|---|---|---|
| 1 | 20 | 24 |
| 2 | 18 | 21 |
| 3 | 16 | 18 |
| 4 | 14 | 15 |
| 5 | 12 | 12 |
| 6 | 10 | 9 |
| 7 | 8 | 6 |

Suppose the prices of the commodity *X* and *Y* are Rs. 2 and Rs. 3, respectively. Now, the revised schedule is as follows:

**TABLE 10.6** Consumer's Equilibrium: In Case of Two Commodities (Revised Schedule)

| Units of Commodities, X and Y | $MU_X/P_X$ | $MU_Y/P_Y$ |
|---|---|---|
| 1 | 10 | 8 |
| 2 | 9 | 7 |
| 3 | 8 | 6 |
| 4 | 7 | 5 |
| 5 | 6 | 4 |
| 6 | 5 | 3 |
| 7 | 4 | 2 |

The consumer equilibrium can be ascertained by comparing the marginal utility of last rupee spent on commodity X and commodity *Y*. This is done by calculating the ratio of the marginal utility of the concerned commodity (*MU*) to the price of that good (*P*). Then the *MU*/*P* for Commodity X and *Y* are equated, subject to the income or budget.

Table 10.5 clarifies that the consumer does not exceed his budget of Rs. 24. The marginal utility per rupee spent on the first unit of commodity *X* is greater than the marginal utility per rupee spent on the first unit of commodity *Y*. The above table reveals that 10 utils is greater than 8 utils. Now, the price of commodity *X* is Rs. 2 per unit, the consumer thus, purchased this first unit of commodity X. The consumer is now left with Rs. 24 – Rs. 2 = Rs. 22 in his budget.

The consumer now again compares *MU*/*P* of the second unit of commodity *X* with *MU*/*P* of the first unit of commodity *Y* (Table 10.6). Since, the $MU_X/P_X > MU_Y/P_Y$. Thus he purchases the second unit of commodity *X* @ Rs. 2 and spends the remaining budget (Rs. 20) on purchase of the first unit of commodity *Y* @ Rs. 3 per unit. Thus, till now 3 units purchased and he has remaining budget of Rs. 17.

Now, the consumer repeats the process and purchases fourth unit of commodity *X* @ Rs. 2. Now, he compares the marginal utility per rupee spent on the fourth unit of commodity *X* with marginal utility per rupee spent on the second unit of commodity *Y*. Because these ratios are both equal to 7 utils, the consumer is indifferent between purchasing the fourth unit of commodity *X* and the second unit of commodity *Y*, so he purchases both and spends remaining budget (Rs. 15) on purchase of fourth unit of commodity *X* @ Rs. 2 and the second unit of commodity *Y* @ Rs. 3. Now, he is left with the budget of Rs. 10 (Rs. 15 – Rs. 2 – Rs. 3).

Now, he will be again indifferent between purchasing the fifth unit of commodity *X* and third unit of commodity *Y* as *MU*/*P* ratio is yielding the same amount of utils (6 utils). So, he spends the remaining amount on purchase of the third unit of commodity *Y* @ Rs 3 and fifth unit of commodity *X* @ Rs. 2, respectively.

Finally, his remaining budget is Rs. 5 (Rs. 10 – Rs. 3 – Rs. 2). Now, he will again be allocating it on the basis of *MU*/*P* ratio. Thus, he reaches equilibrium where he purchases sixth unit of commodity *X* @ Rs. 3 and fourth unit of commodity *Y* @ Rs. 2. At this point, the consumer has exhausted the entire budget of Rs. 24 and has arrived at the consumer equilibrium, where the marginal utilities per rupee spent are equal. By looking at the table it is clear that the consumer decides to purchase 6 units of commodity *X* and 4 unit of commodity *Y*. Therefore, consumer will be in equilibrium when he is buying 6 units of commodity *X* and 4 units of commodity *Y* and will be spending (Rs. 3 × 6 + Rs. 2 × 4) = Rs. 24 on them.

## 10.7 CRITICISM OF CARDINAL UTILITY ANALYSIS

Cardinal utility analysis was criticized heavily on the following grounds:

**1. Consumer is not always rational**

The Marshallian utility analysis assumes that the consumer is a rational decision maker who buys the commodity in order to maximize his level of satisfaction keeping in mind his income constraint. In order to achieve this objective, he calculates the utility and disutility derived from different commodities, and purchases only those which give him greater utility.

**2. Utility cannot be measured cardinally**

The cardinal utility analysis was based on the assumption that utility can be measured in cardinal numbers. Utils was defined as the measuring rod for utility analysis. The analysis defined that utility can be cardinally measured and quantified. It means that a consumer can define his utility in definite numbers. However, utility is a subjective concept and differs from one person to another. Thus, Prof. J. R. Hicks opined that utility is a subjective and psychological concept and cannot be measured cardinally.

**3. Single commodity model is unrealistic**

In the utility analysis, consumer's equilibrium has been explained in case of a single commodity model where the utility of one commodity is regarded independent of the other. The analysis thus regarded substitutes and complementary commodities as one commodity. However, in reality there is a difference between the two, this makes the analysis of utility unrealistic.

**4. Utility analysis assumes the marginal utility of money to be constant**

The utility analysis considers marginal utility of money to be constant. However, MU of money can never be constant. This is because as the quantity of money with the consumer reduces; the consumer gets additional satisfaction from receipt of more units of money. Thus, MU in that case will rise and will never remain constant.

**5. Consumer is not always calculating**

This analysis assumes that consumers keep on calculating the utilities derived from consumption of different units of a commodity. They do so in order to maximize their satisfaction levels. However, in reality the consumers do not calculate in this manner while buying commodities. But the purchase and buying decisions are a function of their income and the prices of the commodities.

**6. Analysis is not applicable in case of indivisible goods**

The utility analysis is applicable in case of divisible commodities like chapatti, fruits, vegetables, etc. It fails to apply in case of indivisible or durable consumer goods like scooter, cooler, television, etc. Hence, the utility analysis is not applicable to indivisible goods.

## Summary

- ✓ There are three approaches to study consumers behaviour. These are:
    - Cardinal utility analysis (Marshall's utility analysis)
    - Ordinal utility analysis (Hicksian utility analysis)
    - Revealed preference theory of demand (Prof. Samuelson's utility analysis)
- ✓ Utility is a psychological phenomenon involving satisfaction of the wants of the consumer. Anything that gives pleasure and satisfaction to the consumer is said to possess utility.
- ✓ The unit of measuring utility was called 'util'.
- ✓ The concept of utility is expressed in three senses:
    - Initial utility
    - Total utility
    - Marginal utility
- ✓ Marginal utility is of three types:
    - Positive marginal utility
    - Zero marginal utility
    - Negative marginal utility

✓ Relationship between total utility and marginal utility is as follows:
  - When *MU* is positive, *TU* increases.
  - When *MU* is zero, *TU* is maximum (point of satiety)
  - When *MU* is negative, *TU* decreases.

✓ The cardinal utility analysis is based on the following assumptions:
  - Rationality
  - Utility is cardinally measurable
  - Constant $MU_m$
  - Diminishing marginal utility
  - Independence of utility
  - Utility is additive
  - No change in personal, social & mental conditions of consumer
  - Constancy of price of the commodity

✓ In cardinal utility analysis two laws are studied:
  - Law of diminishing marginal utility (DMU)
  - Law of equi-marginal utility (EMU)

✓ Law of diminishing marginal utility (DMU) states that as a consumer goes on consuming more and more units of the commodity, the additional satisfaction derived from consumption of an additional unit of the commodity goes on diminishing. A point comes *MU* becomes zero. It is called the 'point of satiety'. After this point any further consumption of the commodity leads to disutility.

✓ The law equi-marginal utility explains that given the limited resources (income) and the prices of the commodity, the consumer allocates these resources in such a manner that he may get maximum satisfaction. According to the law, satisfaction of a consumer is maximized when he makes expenditure on goods in such a way that marginal utility derived from the last rupee spent on each commodity is equal.

✓ Thus, the conditions of consumer's equilibrium under cardinal utility analysis is as follows:
  - For the law of diminishing marginal utility (DMU), the condition is as follows:

$$MU_{\text{Commodity } X} = \text{Price}_{\text{Commodity } X}$$

  - For the law of equi-marginal utility (EMU), the condition is as follows:

$$\frac{MU_X}{P_X} = \frac{MU_Y}{P_Y} = MU_M$$

## Review Questions

1. What do you mean by the law of diminishing marginal utility? Explain its assumptions and limitations.
2. Critically examine the law of diminishing marginal utility.
3. Why the study of law of diminishing marginal utility is important? What are the areas where the law assumes its importance?
4. Explain the theory of consumer behaviour in terms of cardinal utility analysis.
5. Explain the consumer's equilibrium under the law of diminishing marginal utility.
6. Explain the consumer's equilibrium under equi-marginal utility analysis.
7. Explain the law of equi-marginal utility. State the assumptions and limitations of the law.
8. Explain the relationship between *TU* and *MU* with the help of schedule and diagram.
9. Explain determination of consumer's equilibrium when the consumer is consuming:
   (a) Single commodity
   (b) Two or more commodities
10. Critically examine the cardinal approach to theory of consumer behaviour.

# 11 Chapter

# Theory of Consumer Behaviour: Ordinal Utility Analysis

**Learning Objectives**

After going through this chapter, reader would be able to understand:

- ✓ The ordinal approach to analysis of consumer behaviour.
- ✓ The underlying assumptions that lay foundations for ordinal utility analysis.
- ✓ The fundamental concepts of ordinal utility analysis such as indifference curves, marginal rate of substitution, and indifference map.
- ✓ The concept of budget line and analysis of shifts in budget line.
- ✓ The equilibrium determination under ordinal approach to utility analysis.
- ✓ Comparative analysis of cardinal utility analysis and ordinal utility analysis.

## 11.1 INTRODUCTION

In the previous chapter, the cardinal approach to utility analysis was studied. The cardinalists believed that utility is a measureable and quantifiable concept. The theory specified that it can be measured in cardinal numbers. The theory outlined that the consumer can measure utility derived from consumption of the commodities and can give them cardinal numbers. For this purpose, 'utils' was considered the measuring rod for measurement of utility. In contrast, the ordinal school of thought specified that the quantification of utility was impossible and consumer can only rank the various commodities but cannot give them numeric values. Thus, proceeding with the second approach, this chapter discusses another approach of utility analysis, namely, ordinal utility analysis.

## 11.2 ORDINAL APPROACH TO UTILITY ANALYSIS

The concept of ordinal utility analysis was propounded by Prof. J.R. Hicks and Prof. R. G.D. Allen. According to this approach, utility cannot be measured and quantified by the consumer. However, the consumer can only rank the combinations in accordance with his 'scale of preferences'.

Suppose, the consumer consumes two commodities say, *X* and *Y*. The various combinations of two quantities of the commodities that the consumer can consume are marked as *A*, *B*, *C*, *D*, *E*, etc. Thus, a consumer can definitely specify whether he prefers combination *A* to *B*, or *B* to *A* or is indifferent between both of them. Thus, he can only rank the preferred combinations. In this case, the consumer cannot specify by 'how much' satisfaction he is deriving from the consumption of two commodities in numerical values. Thus, according to ordinal approach to utility analysis, the consumer can only specify the qualitative differences in satisfaction levels but cannot specify them quantitatively.

## 11.3 ASSUMPTIONS OF ORDINAL UTILITY ANALYSIS

The ordinal utility analysis or the indifference curve analysis is based on following assumptions:

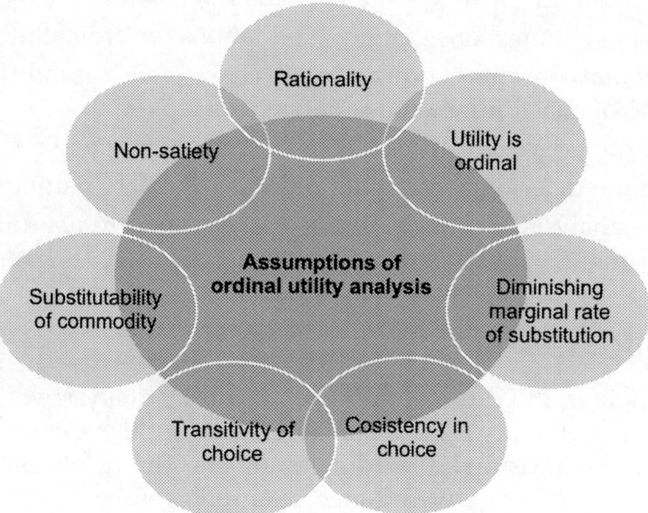


**Fig. 11.1** Assumptions of Ordinal Utility Analysis

1. **Rationality:** The consumer is a rational decision maker, given his money income and prices of the commodity, he allocates him income in such a manner that he gets maximum satisfaction.
2. **Utility is Ordinal:** Utility is not a measureable and quantifiable concept. A consumer can only rank the various combinations of the commodities and can specify which combination gives him more or less satisfaction.
3. **Diminishing Marginal Rate of Substitution:** The rate of substitution of one commodity for the other occurs but at diminishing rate.

4. **Consistency in Choice:** The consumer is assumed to be consistent in choices over a period of time.

   For instance, if the consumer prefers combinations *A* to combination *B* in one time period, then he will not prefer combination *B* over combination *A* in another time period or treat them equal.

   Symbolically, it can be expressed as:

   If Combination *A* > Combination *B* in one period,

   Then,

   Combination *B* > Combination *A* is impossible in another period
5. **Transitivity of Choice:** It is also assumed that the consumer's preferences are not self contradictory. It means that the consumer prefers combination *A* over combination *B*, and prefers combination *B* over combination *C*, it means that he prefers combination *A* over combination *C*. Symbolically it can be expressed:

   If Combination *A* > Combination *B* and

   Combination *B* > Combination *C*,

   This implies that the consumer prefers:

   Combination *A* > Combination *C*
6. **Substitutability of Commodity:** The goods consumed by the consumer are substitutable.
7. **Non-satiety:** It implies that the consumer is a non-satisfied consumer and always tries to move to higher IC in order to get higher satisfaction.

## 11.4 INDIFFERENCE CURVES

### Meaning

It refers to the diagrammatic representation of various combinations of two commodities that give the consumer equal level of satisfaction. Each point on indifference curve represents different quantity combination of the two commodities where the consumer is indifferent. Thus, all the combinations on the same indifference curve are equally pleasing to the consumer and give same level of satisfaction.

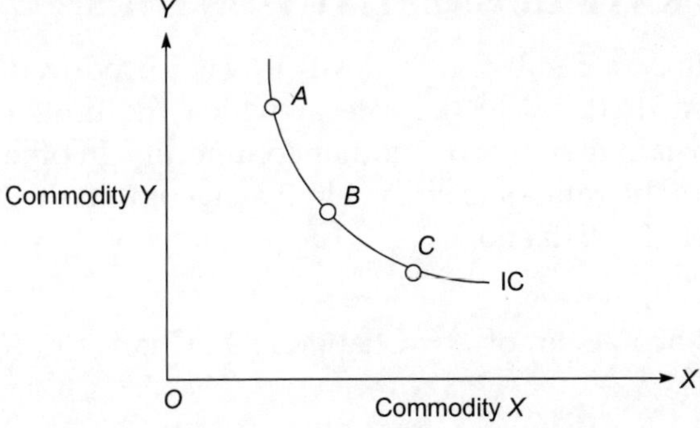


**Fig. 11.2** Indifference Curve

Figure 11.2 reflects that all the quantity combinations of commodity *X* and commodity *Y* are on same indifference curve (*IC*). These have been reflected as *A*, *B* and *C* on *IC*. These quantity combinations show various combinations of commodities *X* and *Y* in which the consumer is indifferent. It means that he treats all these combinations as equally good.

## Indifference Schedule

It refers to the tabular representation of various combinations of two commodities that give the consumer equal level of satisfaction. This has been explained with the help of Table 11.1.

**TABLE 11.1** Indifference Schedule

| Combination | Quantity of Commodity *X* (Tea) | Quantity of Commodity *Y* (Biscuits) | Utility |
|---|---|---|---|
| *A* | 1 | 13 | 100 |
| *B* | 2 | 9 | 100 |
| *C* | 3 | 6 | 100 |
| *D* | 4 | 4 | 100 |
| *E* | 5 | 3 | 100 |

Suppose, the consumer consumes two commodities say, *X* and *Y*. The various quantity combinations of both the commodities have been reflected as combinations *A*, *B*, *C*, *D* and *E*. Combination *A* reflects that the consumer is consuming 1 cup of tea and 13 biscuits, the level of satisfaction remaining same. Similarly, combination *B* reflects that he is consuming 2 cups of tea and 9 biscuits, the level of satisfaction remaining same. In the same manner, the combination *C*, *D* and *E* reflect the quantity combinations of both the commodities which yield same level of satisfaction to the consumer and thus, the consumer is indifferent among them.

## 11.5 MARGINAL RATE OF SUBSTITUTION (MRS)

The concept of marginal rate substitution (MRS) was introduced by Dr. J.R. Hicks and Prof. R.G.D. Allen. It refers to the rate at which the units of commodity are substituted in order to gain the units of another commodity. In other words, marginal rate substitution means the ratio of exchange between commodities *X* and *Y* in order to maintain same level of satisfaction.

It can be represented as:

$$MRS_{XY} = \text{Loss of } Y/\text{Gain of } X = \text{Change in } Y/\text{Change in } X = \Delta Y/\Delta X$$

and

$$MRS_{YX} = \text{Loss of } X/\text{Gain of } Y = \text{Change in } X/\text{Change in } Y = \Delta X/\Delta Y$$

The concept of MRS can be easily explained with the help of schedule given in Table 11.2.

**TABLE 11.2** Marginal Rate of Substitution (MRS)

| Combination | Quantity of Tea | Quantity of Biscuits | Utility | MRS of Tea for Biscuits ($MRS_{TB} = \Delta B/\Delta T$) |
|---|---|---|---|---|
| *A* | 1 | 13 | 100 | – |
| *B* | 2 | 9 | 100 | 4:1 |
| *C* | 3 | 6 | 100 | 3:1 |
| *D* | 4 | 4 | 100 | 2:1 |
| *E* | 5 | 3 | 100 | 1:1 |

In Table 11.2, the consumer is consuming two commodities, viz., tea and biscuits. The five quantity combinations of both the commodities reflect that they provide the same level of satisfaction to the consumer. If he chooses combination *A*, he gets 1 cup of tea and 13 biscuits. The combination *B* reflects that he gets one more cup of tea and for that he is ready to forego 4 biscuits for it to maintain the same level of satisfaction. Thus, MRS is 4:1. In the similar manner, the consumer is willing to sacrifice only 3 biscuits for getting an additional cup of tea. The MRS is 3:1. Likewise, when the consumer moves from combination *D* to *E*, he consumes an additional cup of tea and he forgoes just one biscuit, as it is now relatively less as compared to a situation when it was in plenty. Thus, MRS of tea for biscuits is 1:1. This reflects that marginal rate of substitution is diminishing as the consumer is less prepared to forgo a commodity when it is scarce as compared to the situation when it was available in plenty.

## 11.6 INDIFFERENCE MAP

It refers to the family or a set of indifference curves. Each successive curve farther from the original curve indicates a higher level of total satisfaction. This has been shown diagrammatically in Fig. 11.3.

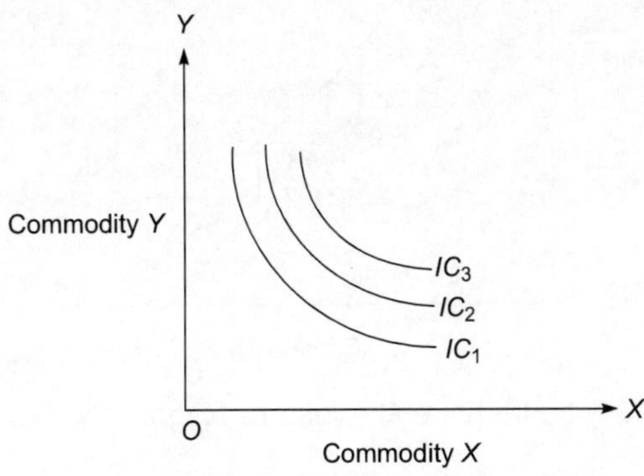


**Fig. 11.3** Indifference Map

In the above diagram, $IC_1$, $IC_2$ and $IC_3$ represent indifference map.

## 11.7 PROPERTIES/CHARACTERISTICS OF INDIFFERENCE CURVES (ICs)

The properties of indifference curves have been shown in Fig. 11.4.

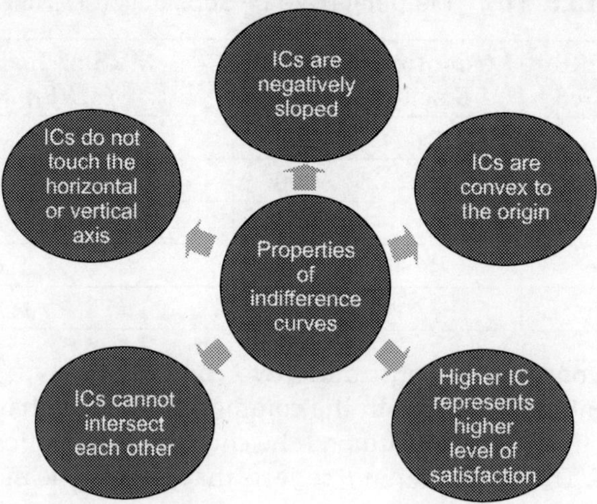


**Fig. 11.4** Properties of Indifference Curves (ICs)

### 1. Indifference Curves are Negatively Sloped

It means that the indifference curves are downward sloping from left to right. This indicates that as the consumer increases the consumption of commodity *X*, he has to forego certain units of commodity *Y* so that the level of satisfaction remains unchanged. This can be understood with the help of following figure 11.5.

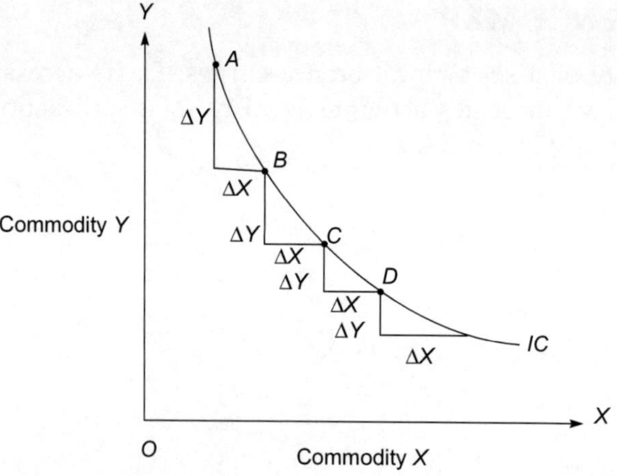


**Fig. 11.5** Indifference Curves are Negatively Sloped

In Fig. 11.5, it is clear that when the consumer wants to increase the units of commodity *X*, he has to forego the units of commodity *Y*, so that the level of satisfaction remains same.

## 2. Indifference Curve are Convex to the Origin

ICs are convex to the origin due to the assumption of diminishing marginal rate of substitution (DMRSxy). It means that the rate at which the consumer substitutes one commodity for the other goes on declining. In other words, as the consumer substitutes commodity *X* for commodity *Y*, the marginal rate of substitution of *X* for *Y* diminishes along the indifference curve.

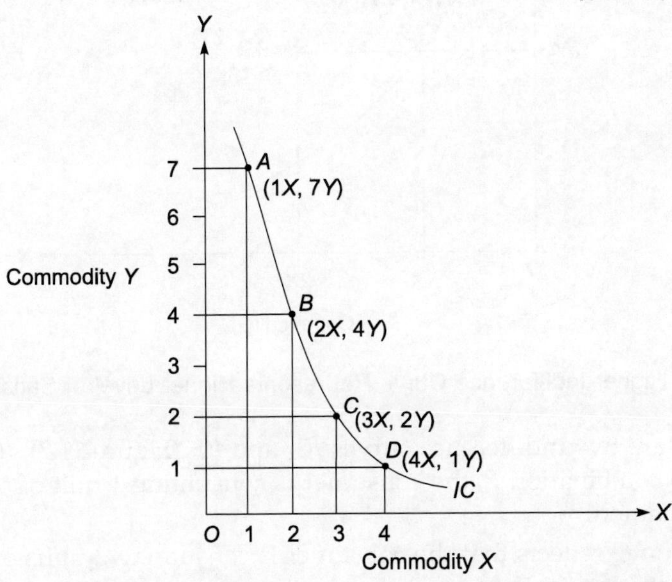


**Fig. 11.6** Indifference Curves are Convex to the Origin

In the above diagram, the units of commodities X and Y are considered on *X*-axis and *Y*-axis, respectively. The consumer initially consumes combination *A* (1*X*, 7*Y*). Now, the consumer wants more of commodity X, for this he has to forgo or sacrifice 3 units of commodity *Y*. This is reflected by combination *B* (2*X*, 4*Y*). The subsequent quantity combinations reflect that the consumer has to sacrifice units of commodity *Y* in order to gain units of commodity X. This is clearly reflected by combinations C (3*X*, 2*Y*) and *D*(4*X*, 1*Y*), respectively. Thus, the consumer prefers more and more of commodity *X* by reducing the units of commodity *Y* but at a declining or diminishing rate.

## 3. Higher Indifference Curve Represents Higher Level of Satisfaction

A higher indifference curve reflects large bundle of commodities and hence more satisfaction. Thus, the indifference curve lying above and to the right of another indifference curve represents a higher level of satisfaction and vice versa.

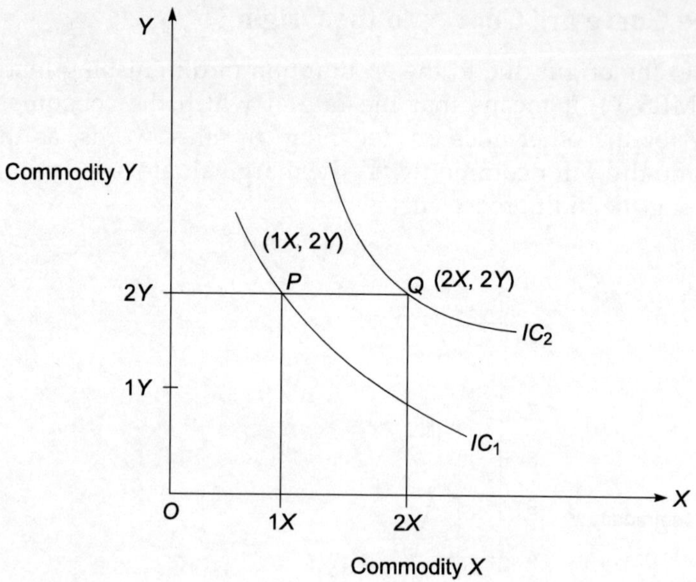


**Fig. 11.7** Higher Indifference Curve Represents Higher Level of Satisfaction

Suppose there are two indifference curves $IC_1$ and $IC_2$ (Figure 11.7). $IC_1$ lies on the left of $IC_2$. At the combination *P*, the consumer is consuming 1 unit of commodity *X* and 2 units of commodity *Y*.

The combination *Q* reflects that the consumer is consuming 2 units of commodity *X* and 2 unit of commodity *Y*.

It can be written as:

$$\text{Combination } P = 1X + 2Y$$

$$\text{Combination } Q = 2X + 2Y$$

According to the assumption of rationality and non-satiety, the consumer will prefer combination *Q* which reflects more of commodity *X* rather than preferring less of it. Thus, the consumer will prefer to have more of commodity *X* and same amount of commodity *Y*. Since, combination *Q* lies on higher *IC*, thus, the consumer will prefer $IC_2$ which represents higher satisfaction.

## 4. Indifference Curves (IC) cannot Intersect each Other

This assumption is proved with the help of absurdity. Suppose, the two ICs, viz., $IC_1$ and $IC_2$ intersect each other at combination *A* (Fig. 11.8).

At $IC_1$,

Combination *A* = Combination *C* (because the combinations on same IC give equal level of satisfaction).

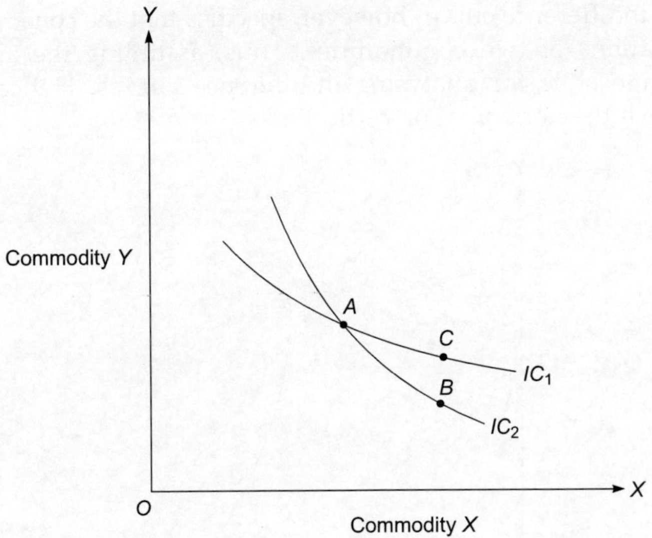


**Fig. 11.8** Indifference Curves Cannot Intersect Each Other

At $IC_2$,

Combination $A$ = Combination $B$ (because the combinations on same $IC$ give equal level of satisfaction).

It means that

Combination $B$ = Combination C (by assumption of transitivity) ...(1)

However, combination $B \neq$ combination C

This is due to fact that combination C has more units of commodity $B$ and the same units of commodity X as compared to combination $B$. In combination $B$, the consumer has comparatively less units of commodity $Y$ and the same units of commodity X.

Thus,

Combination C > Combination $B$.

Thus, equation 1 is not true and gives absurd conclusions. Combination C gives more satisfaction to the consumer. Thus, the basic supposition that two ICs intersect with each other is wrong. Hence, two indifference curves cannot intersect each other.

## 5. Indifference Curves do not Touch the Horizontal or Vertical Axis

This property of indifference curves specifies that the ICs never intersect any of the axis. In this case, there are following possibilities:

- If indifference curve touches $X$-axis ($IC_1$), then the quantity purchased of commodity $Y$ is zero.
- If indifference curve touches $Y$-axis ($IC_2$), then the quantity purchased of commodity X is zero.

The concept of indifference curves however, specifies that the consumer purchases different combinations of two commodities. Thus, assuming the absence of one commodity is impossible for analysing indifference curves. Hence, indifference curves do not touch the horizontal or vertical axis.

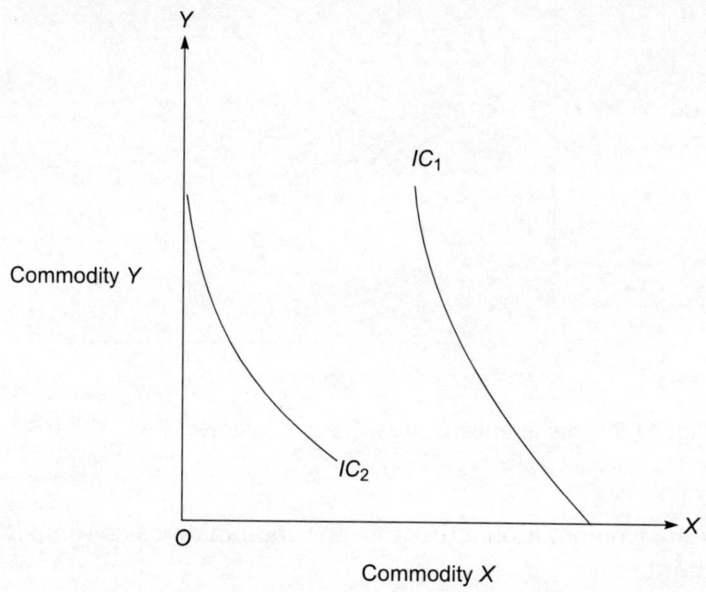


**Fig. 11.9** Indifference Curves do not Touch the Horizontal or Vertical Axis

In the above diagram (Fig. 11.9),

- At $IC_1$, the quantity purchased of commodity $Y$ is zero
- At $IC_2$, the quantity purchased of commodity $X$ is zero

This is contrary to the concept of indifference curves with different combinations of both the commodities. Presuming that the quantity of any of the commodities is zero is outside the purview of IC analysis.

## 11.8 EXCEPTIONAL SHAPES OF INDIFFERENCE CURVES

Indifference curves may make a different shape in certain exceptional cases.

### 1. Linear Indifference Curve: In case of Perfect Substitutes

These are the indifference curves for perfect substitute products. In this case, the commodities can be used in place of each other. These reflect that one unit of commodity $X$ is equally good as one unit of commodity $Y$. These are downward sloping curves (linear curves) and move from left to right. In this case MRS remains constant. This has been shown in Fig. 11.10.

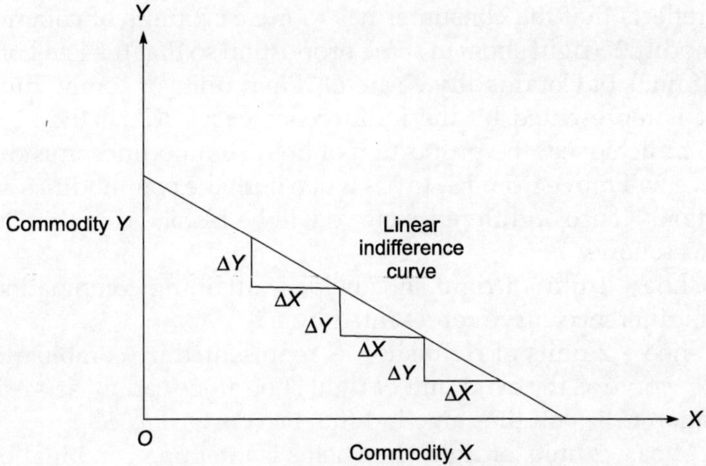


**Fig. 11.10** Indifference Curves in Case of Perfect Substitutes

Figure 11.10 reflects that in order to consume more units of commodity *X*, the consumer has to lose units of commodity *Y*. Thus, indifference curve will be a linear downward sloping curve moving from left to right.

## 2. *L*-Shaped Indifference Curve: In case of Perfect Complements

These are the indifference curves for perfect complementary goods. It means that the commodities are perfectly complemented to each other. Thus, substitutability between commodities is zero. They are used jointly and in a fixed proportion. To increase the level of satisfaction, both units of both commodities are to be increased, holding the proportion constant. In this case, the shape of indifference curve is *L*-shaped. This has been shown in Fig. 11.11.

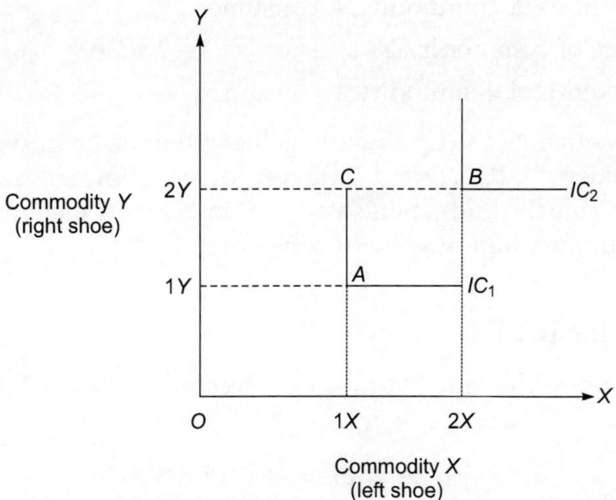


**Fig. 11.11** Indifference Curves in Case of Perfect Complements

Figure 11.11 reflects that the consumer has to increase units of commodity *X* (left shoe) and commodity *Y* (right shoe) in same proportion so that the level of satisfaction remains same. If units of Commodity *X*, are $O_1X$ and units of commodity *Y* are $O_1Y$, then the output is represented by the indifference curve $IC_1$. If the higher level of satisfaction is to be achieved, the proportion of both commodities must be increased. Thus, indifference will move from $IC_1$ to $IC_2$ when both the commodities are increased in same proportion. Hence, indifference curve will be *L*-shaped in this case. This can be understood as follows:

1 unit of left shoe + 1 unit of right shoe helps is attaining combination *A* and the corresponding indifference curve represented by $IC_1$.

1 unit of left shoe + 2 units of right shoe as represented by combination C lies on same indifference curve as the extra unit of right shoe alone cannot serve the purpose. Hence, combination C lies on the same indifference curve, i.e., $IC_1$.

2 units of left shoe + 2 units of right shoe helps is attaining combination B and the corresponding indifference curve represented by $IC_2$ ($IC_2$ is higher indifference curve representing higher level of satisfaction as compared to $IC_1$).

## 11.9 CONCEPT OF BUDGET LINE OR PRICE LINE

A budget line or price line represents the various combinations of two goods that a consumer can purchase given the money income and the prices of commodities. It is also known as price opportunity line or budget constraint line.

**Equation**

$$M = PxQx + PyQy$$

$M$ = Money income of the consumer

$Px$ = Price of commodity *X*

$Qx$ = Quantity of commodity *X* consumed

$Py$ = Price of commodity *Y*

$Qy$ = Quantity of commodity *Y* consumed

Figure 11.12 shows that all the combinations that either lie on or within the budget line, that is, combinations *A*, *B*, *C*, *D* and *E* are considered 'affordable or attainable' and the combinations outside the budget line, that is, *F* and *G* are considered 'unaffordable or unattainable' from the point of view of consumer.

### Slope of Budget Line (BL)

The slope of budget line is the ratio of prices of two commodities and it is symbolically expressed as:

$$\text{Slope of } BL = -Px/Py$$

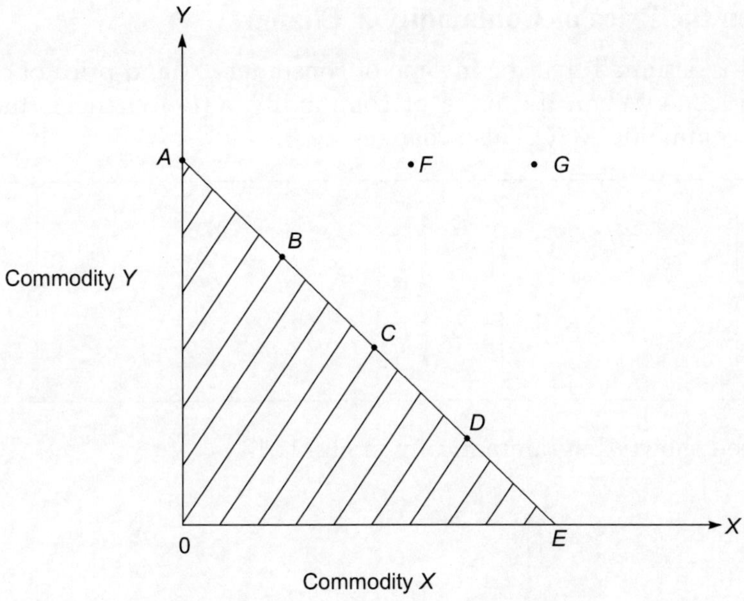


**Fig. 11.12** Budget Line or Price Line

## Characteristics of Budget Line

1. It is always a straight line.
2. It is negatively sloped from left to right.
3. The shape of the budget line depends on the income of the consumer and the prices of the two commodities.
4. The slope of budget line is equal to the ratio of the prices of the two commodities.

## 11.10 SHIFTS IN BUDGET LINE

The shape of the budget line depends on the income of the consumer and the prices of the two commodities. Thus, shift in budget line occurs due to the following factors:

(a) Change in prices of the commodities
(b) Change in income of the consumer

### 11.10.1 Changes in Prices of the Commodities

Keeping the income of the consumer and the price of the other good as constant, when price of one commodity changes, budget line pivots from its original position. There are following cases in this regard:

## Case 1: When the Price of Commodity *X* Changes

In this case, it is assumed that the income of consumer ($Y$) and price of commodity $Y(P_Y)$ remain same. When the price of commodity $X(P_X)$ changes, the quantity demanded of commodity $X(Q_x)$ also changes.

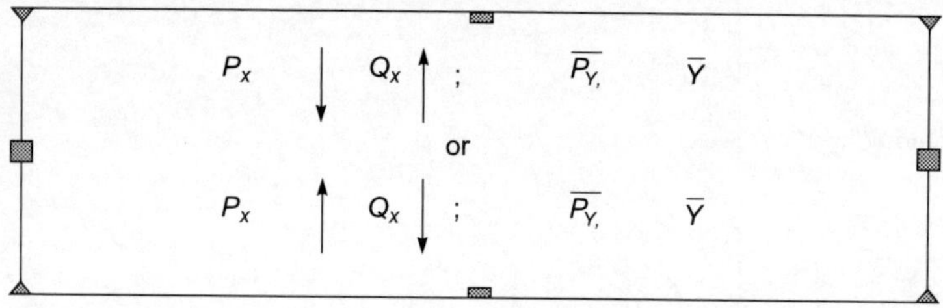


This has been shown diagrammatically in Fig. 11.13.

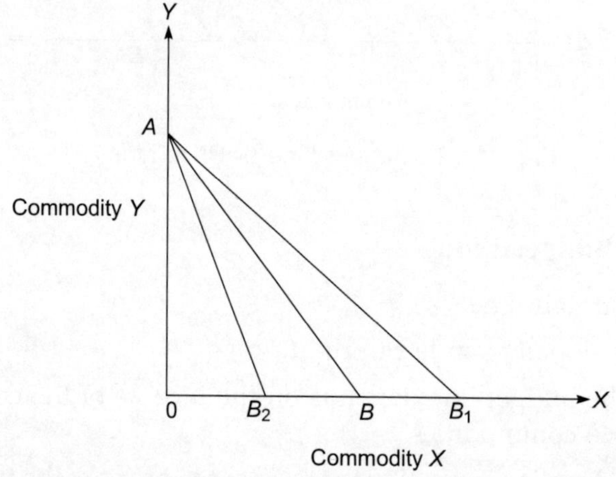


**Fig. 11.13** When the Price of Commodity *X* Changes

This can be explained as under:

Initial budget line = $AB$

**Budget line $AB_2$:** If the price of X rises, price line pivots to $AB_2$ reflecting a decline in quantity demanded as a result of rise in price.

**Budget line $AB_1$:** If the price of X declines, price line pivots to $AB_1$ reflecting rise in quantity demanded as a result of fall in price.

## Case 2: When the Price of Commodity *Y* Changes

In this case, it is assumed that the income of consumer ($Y$) and price of commodity $X(P_X)$ remains same. In Fig. 11.14 it can be seen that when the price of commodity $Y$ changes ($P_Y$), the quantity demanded of commodity $Y(Q_Y)$ also changes.

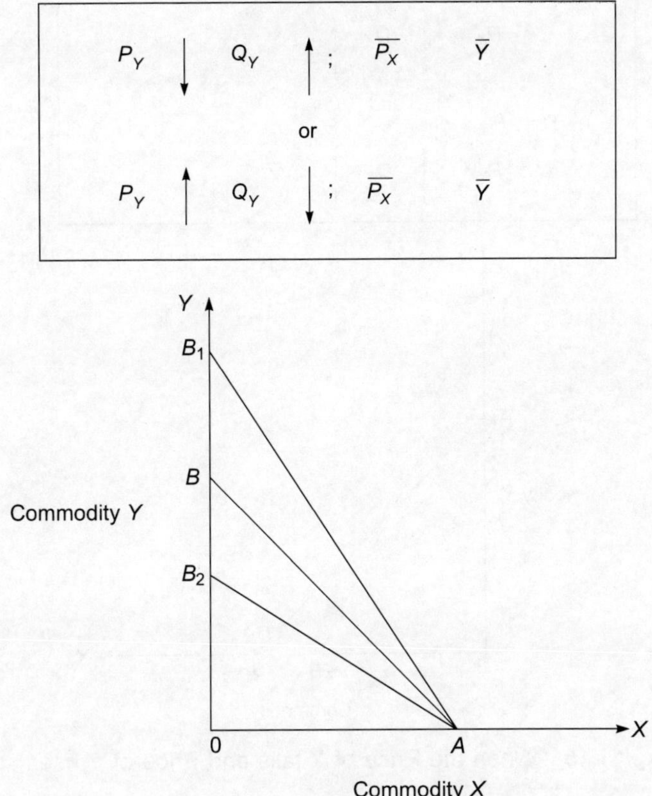


**Fig. 11.14** When the Price of Commodity *Y* Changes

Initial budget Line = *AB*

**Budget line $AB_2$:** If the price of *Y* rises, price line pivots to $AB_2$ reflecting a decline in quantity demanded as a result of rise in price.

**Budget line $AB_1$:** If the price of *Y* declines, price line pivots to $AB_1$ reflecting rise in quantity demanded as a result of fall in price.

## Case 3: When the Prices of Both Commodities Change

In this case, there are two possibilities.

## Case 3a: When the Price of *X* falls and Price of *Y* rises

In this case, it is assumed that the income of consumer remains same. In Fig. 11.15 it can be observed that when the price of commodity *X* falls, the quantity demanded of commodity *X* rises. Similarly, when the price of commodity *Y* rises, the quantity demanded of commodity *Y* falls.

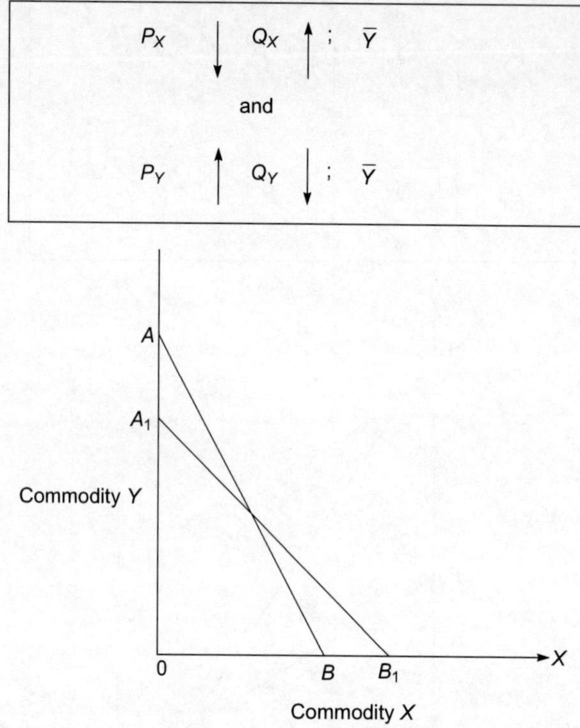


**Fig. 11.15** When the Price of *X* falls and Price of *Y* rises

Initial budget line = *AB*

**New budget line $A_1B_1$**

- When the price of *X* falls, the quantity demanded rises from *OB* to $OB_1$
- When price of *Y* rises, the quantity demanded falls from *OA* to $OA_1$.
- Thus, new budget line is $A_1B_1$

## Case 3b: When the Price of *X* rises and Price of *Y* falls

In this case, it is assumed that the income of consumer remains same. Figure 11.16 makes it clear that when, the price of commodity *X* rises, the quantity demanded of commodity *X* falls. Similarly, when, the price of commodity *Y* falls, the quantity demanded of commodity *Y* increases.

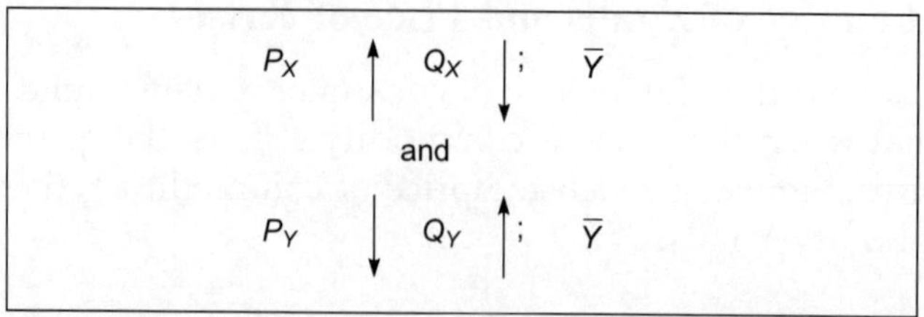

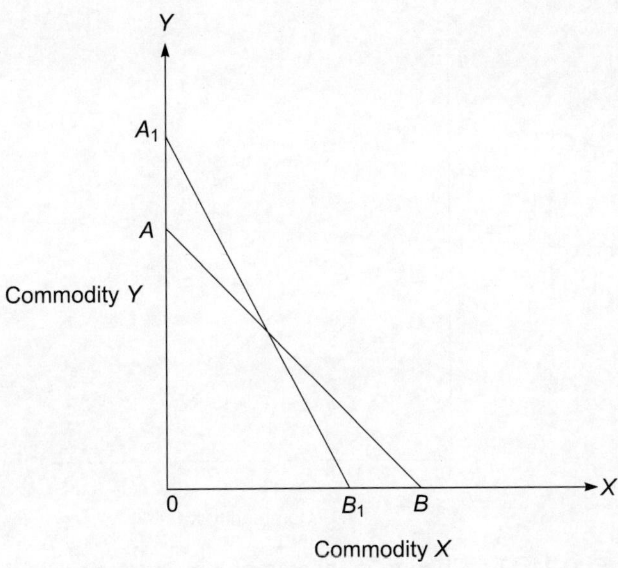


**Fig. 11.16** When the Price of *X* Rises and Price of *Y* Falls

Initial budget line = *AB*

**New budget line $A_1B_1$**

- When the price of *X* rises, the quantity demanded falls from *OB* to $OB_1$
- When price of *Y* falls, the quantity demanded rises from *OA* to $OA_1$. Thus, new budget line is $A_1B_1$.

## 11.10.2 Change in Income of the Consumer

### Case 1: Keeping the prices of two commodities constant, when the consumer's income increases

In this case, the demand increases in case of both the commodities. This is reflected by a parallel outward shift in the budget line.

### Case 2: Keeping the prices of two commodities constant, when the consumer's income decreases

In this case, the demand reduces in case of both the commodities. This is reflected by a parallel inward shift in the budget line.

Case 1 and Case 2 have been reflected in Fig. 11.17.

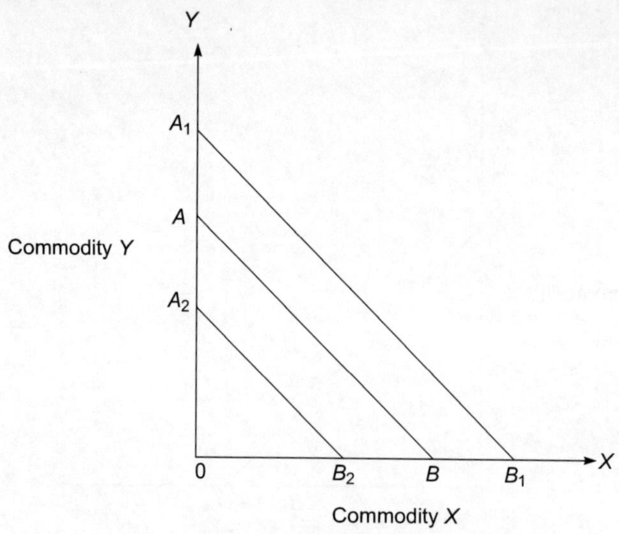


**Fig. 11.17** Change in Income of the Consumer

Initial budget line = $AB$

**Budget line $A_1B_1$**

- An increase in the income shifts the budget line rightward ($A_1B_1$) while the slope of the budget line doesn't change because prices have not changed.

**Budget line $A_2B_2$**

- An increase in the income shifts the budget line leftwards ($A_2B_2$) while the slope of the budget line doesn't change because prices have not changed.

## 11.11 DETERMINATION OF CONSUMERS EQUILIBRIUM UNDER INDIFFERENCE CURVE ANALYSIS

The term "consumer's equilibrium" refers to a situation in which the consumer derives maximum satisfaction given the prices of the commodities and the money income of the consumer.

In case of ordinal approach, "A consumer is said to be in equilibrium at a point where the price line is touching the highest attainable indifference curve from below".

### Assumptions of Consumer's Equilibrium

1. The consumer acts rationally and tries to maximise his satisfaction.
2. The consumer has a well defined indifference map of commodity $X$ and $Y$.
3. The consumer has a fixed money income which is to be spent on purchase of commodities $X$ and $Y$.

3. The prices of commodity $X(P_x)$ and $Y(P_Y)$ are given.
4. Goods are divisible.
5. Good are homogeneous.
6. No change in tastes and habits of consumer.
7. Perfect competition.

## Conditions of Consumer's Equilibrium under Indifference Curve Analysis

The following are the conditions of consumer's equilibrium under indifference curve analysis (Fig. 11.18)

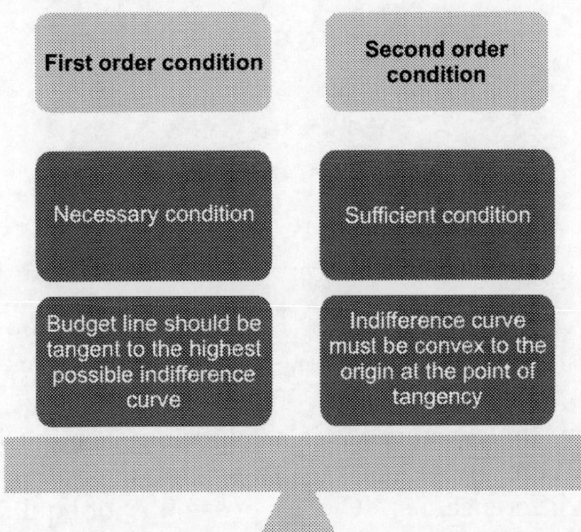


**Fig. 11.18** Conditions of Consumer's Equilibrium under Indifference Curve Analysis

### 1. First Order Condition: Necessary Condition

Budget line should be tangent to the highest possible indifference curve. It means that slope of the indifference curve should be equal to the slope of price line.

It implies that the marginal rate of substitution of commodity $X$ for commodity $Y$ ($MRS_{xy} = \Delta Y/\Delta X$) must be equal to the price ratio of the two goods.

It can be written as:

$$\text{Slope of indifference curve} = \text{Slope of budget line}$$
$$MRS_{xy} = -\text{Price of } X/\text{Price of } Y$$
$$= \Delta Y/\Delta X = -P_x/P_y$$

### 2. Second Order Condition: Sufficient Condition

The second order condition is that the indifference curve must be convex to the origin at the point of tangency.

It means marginal rate of substitution of commodity $X$ for commodity $Y$ ($MRS_{xy} = \Delta Y/\Delta X$) is diminishing.

**Explanation**

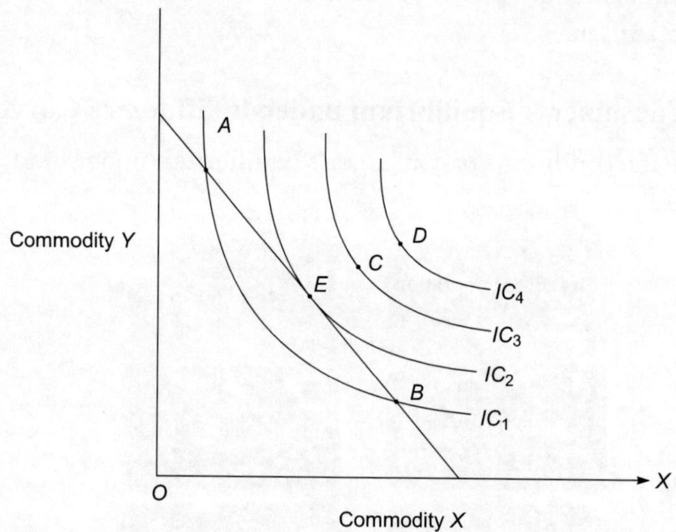


**Fig. 11.19** Consumer's Equilibrium under Ordinal Utility Analysis

In the above diagram, the consumer is in equilibrium at point $E$ where both first and second order conditions are satisfied. At this point, the budget line is tangent to the highest possible indifference, i.e., $IC_2$. The possibility of equilibrium on $IC_3$ and $IC_4$ is ruled out as it is beyond the means as they are outside the budget line. Thus, combination $C$ (on $IC_3$) and $D$ (on $IC_4$) are beyond the means of the consumer and are thus unaffordable combinations.

Any point on the budget line to the left of $E$ (such as combination $A$) and to the right of $E$ (such as combination $B$), lies on lower $IC$ and hence gives lower level of satisfaction than $IC_2$.

Hence, the consumer would like to operate on $IC_2$ and would be in equilibrium at point $E$. In case of deviation from equilibrium the following possibilities may arise:

- If $MRS_{XY} > P_x/P_Y$

  It means that the consumer is willing to purchase more of commodity $X$ than price prevailing in the market. As a result, consumer buys more of $X$ and as a result $MRS$ falls. This decline will be till the equality of MRS and price ratio of two commodities is established.

- ✓ If $MRS_{XY} < P_x/P_Y$

  It means that the consumer is willing to purchase less of commodity $X$ than price prevailing in the market. As a result, consumer buys less of $X$ and as a result MRS rises. This rise will be till the equality of MRS and price ratio of two commodities is established.

## 11.12 CRITICISM OF ORDINAL UTILITY APPROACH

The ordinal approach to utility analysis has been criticized on account of the following grounds.

1. **Unrealistic Assumptions**

   Indifference curve analysis is based on certain assumptions such as rationality and perfect knowledge regarding the preference, etc. However, the purchases are often affected by the tastes, preferences, customs and fashion. In such cases, the consumer does not always act rationally and may not be sure of the choice of preference.

2. **Complex Analysis**

   Indifference curve analysis can be easily applied to two-commodity case. However, the analysis and its interpretation is difficult and complex in case of multiple commodity case.

3. **Imaginary Combinations**

   IC analysis is based at times on imaginary combinations of two commodities that have no meaning for the consumer. Assuming one cup of tea consumed with 13 biscuits, two cups of tea with 9 biscuits and 5 cups of tea with 3 biscuits reflect imaginary and fictitious combinations.

4. **Assumption of Convexity**

   IC analysis assumes that indifference curve is convex to the origin. In reality, marginal rate of substitution of one commodity for the other may not be always diminishing.

5. **Impractical**

   Indifference curve analysis assumes the homogeneity of the commodities which is applicable to perfect competition. However, the market form of such sort does not exist in reality. In real life, there is more prevalence of monopolistic competition and oligopolistic form of market.

## 11.13 COMPARATIVE ANALYSIS OF CARDINAL UTILITY ANALYSIS ANDORDINAL UTILITY ANALYSIS (COMPARATIVE ANALYSIS OF UTILITY AND INDIFFERENCE ANALYSIS)

The cardinal approach to utility analysis believes that utility is a quantifiable concept. It asserts that it is possible on the part of consumer to specify the utility in terms of 'utils' which was considered a measuring rod of utility. In contrast, the ordinal school of thought opines that utility is not a quantifiable concept and is incapable of measurement. It specified that it is only possible on the part of consumer to rank the commodities in order of his choices. But, the consumer cannot specify the extent of satisfaction in numerical values. However, the points of similarity and differences have been specified in Table 11.3.

**TABLE 11.3** Comparative Analysis of Cardinal Utility Analysis and Ordinal Utility Analysis

**Points of Similarity**

1. Both theories lay foundations for the study of consumer behavior.
2. Both approaches assume that consumer is a rational decision maker and aims to maximize his satisfaction level from the consumption of the commodities.
3. Both approaches are based on proportionality rule. This consumer's equilibrium is ascertained in both cases as under:
   In case of cardinal approach, the consumer's equilibrium is ascertained where,

$$\frac{MU_X}{P_X} = \frac{MU_Y}{P_Y} = M_{um}$$

   Thus, the proportion between $MU$ and $P$ are of vital importance.
   In case of ordinal approach, the consumer's equilibrium is ascertained where,

$$MRS_{XY} = -\text{Price of } X/\text{Price of } Y$$
$$= \Delta Y/\Delta X = -P_X/P_Y$$

Thus, the proportion between MRS and $P$ are of vital importance.
In both the cases, the price ratio of two commodities ($P_X/P_Y$) have been considered.

**Points of Difference**

| | Cardinal Utility Analysis | Ordinal Utility Analysis |
|---|---|---|
| Propounder of economic thought | Prof. Marshall | Prof. JR Hicks and Prof. RGD Allen |
| Alternative name | Utility analysis | Indifference curve analysis |
| Crux of analysis | Utility is a measureable and quantifiable concept. | Utility can only be ranked and cannot be measured. |
| Approach | Quantitative | Qualitative |
| Vital components | MU and price | IC and budget line |
| Subject matter | There are two laws studied:<br>(a) The law of diminishing marginal utility<br>(b) The law of equi-marginal utility | Indifference curve and budgetary analysis. |
| Practicability | Less | More |
| The condition of consumer's equilibrium | $\frac{MU_X}{P_X} = \frac{MU_Y}{P_Y} = M_{um}$ | $MRS_{XY} = -\text{Price of } X/\text{Price of } Y = \Delta Y/\Delta X = -P_X/P_Y$ |

## Summary

- ✓ According to ordinal approach to utility analysis, utility cannot be measured and quantified by the consumer. A consumer can only rank the preferred combinations but cannot define the quantum of satisfaction like cardinal utility analysis.
- ✓ Ordinal utility analysis is based on indifference curves.
- ✓ Indifference curves are the diagrammatic representation of various combinations of two commodities that give the consumer equal level of satisfaction.
- ✓ Indifference schedule is the tabular representation of various combinations of two commodities that give the consumer equal level of satisfaction.
- ✓ Marginal rate of substitution (MRS) is the slope of indifference curve. It refers to the rate at which the units of commodity are substituted in order to gain the units of another commodity.
- ✓ An indifference map is the family or a set of indifference curves. Each successive curve farther from the original curve indicates a higher level of total satisfaction.
- ✓ Indifference curves have following properties:
  - ICs are negatively sloped
  - ICs are convex to the origin
  - Higher IC represents higher level of satisfaction
  - ICs cannot intersect each other
  - ICs do not touch the horizontal or vertical axis
- ✓ The exceptional shapes of indifference curves exist in following cases:
  - (a) Perfect substitutes
  - (b) Perfect complements
- ✓ A budget line or price line represents the various combinations of two goods that a consumer can purchase given the money income and the prices of commodities. It is also known as price opportunity line or budget constraint line.
- ✓ The slope of budget line is the ratio of prices of two commodities and it is symbolically expressed as:

$$\text{Slope of } BL = -P_X/P_Y$$

- ✓ Shift in budget line occur due to the following factors:
  - (a) Change in prices of the commodities
  - (b) Change in income of the consumer
- ✓ Under ordinal utility analysis, conditions of consumer's equilibrium are ascertained as follows:
  - (a) First order condition: Necessary condition

    Budget line should be tangent to the highest possible indifference curve. It means that slope of the indifference curve should be equal to the slope of price line.

(b) Second order condition: Sufficient condition

The second order condition is that indifference curve must be convex to the origin at the point of tangency.

## Review Questions

1. What is the ordinal utility approach of consumer behaviour? Explain the assumptions and concept of diminishing marginal rate of substitution.
2. Define indifference curves? What are the assumptions and properties of indifference curve analysis.
3. Define the concept of indifference curves and indifference schedule. What is the normal shape of indifference curve? Are there any exceptions to the normal shapes of indifference curves?
4. 'A consumer will be in equilibrium where budget line is tangent to the highest possible indifference curve'. Explain.
5. Define consumer's equilibrium. What are the conditions of consumer's equilibrium under IC analysis? How equilibrium is determined under indifference approach.
6. What is price line? Explain its role in attaining equilibrium under indifference curve analysis.
7. What happens to the original budget line when there is a change in the following variables:
   (a) Prices
   (b) Income of the consumer
8. Explain the concept of budget line. What are the factors that cause shifts in budget line?
9. Explain graphically the effect of increase in prices of one of the commodities on budget line.
10. Explain graphically the effect of change in income of the consumer on the position of budget line.
11. Explain the consumer's equilibrium under ordinal approach of utility analysis. Also explain the first and second order conditions of consumer's equilibrium.
12. Compare and contrast cardinal utility approach and ordinal utility approach to the theory of consumer's behaviour.
13. Critically examine ordinal utility approach to consumer's behaviour.
14. Write short notes on:
    (a) Budget line
    (b) Diminishing marginal rate of substitution
    (c) Indifference map

# 12 CHAPTER

# Theory of Production and Short-Run Production Analysis

**LEARNING OBJECTIVES**

After going through this chapter, reader would be able to understand:

✓ The meaning and concept of the factors of production.
✓ The time period distinction.
✓ The short- and long-run production functions.
✓ The short-run production analysis in terms of the law of variable proportions.

## 12.1 INTRODUCTION

The aim of every firm is to achieve certain objectives such as maximisation of profit, sales maximisation, growth, expansion of market share, etc. In order to achieve these objectives, the firms need to take production decisions that are relevant for managerial decision-making. These decisions create a framework of operation of production process and relate to economics of production. The economics of production is also known as theory of production or production analysis. These decisions include the following:

- Factor input combination for production process
- The land or area required to carry out production process
- Units of labour required
- The estimation of amount of capital required initially and later on with the progression of production process
- The sources of capital
- The quantum of output to be produced
- Technique of production: Capital or labour intensive
- Type of technology to be used
- The distribution of factor rewards

The present chapter begins with the discussion of meaning of production and factors of production. We then move to study of distinction of time periods in terms of short run and long run. Further the discussion includes the production function analysis. In order to have conceptual understanding of production function, short-run and long-run production functions have been explained. This general discussion is extended to the specific analysis of short-run production analysis. For this purpose, the dynamics related to the law of variable proportions have been explained.

## 12.2 MEANING AND CONCEPT OF PRODUCTION

The analysis of theory of production involves the study of dynamics related to production. This section defines the concept of production. Production refers to the process in which the producer transforms inputs into outputs. The inputs include land, labour, capital (including tools, equipment) and raw material, etc. The output here includes production of goods and generation of services. The firm utilises these factor inputs with the purpose of getting output in the form of goods and services. The concept of production can be understood with the help of the example of computer system manufacture.

For instance, Dell manufactures laptops, tablet PCs, desktop, etc. It may take the following steps to execute the production process:

(a) take a place on lease to run their business or utilise already available space,
(b) ascertain the requirement of finance for producing the output,
(c) hire skilled workforce to execute the production process, and
(d) purchase the requisite material for assembling the final product.

Similarly, Google and Microsoft manufacture software, HP manufactures laptops, printers and other storage devices, Intel manufactures computer processor and other high-end hardware. All these are examples of output of these companies.

Thus, here the inputs are in form of land, skilled workforce, finance, etc., to execute the production process. The output can be in the form of a final product such as laptops, tablet PCs, desktop, software, printers, storage devices, computer processor and other high-end hardware, etc. The output may also be in the form of intermediate product (which is used in further production) like microprocessor. However, production analysis not only includes commodities, it also includes the provision of services.

For instance, if a doctor renders services in a hospital to treat patients, a chartered accountant files the ITR for his clients, the lawyers contests the case of his client. Then all these activities are a part of the services and are a part of output.

## 12.3 FACTORS OF PRODUCTION

A production entity needs to utilise certain factors such as land, labour, capital and entrepreneurial skill to carry out production process. Thus, factors of production refer to the resources that facilitate the production process. They are the building blocks that help in getting output in the form of goods and services. In economics, the major factor inputs are as follows:

- **Land:** In economics, land refers to the factor inputs in the form of natural resources. These include the all gifts of nature, such as rivers, oceans, climate, mountains, fisheries, mines, forests, etc.
- **Labour:** Labour refers to the factor inputs in the form of human resources. It includes the efforts both mental and physical initiated by human beings with the purpose of earning monetary reward or monetary incentive work undertaken for some monetary reward. Thus, all those who render their services for receipt of monetary incentives are known as labour. These include a factory worker, a supervisor, a foreman, a doctor, an engineer, a teacher, a lawyer, etc.
- **Capital:** Capital refers to the factor inputs in form of man-made resources. It includes tools, equipment, machinery, raw materials and means of transport such as roads, railways, canals, etc.
- **Entrepreneur:** The term 'entrepreneur' has been derived from a French word 'Entreprendre' meaning to undertake certain activities. It refers to the factor input that collaborates the other three factors of production viz. land, labour and capital that are scattered at different places. Apart from assembling the other factors of production, the entrepreneur undertakes risks and faces uncertainties in order to maximise his possibility of getting more profits.

## 12.4 FIXED AND VARIABLE FACTORS

The distinction between fixed and variable inputs exists only in the short run. This is because in the long run, all factor inputs become variable or elastic. Thus, in short run, the inputs can be classified into fixed inputs & variable inputs.

✓ **Fixed inputs** are the resources or inputs that remain fixed or constant up to certain level of output. Their supply cannot be increased instantaneously in response to changes in market conditions. Thus, their supply is inelastic in the short run.

*For example:* Buildings, sophisticated machineries, major capital equipment, etc.

✓ **Variable inputs** are the resources or inputs that change with the change in output. It is possible to increase their supply in response to changes in market conditions. Thus, their supply is elastic in the short run.

*For example:* Raw materials and labour services.

## 12.5 SHORT RUN AND LONG RUN

In economics, short run and long run do not refer to any specific time period (such as 3 months, 6 months or a year) on completion of which the new time period commences. The length of time to be considered under short run and long run depends on the nature of the industry and the time period it takes to make all the factors of production as variable. For instance, a business like ironing clothes, long run may be months, quarter or a year. For running a coffee shop, long run may be one year or more. Contrary to this in case of a construction project, long run may be many years to come. In production analysis, the time period is bifurcated under two major heads. These are:

**(a) Short run** refers to the time period in which the quantity of at least one input is fixed or inelastic. These inputs may be land, plant, building, machinery, etc. It is not the time period that is sufficient enough to acquire more of land, plant, building and machinery, etc. Thus, the production can be expanded using only variable inputs like labour and raw materials.

**(b) Long run** refers to a time period in which the supply of all the inputs is variable or elastic. It is the time period that is sufficient enough to acquire more of factor inputs. Thus, their supply can be increased in the long run.

## 12.6 PRODUCTION FUNCTION

In chapter 4, we have studied the demand function. We noticed that the theory of demand discussed the demand function as a functional relationship between demand and determinants of demand. A study of similar kind is done in the theory of production. In theory of production, we study production function as a functional relationship between inputs and output level.

### Meaning

Production function refers to the mathematical relationship between the factor inputs and level of output. It establishes the functional relationship that explains the maximisation of output level using a given set of inputs (keeping the technology constant).

### Assumptions

- There is a given set of factor inputs.
- All the units of factor inputs are homogeneous.
- Technology is invariant and does not change with change in production.

### Mathematical Representation

Mathematically, production function can be represented as:

$$Q = f(L, N, K, T, t)$$

where,

$Q$ = Quantity of output
$L$ = Land
$N$ = Labour
$K$ = Capital
$T$ = Technology
$t$ = Time

The analysis of production function on the basis of time period distinction, extends to the two forms:

(a) Short-run production function
(b) Long-run production function

### 12.6.1 Short-Run Production Function

In this section, we present production function when at least one of the factor inputs is fixed. In such as case, it is not possible to increase output, increase capital or acquire more of land. In such a case, the law of variable proportions operates. Here, increasing returns to variable factors exist because of the abundance of fixed factors as compared to variable factors. On the other side, diminishing returns operate when variable factors are too much as compared to the fixed factors.

### 12.6.2 Long-Run Production Function

In this section, we discuss production function when all the factor inputs become variable. In such as case, it is possible to alter output, invest more capital or acquire more of land. In such a case, the law of returns to scale operates. Here, increasing returns to scale exist because of the economies of scale. On the other side, diminishing returns operate because of diseconomies of scale.

## 12.7 LAW OF VARIABLE PROPORTIONS: SHORT-RUN PRODUCTION ANALYSIS

The law of variable proportion is one of the fundamental laws of production analysis. It relates to the short run in which some factors are fixed and some variable. In this law, it is possible to vary the factor proportion, therefore it is known as the law of non-proportional returns.

### 12.7.1 Statement of the Law

As the producer employs units of only one factor input to a given quantity of fixed factors, the output first increases at increasing rate, then increases at diminishing rate, becomes maximum and eventually declines.

This law is also known as the law of non-proportional returns. This is due to the fact that the proportion between the factors varies in the following manner:

1 land: 1 labour = 1 : 1

1 land: 2 labour = 1 : 2

1 land: 3 labour = 1 : 3

And so on.

### 12.7.2 Assumptions of the Law of Variable Proportions

(i) The law operates in the short run and given period.

(ii) There is a possibility of varying the proportion between the factors.

(iii) The state of technology is assumed to be given and unchanged.

(iv) The units of variable factors are homogeneous in terms of skill, efficiency and expertise to produce a particular product.

(v) Variable factor units are homogeneous or identical in amount and quality.

(vi) Factors of production are indivisible in nature.

(vii) Input prices remain unchanged.

(viii) Output is measured in physical units.

### 12.7.3 Total, Average and Marginal Product Curves

**Total Product (TP)** refers to the total production in a producing unit as a result of employment of one unit of factor (variable factor say labour) while keeping the units of other inputs (capital, land, etc.) as fixed. When no unit of labour is used, *TP* is zero.

**Marginal Product (MP):** From *TP* curves, we derive *MP* curves. It is also known as slope of *TP*. It is defined as change in *TP* by employing one more unit of labour.

$$MP = \frac{\Delta TP}{\Delta L}$$

**Average Product (AP)** is the ratio of *TP* and quantity of labour employed.

$$AP = \frac{TP}{L}$$

where,

$MP$ = Marginal product

$AP$ = Average product

$L$ = Units of labour

### 12.7.4 Three Stages of Production

Considering an agrarian situation, where land is the fixed factor and labour is the variable factor. The farmer is engaged in production of wheat. The production of wheat in this case can be increased only by employing additional units of variable factor. The law has been further explained as under three stages (Fig. 12.1).

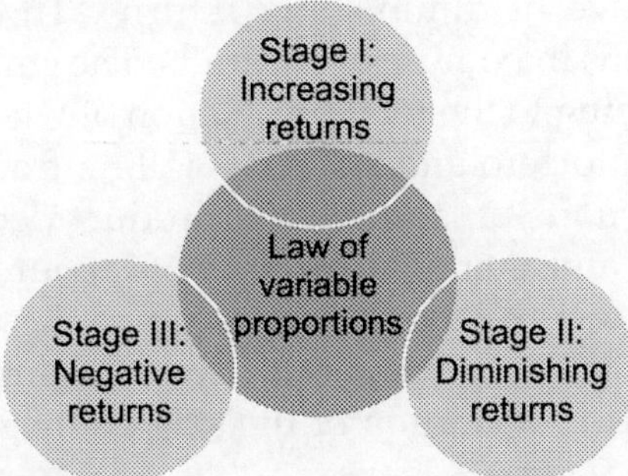


**Fig. 12.1** Three Stages of Production

- ✓ Stage I: Increasing returns to variable factor
- ✓ Stage II: Diminishing returns to variable factor
- ✓ Stage III: Negative returns to variable factor

**Table 12.1** Three Stages of Production

| Units of Fixed Factor (land) | Units of Variable Factor (labour) | *TP* | *AP* | *MP* | Stages of Production | Description |
|---|---|---|---|---|---|---|
| 1 | 1 | 20 | 20 | 20 | Increasing returns | $MP > AP$ |
| 1 | 2 | 50 | 25 | 30 | | |
| 1 | 3 | 90 | 30 | 40 | | |
| 1 | 4 | 120 | 30 | 30 | | $MP = AP$ |
| 1 | 5 | 140 | 28 | 20 | Diminishing returns | $MP = 0$ |
| 1 | 6 | 150 | 25 | 10 | | |
| 1 | 7 | 150 | 21.3 | 0 | | |
| 1 | 8 | 140 | 17.5 | –10 | Negative returns | $MP$ = –ve |
| 1 | 9 | 120 | 13.3 | –20 | | |
| 1 | 10 | 90 | 9 | –30 | | |

Table 12.1 reflects that when 3 units of labour are applied to units of fixed factor, total product increases at an increasing rate. Beyond the third unit, total product increases but at diminishing rate. Further, the analysis of marginal product of labour reflects that it initially rises but beyond the use of three units of labour, it starts diminishing. Throughout the analysis, *AP* continues to rise and is maximum at the end of this stage. This stage is known as the stage of increasing returns to factor.

The next stage is the stage of diminishing returns. Throughout this stage, *TP* continues to rise and attains its maximum at 150 units. The employment of seven units of labour does not add anything to the total production of wheat. Hence, the marginal product of labour has fallen to zero and *AP* starts falling from 25 units to 21 units.

Beyond the use of seven units of labour, total product declines in absolute terms from 150 units to 140 units and marginal product of labour takes a negative value. Regarding the average product of labour, it rises up to the use of the third unit of labour and beyond that it is falling throughout. Thus, the employment of eighteenth unit of variable factor results in operation of the stage of negative returns.

## Three Stages of the Law of Variable Proportions: Diagrammatic Representation

These stages are illustrated in the Figure 12.2 where labour is measured on the *X*-axis and output on the *Y*-axis.

**Stage 1. Stage of Increasing Returns to Factor**

- In this stage, total product increases at an increasing rate up to a point F. This is because the application to variable factors to a given quantity of fixed factors increases the efficiency of fixed factors.
- After point *F*, the *TP* increases but at diminishing rate.
- The point *F* is known as the point of inflexion. It is the point where the curvature of *TP* curve changes and it starts increasing at diminishing rate rather than rising at increasing rate.
- Vertically downwards towards the *X*-axis, *MP* is maximum at this point.
- When *TP* is rising at increasing rate, *MP* rises and when *TP* rises at diminishing rate, then MP falls.
- In this stage, *AP* increases throughout.
- The stage comes to an end where:
  (a) *TP* is rising at diminishing rate,
  (b) *MP* is declining but positive, and
  (c) *AP* reaches the point of maximum.

**Stage 2. Stage of Diminishing Returns**

- In this stage, total product continues to increase but at a diminishing rate. This is because the fixed factor becomes inadequate as compared to the quantity of the variable factors.

- Both the marginal product and average product of labour are diminishing but are positive.
- The stage comes to an end where:
  (a) *TP* reaches its maximum at point *H*.
  (b) Marginal product of labour is zero at point *M* which corresponds to the maximum point *H* of the total product curve (*TP*).
  (c) Average product of labour is still declining but is positive.
- This stage is most relevant from producer's point of view because the firm will seek to produce in this range.

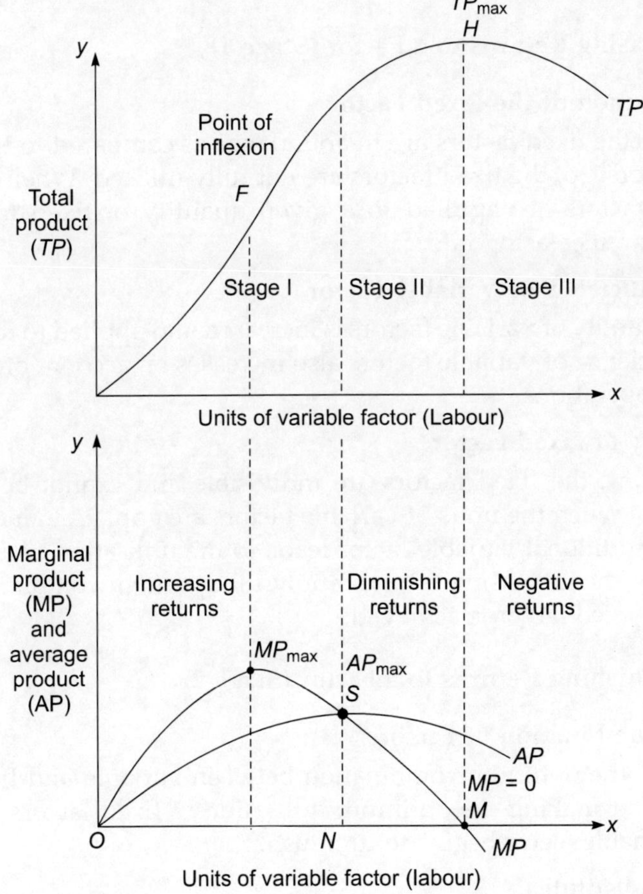


**Fig. 12.2** Three Stages of Production under the Law of Variable Proportions

### Stage 3. Stage of Negative Returns

- In this stage, total product declines in absolute terms and hence, slopes downwards. This is because the proportion of variable factor (labour) is too much as compared to the quantity of fixed factors. Due to this, the variable factors are not utilised efficiently.

- Marginal product becomes negative and lies below *X*-axis.
- *AP* continues to fall but is positive.

### 12.7.5 Reasons of Operation/Causes of Operation of Law of Variable Proportions

The reasons of operation of the law of variable proportion relate to each stage of the production process. Thus, various reasons for 3 phases of the law of variable proportions are as follows.

**Reasons for Increasing Returns to a Factor (Stage 1)**

1. **Better Utilization of the Fixed Factor**

   In this stage, the fixed factors are in abundance as compared to the quantity of variable factors. So, the fixed factors are not fully utilised. When the quantities of variable factors are applied to a given quantity of fixed factors, output increases at an increasing rate.

2. **Increased Efficiency of Variable Factor**

   When the quantity of variable factors is increased and applied to the fixed factor, then the efficiency of variable factors also increases on account of specialisation in business operations.

3. **Indivisibility of Fixed Factor**

   Under this law, the fixed factors are indivisible and cannot be divided into smaller units. When the units of variable factors are applied to indivisible fixed factor, then additional variable factor leads to the utilisation of available fixed factors. Thus, the increasing returns apply till optimum combination between variable and fixed factor is achieved.

**Reasons for Diminishing Returns to a Factor (Stage 2)**

1. **Optimum Combination of Factors**

   In this stage, the optimum combination between variable and fixed factors is achieved. After making the optimum utilisation of fixed factors, the marginal return of variable factor begins to diminish.

2. **Imperfect Substitutes**

   Imperfect substitutability is one of the reasons of diminishing returns to a factor. It means that the fixed and variable factors are imperfect substitutes of one another. In other words, if we want to replace labour in place of capital or capital in place of labour that can be done but till a particular limit. Beyond a specific limit, they cannot be substituted which leads to diminishing returns.

**Reasons for Negative Returns to a Factor (Stage 3)**

1. **Limitation of Fixed Factor**

   In this stage, the units of fixed factors have become scarce as compared to the units of variable factors and their units cannot be increased in short run which leads to the operation of negative returns to a factor.

2. **Poor Coordination between Variable and Fixed Factors**

   The numbers of variable factor have become too large in relation to fixed factors that the coordination issues arises between variable and fixed factor. As a result, *TP* falls in absolute terms instead of rising and *MP* becomes negative.

3. **Decrease in Efficiency of Variable Factor**

   In this stage, the units of variable factor become so large that the advantages of specialization and division of labour start diminishing. As a result the diminishing returns to variable factors occur.

### 12.7.6 Relevant Stage of Operations

A rational producer likes to operate in stage II of labour. This is on account of the following reasons:

- **Reasons for not operating in Stage III:**

  **Reason 1:** In Stage III, *MP* is negative. It means that more output can be produced by using less of labour.

  **Reason 2:** Variable factors have become too excessive in relation to fixed factors that they obstruct each other. It leads to poor coordination between variable and fixed factors.

  **Reason 3:** With the continuous increase in units of variable factor, the advantages of specialization and division of labour start diminishing. It results in inefficiency of variable factor.

  Therefore the producer would not like to operate in this stage.

- **Reasons for not operating in Stage I:**

  **Reason 1:** In stage I, *MP* of land is negative as it corresponds to the third stage III of capital.

  **Reason 2:** Fixed factors have become too excessive in relation to variable factors that they are not being utilised properly.

### Producer's Preference for Stage II

**Reason 1:** *MP* of both factors is positive though declining.

**Reason 2:** Optimum combination of fixed and variable factors is attained as the variable factors are able to make optimum utilisation of fixed factors.

The producer will keep on employing the extra units of variable factors to the fixed factors till the extra revenue generated from sale of output is greater than the extra cost of hiring labour.

Now, the two concepts that require understanding are:

1. Extra revenue from sale of output
2. Extra cost of hiring labour

**1. Extra Revenue from Sale of Output**

It is known as marginal revenue productivity (*MRP*).

This is calculated by multiplying marginal product (*MP*) from employment of an additional unit of labour with marginal revenue (*MR*) from sale of extra output produced.

$$MRP = MR \times MP$$

**2. Extra Cost of Hiring Additional Units of Labour**

Increase in total cost ($\Delta TC$) as a result of employment of an additional unit of labour ($\Delta L$).

$$MCL = \frac{\Delta TC}{\Delta L}$$

Thus, the producer will employ the units of variable factors as long as $MRP > MCL$ and till $MRP = MCL$.

## Summary

- ✓ Production refers to the process in which the producer transforms inputs into outputs.
- ✓ The inputs in production process include land, labour, capital (including tools, equipment) and raw material, etc. The output here includes production of goods and generation of services.
- ✓ In production process, fixed as well as variable inputs are utilised.
  - Fixed inputs are the resources or inputs that remain fixed or constant up to certain level of output. Their supply is inelastic in the short run.
  - Variable inputs are the resources or inputs that change with the change in output. Their supply is elastic in the short run.
- ✓ In economics, the study of time period is done under the following heads: short run and long run.
  - Short run refers to the time period in which the quantity of at least one input is fixed or inelastic.

  - Long run refers to a time period in which the supply of all the inputs is variable or elastic.

- ✓ Production function refers to the mathematical relationship between the factor inputs and level of output. It establishes the functional relationship that explains the maximisation of output level using a given set of inputs (keeping the technology constant).
- ✓ The law of variable proportions states that as the producer employs units of only one factor input to a given quantity of fixed factors, the output first increases at increasing rate, then increases at diminishing rate, becomes maximum and eventually declines.
- ✓ There are three stages of production under the law of variable proportions:
  - Stage I: Increasing returns to variable factor
  - Stage II: Diminishing returns to variable factor
  - Stage III: Negative returns to variable factor
- ✓ Among the three stages, a rational producer likes to operate in stage II as here *MP* of both the factors is positive.
- ✓ The producer will keep on employing the extra units of variable factors to the fixed factors till the extra revenue generated from sale of output is greater than extra cost of hiring labour. He will stop the employment of additional factors where extra cost of hiring labour starts exceeding extra revenue generated from sale of output.

## Review Questions

1. Explain the law of variable proportions with assumptions and reasons. In which stage, a rational consumer would like to operate and why?
2. Write short notes on:
   (a) Point of inflexion
   (b) Short run and long run
   (c) Fixed and variable factors
   (d) Production function
3. How do total product, average product and marginal product change due to a change in the use of one input, keeping other inputs constant? Explain with the help of schedule and diagram.
4. Explain the relationship between *TP*, *AP* and *MP* of factor inputs with schedule and diagram.
5. Explain the law of variable proportions with the help of *TP* and *MP* curves.
6. Explain the likely behaviour of *TP* and *MP* when for increasing production only one input is increased while other inputs are kept constant.

7. Show the various stages of production through short-run production analysis. Explain using schedule and diagram.
8. What is law of variable proportions? Give the reasons of operation of the law.
9. Explain the law of returns to factor with *TP* and *MP* schedule.
10. Explain the law of non-proportional returns. What are the causes of change in the behaviour of *TP*, *AP* and *MP* curves.

# 13 CHAPTER

# Isoquant Approach and Long-Run Production Analysis

**LEARNING OBJECTIVES**

After going through this chapter, reader would be able to understand:

- ✓ The concept of isoquants, isoquant schedule and isoquant map.
- ✓ The attributes of isoquants in terms of properties of isoquants.
- ✓ The exceptional shapes of isoquants.
- ✓ The slope of isoquant in terms of marginal rate of technical substitution.
- ✓ The long-run production analysis as defined by the law of returns to scale.
- ✓ The least cost combination of factors with the help of isoquant analysis, iso cost line and the expansion path.
- ✓ The points of difference between returns to factor and returns to scale.

## 13.1 INTRODUCTION

In chapter 12, the economics of production was discussed in terms of general concepts such as production, factors of production, time period distinction, production function analysis, etc. However a major analysis that unfurls the dynamics related to short-run production function was discussed. Thus, the law of variable proportions was discussed. The law explains the theory of production when at least one of the factors is fixed. In this chapter, we move further and pave our way to the long-run production analysis. In long-run production analysis, we assume that all the factors of production become variable. This is on account of the fact that long run is the time period that is sufficient enough to acquire more of land, investment of more capital, employ more labour, etc. Thus, none of the factors is fixed in the long run. In order to explain the production analysis in the long run, the present chapter will discuss the operation and working of the law of returns to scale.

The chapter initially discusses the concept of isoquants, isoquant schedule and isoquant map. Further, the properties of isoquants and the exceptional shapes of isoquants have been discussed. Then we move on to the study of long-run production analysis in terms of the law of returns to scale. Thereafter, the least cost combination of factors with the help of isoquant analysis, isocost line and the expansion path have been discussed. In the last section, the areas of difference between returns to factor and returns to scale have been explained.

## 13.2 ISOQUANTS AND ISOQUANT MAP

### Isoquants

Isoquant is composed of two words: 'Iso' means 'equal' and 'quant' means 'quantity'. It is the diagrammatic representation of various combinations of two factor inputs (say labour and capital) that can produce the same output. It is also known as a production indifference curve.

Just as the indifference curve shows the diagrammatic representation of various combinations of two commodities that give the consumer the same amount of satisfaction, in the same manner an isoquant indicates the various combinations of two factors of production which give the producer the same level of output.

Table 13.1 shows a hypothetical isoquant schedule of a firm producing 100 units of a commodity. On the basis of the schedule, the isoquant takes the following form:

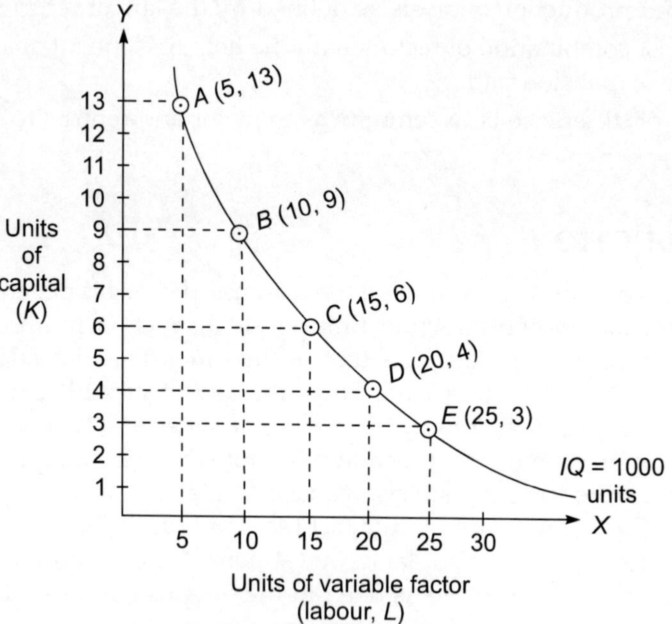


**Fig. 13.1** Isoquant Curve

## Isoquant Schedule

An isoquant schedule indicates the various combinations of two factors of production which give the producer the same level of output. This has been explained with the help of Table 13.1.

**TABLE 13.1** Isoquant Schedule

| Combination | Units of Labour | Units of Capital | Total Output (in units) |
|---|---|---|---|
| *A* | 5 | 13 | 1000 |
| *B* | 10 | 9 | 1000 |
| *C* | 15 | 6 | 1000 |
| *D* | 20 | 4 | 1000 |
| *E* | 25 | 3 | 1000 |

Table 13.1 reflects that labour units are measured along the *X*-axis and capital units on the *Y*-axis. The combination *A* reflects that the producer is employing 5 units of labour and 13 units of capital in order to produce 1000 units of a product. In similar manner, the same level of output (1000 units) is produced using 10 units of labour and 9 units of capital. Moving further, combination *C* reflects 15 units of labour and 6 units of capital; combination *D* is combination of 20 units of labour and 4 units of capital; and combination *E* shows 25 units of labour and 3 units of capital to yield the same output of 1000 units. By joining all these combinations, we get an isoquant curve.

## Isoquant Map

An isoquant map is the family or a set of a number of isoquant representing different amounts of output. Higher the isoquant, higher the level of output produced by the producer. This has been shown in Figure 13.2.

In Figure 13.2, the curves, $IQ_1$, $IQ_2$, $IQ_3$, $IQ_4$, $IQ_5$ collectively show an isoquant map. The analysis of above isoquant map is as follows:

$IQ_1$ yields 1000 units of product
$IQ_2$, yields 2000 units of product
$IQ_3$, yields 3000 units of product
$IQ_4$, yields 4000 units of product
$IQ_5$, yields 5000 units of product

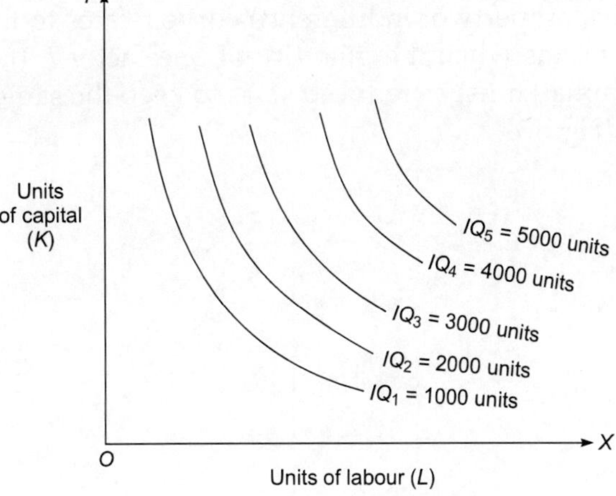


**Fig. 13.2** Isoquant Map

Each combination on same isoquant reflects same level of output whereas a higher isoquant reflects the higher level of output that can be produced using different combinations of the two factors.

## 13.3 PROPERTIES OF ISOQUANTS

Properties of Isoquants (IQs) are similar to those of indifference curves. These have been mentioned in Fig. 13.3 as:

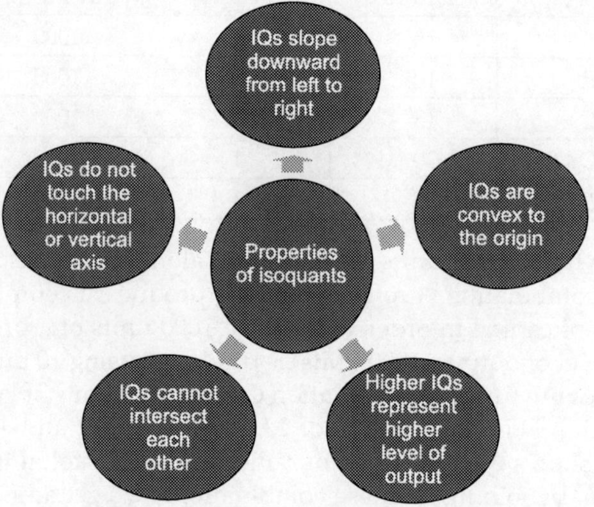


**Fig. 13.3** Properties of Isoquants

### 1. Isoquants are Downward Sloping from Left to the Right

This property of indifference curve relates to the negatively slope of isoquant curve. It means when the quantity of one factor *L* (labour) is increased, the quantity of *K* (capital) must be reduced so as to keep the same level of output. This has been shown in Fig. 13.4.

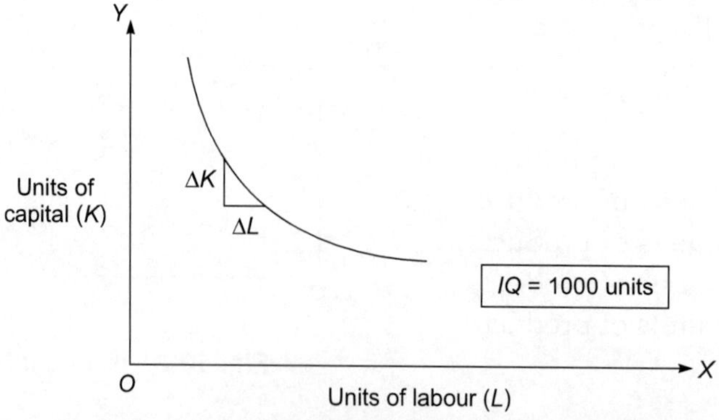


**Fig. 13.4** IQs Slope Downward from Left to Right

Figure 13.4 depicts that an isoquant (*IQ*) is negatively sloped curve. This curve shows that as the amount of labour is increased, the units of capital (*K*) have to be reduced so that level of output of 1000 units remains constant.

## 2. Each Isoquant is Convex to the Origin

The convexity of isoquant curve is attributed to the marginal rate of technical substitution. It means that as the producer employs more and more units of labour in order to produce a given level of output, some units of capital are to be sacrificed. However, this rate of sacrifice is at diminishing rate. Thus, as a producer gains more and more units of labour smaller and smaller units of capital for additional units of labour are sacrificed. This leads to convexity of isoquant curve. This has been shown in Figure 13.5.

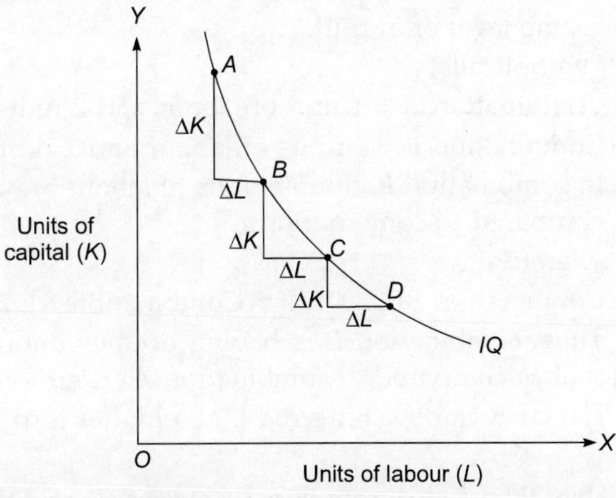


**Fig. 13.5** IQs are Convex to the Origin

## 3. Higher Isoquant Represents a Higher Output Level

Another property of isoquant is that an isoquant that appears on the right represents a higher output level. It is on account of the reason that the higher isoquant will either have more units of one or both the factors of production. This is clearly evident from the following diagram:

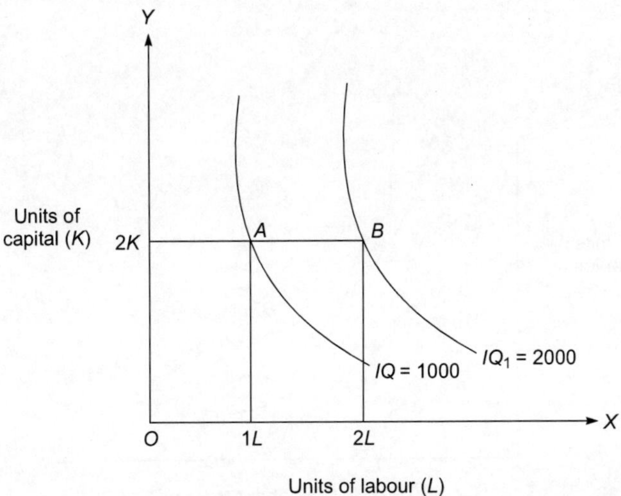


**Fig. 13.6** Higher *IQ* Represents a Higher Output Level

Figure 13.6 can be interpreted in the following manner:

At *IQ*

Combination *A* represents 1 unit of labour and 2 units of capital that produces the same level of output.

At $IQ_1$

Combination *B* represents 2 units of labour and 2 units of capital that produces the same level of output.

Symbolically,

Combination $A$ = 1 unit of labour and 2 units of capital

Combination $B$ = 2 units of labour and 2 units of capital

In combination *B*, double units of labour are used and the same amount of capital as compared to combination *A*.

Therefore,

Combination $B(2L + 2K) >$ Combination $A(1L + 2K)$

Thus, combination *B* is having double amount of labour, though the amount of capital as compared to combination *A*. Therefore, it will yield a higher output.

Hence, it can be conferred that a higher isoquant shows a higher level of output.

## 4. No Two Isoquants can Intersect Each Other

The two isoquants never intersect with each other. This property can be proved by contradiction.

In Fig. 13.7, let us suppose two isoquants $IQ_1$ and $IQ_2$ cut each other.

On the isoquant $IQ_2$

Combination $A$ = Combination C (both lie on same indifference curve).

On the isoquant $IQ_1$,

Combination $B$ = Combination C (both lie on same indifference curve).

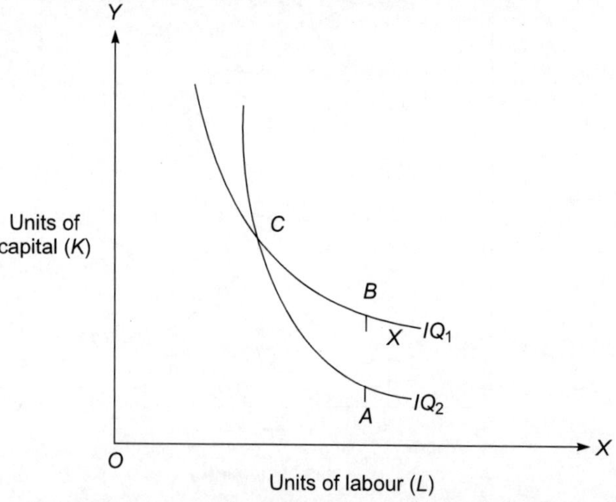


**Fig. 13.7** IQs Cannot Intersect Each Other

Thus,

$$\text{Combination } A = \text{Combination } C$$
$$\text{Combination } B = \text{Combination } C$$

It follows from the above that

$$\text{Combination } A = \text{Combination } B$$

But this is not true and Combination $B$ > Combination $A$ (because it employs more units of capital but same units of labour as combination $B$ which results in higher output).

Thus, the supposition that two isoquants intersect with each other is not correct and leads to absurd conclusions.

## 5. Isoquants do not Touch the Horizontal or Vertical Axis

No isoquant can touch either axis. This property can be understood with the help of following two cases.

**(a) If an isoquant touches *X*-axis (Fig. 13.8)**

It means that the product is being produced with the help of labour alone without using capital. This is absurd as the concept of isoquants means that specific combination of both the factors of production are employed in order to produce output. To presume that the entire output is produced using units of labour and no capital is something not consistent with the meaning of isoquant.

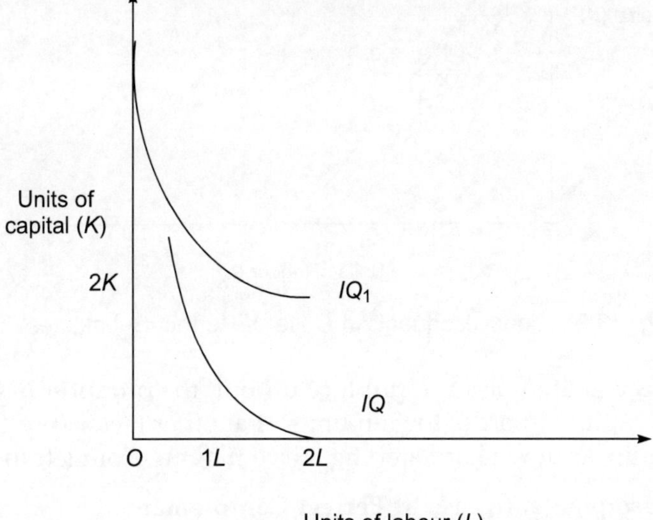


**Fig. 13.8** IQs do not Touch the Horizontal or Vertical Axis

**(b) If an isoquant touches *Y*-axis (Fig. 13.8)**

It means that the product is being produced with the help of capital alone without using labour. However, the concept of isoquants means that a specific combination of both the factors of production is employed in order to produce output. Thus, Isoquants can never touch *Y*-axis.

In the above diagram, the *IQ* is touching *X*-axis and $IQ_1$ is touching *Y*-axis indicating no use of capital and labour respectively. This is contrary to the concept of isoquants. Thus, *IQ* and $lQ_1$ cannot be isoquants, as shown in Figure 13.8.

## 13.4 EXCEPTIONS TO NORMAL SHAPE OF ISOQUANTS

**1. Linear Isoquant: In case of Perfect Substitutes**

These are the isoquants for perfect substitute factors. It means that the factors that have perfect and unlimited substitutability. In this case the factors can be used in place of each other. These reflect that one unit of labour is equally good as one unit of capital. These are downward sloping curves linear curves and move from left to right. In this case MRTS remains constant. This has been shown in Fig. 13.9.

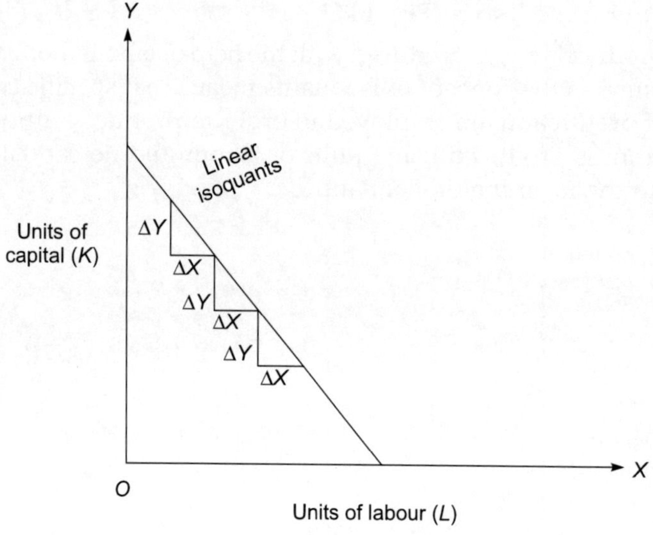


**Fig. 13.9** Linear Isoquant: In Case of Perfect Substitutes

Figure 13.9 reflects that in order to produce output, the producer has to lose units of one factor (say, capital) in order to gain units of another factor (say, labour). Thus, isoquant will be a linear downward sloping curve moving from left to right.

**2. Input-Output Isoquants: In case of Perfect Complements**

These are the isoquants for perfect complementary products. It means that the factors are perfectly complemented to each other. Thus, substitutability between factors is zero. They are used jointly and in a fixed proportion. To increase output, both factors are to be increased holding the proportion constant. In this case, the shape of isoquant is *L*-shaped.

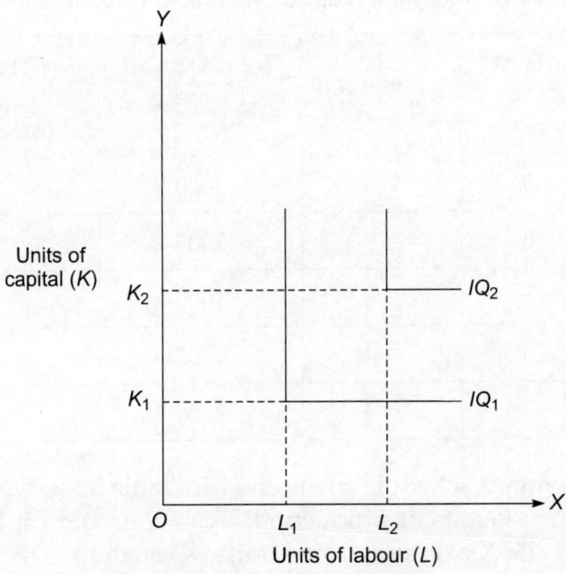


**Fig. 13.10** Input-Output Isoquant: In Case of Perfect Complements

Figure 13.10 reflects that in order to produce output the producer has to increase units of labour and capital in same proportion. If units of labour are $OL_1$ and units of capital are $OK_1$, then the output is represented by the isoquant $IQ_1$. If the higher level of output is to be achieved, the proportion of both factors must be increased. Thus, isoquant will move from $IQ_1$ to $IQ_2$ when both the factors are increased in same proportion. Hence, isoquant will be *L*-shaped in this case.

## 13.5 MARGINAL RATE OF TECHNICAL SUBSTITUTION

It refers to the rate at which the units of one factor (say, capital) are substituted in order to gain one additional unit of another factor (say, labour) so that the level of output remains same. In other words, marginal rate substitution means the ratio of exchange between two factor inputs (say, labour and capital) in order to produce same level of output.

It can be represented as:

$$MRTS_{LK} = \text{Loss of } K/\text{Gain of } L = \text{Change in } K/\text{Change in } L = \Delta K/\Delta L$$

and

$$MRTS_{KL} = \text{Loss of } L/\text{Gain of } K = \text{Change in } L/\text{Change in } K = \Delta L/\Delta K$$

It can be understood with the help of the following isoquant schedule given in Table 13.2.

**TABLE 13.2** Marginal Rate of Technical Substitution *LK*

| Combination | Units of Labour | Units of Capital | Total Output (in units) | *MRTS* of Labour for Capital ($MRTS_{LK} = \Delta K/\Delta L$) |
|---|---|---|---|---|
| *A* | 5 | 13 | 1000 | – |
| *B* | 10 | 9 | 1000 | 4:5 |
| *C* | 15 | 6 | 1000 | 3:5 |
| *D* | 20 | 4 | 1000 | 2:5 |
| *E* | 25 | 3 | 1000 | 1:5 |

Considering the isoquant schedule mentioned in Table 13.2, we can see that the producer is utilising two factors of production say, labour and capital. Labour units ($L$) are measured along the $X$-axis and capital units ($K$) on the $Y$-axis. The combination $A$ reflects that the producer is employing 5 units of labour and 13 units of capital in order to produce 1000 units of a product. In similar manner, the same level of output (1000 units) is produced using 10 units of labour and 9 units of capital as reflected by combination $B$. Here, the producer foregoes 4 units of capital in order to gain 5 units of labour in order to maintain the same level of output. Thus, $MRTS_{LK}$ is 4:5.

Moving further, combination $C$ reflects 15 units of labour and 6 units of capital. He gets 5 units of labour and for that he is ready to forego 3 units of labour. Here, $MRTS_{LK}$ is 3:5. Combination $D$ is combination of 20 units of labour and 4 units of capital; thus $MRTS_{LK}$ is 2:5 and combination $E$, 25 units of labour and 3 units of capital to yield the same output of 1000 units. Therefore, $MRTS_{LK}$ is 1:5.

This reflects that marginal rate of technical substitution is diminishing as the producer is less prepared to forgo units of a factor when it is scarce as compared to the situation when it was available in plenty.

## 13.6 LAW OF RETURNS TO SCALE LONG-RUN PRODUCTION ANALYSIS

It refers to the long-run production law that studies the behaviour of output when all the factors of production are subject to change. In the long run, all factors are variable. The production can thus be increased by increasing all inputs in the production process. No factors remain fixed in the long run. Thus, a firm can change its scale of operations. It means that all the factor inputs are increased in the same proportion, thus the factor proportion remains same.

Under this law, the input and output behaviour exhibits three possibilities:

- Total output increases more than proportionately when the inputs rise
- Total output increases proportionately as the inputs rise
- Total output increases less than proportionately as the inputs rise

Corresponding to this input-output behaviour, there are three cases of returns to scale. These are shown in Fig. 13.11.

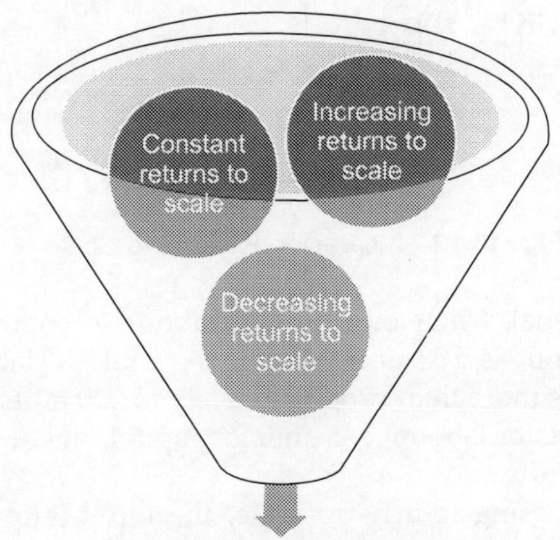


**Fig. 13.11** Three Cases of Returns to Scale

**1. Increasing Returns to Scale**

When as a result of change in inputs, the output of a firm increases more than proportionately, the increasing returns to scale is said to exist.

In other words, if the amount of inputs is doubled and the output increases by more than double, it is said to be an increasing returns to scale. It can be understood with the help of Table 13.3.

**TABLE 13.3** Increasing Returns to Scale

| Units of Labour | Units of Capital | Factor Proportion | Total Product (in units) |
|---|---|---|---|
| 1 | 1 | 1:1 | 100 |
| 2 | 2 | 2:2 | 220 |
| 3 | 3 | 3:3 | 360 |

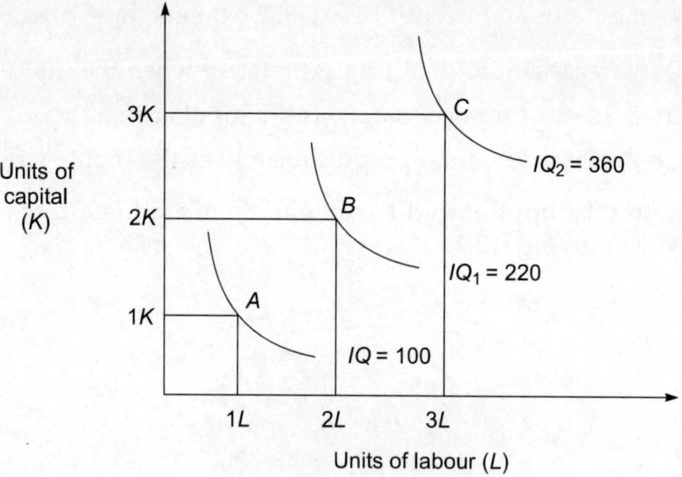


**Fig. 13.12** Increasing Returns to Scale

Figure 13.12 shows that when one unit of labour is combined with one unit of capital, the total output is 100 units. When the units of labour and capital are doubled, the output rises more than proportionately to 220 units. Similarly, when the producer employs 3 units of labour to 3 units of capital, the output rises more than proportionately to 360 units.

Thus, in case of increasing returns to scale, the input-output relationship is as follows:

100 units of output require $1L + 1K$; represented by $IQ$
220 units of output require $2L + 2K$; represented by $IQ_1$
360 units of output require $3L + 3K$; represented by $IQ_2$

**2. Constant Returns to Scale**

When as a result of change in inputs, the output of a firm increases proportionately, the constant returns to scale is said to exist.

In other words, if the amount of inputs is doubled and the output is also doubled, constant returns to scale is said to exist. It can be understood with the help of Table 13.4.

**TABLE 13.4** Constant Returns to Scale

| Units of Labour | Units of Capital | Factor Proportion | Total Product (in units) |
|---|---|---|---|
| 1 | 1 | 1:1 | 100 |
| 2 | 2 | 2:2 | 200 |
| 3 | 3 | 3:3 | 300 |

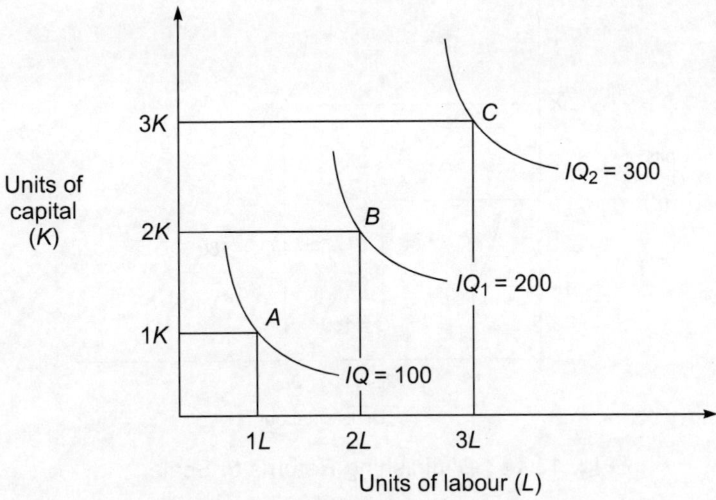


**Fig. 13.13** Constant Returns to Scale

Figure 13.13 shows that when one unit of labour is combined with one unit of capital, the total output is 100 units *IQ*. When the units of labour and capital are doubled, the output doubles to 200 units. Similarly, when the producers employ 3 units of labour to 3 units of capital, the output rises to 300 units.

Thus in case of constant returns to scale, the input-output relationship is as follows:

100 units of output require $1L + 1K$; represented by $IQ$

200 units of output require $2L + 2K$; represented by $IQ_1$

300 units of output require $3L + 3K$; represented by $IQ_2$

### 3. Diminishing Returns to Scale

When as a result of change in inputs, the output of a firm increases less than proportionately, the increasing returns to scale is said to exist.

In other words, if the amount of inputs are doubled and the output increases by less than double, it is said to be an increasing returns to scale. It can be understood with the help of Table 13.5.

**TABLE 13.5** Diminishing Returns to Scale

| Units of Labour | Units of Capital | Factor Proportion | Total Product (in units) |
|---|---|---|---|
| 1 | 1 | 1:1 | 100 |
| 2 | 2 | 2:2 | 180 |
| 3 | 3 | 3:3 | 240 |

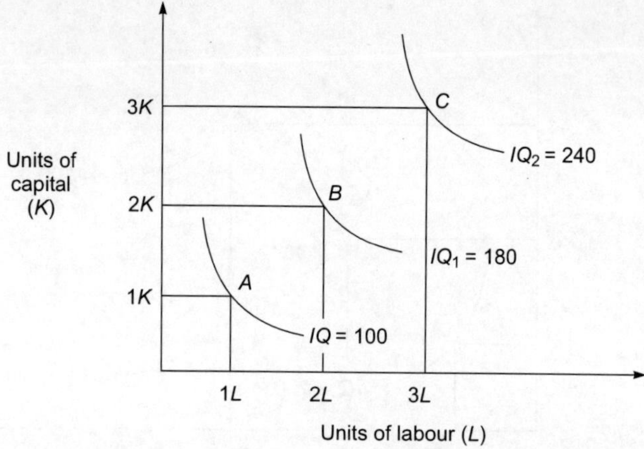


**Fig. 13.14** Diminishing Returns to Scale

Figure 13.14 shows that when one unit of labour is combined with one unit of capital, the total output is 100 units. When the units of labour and capital are doubled, the output increases to 180 units which is less than proportionate to the change in input. Similarly, when the producer employs 3 units of labour to 3 units of capital, the output rises to 240 units.

Thus in case of diminishing returns to scale, the input-output relationship is as follows:

100 units of output require $1L + 1K$; represented by $IQ$

180 units of output require $2L + 2K$; represented by $IQ_1$

240 units of output require $3L + 3K$; represented by $IQ_2$

## Causes of Increasing Returns to Scale

1. **High degree of specialisation and division of labour:** With the expansion in the scale of production, there is a scope of division of labour which requires the division of entire task into small tasks of similar nature. This leads to specialisation and efficiency of operations. This results in increasing returns to scale of business operations.
2. **Internal economies of production:** As the scale changes, the firms may install sophisticated machines, get easy access to finances, borrow money cheaply, procure the services of more efficient manager and workers, etc. All these economies result in increasing the returns to scale.
3. **External economies:** With the expansion of the industry and concentration of firms at one place the following benefits are available:
   - Availability of skilled labour
   - Access to credit facility
   - Transport facilities

   Thus these external economies are also the cause of increasing returns to scale.

### Causes of Constant Returns to Scale

1. It is said to occur when internal economies enjoyed by a firm are neutralised by internal diseconomies in a manner that output increases in the same proportion as increase in input.
2. Another reason is the balancing of external economies and external diseconomies. Thus, the returns to scale are constant.

**Causes of Decreasing Returns to Scale (DRS):** All these factors tend to raise costs and the expansion of the firms leads to diminishing returns to scale so that doubling the scale would not lead to doubling the output.

1. **Imperfect factor substitutability:** The factors of production can be used in place of each other to a certain limit. After reaching a particular level the factor units cannot be used in place of each other. Thus, the DRS rise in the production process.
2. **Unhealthy management and organization:** After a level, with the increase in scale of operations, the following problems arise:
   - The problem of coordination and cooperation
   - Low motivation of employees
   - Unwanted delay in decision making

As a result, the DRS rise in the production process.

## 13.7 PRODUCER'S EQUILIBRIUM/ LEAST COST COMBINATION OF FACTORS/CHOICE OF OPTIMAL FACTOR COMBINATION

It is one of the important aspects of the theory of production. It helps in analysing those combinations of factors that can help in maximising profit given the cost constraint. The least cost combination in producer's equilibrium refers to a firm producing the maximum possible output from a given cost and producing a given level of output with the minimum cost.

In this case, the producer faces two situations:

Situation 1: To minimise cost for a given output
Situation 2: To maximise output for a given cost.

### *Assumptions*

The producer's equilibrium is based on the following assumptions:

1. The firm aims at profit maximisation.
2. There are only two factors of production, namely, labour and capital.
3. All units of labour and capital are homogeneous.
4. The prices of labour ($w$) and that of capital ($r$) are given and constant.

5. The cost outlay is given.
6. The firm produces a single product.
7. There is perfect competition in the factor market.

## Condition of Equilibrium

It occurs at a point where the isocost line is tangent to the isoquant curve. In this regard, there are two conditions for the equilibrium of the firm.

### 1. The First Order Condition

It means that the isocost line is tangent to the isoquant curve. In other words, the slope of the isocost line must equal to the slope of the isoquant curve.

Slope of isoquant = Slope of isocost line

$$MTRS_{LK} = \frac{P_L}{P_K}$$

$$\frac{\Delta K}{\Delta L} = \frac{P_L}{P_K}$$

### 2. The Second Order Condition

It means that at the point of tangency, the isoquant curve must be convex to the origin. This requires the analysis of two major aspects:

1. Isoquant curve
2. Isocost curve

1. **Isoquant Curve:** It is the diagrammatical representation of various combinations of two factors of production which give the producer the same level of output.
2. **Isocost Lines:** These are the diagrammatic representations of different combinations of two factor inputs that a firm can buy given the money and the prices of each factor input. These curves are also known as outlay lines or factor-cost lines, etc.

The producer's equilibrium is attained where the isocost line is tangent to an isoquant with the least cost combination of the two factors for producing a given output. However, the specific analysis of producer's equilibrium relates to the following situations.

### Situation 1: To Minimise Cost for a given Output

Figure 13.15 reflects that there are three isocost lines representing the different combinations of two factor inputs (say, labour and capital) that a firm can buy given the money and the prices of each factor input. These isocost lines are *EF*, *GH* and *KP*. Let *IQ* be the isoquant that reflects the production of 200 units. The analysis is as follows:

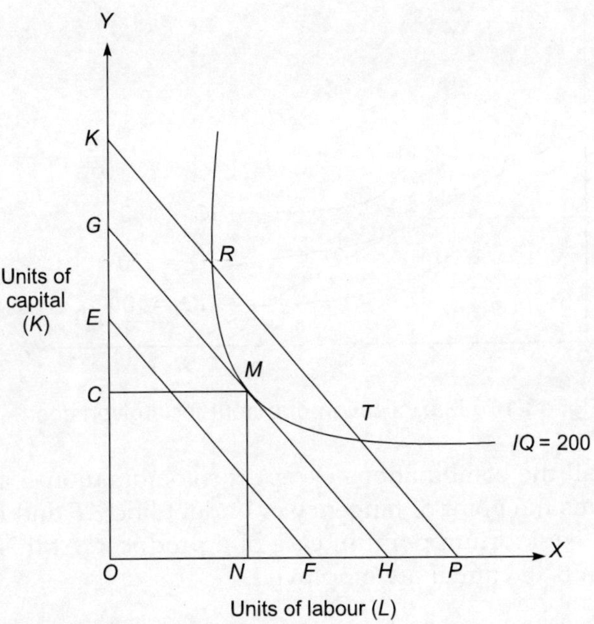


**Fig. 13.15** Minimisation of cost for a given output

### At budget line *EF*

Any point within or on *EF* represents the factor combination that is affordable to the producer but represents less output than 200 units.

### At budget line *KP*

*R* and *T* are the points that produce an output of 200 units but is unaffordable from producer's point of view.

### At budget line *GH*

Budget line *GH* is tangent to the isoquant *IQ*. *M* is the point of tangency where producer's equilibrium is attained. Thus, point *M* is the point of least cost combination where *OL* units of labour and *OC* units of capital are employed.

## Situation 2: To Maximise Output for a Given Cost

In Figure 13.16, it can be seen that the isoquants are represented by $IQ_1$, $IQ_2$, $IQ_3$ representing the output level at 100 units, 150 units and 180 units, respectively. Let *AB* be the iso cost lines representing outlay of Rs 300. The analysis is as follows:

At isoquant $IQ_1$, the output level is 100 units, however the producer can produce more output than 100 units, so would not like to operate on $IQ_1$.

At Isoquant $IQ_3$, the output level is 180 units, which represents more output but is unaffordable from producer's point of view.

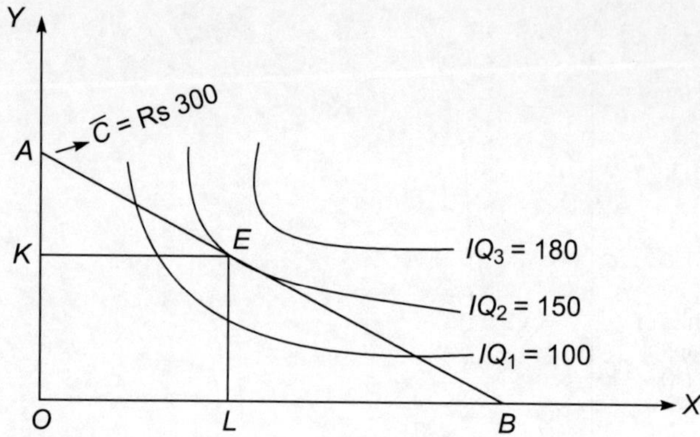


**Fig. 13.16** Maximisation of output for a given cost

At isoquant $IQ_2$, all the combinations except the combination *E* are unaffordable. The point *E* represents the point of tangency of budget line *AB* and the isoquant $IQ_2$. Thus, point *E* is the equilibrium point in case of a producer. At this point, *OL* units of labour and *OK* units of capital are employed.

## 13.8 EXPANSION PATH

In the long run, all the factors of production are variable. The firm plans to the business operations such that costs are minimised and the revenue is maximised. Thus, the motive is to achieve maximum profits. In order to achieve the profit maximisation objective, firm changes the factors proportions and its total outlay, while relative factor prices remain constant. In this direction, the concept of expansion path has been introduced.

### Meaning of Expansion Path

It is the locus of different points of firm's equilibrium when it changes its total outlay and moves to higher isoquant curves, relative factor prices remaining constant. Thus, the relative wage rate (*w*) and rate of interest of capital (*r*) remain same. The optimal expansion path is determined by the points of tangency of successive isocost lines and successive isoquants.

#### *Assumptions*

1. There are two factors of production, labour (*L*) and capital (*K*).
2. Both labour and capital are variable as it is long run.
3. The units of factors of production are homogeneous.
4. The price of labour (*w*) and price of capital (*k*) is constant.

### *Explanation*

Now, the firm tries to either maximise its profits or to have the least cost combination. For this it utilises different isocost lines and isoquant curves. Isocost lines reflect the cost structure while isoquant represents the level of output. In order to find expansion path, the point of tangency between an isocost line and an isoquant curve is ascertained. The determination of expansion path can be understood with the help of Fig. 13.17.

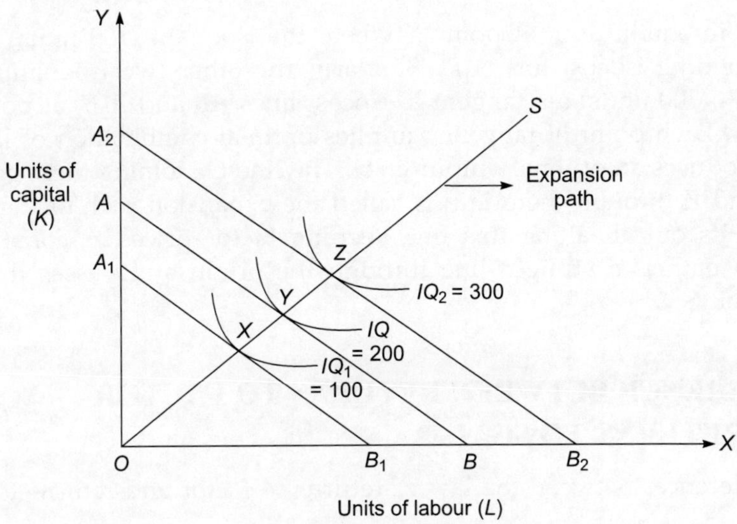


**Fig. 13.17** Expansion Path

This is explained with the help of table given below:

**TABLE 13.6** Expansion Path

| Isocost Lines | Isoquants | Output Levels | Equilibrium Point | Expansion Path |
|---|---|---|---|---|
| $A_2B_2$ | $IQ_2$ | 300 units | *Z* | *OS* |
| *AB* | *IQ* | 200 units | *Y* | |
| $A_1B_1$ | $IQ_1$ | 100 units | X | |

## Isocost Line

There are three isocost lines namely: $A_2B_2$, *AB* and $A_1B_1$. The isocost line $A_2B_2$ shows higher total outlay than the line *AB*. Similarly, *AB* has higher total outlay than the line $A_1B_1$. These isocost lines are parallel indicating the constancy of factor prices. This can be written as:

$$A_2B_2 > AB > A_1B_1$$

## Isoquants

There are three isoquants, namely: $IQ_2$, $IQ$ and $IQ_1$. They represent the following output levels:

$$IQ_2 = 300 \text{ units}$$
$$IQ = 200 \text{ units}$$
$$IQ_1 = 100 \text{ units}$$

The firm is in equilibrium at point $X$ where the isoquant (100 units) is tangent to its corresponding isocost line $A_1B_1$. Similarly, the other two isoquants, $AB$ (200 units) and $A_2B_2$ (300 units) are tangent to isocost lines $AB$ and $A_2B_2$ at points $Y$ and $Z$, respectively. Each point of tangency implies optimal combination of labour and capital that produces an optimal output level. The line $OS$ joining these equilibrium points $X$, $Y$ and $Z$ through the origin is called the expansion path of the firm. The firm expands its output along this line keeping factor prices as constant. Thus, the expansion path is a straight line through the origin and passes through the equilibrium points.

## 13.9 DIFFERENCE BETWEEN RETURNS TO FACTOR AND RETURNS TO SCALE

The major differences between the law of returns to factor and returns to scale are listed in Table 13.7.

**TABLE 13.7** Comparison between Returns to Factor and Returns to Scale

| Area of Difference | Law of Returns to Factor | Law of Return to Scale |
|---|---|---|
| Time period | It relates to short-run phenomenon. | It relates to long run. |
| Variability of factors | At least one of the factors is fixed. | All factors vary and none of the factors is fixed. |
| Factor proportion | The factor proportion varies | Factor proportion does not vary. |
| Three stages | The three stages are:<br>• Increasing returns to factor<br>• Diminishing returns to factor<br>• Negative returns to factor | The three possibilities are:<br>• Increasing returns to scale<br>• Constant returns to scale<br>• Negative returns to scale |
| Input-output relationship | It tells the relationship between variable factors and output. | It tells the relationship between all factors of production and output. |

## Summary

✓ An isoquant is the diagrammatic representation of various combinations of two factor inputs that can produce the same output. It is also known as a production indifference curve.

✓ An isoquant schedule indicates the various combinations of two factors of production which give the producer the same level of output.

✓ An isoquant map is the family or a set of a number of isoquant representing different amounts of output.

✓ The properties of isoquants are as follows:
- IQs slope downward from left to right
- IQs are convex to the origin
- Higher IQ represents higher level of output
- IQs cannot intersect each other
- IQs do not touch the horizontal or vertical axis

✓ There are two exceptions to the normal shape of isoquants:
- Linear isoquant: In case of perfect substitutes
- Input-output isoquants: In case of perfect complements

✓ Marginal rate of technical substitution refers to the rate at which the units of one factor (say capital) are substituted in order to gain one additional unit of another factor (say, labour) so that the level of output remains same. It is the slope of isoquant curve.

✓ The law of returns to scale is a production law applicable in the long run. Under this law, the input and output behaviour exhibits three possibilities:
- Total output increases more than proportionately when the inputs rise.
- Total output increases proportionately as the inputs rise.
- Total output increases less than proportionately as the inputs rise.

Corresponding to each possibility, the law is subdivided among the following:
- Increasing returns to scale
- Constant returns to scale
- Decreasing returns to scale.

✓ The least cost combination in producer's equilibrium refers to a firm producing the maximum possible output from a given cost and producing a given level of output with the minimum cost.

✓ There are two conditions of producer's equilibrium:
- The first order condition means that the isocost line is tangent to the isoquant curve.
- The second order condition means that at the point of tangency, the isoquant curve must he convex to the origin.

✓ It is the locus of different points of a firm's equilibrium when it changes its total outlay and moves to higher isoquant curves, relative factor prices remaining constant.

## Review Questions

1. What are isoquants? Explain the concept by elucidating the properties.
2. Use isoproduct and isocost lines to explain the following:
   (a) Minimisation of cost for a given output
   (b) Maximisation of output for a given cost.
3. Explain the law of returns to scale with the help of diagram.
4. Explain increasing constant and diminishing returns to scale with the help of isoquant analysis.
5. Explain the properties of isoquant curves. Also explain the cases where the normal shape of isoquants does not apply.
6. Explain diagrammatically the concept of expansion path.
7. Explain using isoquants, how a producer chooses the optimal combination of factors.
8. Elucidate how the least cost combination of factors would be attained in production analysis?
9. Explain diagrammatically how a producer will choose optimal factor combination given the prices of factor inputs.
10. Explain the conditions of producer's equilibrium with assumptions. Also explain how a producer will minimise cost for a given level of output.
11. Explain the difference between law of returns to factor and law of returns to factor.
12. Write short notes on the following:
    (a) Isoquant map
    (b) Isocost lines
    (c) Exceptional shapes of isoquant curves.

# 14 Chapter

# Introduction to Theory of Costs

**Learning Objectives**

After going through this chapter, reader would be able to understand:

- ✓ The concept of cost and various types of costs that are involved in production and distribution of the commodities.
- ✓ The concept of cost function.
- ✓ Short-run and long-run cost curves.
- ✓ Economies and diseconomies of scale.

## 14.1 INTRODUCTION

The main aim of every business entity is to maximize the level of profits. The profit is the earning over and above the cost incurred in production and selling of the product. It is the difference between revenue and cost. Thus, the cost component assumes immense importance as it is one of the components that determine the profit. Thus, cost occupies an important place in managerial decision-making. In this chapter, we examine the concept of cost and the cost distinction. Then we move to the study of cost where the conventional analysis of cost in short-run and long-run has been made. Subsequently, the reasons for U shape of long-run average cost curve and the derivation of long-run marginal curves have been explained. Finally, the chapter concludes with the understanding of U shape of LAC with the help of economies and diseconomies of scale.

## 14.2 CONCEPT OF COST

The cost refers to the total expenditure involved in order to produce and sell a specific quantity of output. In a business concern, the production of a commodity may lead to incurring of expenditure on purchase of raw materials, installation of plant and machinery, payment of wages of workers and salaries of employees, rent of building, insurance premium, payment of taxes, etc. In addition, funds are also spent on advertisement and sales promotion techniques. The motive here is to position the product in the minds of the consumers. Thus, the study of cost is an important criterion as it involves outlays which may affect the overall profitability of a business concern.

## 14.3 TYPES OF COST

The various types of cost have been described as under:

1. **Fixed Costs**

   Fixed costs are the costs that do not change or vary with the level of output. It means that they remain same whether the level of output is more, less or zero. In economics, the concept of fixed cost is studied in short run as in long run all the costs become variable.

   These include:

   (i) Rent of the building
   (ii) Cost of managerial and administrative staff
   (iii) Depreciation of machinery

2. **Variable Costs**

   Variable costs are the costs that vary with the level of output. It is directly related with the variations in output. The more the output level, the more is the magnitude of variable cost and vice versa.

   These include:

   (i) Cost of raw materials
   (ii) Fuel charges
   (iii) Routine maintenance expenditure

3. **Direct Cost**

   Direct costs are expenses that can be attributed to a specific product, department or project. It includes direct material (raw materials), direct labour (wages) and direct expenses (octori, carriage, freight etc).

4. **Indirect Cost**

   Indirect costs are the expenses that cannot be attributed to a specific product, department or project. They are associated with the provision of a product to customers and are calculated after direct costs have been computed. It includes indirect material rather than raw material, indirect labour expenses (salaries) payment of excise duty, payment of corporate tax, etc.)

5. **Private Costs**

These are the monetary payments made by individuals or firms. In case of the individuals, these include expenses on food, clothing, shelter, maintenance of hygiene, gaining of education, entertainment expense or any other expense that is incurred in order to ensure and elevate the level of living. In case of a business firm, these may include expenses such as acquisition of raw material, employment of skilled and unskilled labour, rent, insurance premium, etc.

6. **Social Cost**

It includes the private cost and the costs which are borne by society at large. The cost that is borne by the society includes any loss or damage to the society which is attributed to the operations of the firm.

*For example:* If the conduct of business operations causes air pollution which indirectly leads to air pollution, then the society is at losing end and is paying penalty for which it is not responsible. On the other side, the erring firm is not bearing the disutility caused by its operations in an economy. Thus, such cost is added to the private cost to find the social cost of producing the product. Another example includes water pollution from oil refineries, noise pollution from factories, and the like.

7. **External Cost**

It refers to that part of social cost that is not borne the firm. For example: The expenditure on development of roads, bridges, flyovers, underpasses which facilitate transportation of raw material, semi-finished and finished stock. Another example of external cost can be good sewage system and street lights, etc. The firm does not bear the cost but gets benefits from such facilities.

8. **Explicit Costs**

Explicit costs refer to the actual expenditure made by the firm in order to hire, rent or purchase the input it requires in order to produce a product. They are known as accounting cost or money cost, as they represent the actual monetary payment made by a firm.

These include:

- Acquisition of raw material
- Payment of rent
- Payment of wages and salaries
- Purchase of stationery items

9. **Implicit Costs**

It refers to the value of the inputs owned and used by the firm in its own production activity. These are possessed and supplied by the entrepreneur himself. There is no contractual obligation for payment to anyone else in order to obtain these factor units. These are not recorded in the books of accounts and are also known as imputed costs.

These include:

- The rent of owned land used for production process rather than renting it out to others.
- Wages of labour rendered by the entrepreneur himself.
- Interest for use of owned capital rather than using it for lending out to others and earn interest over it.

**10. Accounting Cost**

Accounting Cost refers to all such business expenses that are made in the form of money and are recorded in the book of accounts. Such expenses or costs are also known explicit costs.

The examples include

- Cost of raw materials
- Payment of wages and salaries
- Payment of taxes
- Overhead expenses
- Payment of telephone bill
- Payment of electricity bill
- Sales promotion expenses

When such business expenses or accounting expenses are deducted from the sales income of any firm the accounting profit is obtained. It may be written as:

Accounting profit = Total revenues - Accounting cost

**11. Economic Cost**

Economic Cost includes both accounting cost as well as the opportunity cost of a business firm. Economic cost and economic profit are thus calculated as follows:

Economic cost = Accounting cost (explicit costs) + Opportunity cost

and

Economic profit = Total revenues – (Accounting cost + Opportunity cost)
= Total revenues – Accounting cost – Opportunity cost

But, Accounting profit = Total revenues – Accounting cost

Thus,

Economic profit = Accounting profit – Opportunity cost

**12. Opportunity Cost**

The concept of opportunity cost occupies an important place in managerial decision-making related to choice of projects, employment of factors of production, etc. The opportunity cost is the cost of next best alternative foregone.

It refers to the reward that factor could have earned in the next best alternative occupation. To avoid double counting only the best alternative is regarded as opportunity cost.

***For example:*** If an employee getting a salary of Rs. 20,000 in its Firm *A*. If he applies in Firm *B*, there he is offered a salary amounting to Rs. 15000. Then his choice of working in Firm *A* has the opportunity cost amounting to Rs. 15000.

13. **Controllable Costs**

    Controllable costs are those which can be controlled or regulated through the effort of corporate executives. These costs can be controlled if a correct decision is taken at the right time.

    ***For example:*** Inventory costs can be controlled at the shop level, etc.

14. **Non-controllable Costs**

    Non-controllable costs are those which are beyond the control of corporate executives and cannot be controlled despite their best efforts.

    ***For example:*** Costs due obsolesce and depreciation.

15. **Short-run Costs**

    These are the costs that are associated with the change in output. In the short run, the production function contains both fixed factor input and variable inputs. These are the costs that vary in relation to the variation in the variable input component only.

16. **Long-run Costs:** The long-run costs are associated with the changing scale of output. In the long run, the production function is based on all variable factor inputs. Thus, the costs of all variable inputs are the long-run costs.

## 14.4 COST FUNCTION

It shows the functional relationship between output and the cost incurred. It is derived from production function. When we include the cost of the factors of production, we obtain the cost function.

It can be expressed as:

$$C = F(Qf \cdot Pf)$$

where,

$C$ = Cost incurred

$F$ = Functional relationship

$Qf$ = Quantity of factor of production

$Pf$ = Price of factor of production

## 14.5 SHORT-RUN COST CURVES/BEHAVIOUR OF COSTS IN THE SHORT RUN

The study of short run is done under three heads:

(a) Total cost curves
(b) Average cost curves
(c) Marginal cost curves

### (a) Total Cost Curves

In short run, the firm has three categories of total cost curves. These are:

1. Total fixed costs (TFC)
2. Total variable costs (TVC)
3. Total costs (TC)

**1. Total Fixed Costs (TFC)**

These are the costs related with the volume of output and are incurred irrespective of output level.

These include:

- Payment of rent
- Payment of taxes
- Insurance premium
- Interest on loan
- Salary of permanent staff

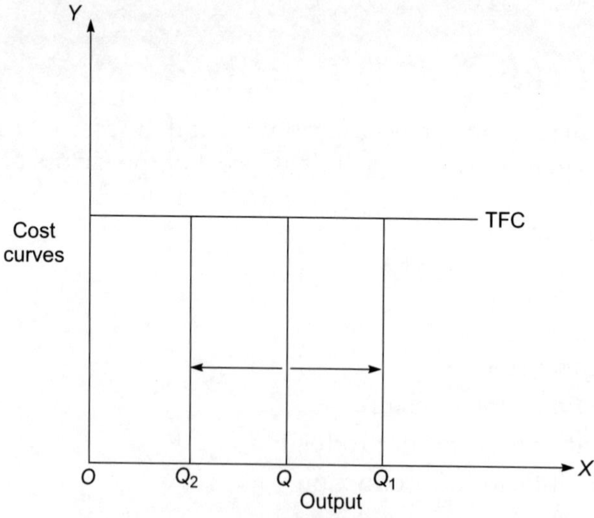


**Fig. 14.1** Total Fixed Cost

Figure 14.1 reflects that TFC curve is a horizontal straight line parallel to X-axis showing that TFC is same at all levels of output. TFC is constant even when the output level is zero.

## 2. Total Variable Costs (TVCs)

It refers to the cost that varies with the level of output. It means that the variable cost increases with the increase in output and reduces with reduction in output. It starts from the origin indicating that when the output is zero, variable cost is also zero.

These include:

- Payment for raw materials
- Labour cost
- Use of power depreciation associated with the use of the plant and equipment
- Excise duties

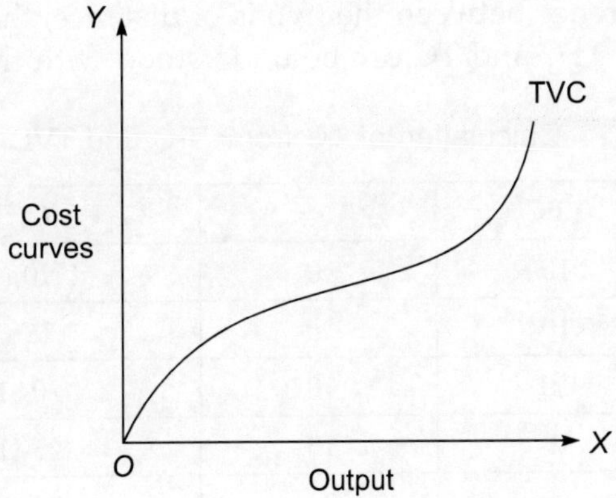


**Fig. 14.2** Total Variable Cost

It can be seen in Fig. 14.2 that TVC is an inverse 'S'-shaped curve due to the operation of law of variable proportions. That is, if TVC increases at diminishing rate because of increasing returns to variable factor and eventually increases at an increasing rate because of diminishing returns to variable factor.

## 3. Total Costs (TC)

Total costs (TCs) are the summation of total fixed costs (TFCs) and total variable costs (TVCs) at various levels of output.

That is,

$$TC = TFC + TVC$$

It may be represented as:

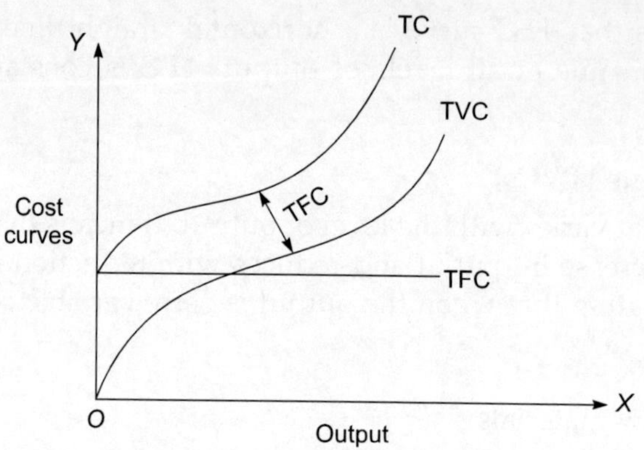


**Fig. 14.3** Total Cost Curve

Since, TFC remains fixed irrespective of level of output, the changes in TC are therefore induced by TVC. Figure 14.3 reflects that the shape of the TVC and TC are identical. The only difference between the two is of distance, that is, total fixed cost.

The concepts of TVC, TFC and TC can be understood with the help of Table 14.1.

**TABLE 14.1** Calculation of TC from TFC and TVC Curves

| Output | TFC | TVC | TC (TFC + TVC) |
|---|---|---|---|
| 0 | 10 | 0 | 10 (10 + 0) |
| 1 | 10 | 6 | 16 (10 + 6) |
| 2 | 10 | 10 | 20 (10 + 10) |
| 3 | 10 | 15 | 25 (10 + 15) |
| 4 | 10 | 24 | 34 (10 + 24) |
| 5 | 10 | 35 | 45 (10 + 35) |

It may be seen from the Table 14.1 that TFC is constant at each level of output. The curves TFC and TC are initially rising at diminishing rate and then rising at increasing rate. Finally, TC is the submission of TVC and TFC curves.

**Relationship among TC, TFC and TVC**

Figure 14.3 reflects the relationship among TC, TFC and TVC in the following manner:

1. Total cost curve is derived by vertically adding up TVC and TFC curves.
2. TFC curve is independent of level of output and hence is represented by horizontal line parallel to X-axis.
3. TC and TVC curves are inverse *S*-shaped curves. This is due to the law of variable proportions. Therefore, both the curves initially increase at a decreasing rate, but after a point increase at an increasing rate.

4. TC varies in the same proportion as the TVC. In other words, the change in total cost is entirely due to changes in the total variable costs as fixed cost remains same at each level of output.
5. The distance between TC and TVC is the TFC, which remains same at all levels of output.
6. The distance between TC and TFC is the TVC, which varies with the levels of output.

The concepts of TFC, TVC, TC, AFC, AVC, ATC and MC can be understood with the help of Table 14.2.

**TABLE 14.2** Tabular Representation of TFC, TVC, TC, AFC, AVC and ATC Curves

| Q | TFC | TVC | TC | AFC | AVC | ATC |
|---|---|---|---|---|---|---|
| 0 | 25 | 0 | 25 | – | – | – |
| 1 | 25 | 25 | 50 | 25 | 25 | 50 |
| 2 | 25 | 40 | 65 | 12.5 | 20 | 32.5 |
| 3 | 25 | 50 | 75 | 8.33 | 16.67 | 25 |
| 4 | 25 | 60 | 85 | 6.25 | 15 | 21.25 |
| 5 | 25 | 80 | 105 | 5.00 | 16 | 21 |
| 6 | 25 | 110 | 135 | 4.16 | 18.33 | 22.49 |
| 7 | 25 | 150 | 175 | 3.57 | 21.43 | 25 |
| 8 | 25 | 300 | 325 | 3.12 | 37.5 | 40.62 |
| 9 | 25 | 500 | 525 | 2.77 | 55.55 | 58.32 |
| 10 | 25 | 900 | 925 | 2.50 | 90 | 92.5 |

Examination of Table 14.2 gives us the following observations regarding the total costs.

## (b) Average Cost Curves

In short run, the firm has three categories of unit costs. These are:

1. Average fixed cost (AFC)
2. Average variable cost (AVC)
3. Average total cost (ATC)

### 1. Average Fixed Cost (AFC)

It refers to per unit fixed cost of production. It is calculated by dividing TFC by the total output. It may be written as:

$$AFC = TFC/TQ$$

Calculation of AFC is shown in Table 14.3.

**TABLE 14.3** Calculation of AFC

| Output (units) | TFC (Rs.) | AFC (Rs.) |
|---|---|---|
| 0 | 10 | – |
| 1 | 10 | 10 |
| 2 | 10 | 5 |
| 3 | 10 | 3.33 |
| 4 | 10 | 2.25 |
| 5 | 10 | 2 |

It can be seen from Table 14.3 that AFC decreases as output increases. It can be seen that at zero level of output, TFC is Rs. 10 at each level of output. AFC curve represents a rectangular hyperbola. This is shown diagrammatically as:

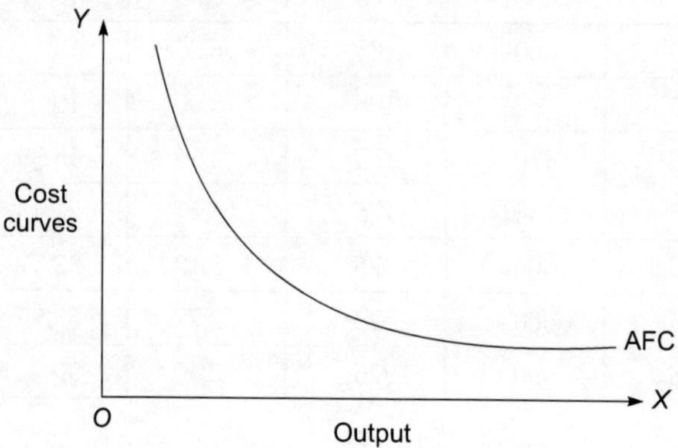


**Fig. 14.4** Average Fixed Cost

It can be seen from Fig. 14.4 that AFC approaches both the axes but never becomes zero. This is due to the fact that TFC can never be zero, thus its average cannot be zero as well.

**2. Average Variable Cost (AVC)**

It is calculated by dividing TVC by the total output. It is per unit cost of variable factors of production. AVC first decreases and then increases as the output increases. It is represented as follows:

$$AVC = TVC/TQ$$

Calculation of AVC is shown in Table 14.4.

**TABLE 14.4** Calculation of AVC

| Output | TVC | AVC |
|---|---|---|
| 0 | 0 | – |
| 1 | 6 | 6 |
| 2 | 10 | 5 |
| 3 | 15 | 5 |
| 4 | 24 | 6 |
| 5 | 35 | 7 |

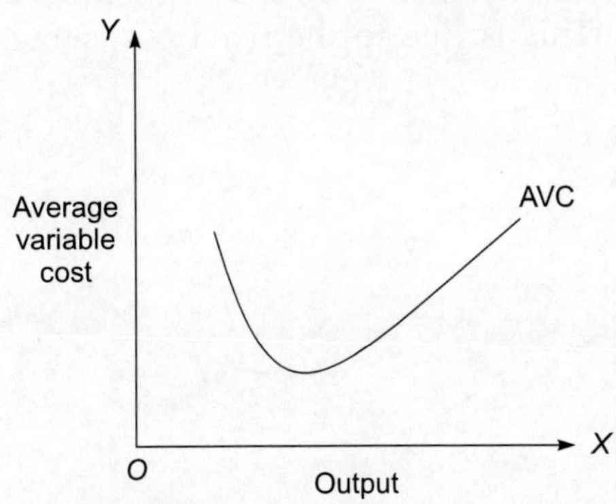


**Fig. 14.5** Average Variable Cost

It can be seen from Fig. 14.5 that AVC curve is dish-shaped or U-shaped. This is because of the law of variable proportions. It initially falls and remains constant for a while and finally starts rising. AFC initially falls because of increasing returns to variable factor and after attaining minima starts rising due to diminishing returns to the variable factor.

### 3. Average Total Cost (ATC)/ Average Cost (AC)

It refers to per unit cost of production. It is the sum of average fixed cost (AFC) and average variable cost (AVC). It is represented as follows:

$$AC = \frac{TC}{Q}$$

or

$$AC = AFC + AVC$$

AC decreases in the beginning as both the components decrease initially. After a point, AVC starts increasing. The rise in AVC outweighs the influence of ever decreasing AFC. As a result, ATC is pulled up along with AVC.

### Relationship among AC, AFC and AVC

Figure 14.6 reflects the relationship among AC, AFC and AVC in the following manner:

1. AC is the vertical summation of AVC and AFC. Thus, its shape is affected by the shape of both the curves.
2. AC curve always lies above AVC because it includes both AFC and AVC.
3. In case of AVC, the point of minima is reached earlier as compared to ATC curve. This is due to the fact that when AVC attains its minimum, another component of ATC, that is AFC, still continues to fall, as a result ATC attains its point of minima after AVC.
4. With an increase in output, the ATC and AVC tend to converge but never intersect each other. This is due to the fixed cost which tends to reduce but never becomes zero.

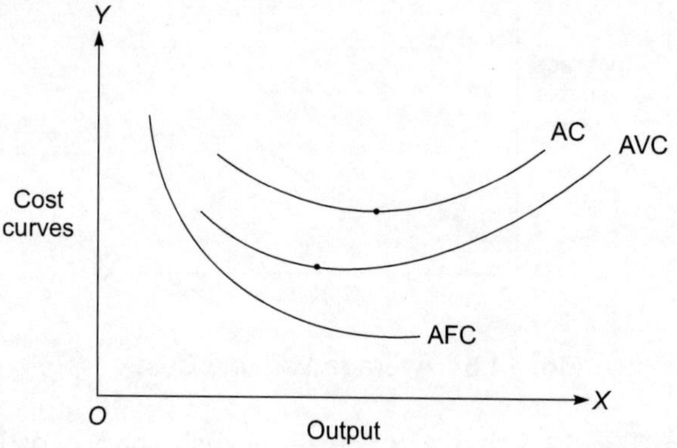


**Fig. 14.6** Relationship Among AC, AFC and AVC

## (c) Marginal Cost Curve

### Marginal Cost (MC)

Marginal cost is the addition made to the total cost when one more unit of output is produced. Marginal cost is the rate of change in total costs with respect to change in the level of output. Therefore, marginal cost at any level of output is the slope of the total cost curve at the corresponding point. Thus, MC can be defined as:

$$MC = TC_n - TC_{n-1} \quad \text{...(14.1)}$$

where,

MC = Marginal cost curve, $TC_n$ = Total cost of n units, $TC_{n-1}$ = Total cost of n – 1 units

It can also be defined as:

$$MC = \Delta TC/\Delta Q$$

where,

$$\Delta TC = \text{Change in total cost, } \Delta Q = \text{Change in quantity}$$

In the short run, the marginal cost is independent of fixed cost and is directly related to the variable cost. This can be understood from equation (14.1) as follows:

$$MC = TC_n - TC_{n-1} \text{ (from equation 14.1)}$$

$$MC = (TVC_n + TFC_n) - (TVC_{n-1} + TFC_{n-1})$$

Since, $TFC_n = TFC_{n-1}$ (because fixed cost remains same in n period and n – 1 period) Thus, the above equation becomes:

$$MC = (TVC_n + TFC_n) - (TVC_{n-1} + TFC_n)$$

$$MC = TVC_n + TFC_n - TVC_{n-1} - TFC_n$$

Cancelling the positive and negative values of $TFC_n$, we get

$$MC = TVC_n - TVC_{n-1}$$

Similarly, since MC is independent of fixed cost in short run, therefore we have:

$$MC = \Delta TVC/\Delta Q$$

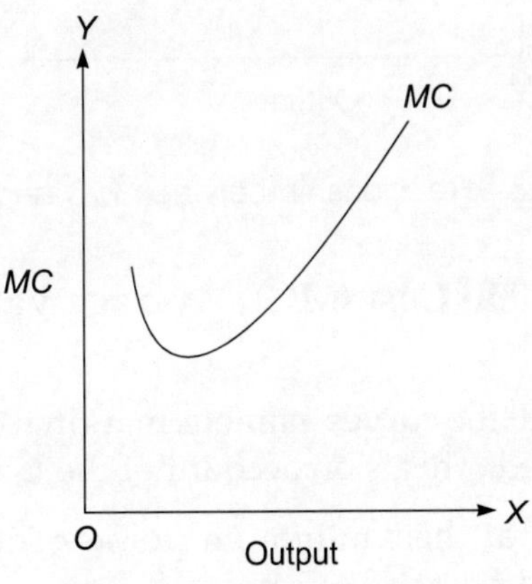


**Fig. 14.7** Marginal Cost

It can be seen from Fig. 14.7 that MC is U shaped. This is on account of the law of variable proportions. This can be understood as follows:

- When marginal product (MP) increases following increasing returns to factor, MC tends to fall.
- When marginal product (MP) becomes maximum, MC attains its minimum.
- When marginal product (MP) declines following diminishing returns to factor, MC tends to rise.

## Relationship between Marginal Cost (MC) and Average Cost (AC)

There is a unique relationship between AC and MC that has been described in Fig. 14.8 as below:

1. When AC is minimum, MC is equal to AC. Thus MC intersects AC at its lowest point.
2. When AC is falling, MC is always below AC. In fact, it is the MC that pulls down AC along with it. The point to note here is that MC may be rising, but will remain below AC.
3. When AC is rising, MC must be above AC.

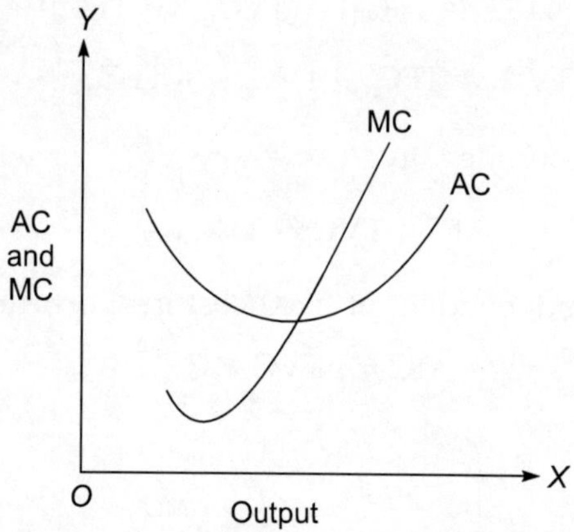


**Fig. 14.8** Relationship between MC and AC

## Relationship among Marginal Cost (MC), Average Variable Cost (AVC), and Average Cost (AC)

It can be seen from Fig. 14.9, all the curves, namely, marginal cost, average variable cost and average cost are U-shaped. This is on account of the law of variable proportions.

- MC cuts AC and AVC at their minimum points. The minimum point of MC comes before minimum point of AC and AVC.
- The point of minima is attained at first in case of AVC and then AC curve. This is due to continuous fall in the AFC. In other words, the minimum point of AC always lies on the right of minimum point of AVC curve.
- When MC < AC and AVC, MC pulls both of them downwards.
- When MC > AC and AVC, MC pulls both of them upwards.
- AC > AVC as AC is the summation of both
  AVC and AFC. Thus, by adding AFC to AVC curve, we arrive at AC curve, Thus, AC curve is at a position indicating higher cost as compared to AVC.

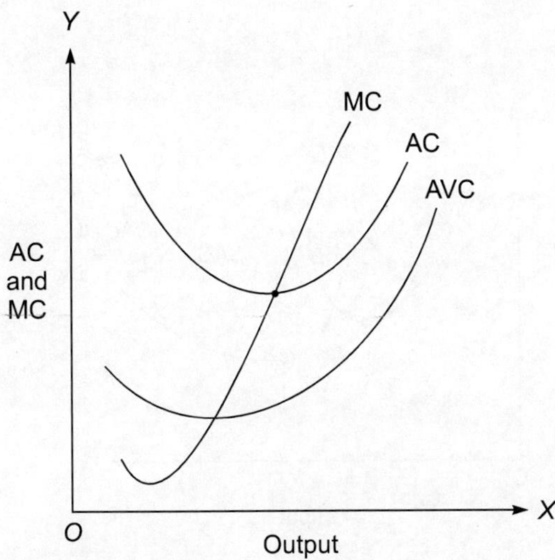


**Fig. 14.9** Relationship between MC, AVC and AC

## 14.6 LONG-RUN COST CURVES

In long run, all the factors of production become variable. It is the time period that is sufficient enough to acquire more of land and employ more of labour, skilled or unskilled. In addition, more capital can be invested in the form of funds, machines, tools and equipment. By this time there is also an improvement in entrepreneurial skill due to length of time period. Thus, all costs are variable in the long run and there is no fixed costs.

However, there is no universally applicable time period to define long run. It may vary from one industry to another. In some industries like photocopying, the long run may be a few months or quarter. For others, which are capital intensive, like construction, communication network, long run may relate to several years.

The long-run cost curves represent the cost structure of an organization when all the inputs are variable. In long run, average cost is calculated using long run total cost (LTC) divided by the level of output (Q). Long run average cost depicts the least possible average cost for producing all possible levels of output. The analysis of long-run average cost (LAC) curve is done by analyzing short-run cost curves.

### Derivation of Long Run Average Cost Curve

Suppose, we consider five short-run average cost curves as defined by $SAC_1$, $SAC_2$, $SAC_3$, $SAC_4$ and $SAC_5$. These curves are also called plant curves. This is due to the fact that in the short run, plant is fixed and each short-run average cost curve corresponds to a particular plant. This has been explained in Fig. 14.10.

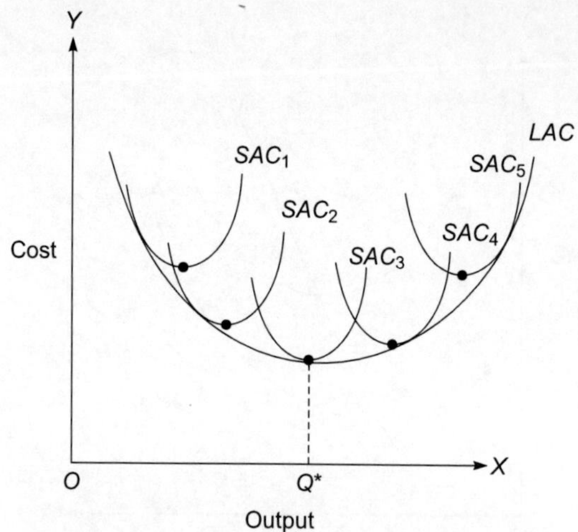


**Fig. 14.10** Long-Run Average Cost Curve

In short run, the firm can operate on any short-run average cost curve (SAC), given the size of the plant. In the long run, the firm will try to produce a given level of output where cost would be minimum.

Figure 14.10 shows that the five SACs as defined by $SAC_1$, $SAC_2$, $SAC_3$, $SAC_4$ and $SAC_5$ have been drawn in such a manner that $SAC_1$ lies at a higher position as compared to $SAC_2$. Similarly, $SAC_2$ lies at higher position as compared to $SAC_3$. This is on account of economies of scale (refer section 14.7) that the short-run cost curves are following a falling trend. Further, after attaining minima at $SAC_3$, the cost curves tend to rise from $SAC_4$ and then to $SAC_5$. Here, $SAC_5$ is a higher curve as compared to $SAC_4$. This shows that diseconomies of scale (refer section 14.7) have emerged which further pushes up short-run cost curves.

Now, the long-run average cost curve (LAC) is locus of all tangency points with short-run average cost curves (SACs). However, the firm will decide to produce particular output where it has minimum costs. Since, a lot of analysis and decision-making is involved at this stage, it is for this reason also called 'planning curve'. In addition, it takes in its ambit the short-run cost curves and envelopes them. It is for this reason that LAC curve is also known as 'envelop curve'.

Figure 14.10 makes it clear that the long-run average cost curve (LAC) first falls, becomes minimum and then starts rising. Thus, LAC is a U shaped curve. As explained above, the reasons for declining portion of LAC is economies of large scale production and rising portion are diseconomies of large-scale production. These are also known as economies and diseconomies of scale (refer section 14.7).

## Long-Run Marginal-Cost Curve (LMC)

In long run, the marginal cost curve is derived from short-run marginal cost curves. The LMC is obtained from the point of intersection of SMC with the vertical lines drawn from the point of tangency of corresponding SAC and LAC curve to the horizontal axis (X-axis).

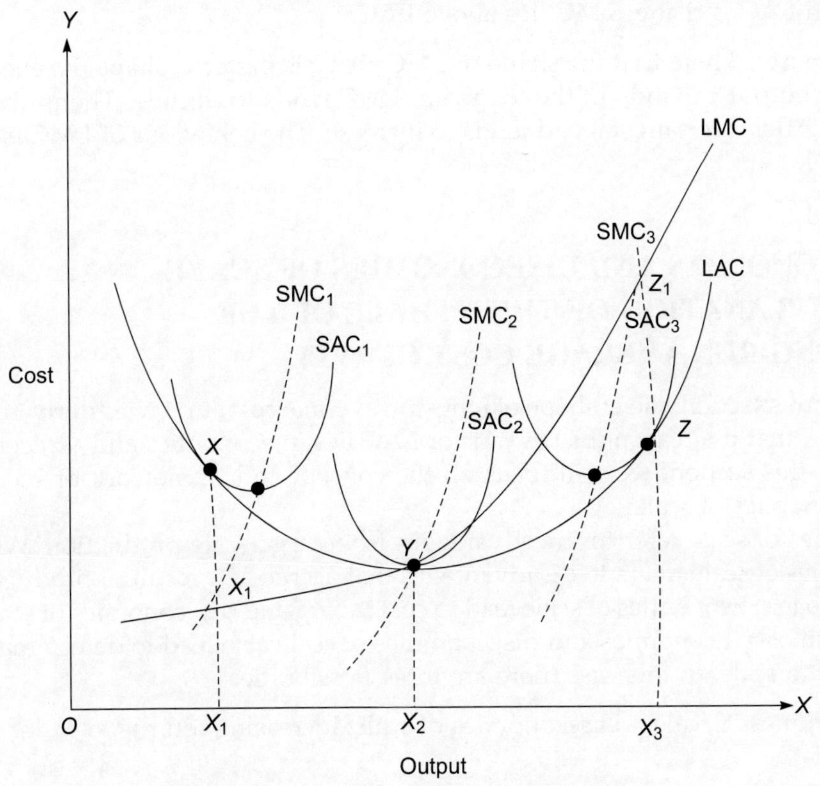


**Fig. 14.11** Long Run Marginal Cost Curve

Figure 14.11 shows the derivation of long-run marginal cost curve (LMC) with the help of long-run average cost curve (LAC) which envelops a set of short-run average (SAC) and marginal cost curves (SMCs).

## Derivation of LMC

At $OX_1$ output, LAC is tangent to $SMC_1$, point X is obtained at their intersection. In order to obtain the first point of LMC, a line is drawn from point X to the output axis and see where it intersects LAC. Thus, we obtain the first point of LMC as denoted by $X_1$. To produce $OX_2$ output, the firm operates at point Y, where LAC is tangent to $SAC_2$ and $SMC_2$. Thus, the second point of LMC is obtained at point Y.

To produce $OX_3$, it can be observed that LAC is tangent to $SMC_3$. Thus, point $Z_1$ is obtained by vertically extending the line where LAC intersects $SAC_3$.

The above figure shows that LAC and LMC have the following relationship:

1. When LAC is decreasing, LMC lies below LAC.
2. When LMC is equal to LAC, LAC is at its minimum point.
3. When LAC is rising, LMC lies above LAC.

It is to be noted here that the shape of LMC curve is flatter U shape. It reflects that initially as output expands in the long run, LMC tends to decline. Then it becomes minimum. After a certain stage, it tends to increase. The behaviour of LMC is shown in Fig. 14.11.

## 14.7 ECONOMIES AND DISECONOMIES OF SCALE (EXPLANATION OF THE U SHAPE OF THE LONG-RUN AVERAGE COST CURVE)

In the previous section, the U shape of long-run average cost curve was derived. It was also defined that the reason for U shape of LAC lies in economies and diseconomies of scale. In this section, we will focus on the concept and framework of economies and diseconomies of scale.

Economies of scale refer to the advantages from large-scale production. Whereas, diseconomies of scale refers to disadvantages that accrue as a result of production on large scale basis. Economies of scale lead to cost saving and diseconomies of scale lead to the rise in cost. Economies and diseconomies of scale also lead to determination of the returns to scale. In this case there are three possibilities:

- Economies of scale > Diseconomies of scale; increasing returns to scale are said to exist.
- Economies of scale = Diseconomies of scale; constant returns to scale are said to exist.
- Diseconomies of scale > Economies of scale; diminishing returns to scale are said to exist.

The chapter proceeds with discussion on economies of scale. These have been bifurcated under internal and external economies of scale. This has been followed by the explanation of diseconomies of scale which have again been explained in terms of internal and external diseconomies of scale.

### 14.7.1 Economies of Scale

As defined above, economies of scale are advantages from large-scale production. These advantages are availed in the form of cost benefits by expanding the scale of production. It finally results in reduction of the long-run average (unit) costs of production. These reduced costs give business a competitive advantage or an edge over other firms. The economies of scale are classified in Fig. 14.12.

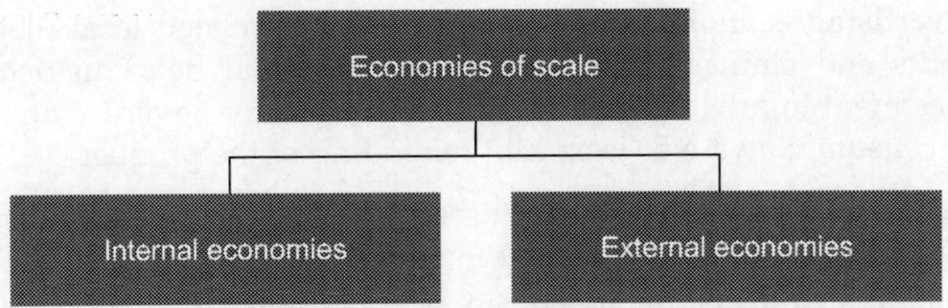


**Fig. 14.12** Economies of Scale

## (a) Internal Economies of Scale

1. **Production/Technical Economies of Scale:** These are the benefits that are related to the production aspect of working of a firm. They are of following nature.

   **(a) Investment in Expensive and Sophisticated Machinery:** In long run, a firm can always avail the benefit of investment in expensive and sophisticated machinery. Though it involves onetime cost but huge and recurring benefits follow thereafter. These benefits are in the form of production of more units, reduction in labour cost, reduction in time involved in production of the product, etc.

   **(b) Division of Labour and Efficiency of Business Operations:** In case of large entities, the complex tasks can be divided and subdivided into smaller tasks of specialized nature. As a result, every employee knows what is expected from him/her. This results in efficiency of business operations as the concerned person is responsible for the task that is allocated to him or her. Example includes:
   The **division of labour** in production of motor vehicles, selling of insurance schemes, selling of mutual funds and in telecommunication sector.

   **(c) Benefits of Backward Integration and Forward Integration:** Benefits of Backward Integration may be in the form of developing own source of raw material such as a coffee making company may own its own cocoa plant.

   On the other hand, benefits of forward integration may be in the form of owning retail outlet or distribution system. For example, a company that is engaged in production of floor tends to have ownership of bakery.

2. **Marketing Economies of Scale:** These benefits are related to the marketing aspect of working of a firm. They are of following nature:

   - **Availing monopsony power** refers to the powers that are in the hands of buyers of the product. It can be availed in the form of purchase of inputs or material in bulk at negotiated or discounted prices.

- **Advertising economies** involve the decisions related to available funds, profits and similar activities of competitors. It helps in deciding the investment in advertisement and the intensity of advertisement to make the consumer aware or keep him reminding of the product.

3. **Managerial Economies of Scale** are the benefits that are related to the managerial working of a firm. They are of following nature.

   **Functional distribution:** In large business organisations, separate departments can be created so as to attain the efficiency of business organisations. These include: production department, sales department, personnel department, finance department and so on. The creation of different departments clearly defines the role of each manager or employee in the organisation. The proper coordination within a department and between the departments is a key to more efficient working of the firm.

4. **Mechanization Economies:** Large firms can use more innovation techniques that involve use of technology. This results in reducing the cost of information flow substantially.

5. **Financial Economies of Scale:** The large firms have the following financial economies of scale as compared to smaller firms:
   - Preference in getting credit over small borrowers. This is on account of greater credibility, ability to pay debts on time and reduced possibility of doubtful debts or non-performing assets as compared to a smaller firm.
   - Apart from enhanced volume of credit, the large firms gain benefit in terms of favourable borrowing rates.

6. **Network Economies of Scale:** The large scale organisations can also avail benefits through creation of websites, e-advertisements and use of e-commerce to promote their product.

7. **Risk and Survival Economies:** A large firm is generally financially strong and more balanced as far as sustenance in situations of uncertainties and risk is concerned. In addition, they undertake research and development (R&D) to economise cost of production and improve quality of products.

### (b) External Economies of Scale

It may be in following form:

- **Development of R&D:** Development of Research and Development facility in local universities that helps the local business in that area.
- **Development of Infrastructure:** Investment by local authority for development of infrastructure that helps in improving the transport network.

### 14.7.2 Diseconomies of Scale

The diseconomies of scale are classified in Fig. 14.13.

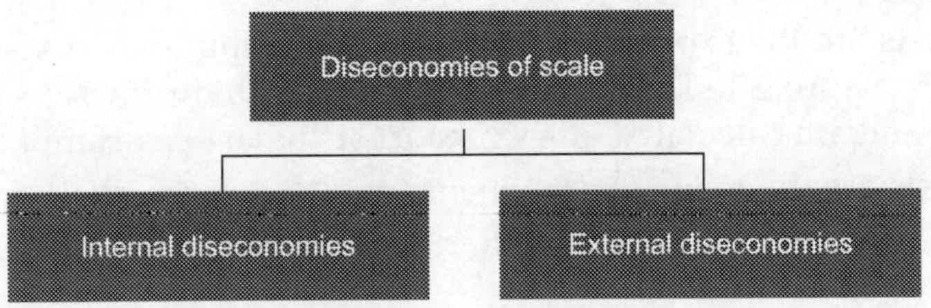


**Fig. 14.13** Diseconomies of Scale

It may be caused by:

**(a) Internal Diseconomies**

**Loss of Coordination and Cooperation** – Large business firms tend to have large number of employees. With enhanced number of employees, it becomes difficult to exercise control over the employees. As a result problem of coordination and cooperation persists. This results in reduction of productivity and efficiency of the workers due to which the business concern is at losing end.

1. **Confusion and Chaos:** The absence of coordination and cooperation leads to confusion and chaotic situations in the organization. As a result the performance of business is negatively affected.
2. **Managerial Inefficiency Diseconomies:** The expansion of scale results in managerial inefficiencies. This is due to the fact that expansion of production scale results in the dilution of personal communication between owners, managers and labour. Thus, managerial inefficiencies crop up.
3. **Labour Inefficiency:** It occurs on account of excess of labour which may lead to loss of control and reduction in productivity.

**(b) External Diseconomies**

1. **Diseconomies of Pollution:** If firms localise in a particular area, then there is a rise in social cost of production in terms of spread of pollution, viz., air, water and noise.
2. **Diseconomies of High Factor Prices:** When the industries tend to concentrate at one place, the suppliers tend to supply the product at enhanced prices which leads to diseconomies of high factor prices.

## Summary

- ✓ The cost refers to the total expenditure involved in order to produce and sell specific quantity of output.
- ✓ Fixed costs are the costs that do not change or vary with the level of output. The concept of fixed cost is studied in short run as in long run all the costs become variable.

- ✓ **Variable costs** are the costs that vary with the level of output.
- ✓ Direct costs are expenses that can be attributed to a specific product, department or project.
- ✓ Indirect costs are the expenses that cannot be attributed to a specific product, department or project. They are associated with the provision of product to customers and are calculated after direct costs have been computed.
- ✓ **Private costs** are the monetary payments made by individuals or firms.
- ✓ Social cost includes the private cost and the costs which are borne by society at large.
- ✓ **External cost** refers to that part of social cost that is not borne the firm.
- ✓ Explicit costs refer to the actual expenditure made by the firm in order to hire, rent or purchase the input it requires in order to produce a product. They are also known as accounting cost or money cost.
- ✓ Implicit cost refers to the value of the inputs owned and used by the firm in its own production activity.
- ✓ Accounting cost refers to all such business expenses that are made in the form of money and are recorded in the book of accounts.
- ✓ Economic cost includes both accounting cost as well as the opportunity cost of a business firm.
- ✓ Opportunity costs: These are the costs of next best alternative foregone.
- ✓ Controllable costs are those which can be controlled or regulated through the effort of corporate executives. These costs can be controlled if a correct decision is taken at the right time.
- ✓ Non-controllable costs are those which are beyond the control of corporate executives and cannot be controlled despite their best efforts.
- ✓ TFC curve is independent of level of output and hence is represented by horizontal line parallel to X-axis.
- ✓ TC and TVC curves are inverse S-shaped curves.
- ✓ AFC curve represents a rectangular hyperbola. AVC curve is dish shaped or U-shaped.
- ✓ MC is U shaped.
- ✓ The long-run average cost curve (LAC) is the locus of all tangency points with short-run average cost curves (SACs).
- ✓ The LMC is obtained from the point of intersection of SMC with the vertical lines drawn from the point of tangency of the corresponding SAC and LAC curves to the horizontal axis (X-axis).
- ✓ Economies of scale refer to the advantages from large-scale production. Whereas, diseconomies of scale refer to disadvantages that accrue as a result of carrying production on large scale.

## Review Questions

1. Define the concept of cost. Explain the behaviour of cost curves in the short run.
2. Explain the relationship among average cost, average variable cost and marginal cost.
3. As the level of output rises, AC and AVC tend to come close but never meet. Explain.
4. 'Long run average cost curve is derived from short-run average cost curve'. Explain.
5. Explain diagrammatically the derivation of long-run marginal cost curve.
6. Explain how long-run marginal cost curve is derived with the help of suitable diagrams.
7. Explain the relationship between/among the following:
   (a) AC and MC
   (b) AC, AVC and MC
8. Distinguish between the following:
   (a) Explicit cost and implicit cost
   (b) Accounting cost and economic cost
   (c) Fixed cost and variable cost
   (d) Private cost and social cost
   (e) Accounting profit and economic cost
9. Write short notes on the following:
   (a) External cost
   (b) Controllable cost
   (c) Economic profit
10. Why long-run average cost curve is U shaped? Explain the reason in the light of concept of economies and diseconomies of scale.

## CASE STUDY 1: PERASENSHA (1982)

Perasensha was established in 1982 with the motive to provide excellent quality stationery to the consumers. It initially started manufacturing general pencils and further added product with variations like professional pencils, coloured pencils, pencils with rubber on one side, etc. Since the product quality was good, it received positive response from the consumers of all age groups. Ten years later, the company expanded to include erasers, sharpeners, art materials, instrument sets, etc. A lot of work was done on company's products and finally the company earned a good name for itself. Gradually, in the wake of enhanced demand, the company hired more workers and purchased sophisticated machineries that were able to produce more products and meet the professional commitments. In the pencil segment, the company wishes to introduce a new product that is 'Grip pencils'. These are the pencils that have an attractive gripper at beginning of pencil and especially designed the product to facilitate writing skills of kids with 3 plus years age group. The product aimed to make the "reluctant writers" write. The price per box is kept at Rs. 20 and in all there were 10 pencils, one eraser and a sharpener in the pencil box. The firm's cost function is as follows:

$$C = 4 + 4Q + Q^2$$

## Questions

1. Following MR-MC approach, ascertain the quantity of the commodity that would be sold in the market when the price is kept as follows:
   (a) Rs. 20 per box
   (b) Rs. 10 per box
   (c) Rs. 30 per box
2. Ascertain the total variable cost when the product is sold at Rs. 20 in the market.
3. Do you think that the company's decision to produce 'Grip pencils' is desirable? Justify.
4. Do you think that the company is making supernormal profits in short run?
5. Show diagrammatically the short-run equilibrium position of said company.

## CASE STUDY 2: COST ANALYSIS AT M/S CARRETO (2016)

M/S Carreto commenced its business of assembling the hardware components of personal computers and selling the final product to the consumers. Fifty employees were hired by the company from June 10 till July 25, 2016 in order to execute orders. Gradually, it was recognized that the company was incurring losses and was performing poorly on sales front. It was realized that the company is losing its revenue and this was followed by the decline in the profitability. The loss in profitability was partly on account of heavy fixed cost and the high salary demands of the employees. The company also realized that it was giving 1.5 times salary as compared to its rivals. Thus, in the wake of rising losses, the company decided to lay off eight employees as it was finding difficult to pay them.

The General Manager of the company told the employees "Since the business is not reviving and we are facing severe financial constraints, we have decided to remove non-performing workers from our payrolls".

## Questions

1. Considering the cost analysis of the company, identify the two fixed costs and two variable costs that the company would incur.
2. Do you think that the costs overruns of company are on account of wrong salary negotiations with employees?
3. What should the company do in order to increase the revenue of the company?
4. What problems might the company face by reducing the employee base?

# 15 CHAPTER

# Price and Output Decisions Under Perfect Competition

**LEARNING OBJECTIVES**

After going through this chapter, reader would be able to understand:

- ✓ The meaning of market and market structures.
- ✓ The concept of perfectly competitive market structure.
- ✓ The assumptions that establish the base for perfect competition.
- ✓ The distinction between pure and perfect competition.
- ✓ Price and output decisions under perfect competition.
- ✓ Short-run and long-run equilibrium analysis of perfectly competitive firm.

## 15.1 INTRODUCTION

In this chapter, we will discuss the price and output determination under first form of market structure that is perfect competition. The chapter begins with defining the concept of markets and gives an introduction of market structures. Further, the meaning of perfect competition and the fundamental assumptions that formulate the basis of this form of market structure have been discussed. In this market form, all firms sell an identical product that is why the industry is a price maker and the firm is a price taker.

Generally, there is a myth that there is no difference between pure competition and perfect competition. Thus, the chapter moves further with the explanations related to the conceptual differences between pure competition and perfect competition. Then we go on to determine the price and quantity relationships in short and long run under perfect competition. In short run, the outcomes of production process have been discussed in the form of three possibilities. These are supernormal profits, normal profits and losses. However, there is a change in long run. In long run, a perfectly competitive firm earns only normal profits due to the assumption of free entry and exit. However, it is a hypothetical form of market structure. Its study is imperative for understanding the comparative analysis between other real market forms.

## 15.2 CONCEPT OF MARKET

In common parlance, the term "market" refers to a particular place where goods are exchanged for a value, that is, the price. It is the place where purchase and sales are executed. However, in economics, it has been defined in a much wider perspective. In economics, the term "market" does not accommodate the concept of coverage of particular place but of entire area or region or network where buyers and sellers of a product are spread and are connected. The concept of market takes into account the contemporary channels of communication, expansion of transportation facilitates and points towards digital marketing and expansion of e-commerce.

## 15.3 INTRODUCTION TO MARKET STRUCTURES

Market structure refers to overall composition, mechanism of working and extent of competition among the market players. The concept of market structure is applicable to both commodity market and service (factor) market. However, the present chapter and forthcoming three chapters focus on commodity or product market. On the basis of competition, a market can be classified under the following heads:

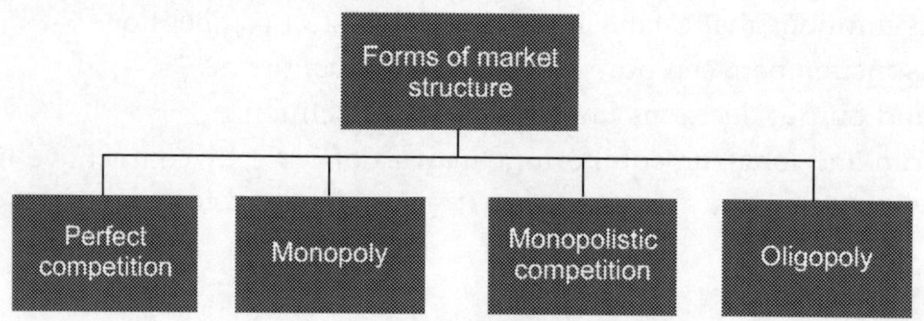


**Fig. 15.1** Forms of Market Structure

These are known as the forms of market structure.

## 15.4 MEANING OF PERFECT COMPETITION

Perfect competition refers to a market structure which is characterized by large number of buyer and sellers where the sellers are selling homogeneous products. In such a market structure, free entry and exit is permitted. This model of market structure presumes that it is easy for new firms to enter and for existing ones to leave the market.

## 15.5 ASSUMPTIONS/FEATURES OF PERFECT COMPETITION

The following are the assumptions or main features of perfect competition.

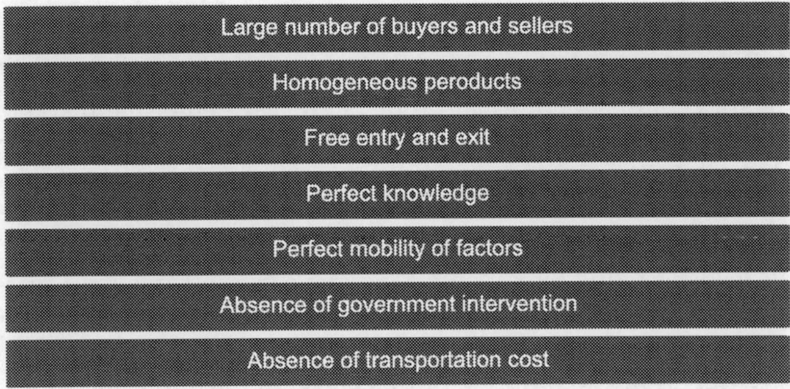


**Fig. 15.2** Assumptions of Perfect Competition

**1. Large Number of Buyers and Sellers**

- The number of buyers and sellers is so large that none of them is in a position to influence the level of prices.
- Since the number of sellers is large, the output produced by each seller constitutes a insignificant portion of the total industrial output.
- Industry is the price maker, it determines the prices though the market forces of demand and supply.
- In this market form, the firm (seller) is a price taker and not price maker. This is because the price is determined by industry and the firms take that price from industry and can sell any output at that prevailing price.
- Similarly, every buyer has to accept the price decided by market forces of demand and supply. Hence, all buyers are price takers and not price makers.

**2. Homogeneous (identical/ similar) Products**

- The products are homogeneous in the sense that they are perfectly identical to each other.
- There are no real or artificial (pecuniary) differences among the products of two sellers.
- All products are perfectly similar in terms of shape, size, quality, colour, taste, ingredients, etc.
- This ensures the prevalence of single or uniform price in the market.

3. **Free Entry and Exit**
   - There are no restrictions on entry of new firms and exit of the existing firms.
   - When there are supernormal profits, new firms enter the market with the purpose of absorbing the excess profit. This results in increase in supply of the product. A rise in supply results in fall of price. The prices reduce to such a level till they come to a normal level.
   - When profits are low or losses occur, some firms may exit the market. This leads to reduction in supply. So, the existing firms raise prices of the product which results in increase in revenue and thus the level of profits goes up. This happens till the normal level of profit is ensured.
   - Thus, due to the assumption of free entry and exit, normal profit prevails in long run under perfect competition.
4. **Perfect Knowledge**
   - Buyers and sellers are fully aware of current and future market prices.
   - None of the buyers will pay price higher than the market price and none of the sellers will charge lower price than the market price.
5. **Perfect Mobility of Factors**
   - All factors can be moved from one place to another and from one region to another.
   - The labour can move from one job to another and low-paid to a high-paid industry.
6. **Absence of Government Intervention**
   - The market is controlled by the forces of demand and supply.
   - There is no government intervention or interference.
   - Hence, there are no taxes, subsidies, tariffs, rebates, licensing policy, etc.
7. **Absence of Transportation Cost**
   - There is complete absence of transport costs in carrying of product from one place to another.
   - This ensures existence of single price in market.
   - This is on account of the reason that if transport costs are added to the price of the product, then each homogeneous product will tend to have different prices.
   - Thus, a seller with low transportation cost will have lower final price and the one with higher transportation cost with a higher final price of the product.
   - Thus, it is presumed that buyers and sellers are close to market, hence, transport cost is nil.

## 15.6 DISTINCTION BETWEEN PURE AND PERFECT COMPETITION

Apparently, there is no distinction between pure and perfect competition. However, in reality, there is a demarcation. Pure competition is a market form that qualifies the first three features or assumptions of perfect competition. These are:

- Large number of buyers and sellers
- Homogeneous (identical/similar) products
- Free entry and exit

When these features are supplemented by four additional features, then perfect competition comes into existence. These four features are:

- Perfect knowledge
- Perfect mobility of factors
- Absence of government intervention
- Absence of transportation cost

The features of pure competition and perfect competition have been represented in Fig. 15.3 as follows:

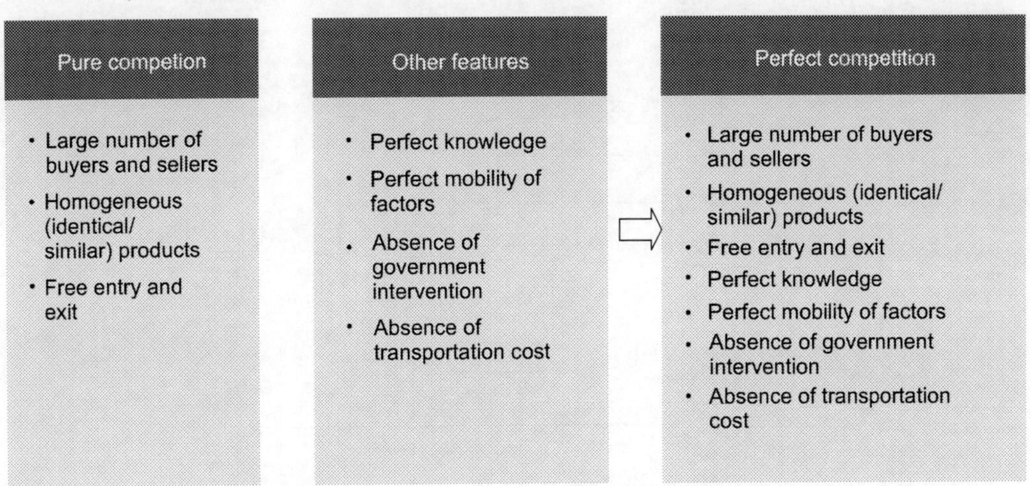


**Fig. 15.3** Pure Competition vs Perfect Competition

## 15.7 PRICE AND OUTPUT DECISIONS UNDER PERFECT COMPETITION

In perfect competition, the price and output are determined by the industry. Industry in such a case is the price maker and the firm is the price taker. The industry utilizes the dynamics of demand (buyer's side) and supply (seller's side) in order to determine the price. Therefore, the buyers are represented by demand curve and the firms are represented by supply curve.

The demand curve indicates:

- The ability and willingness of the consumers to purchase a product
- The taste and preferences of consumers
- Ability of the consumer to pay the price
- Willingness to part with the funds

Similarly, the supply curve indicates

- The ability and willingness of the firm to sell a product
- The cost conditions
- The price at which the product would be sold

Thus, both buyers and sellers assume equal role in the determination of price. Figure 15.4 shows the determination of equilibrium price in the following manner:

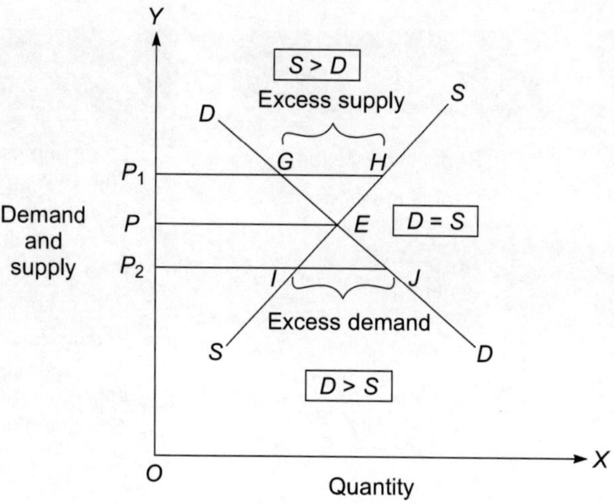


**Fig. 15.4** Price Determination under Perfectly Competitive Industry

In the above figure, the demand curve (*DD*) and supply curve (*SS*) are intersecting at point *E* where equilibrium price (*OP*) and output (*OQ*) is ascertained. The price and output remains unchanged till demand and supply remain constant.

At price $OP_1$, since supply is more than the demand, therefore there is excess supply as denoted by *GH*. Similarly, when the price is $OP_2$, the demand is more than the supply, therefore there is excess demand as denoted by *IJ*.

However, the price determination under perfectly competitive firm is as follows:

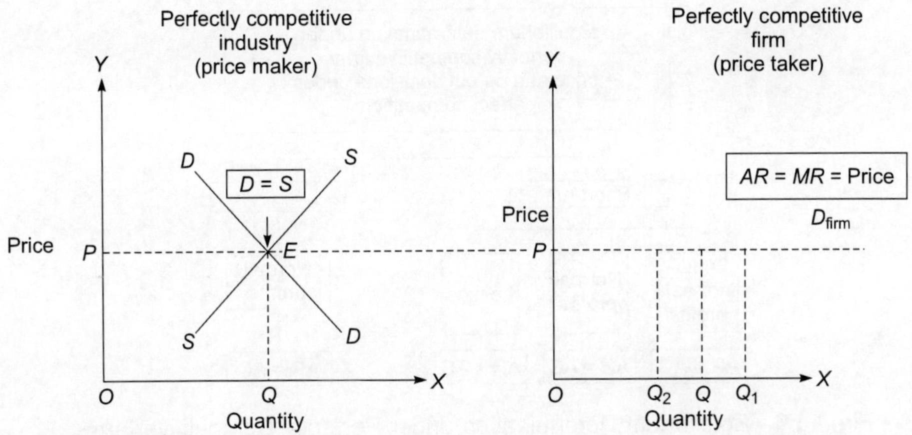


**Fig. 15.5** Price Determination under Perfectly Competitive Firm

In Fig. 15.5, demand curve of industry is reflected by *DD* which intersects supply curve of industry *SS* at point *E*. At this equilibrium price, the *OP* is the equilibrium price and *OQ* is the equilibrium output.

Since, industry is the price maker and the firm is the price taker, the price determined by industry will be taken by the firm. Thus, *OP* will be the price at which each firm under perfectly competitive firm will sell the output. The firm can neither increase or decrease price because it has been determined by the industry. Thus, at this price (*OP*), it can sell more ($OQ_1$) units or less ($OQ_2$) units.

The firm's demand curve is parallel to *X*-axis, signifying that the firm can sell any output at the prevailing price (*OP*). It is to be noted here that the firm's demand curve is also known as its *AR* curve and *MR* curve. *AR* and *MR* curves in case of perfectly competitive firm are parallel to *X*-axis. Since, perfectly competitive firms sell additional units of output at the same price, marginal revenue curve coincides with average revenue curve. Thus, at *OP* price, following relationship is established in case of perfectly competitive firm:

$$P = AR = MR.$$

## 15.8 SHORT-RUN EQUILIBRIUM OF THE FIRM/SHORT-RUN PRICE AND OUTPUT DECISIONS UNDER PERFECT COMPETITION

### Meaning of Equilibrium

The term equilibrium refers to a phenomenon which means the 'state of rest or balance and where there is no tendency to change'. A firm is said to be in equilibrium when it has no tendency either to expand or to contract its output. A firm is in equilibrium when it is earning maximum profit. The equilibrium determination is mainly studied in consonance with two time periods: short run and long run. It has been shown with the help of Fig. 15.6.

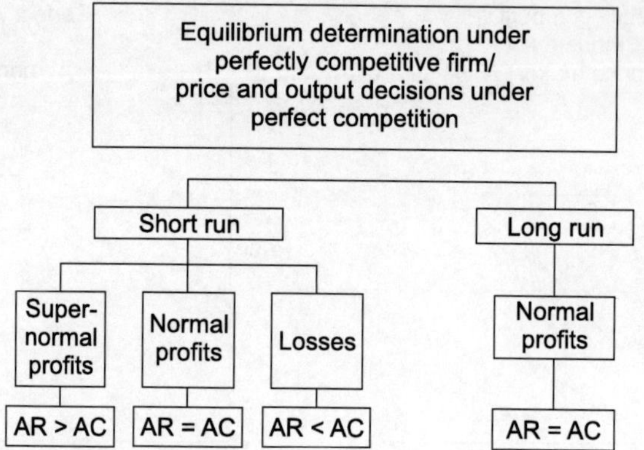


**Fig. 15.6** Equilibrium Determination under Perfectly Competitive Firm

## Conditions of Equilibrium

A firm would be in equilibrium when the following two conditions are fulfilled:

1. $MR = MC$ (First order condition for equilibrium – Necessary condition)
2. $MC$ curve cuts $MR$ curve from below (Second order condition for equilibrium – Sufficient condition)

## Equilibrium of the Firm in the Short Period

Short run means a time period in which the production can be changed by changing units of variable factors such as labour and raw material, while the units of fixed factors like capital, machinery, land, equipment remaining unchanged. Moreover, in the short run, new firms can neither enter the industry nor the existing firms can leave it.

Thus, under short run, the following cases of equilibrium determination exist:

**Case I:** Supernormal profits

**Case II:** Normal profit

**Case III:** Losses

**Case IV:** Shut down point

These cases have been explained as under:

### Case I: Supernormal profits ($AR > AC$)

A firm in equilibrium earns supernormal profits when there is excess of average revenue over the average cost. However, in order to qualify for equilibrium the following conditions must be satisfied.

- Marginal revenue is equal to marginal cost.
- Marginal cost curve cuts marginal revenue curve from below.

The diagrammatic representation of equilibrium determination has been shown in Fig. 15.7.

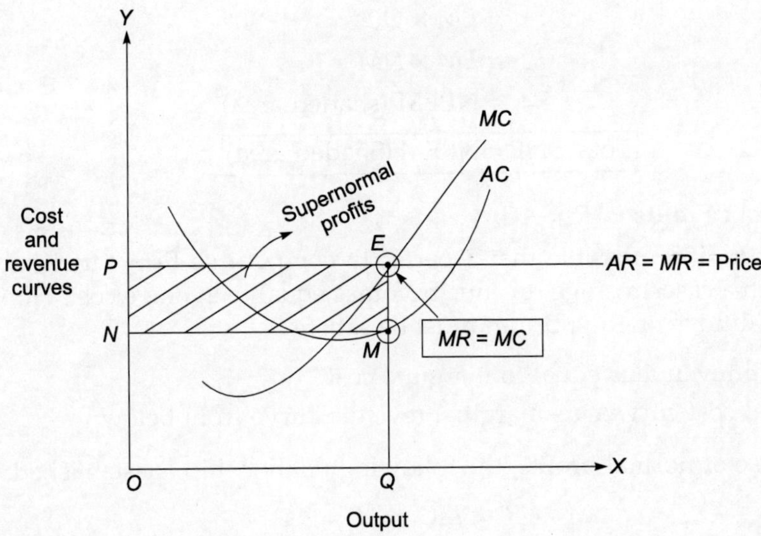


**Fig. 15.7** Determination of Supernormal Profits under Perfect Competition

The above diagram can be explained in the following manner:

1. Under perfectly competitive firm, since the firm is a price taker not price maker, Price = Average revenue = Marginal revenue and it is reflected by a straight line that is parallel to the *X*-axis.
2. *AC* and *MC* are short-run average and marginal cost curves of the firm. *AC* curve lies below *AR* curve.
3. The firm's equilibrium will be at point *E* when the conditions of equilibrium are satisfied.
4. A perpendicular parallel to the *Y*-axis is drawn from the equilibrium point *E* that connects the *X*-axis at *Q*. Here, equilibrium price (*OP*) and equilibrium quantity (*OQ*) are determined.

## DETERMINATION OF SUPERNORMAL PROFIT (SNP)

$$\text{SNP per unit} = AR - AC \quad \ldots(15.1)$$

where,

$$AR = EQ = OP$$
$$AC = MQ = ON$$

Substituting value of *AR* and *AC* in equation (15.1) we get,

$$\text{SNP per unit} = EQ - MQ$$
$$= EM$$
$$\text{Total SNP} = \text{SNP per unit} \times \text{Quantity sold}$$

$$= EM \times OQ$$
$$= EM \times NM$$
$$= \text{NPEM (shaded area)}$$

$$\boxed{\text{Total SNP} = \text{NPEM (Shaded area)}}$$

**Case II: Normal Profits (*AR* = *AC*)**

In the short run, it is possible that a perfectly competitive firm earns only normal profits. In such a case, average revenue becomes equal to average cost. However, the following conditions of equilibrium must be satisfied:

- Marginal revenue is equal to marginal cost.
- Marginal cost curve cuts marginal revenue curve from below.

Thus, in case of normal profits, the following relationship is established:

$$MR = MC = AR = AC$$

The diagrammatic representation of equilibrium determination has been shown in Fig. 15.8.

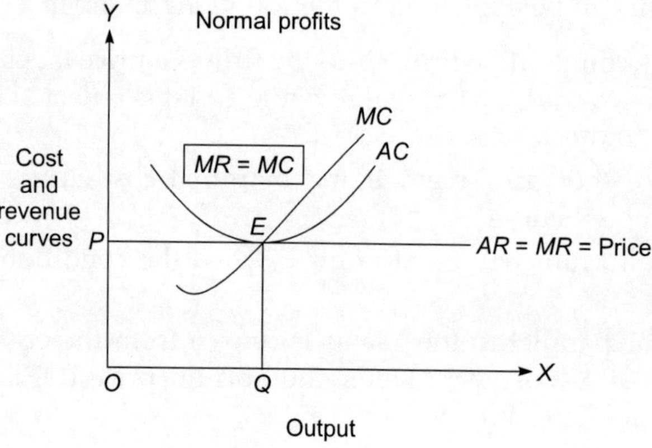


**Fig. 15.8** Determination of Normal Profits under Perfect Competition

The above diagram can be explained in the following manner:

1. Under perfectly competitive firm, since the firm is a price taker not price maker, Price = Average revenue = Marginal revenue and it is reflected by a straight line that is parallel to the *X*-axis.
2. *AC* and *MC* are short-run average and marginal cost curves of the firm. At *OQ* level of output the firms, *AC* curve is tangent to *AR* curve.
3. At equilibrium, in case of normal profits,

$$MR = MC = AR = AC$$

4. The firm's equilibrium will be at point *E* when the conditions of equilibrium are satisfied.

5. A perpendicular parallel to the $Y$-axis is drawn from the equilibrium point $E$ that connects the $X$-axis at $Q$. Here, equilibrium price ($OP$) and equilibrium quantity ($OQ$) are determined.

## DETERMINATION OF NORMAL PROFITS (NP)

$$\text{NP per unit} = AR - AC \qquad \ldots(15.2)$$

where,

$$AR = OP = EQ$$
$$AC = OP = EQ$$

Substituting value of $AR$ and $AC$ in equation (15.2) we get,

$$\begin{aligned} \text{NP per unit} &= EQ - EQ \\ &= 0 \\ \text{Total NP} &= \text{NP per unit} \times \text{Quantity Sold} \\ &= 0 \times OQ \\ &= 0 \\ \boxed{\text{Total NP} = 0} \end{aligned}$$

**Case III: Losses ($AR < AC$)**

A firm in equilibrium may incur losses when there is excess of average cost over the average revenue. However, in order to qualify for equilibrium the following conditions must be satisfied.

- Marginal revenue is equal to marginal cost.
- Marginal cost curve cuts marginal revenue curve from below.

The diagrammatic representation of equilibrium determination has been shown in Fig. 15.9.

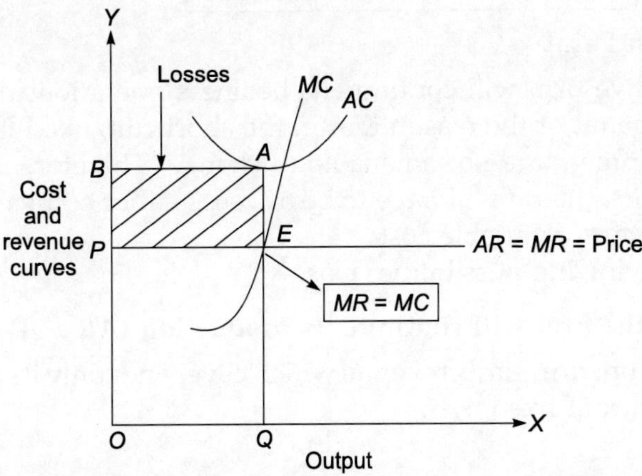


**Fig. 15.9** Determination of Losses under Perfect Competition

The above diagram can be explained in the following manner:

1. Under perfectly competitive firm, since the firm is a price taker not price maker, Price = Average revenue = Marginal revenue and it is reflected by a straight line that is parallel to the *X*-axis.
2. *AC* and *MC* are short-run average and marginal cost curves of the firm. *AC* curve lies above *AR* curve.
3. The firm's equilibrium will be at point *E* when the conditions of equilibrium are satisfied.
4. A perpendicular parallel to the *Y*-axis is drawn from the equilibrium point *E* that connects the *X*-axis at *Q*. Here, equilibrium price (*OP*) and equilibrium quantity (*OQ*) are determined.

## DETERMINATION OF LOSSES

$$\text{Loss per unit} = AC - AR \qquad \ldots(15.3)$$

where,

$$AC = AQ = OB$$
$$AR = EQ = OP$$

Substituting value of *AR* and *AC* in equation (15.3), we get

$$\begin{aligned} \text{Loss per unit} &= OB - OP \\ &= BP \\ \text{Total Loss} &= \text{Loss per unit} \times \text{Quantity Sold} \\ &= BP \times OQ \\ &= BP \times PE \text{ (as } OQ = PE) \\ &= PBAE \text{ (shaded area)} \end{aligned}$$

$$\boxed{\text{Total loss} = PBAE \text{ (shaded area)}}$$

**Case IV: Shut-Down Point**

A perfectly competitive firm will continue its business operations despite incurring losses. This is on account of the reason that in the short run, fixed factors like plant, machinery and equipment are not amenable to change. Therefore, if the firm stops production due to loss, then it will have to bear losses either equivalent to fixed cost or fixed cost plus a part of variable cost.

In this case, the following possibilities exist.

**Sub-Case I: Where the firm will continue its production (*AR* > *AVC*).**

**Condition:** In short run, firm earns revenue which covers not only its average variable cost but also some part of fixed cost.

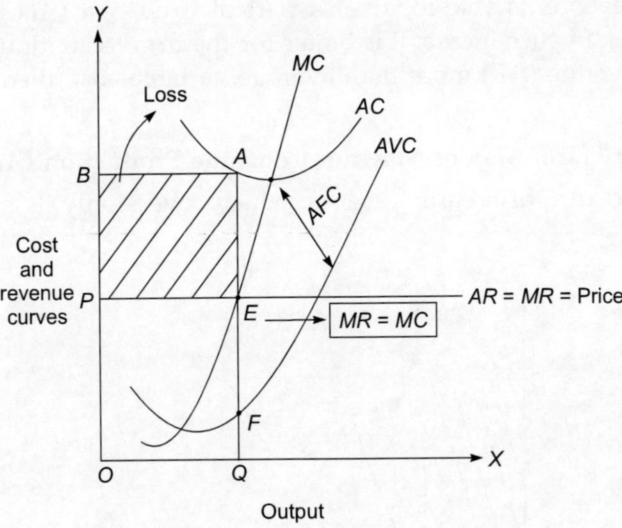


**Fig. 15.10** Where the Firm Will Continue Production

Figure 15.10 can be explained in the following manner:

1. Under perfectly competitive firm, since the firm is a price taker not price maker, Price = Average revenue = Marginal revenue and it is reflected by a straight line that is parallel to the *X*-axis.
2. *AC*, *AVC* and *MC* are short-run average and marginal cost curves of the firm. Minimum point on *AVC* is attained before attaining the minimum point on *AC* curve. *MC* curve passes through minimum of *AVC* and then it intersects *AC* curve at its minima.
3. The firm's equilibrium will be at point *E* when the conditions of equilibrium are satisfied.
4. A perpendicular parallel to the *Y*-axis is drawn from the equilibrium point *E* that connects the *X*-axis at *Q*. Here, equilibrium price (*OP*) and equilibrium quantity (*OQ*) are determined.
5. A perpendicular parallel to the *Y*-axis is drawn from the equilibrium point *E* upwards and it intersects *AC* curve at point *A*.

## Calculation

Loss = *AEPB*

*AFC* = *AF*

*AVC* = *FQ*

*AR* = *EQ*

*AR* = *EF* (a part of fixed cost) + *FQ* (entire variable cost)

It means that revenue is able to cover a part of fixed cost (*AFC*) and the entire variable cost (*AVC*). In such a case, it is better for the firm to continue to produce so long as it earns revenue (*AR*) more than average variable cost, then firm will incur minimum losses.

**Sub-Case II: Where Firm May or May not Continue Production (*AR* = *AVC*).**

**Condition:** In short run, firm earns revenue which covers only its average variable cost.

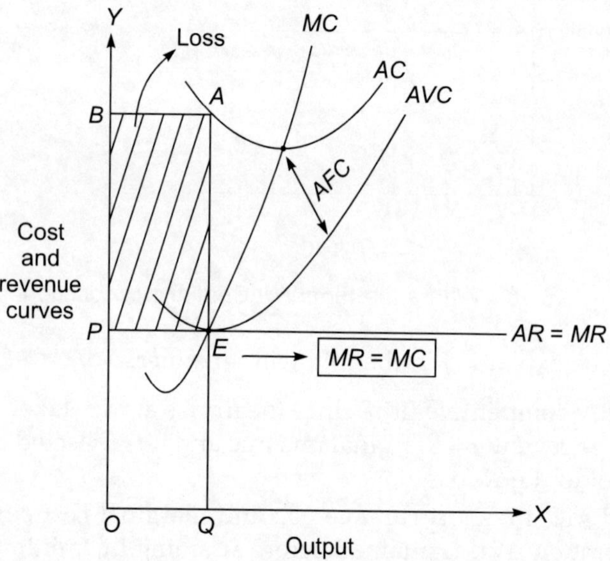


**Fig. 15.11** Where Firm May or May not Continue Production

Figure 15.11 can be explained in the following manner:

1. Under perfectly competitive firm, since the firm is a price taker not price maker, Price = Average revenue = Marginal revenue and it is reflected by a straight line that is parallel to the *X*-axis.
2. *AC*, *AVC* and *MC* are short-run average and marginal cost curves of the firm. Minimum point on *AVC* is attained before attaining the minimum point on *AC* curve. *MC* curve passes through minimum of *AVC* and then it intersects *AC* curve at its minima.
3. The firm's equilibrium will be at point *E* when the conditions of equilibrium are satisfied.
4. A perpendicular parallel to the *Y*-axis is drawn from the equilibrium point *E* that connects the *X*-axis at *Q*. Here, equilibrium price (*OP*) and equilibrium quantity (*OQ*) are determined.
5. A perpendicular parallel to the *Y*-axis is drawn from the equilibrium point *E* upwards and it intersects *AC* curve at point *A*.

**Calculation**

$$Loss = BAEP$$
$$AFC = AE$$
$$AVC = EQ$$
$$AR = EQ$$

Here,

$$AR = AVC = EQ$$
$$AR = EQ \text{ (entire variable cost)}$$

Thus,

$$Loss = \text{Fixed cost} = BAEP$$

In such a case, firm may or may not shut down its business operations.

It means that revenue is able to cover the entire variable cost (*AVC*) and loss is equal to the fixed cost. In such a case, firm does not continue its business operations, then also it has to bear loss equal to fixed cost or if it continues its business operations, then also loss is equal to fixed cost (*BAEP*). Thus, in such a case, firm may or may not shut down its business operations.

**Sub-Case III: Where Firm will Definitely Shut Down its Production: The Shut Down Condition (*AR* < *AVC*)**

**Condition:** In short run, firm earns revenue but is not able to cover the entire fixed cost (*AFC*) and a part of variable cost (*AVC*).

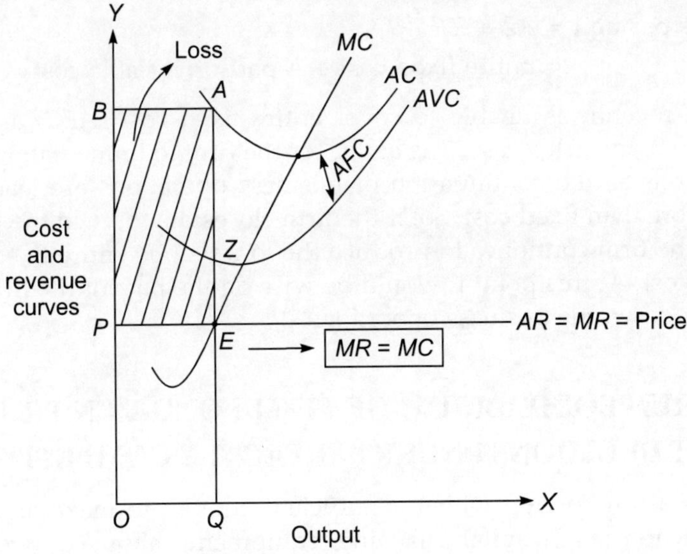


**Fig. 15.12** The Shut Down Condition

Figure 15.12 can be explained in the following manner:

1. Under perfectly competitive firm, since the firm is a price taker not price maker, Price = Average revenue = Marginal revenue and it is reflected by a straight line that is parallel to the *X*-axis.
2. *AC*, *AVC* and *MC* are short-run average and marginal cost curves of the firm. Minimum point on *AVC* is attained before attaining the minimum point on *AC* curve. *MC* curve passes through minimum of *AVC* and then it intersects *AC* curve at its minima.
3. The firm's equilibrium will be at point *E* when the conditions of equilibrium are satisfied.
4. A perpendicular parallel to the *Y*-axis is drawn from the equilibrium point *E* that connects the *X*-axis at *Q*. Here, equilibrium price (*OP*) and equilibrium quantity (*OQ*) are determined.
5. A perpendicular parallel to the *Y*-axis is drawn from the equilibrium point *E* upwards and it intersects *AC* curve at point *A* and *AVC* curve at point *Z*.

**Calculation**

$$\text{Loss} = PBAE$$
$$AFC = AZ$$
$$AVC = ZQ$$
$$AR = EQ$$
$$\text{Loss per unit} = AE$$
$$\text{Loss per unit} = AZ + ZE$$
$$= \text{Entire fixed cost} + \text{A part of variable cost}$$

It means that revenue is unable to cover entire fixed cost (*AFC*) and a part of variable cost (*AVC*). In such a case, it is better for the firm to immediately shut down business operations as the continuation of business operations are leading to loss which is even more than fixed cost. So, if the firm closes down, then the loss is equal to fixed cost. If the firm continues to produce the loss will be entire fixed cost and a part of variable cost. At this point it would be wise on the part of the firm to reduce losses by closing down the business operations.

## 15.9 LONG-RUN EQUILIBRIUM OF FIRM/LONG-RUN PRICE AND OUTPUT DECISIONS UNDER PERFECTLY COMPETITIVE FIRM

Long run means a time period which is sufficient enough to make adjustments in factors of production (e.g., capital, machine, equipment, labour) as well as in the number of firms. On one side, it is sufficiently long to make changes in all factors of production. On the other side, new firm can enter the industry to compete with the existing firms in long run.

A perfectly competitive firm is in equilibrium, when the following marginal conditions are satisfied:

1. $MC = MR$
2. $MC$ curve must cut $MR$ curve from below.

But for the firm to be in long-run equilibrium, besides the equality of $MC$ and $MR$, there must be equality of $AR$ and $AC$. Thus, it can be inferred that in long run the equality of the following is required:

$$MR = MC = AR = AC$$

It means that in long run, the perfectly competitive firm will get only normal profits. The reasons have been reflected with the help of Fig. 15.13.

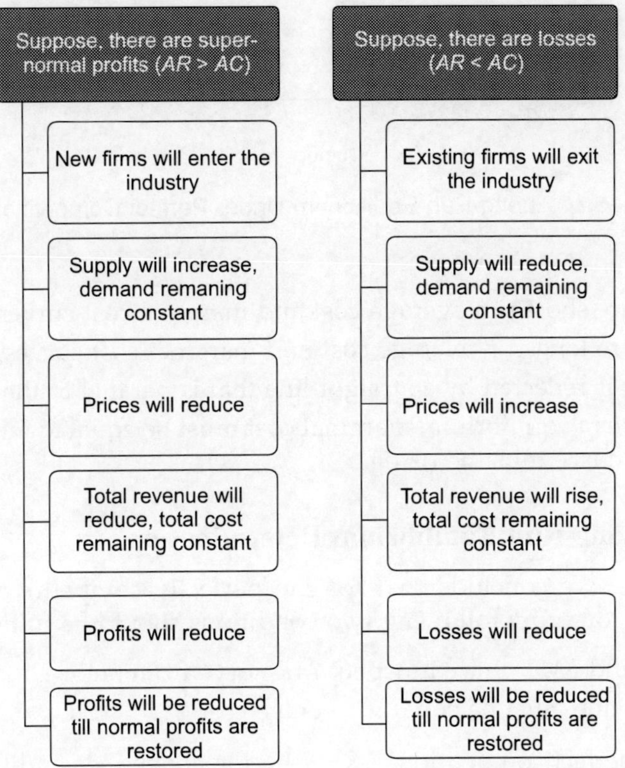


**Fig 15.13** Reasons of Normal Profits in Long Run under Perfect Competition

Thus, the firms will get only normal profit, in the long run.

**Equilibrium Determination**

In the long run, firms are in equilibrium when they produce at the minimum point of their long run $AC$ curve ($LAC$). In addition $LAC$ must be tangent to the demand curve ($AR$). This condition leads to earning normal profits in long run. The long-run equilibrium determination under perfectly competitive firm has been shown in Fig. 15.4.

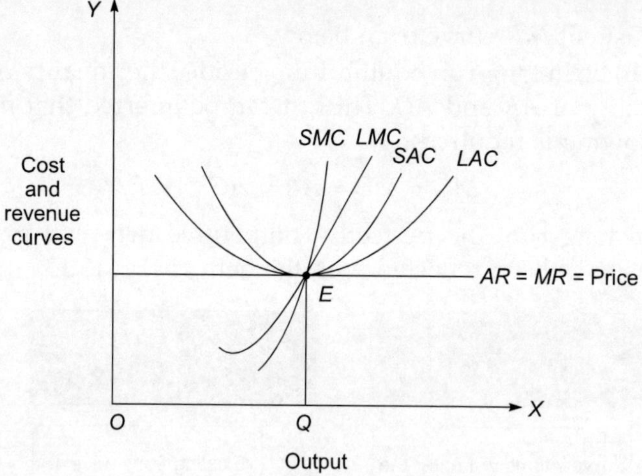


**Fig. 15.14** Long-Run Equilibrium Under Perfect Competition

In Fig. 15.14,

*SAC* and *SMC* are short-run average cost and marginal cost curves, respectively.

*LAC* and *LMC* are long-run average cost and marginal cost curves, respectively.

*AR* = *MR* and it is reflected by a straight line that is parallel to the *X*-axis.

For the firm to be in equilibrium, marginal cost must be equal to marginal revenue and marginal cost curve must be rising.

## Conditions for Long-Run Equilibrium Determination

From this analysis, we conclude that for the perfectly competitive firm to be in equilibrium in the long run, following two conditions should be fulfilled.

(i) *LMC* = *MR* and *LMC* curve must cut *MR* curve from below.

(ii) Average revenue must be equal to average cost (*AR* = *LAC*).

Because in the perfect competition, *AR* = *MR*, the above the condition can also be written as:

$$\text{Price} = AR = MR = LMC = LAC.$$

$$\text{Price} = LMC = LAC$$

Since, there is one point where the short-run average and marginal curves meet the long-run curves. It is known as equilibrium point *E*. Thus, at *E* the following relationships are established:

$$\text{Price} = AR = MR = SAC = SMC = LAC = LMC$$

The relationship between *MC* and *AC* also reveals that *MC* curve cuts *LAC* curve at its minimum point.

These conditions for long-run equilibrium of the firm can also be written as:

Price = *LMC* = Minimum long-run average cost

## Summary

- ✓ Market represents the entire area or region or network where buyers and sellers of a product are spread and are connected.
- ✓ There are four forms of market structure
  - Perfect competition
  - Monopoly
  - Monopolistic competition
  - Oligopoly
- ✓ Perfect competition refers to a market structure which is characterized by a large number of buyer and sellers where the sellers are selling homogeneous products.
- ✓ Pure competition is characterized by the following features:
  - Large number of buyers and sellers
  - Homogeneous products
  - Free entry and exit
- ✓ When the following features are added to pure competition, perfect competition comes into existence. These four features are as follows:
  - Perfect knowledge
  - Perfect mobility of factors
  - Absence of government intervention
  - Absence of transportation cost
- ✓ Under perfect competition, the industry is the price maker and firm is the price taker. The price in industry is determined by the intersection of demand and supply curves. The firms can sell output at the prevailing price that has been determined by the industry.
- ✓ *AR* and *MR* curves in case of perfectly competitive firm are a line parallel to *X*-axis.
- ✓ A firm would be in equilibrium when the following two conditions are fulfilled:
  - *MR* = *MC* (First order condition for equilibrium – Necessary condition)
  - *MC* curve cuts *MR* curve from below (Second order condition for equilibrium – Sufficient condition)

- ✓ Under short run, the following cases of equilibrium determination exist :
  - Supernormal profit
  - Normal profit
  - Losses
  - Shut-down point
- ✓ In long run, the perfectly competitive firm will get only normal profits due to the assumption of free entry and exit.
- ✓ The conditions for long-run equilibrium determination under perfectly competitive firm are as follows:
  - *LMC* = *MR* and *LMC* curve must cut *MR* curve from below.
  - Average revenue must be equal to average cost (*AR* = *LAC*).
- ✓ The conditions for long-run equilibrium of the firm can also be written as:

Price = *LMC* = Minimum long-run average cost

## Review Questions

1. Explain the short and long-run equilibria determination under perfect competitive firm.
2. Elaborate the price and output determination in case of perfect competition.
3. Why a perfect competitive firm earns only normal profits in long run. Explain with reasons.
4. What are the features of perfect competition? Distinguish between pure and perfect competition.
5. Is there any difference between pure and perfect competition? If yes, what is the points of difference between these two?
6. Explain the statement "Under perfect competition, the industry is the price maker and firm is the price taker".
7. Explain the short-run equilibrium of perfect competition firm. What are the necessary and sufficient conditions of equilibrium determination?
8. When would a perfectly competitive firm close down in short run?
9. Under what conditions would a firm continue to produce in short run despite of incurring losses.
10. What are the conditions of equilibrium determination under perfect competition in the long run? Prove that in the long run, price is equal to long-run average and marginal cost.
11. What is the best level of output of a perfect competitive firm in long run?
12. Is there any difference in equilibrium determination in short and long run under perfect competition? If yes, bring out the cases of equilibrium determination in this regard.

## CASE STUDY: PERFECT COMPETITION IN CREDIT CARD INDUSTRY (AUGUST, 2015)

In 1997, over $700 billion purchases were charged on credit cards, and this total is increasing at a rate of over 10 per cent a year. At first glance, the credit card market would seem to be a rather concentrated industry. Visa, MasterCard and American Express are the most familiar names, and over 60 per cent of all charges are made using one of these three cards. But on closer examination, the industry seems to exhibit most characteristics of perfect competition.

Consider first the size and distribution of buyers and sellers. Although Visa, Mastercard and American Express are the choices of the majority of consumers, these cards do not originate from just three firms. In fact, there are over six thousand enterprises (primarily banks and credit unions) in the US that offer charge cards to over 90 million credit card holders. One person's Visa card may have been issued by his company's credit union in Los Angeles, while a next door neighbour may have acquired hers from a Miami Bank when she was living in Florida.

Credit cards are a relatively homogeneous product. Most Visa cards are similar in appearance, and they can all be used for the same purposes. When the charge is made, the merchant is unlikely to notice who it was that actually issued the card. Entry into and exit from the credit card market is easy as evidenced by the 6000 institutions that currently offer cards. Although a new firm might find it difficult to enter the market, a financially sound bank, even one of modest size, could obtain the right to offer a MasterCard or a Visa card from the present companies with little difficulty. If the bank wanted to leave the field, there would be a ready market to sell its accounts to other credit card suppliers. Thus, it would seem that the credit card industry meets most of the characteristics for a perfectly competitive market.

*Source:* Live Economics (August 31, 2015). Perfect Competition in Credit Card Industry. Retrieved from http://bkmiba.blogspot.com/2015/08/case-study-perfect-competition-in.html on November 15, 2019.

### Questions

1. What are the characteristics of perfect competition that are exhibited by the credit card industry?
2. Do you think the same competitive state is applicable to the Indian scenario?
3. Do you think that the rise in commercial activities and the growing malls have impacted the credit card market?

16 CHAPTER

# Price and Output Decisions Under Monopoly

**LEARNING OBJECTIVES**

After going through this chapter, reader would be able to understand:

- ✓ The meaning and assumptions that formulate the base of monopoly market structure.
- ✓ The types of monopoly market structure.
- ✓ The short-run price and output decisions under pure or simple monopoly.
- ✓ The long-run price and output decisions under pure or simple monopoly.
- ✓ The concept, types and degrees of price discrimination.
- ✓ Price-output determination under discriminating monopolist.

## 16.1 INTRODUCTION

In this chapter, we move our discussion to another form of market structure, that is, monopoly. The chapter begins with a basic discussion on the concept of monopoly and specifies the underlying assumptions behind this market form. Further, the discussion on the kinds of monopoly market structure has been done so as to have the holistic view of monopoly. In order to understand that price and output determination under monopoly, the chapter further discusses the revenue and cost curves. In this market form, there is a single seller selling products which have no close substitutes. The presence of a single seller lapses the distinction between firm and industry.

The chapter moves further with determination of short-run equilibrium under pure or simple monopoly. In short run, the three possibilities in terms of supernormal profits, normal profits and losses have been discussed. Then we go on to determine the long-run equilibrium under pure or simple monopoly. Moving further, the concept, types and degrees of price discrimination have been discussed. In the last section, price-output determination by discriminating monopolist operating in different markets has been discussed. It is again a hypothetical market form but to explain the concept, the examples of Indian Railways, electricity, communication, etc., are given to understand the concept of monopoly market structure.

## 16.2 MEANING OF MONOPOLY

It is an extreme form of imperfect competition. The word monopoly derives from two Greek words: 'mono' means 'single' and 'poly' means 'seller'. Thus, monopoly means a market structure that is characterized by existence of a single producer or single seller. The seller being single produces or sells a product which has no close substitute. The person who has monopoly power is known as monopolist. He has no competitors or rivals. In absence of competition, he dictates price. Thus, he is the price maker and can fix the price. There are strong barriers to entry into the industry. As a result, seller has full control over the supply of the commodity. In absence of any other competitive firm, the difference between firm and industry disappears. Hence, firm is the industry itself.

## 16.3 ASSUMPTIONS/FEATURES OF MONOPOLY

1. **Existence of a Single Seller and Large Number of Buyers**

   In case of monopoly form of market structure, a single firm produces and sells a particular commodity or a service. It has two implications:

   1. The distinction between firm and industry vanishes as industry is the composition of many firms and here the firm is the sole seller. Thus, firm itself is the industry.
   2. The existence of no other seller except the monopolist points that the buyers' bargaining power would be weak or almost nil.

2. **Products with No Close Substitutes**

   - A monopolist would be called a monopolist only and only when the product he is producing have no close substitutes.
   - In such a case, the cross elasticity of demand exhibiting the relationship between price of a commodity (say, commodity $X$) and quantity of substitute commodity (say, commodity $Y$) is almost nil.
   - In case, there is a product for which the close substitutes are available then there will be dilution of monopoly powers and it will cease to exist.

3. **Strong Entry Barriers**

   - In a monopoly market, strong barrier on the entry of new firms exist. No other seller can enter the market for whatever reasons.
   - In absence of any competition, monopolist has absolute control over the production and sale of the commodity.

4. **Nature of Demand Curve**

   - The demand curve in case of monopoly form of market is a downward sloping demand curve. This is because the entire demand of the consumers for a product goes to the monopolist.

- Thus, a monopolist can sell higher output at reduced price and can sell lower output at higher price. This is reflected by a downward sloping demand curve that expresses that the price (*AR*) goes on falling as sales are increased.
- In monopoly, *AR* curve slopes downward from left to right. Regarding *MR* curve, *MR* lies below *AR* curve and falls twice the rate as *AR* curve.

5. **Profit Maximization Motive**

A monopolist is a price maker and can fix either output or the price. He has strong control over the price of his product. Thus, he utilizes this motive in order to derive maximum profits.

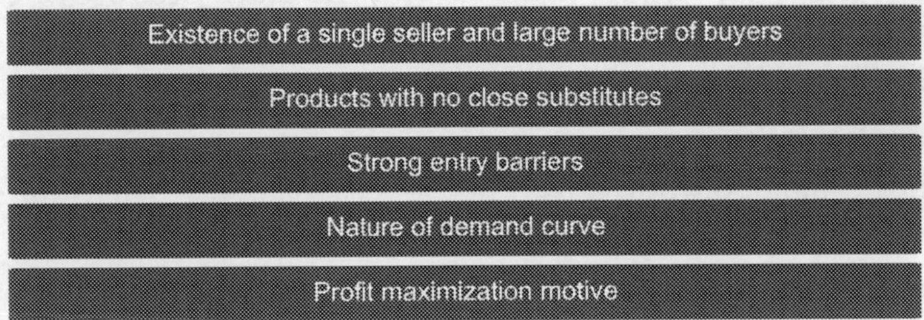


**Fig. 16.1** Assumptions of Monopoly

## 16.4 KINDS OF MONOPOLY

The types of monopoly form of market structure have been reflected in Fig. 16.2.

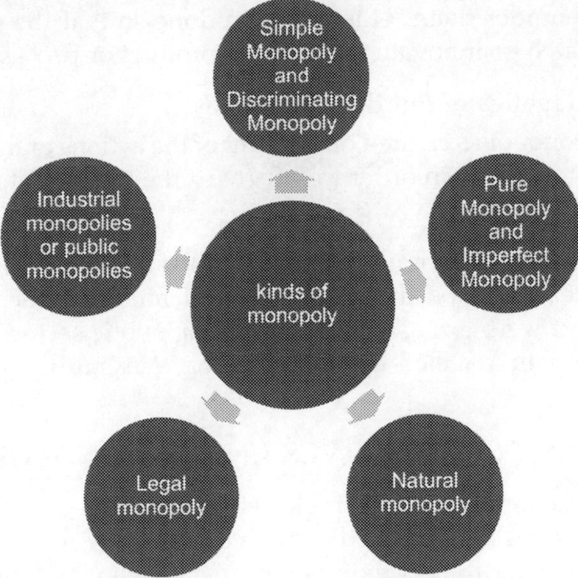


**Fig. 16.2** Kinds of Monopoly

1. **Simple Monopoly and Discriminating Monopoly**
   - **Simple monopoly** is a market structure in which the monopolist charges uniform price for a given product from its buyers.
   - **Discriminating monopoly** is a market structure in which the monopolist charges different price for same product from different buyers.
2. **Pure Monopoly and Imperfect Monopoly**
   - **Pure or simple monopoly** is a rare form of monopoly form of market where the seller enjoys an absolute monopoly power and has strong control over the supplies. It is also called simple monopoly.
   - **Imperfect monopoly** refers to a single firm which produces a commodity having no close substitutes. In this case, the extent or degree of monopoly is less than perfect.
3. **Natural Monopoly**

   It refers to the monopoly power awarded as a gift of nature. This is the monopoly enjoyed as a result of advantage in terms of factor endowments.

   ***For example:*** Canada has got monopoly in nickel production.
4. **Legal Monopoly**

   The monopoly acquired as a result of operation of law or the legal provisions is known as legal monopoly.

   ***For example:*** The prevalence of legal provisions on intellectual properties like patents, trade-marks, copyrights prohibits the potential competitors to imitate the works done under them. This has been done so that the genuine work of those who research or innovate a particular product or process is protected.
5. **Industrial Monopolies or Public Monopolies**

   These are the monopolies created on account of the actions of the government or any other statutory body in order to safeguard the overall interest of economy as a whole.

   ***For example:*** The new economic policy of 1991 led to reservation policy wherein certain industries like arms and ammunition, defense, atomic energy, railways and air transport were exclusively reserved for public sector. This resulted in industrial monopolies created through statutory measures.

## 16.5 REVENUE AND COST CURVES UNDER MONOPOLY

Under monopoly, a monopolist is the single seller and thus, aims to maximize his profits. A monopolist faces a downward sloping demand (or *AR*) curve. This is due to the fact that he can lower the price of the product to sell more and can sell less at an enhanced price. In addition, marginal revenue curve is also downward sloping. This has been reflected as follows:

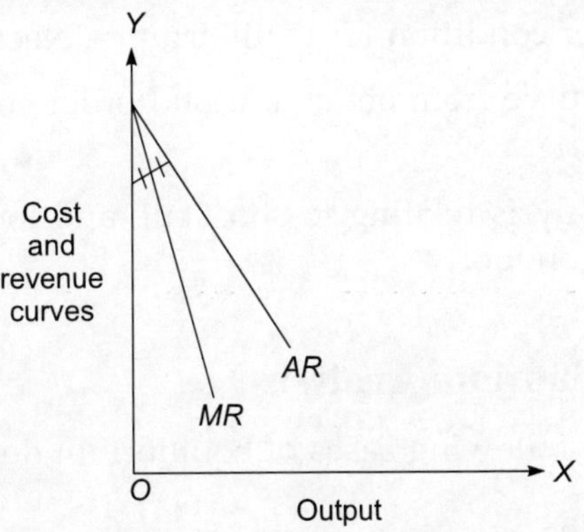


**Fig. 16.3** *AR* and *MR* Curves under Monopoly

In Fig. 16.3, *AR* curve is a downward sloping steep curve from left to right. Marginal revenue (*MR*) curve is also downward sloping and lies below the average revenue curve. In addition, the *MR* curve falls twice the rate as *AR* curve. The monopolist will use these *AR* and *MR* curves along with the conventional 'U shaped' cost curves to arrive at equilibrium. The cost curves have been considered directly for equilibrium analysis under Section 16.6 and 16.7.

## 16.6 SHORT-RUN EQUILIBRIUM UNDER MONOPOLY FIRM/SHORT-RUN PRICE AND OUTPUT DECISIONS UNDER MONOPOLY

The equilibrium determination is mainly studied in consonance with two time periods: short run and long run. It has been shown with the help of Fig. 16.4.

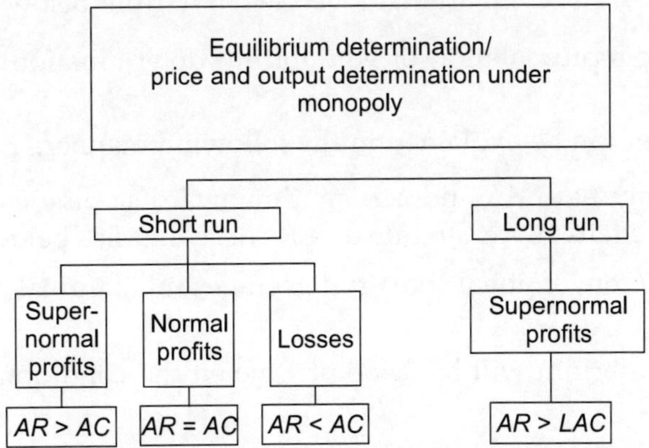


**Fig. 16.4** Equilibrium Determination under Monopoly

However, the marginal conditions of equilibrium are same, like perfect competition. These are:

1. *MR* = *MC* (First order condition for equilibrium – Necessary condition)
2. *MC* curve cuts *MR* curve from below (Second order condition for equilibrium – Sufficient condition)

However, the innate analysis relating to short run and long run varies in case of perfect competition and monopoly.

### 16.6.1 Short-Run Equilibrium Analysis

Thus, under short run, the following cases of equilibrium determination exist:

**Case I:** Supernormal profits

**Case II:** Normal profit

**Case III:** Losses

These cases have been explained as under.

**Case I: Supernormal Profits (*AR* > *AC*)**

A monopolist earns supernormal profits if the price (*AR*) charged by him supercedes the average cost (*AC*). Thus, a firm is said to be making supernormal profits if *AR* > *AC*. In this case, the price charged by the firm covers all the costs and also generates a surplus over the expenditure. Hence, it is called supernormal profits.

However, in order to qualify for equilibrium the following conditions must be satisfied.

- Marginal revenue is equal to marginal cost.
- Marginal cost curve cuts marginal revenue curve from below.

The diagrammatic representation of equilibrium determination has been shown in Fig. 16.5.

The above diagram can be explained in the following manner:

1. Under monopoly, both *AR* and *MR* are downward sloping curves from left to right. *MR* curve falls twice the rate as *AR* curve and lies below it.
2. *AC* and *MC* are conventional short-run average and marginal cost curves of the firm.
3. The firm's equilibrium will be at point *E* when the conditions of equilibrium are satisfied.
4. A perpendicular parallel to the *Y*-axis is drawn from the equilibrium point *E* that connects the *X*-axis at *Q*. Here, equilibrium quantity (*OQ*) is determined.

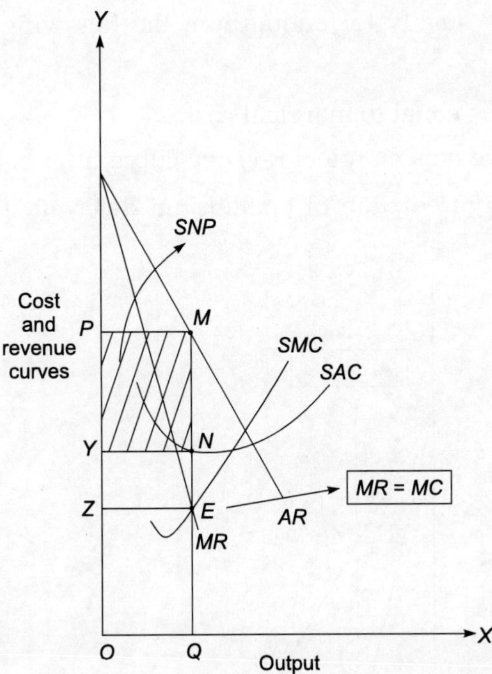


**Fig. 16.5** Determination of Supernormal Profits under Monopoly

## DETERMINATION OF SUPERNORMAL PROFIT (SNP)

$$\text{SNP per unit} = AR - AC \qquad \ldots(1)$$

where,

$AR = MQ = OP$

$AC = NQ = OY$

Substituting value of *AR* and *AC* in equation (1) we get,

$$\begin{aligned} \text{SNP per unit} &= OP - OY \\ &= PY \\ \text{Total SNP} &= \text{SNP per unit} \times \text{Quantity sold} \\ &= PY \times OQ \\ &= PY \times YN \\ &= YPMN \text{ (shaded area)} \end{aligned}$$

**Total SNP = *YPMN* (Shaded area)**

**Case II: Normal Profits (*AR* = *AC*)**

A monopolist earns normal profits when the average revenue (*AR*) is equal to average cost (*AC*). It means that the price (*AR*) covers the costs (*AC*). Normal profit is also called 'no profit no loss' condition or breakeven point in managerial economics.

However, in order to qualify for equilibrium the following conditions must be satisfied.

- Marginal revenue is equal to marginal cost.
- Marginal cost curve cuts marginal revenue curve from below.

The diagrammatic representation of equilibrium determination has been shown in Fig. 16.6.

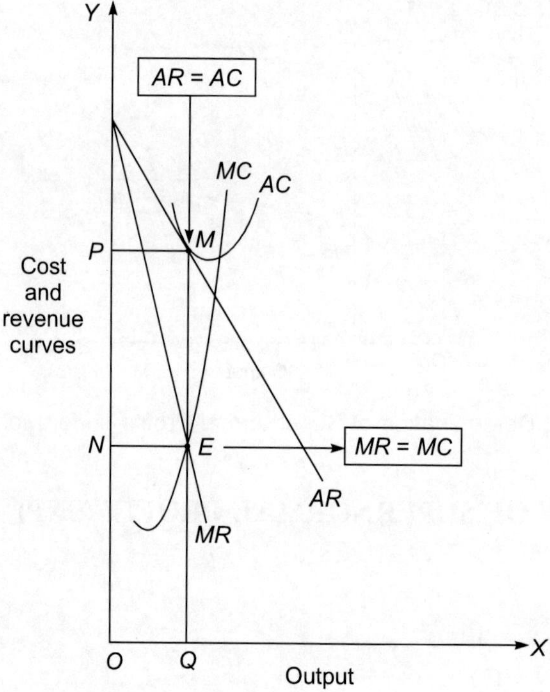


**Fig. 16.6** Determination of Normal Profits under Monopoly

The above diagram can be explained in the following manner:

1. Under monopoly, both *AR* and *MR* are downward sloping curves from left to right. *MR* curve falls twice the rate as *AR* curve and lies below it.
2. *AC* and *MC* are conventional short-run average and marginal cost curves of the firm.
3. The firm's equilibrium will be at point *E* when the conditions of equilibrium are satisfied.
4. A perpendicular parallel to the *Y*-axis is drawn from the equilibrium point *E* that connects the *X*-axis at *Q*. Here, equilibrium quantity (*OQ*) is determined.

## DETERMINATION OF NORMAL PROFITS (NP)

$$NP \text{ per unit} = AR - AC \quad \ldots(1)$$

where,

$$AR = MQ = OP$$
$$AC = MQ = OP$$

Substituting value of $AR$ and $AC$ in equation (1) we get,

$$NP \text{ per unit} = OP - OP$$
$$= 0$$
$$\text{Total } NP = \text{SNP per unit} \times \text{Quantity sold}$$
$$= 0 \times OQ$$
$$= 0$$

**Total $NP$ = 0**

### Case III: Losses ($AR < AC$)

A monopoly firm is said to incur losses if, the average cost ($AC$) supercedes the average revenue ($AR$). However, in order to qualify for equilibrium the following conditions must be satisfied.

- Marginal revenue is equal to marginal cost.
- Marginal cost curve cuts marginal revenue curve from below.

The diagrammatic representation of equilibrium determination has been shown in Fig. 16.7.

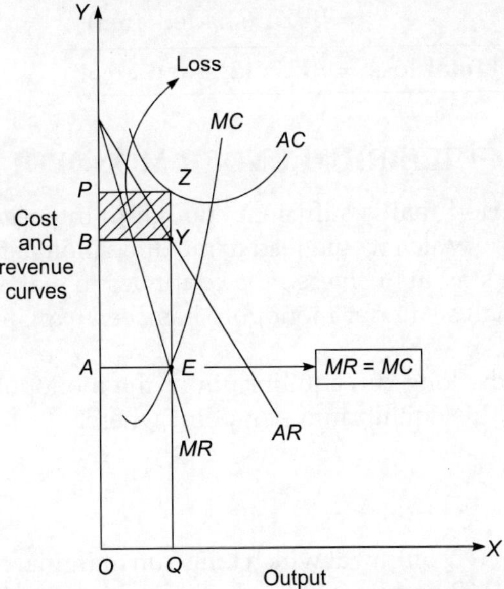


**Fig. 16.7** Determination of Losses under Monopoly

The above diagram can be explained in the following manner:

1. Under monopoly, both *AR* and *MR* are downward sloping curves from left to right. *MR* curve falls twice the rate as *AR* curve and lies below it.
2. *AC* and *MC* are conventional short-run average and marginal cost curves of the firm.
3. The firm's equilibrium will be at point *E* when the conditions of equilibrium are satisfied.
4. A perpendicular parallel to the *Y*-axis is drawn from the equilibrium point *E* that connects the *X*-axis at *Q*. Here, equilibrium quantity (*OQ*) is determined.

## DETERMINATION OF LOSSES

$$\text{Loss per unit} = AC - AR \qquad \text{...(16.1)}$$

where,

$$AC = ZQ = OP$$
$$AR = YQ = OB$$

Substituting value of *AR* and *AC* in equation (16.1), we get

$$\begin{aligned} \text{Loss per unit} &= OP - OB \\ &= PB \\ \text{Total loss} &= \text{Loss per unit} \times \text{Quantity sold} \\ &= PB \times OQ \\ &= PB \times BY \\ &= \text{BPZY (shaded area)} \end{aligned}$$

**Total loss = BPZY (Shaded area)**

## 16.7 LONG-RUN EQUILIBRIUM UNDER MONOPOLY FIRM

Long run is the time period that is sufficient enough to intensively use the existing plant or acquire a new one which would lead to maximization of the profits. However, a monopolist would not stay in business if he continues to make losses for long. The long-run equilibrium analysis under monopoly has been explained with the help of Fig. 16.8.

Figure 16.8 portrays the long-run equilibrium of the monopolist. In the long run, the monopolist will find his equilibrium at a point where,

1. *LMC* = *MR*
2. *LMC* cuts *MR* from below

He is in equilibrium at *OQ* output at which long-run marginal curve *LMC* intersects marginal revenue curve *MR* and he will be charging price equal to *MQ* or *OP*.

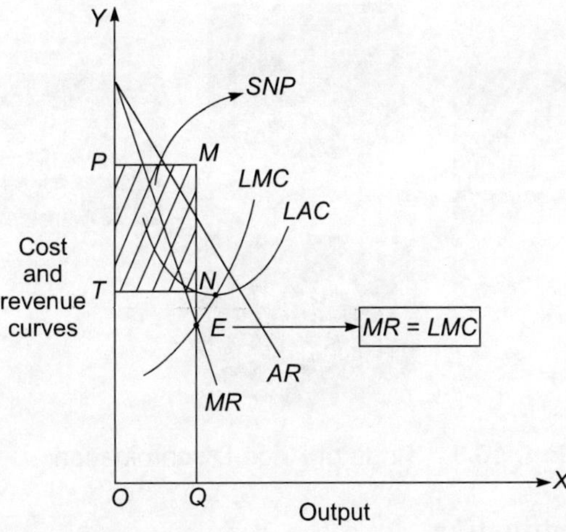


**Fig. 16.8** Determination of Long-Run Equilibrium under Monopoly Firm

## DETERMINATION OF SUPERNORMAL PROFIT (SNP)

$$SNP \text{ per unit} = AR - AC \quad \ldots(1)$$

where,

$$AR = MQ = OP$$
$$AC = NQ = OT$$

Substituting value of *AR* and *AC* in equation (1) we get,

$$SNP \text{ per unit} = OP - OT$$
$$= PT$$
$$\text{Total } SNP = SNP \text{ per unit} \times \text{Quantity sold}$$
$$= PT \times OQ$$
$$= PT \times TN$$
$$= TPMN \text{ (Shaded area)}$$

**Total *SNP* = *TPMN* (Shaded area)**

## 16.8 PRICE DISCRIMINATION OR DISCRIMINATING MONOPOLIST

Price discrimination refers to the practice of selling the same product at different prices to different buyers. Robinson defines it as "charging different price for the same product or same price for differentiated product".

### Kinds of Price Discrimination

Price discrimination may be divided under the following heads (Fig. 16.9):

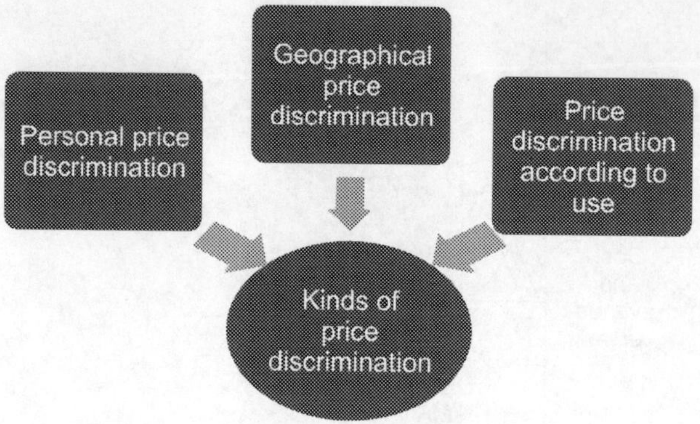


**Fig. 16.9** Kinds of Price Discrimination

### 1. Personal Price Discrimination

Personal price discrimination is said to exist when the seller charges different prices from different persons for the same commodity or service.

***For example:***

- In salon, the price charged by barber may be less for a child and more for an adult.
- A doctor may charge high fees for consultation from a rich patient but may charge less or no fee from a poor patient.
- A vegetable seller may charge different prices from different customers for same product.

### 2. Geographical Price Discrimination

Geographical price discrimination is said to exist when the seller charges different prices for people of different localities. Hence, in such a case, the seller discriminates between the customers on the basis of geographic region or area; it is known as geographical price discrimination. In this case, a seller may charge different prices in domestic and international markets.

**For instance:**

- A seller may charge low price from local people but more from foreign tourists.
- A seller of apparel may charge more prices in South Delhi as compared to west or east Delhi.

### 3. Price Discrimination According to Use

Price discrimination according to use is said to exist when the same commodity is put to different uses.

**For example,** electricity is usually sold at a higher rate for industrial than for domestic purposes.

## Degrees of Price Discrimination

Price discrimination has been defined in terms of three degrees which are as follows:

1. First degree of price discrimination
2. Second degree of price discrimination
3. Third degree of price discrimination

### 1. First Degree of Price Discrimination

- First degree of price discrimination is also known as 'take it or leave it policy'.
- In this case, the monopolist charges different prices for each unit of commodity from different customers.
- Here, the seller has the motive of exploiting the consumer's desire. Thus, he charges a price equal to what the consumer is willing to pay.
- When the consumer actually pays a price that is equal to the amount that he is willing to pay, consumer is left with no surplus.
- Thus, it is perfect price discrimination, which involves maximum possible exploitation of each buyer as the consumer is left with zero consumer surplus.

*For example:* Fixed price shops follow, take it or leave it policy 'and consumer is left with no surplus.

### 2. Second Degree of Price Discrimination

- It is also known as block pricing strategy.
- In the second degree of price discrimination, the quantities are divided into different lots. Then each lot (of quantities) is sold at a different price.

*For example:* Railway and airways

### 3. Price Discrimination of the Third Degree

- It is the price discrimination that exists in reality.
- It occurs when the seller divides his buyers into sub-markets or groups and charges a different price in each sub-market or group.
- Thus, this type of price discrimination is according to the customer or the target group.

*For example:*

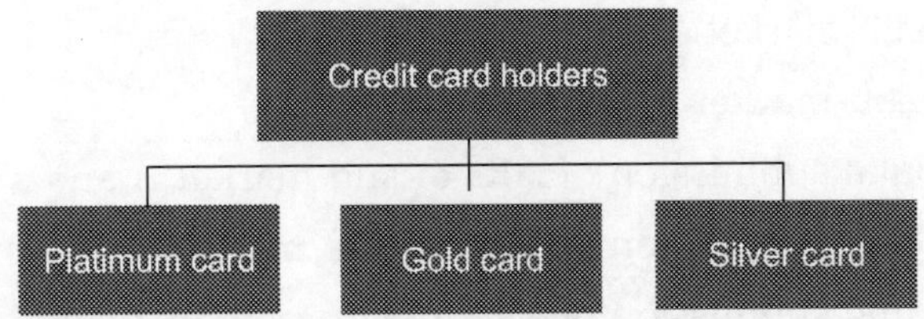


**Fig. 16.10** Example of Price Discrimination of the Third Degree

Thus, different prices are charged for same commodity (credit card), the highest price from platinum card holders and the lowest from silver card holders.

## 16.9 PRICE-OUTPUT DETERMINATION UNDER DISCRIMINATING MONOPOLY

The discriminating monopolist is the one who discriminates between the customers on the basis of price. Here, the motive is to extract the maximum profits from the market. In order to understand the working of discriminating monopolist, let us assume that the monopolist is operating his business activities in two sub-markets:

Sub-market A: Has low elasticity of demand
Sub-market B: Has high elasticity of demand

The graphical representation of price-output determination under conditions of discriminating monopoly operating in two markets *A* and *B* with different price elasticities has been shown in Fig. 16.11.

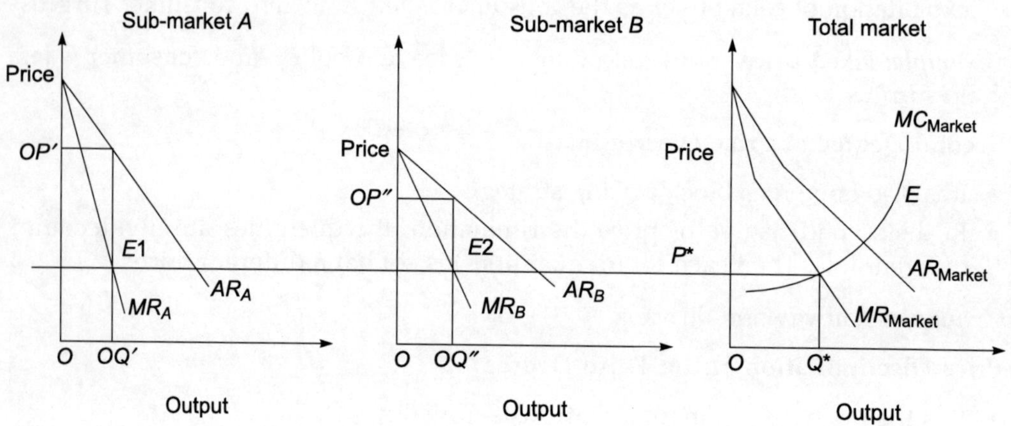


**Fig. 16.11** Price-output Determination under Discriminating Monopoly

Figure 16.11 can be explained in the following manner:

$AR_A$ = *AR* of sub-market *A*

$MR_A$ = *MR* of sub-market *A*

$AR_B$ = *AR* of sub-market *B*

$MR_B$ = *MR* of sub-market *B*

$AR_{\text{market}}$ = Horizontal submission of ARs of sub-market *A* and sub-market *B*

$MR_{\text{market}}$ = Horizontal submission of MRs of sub-market *A* and sub-market *B*

$MC_{\text{market}}$ = Horizontal submission of MCs of sub-market *A* and sub-market *B*

The equilibrium would be attained where,

1. $MR_{market}$ is equal to $MC_{market}$, and
2. $MC_{market}$ cuts $MR_{market}$ from below.

Therefore, *OP* is the equilibrium price and *OQ** is the equilibrium output.

Now, this total output (*OQ**) will be distributed among both the sub-markets. This will be done in the following manner:

1. By equating $MC_{market}$ with $MR_A$
2. By equating $MC_{market}$ with $MR_B$

Thus, here marginal revenues in two markets are equal and at the same time they should be equal to the marginal cost.

Hence, following output levels and price relationships would be observed in each market (Table 16.1):

**TABLE 16.1** Output-Price Relationships

| Type of Sub-market | Price | Output |
|---|---|---|
| Sub-market *A* (low elasticity of demand) | *OP′* | *OQ′* |
| Sub-market *B* (high elasticity of demand) | *OP″* | *OQ″* |

Price is higher in market *A* where the demand is less elastic than in market *B* where the demand is more elastic. Thus, it can be concluded that a profit maximizing monopolist charges different prices and supplies different quantities in the sub-markets having different price elasticities.

## Summary

✓ Monopoly means a market structure that is characterized by existence of a single producer selling a product which has no close substitutes.

✓ The kinds of monopoly are as follows:
- Simple monopoly and discriminating monopoly
- Pure monopoly and imperfect monopoly
- Natural monopoly
- Legal monopoly
- Industrial monopolies or public monopolies

✓ In case of monopoly, revenue and cost curves are as follows:
- *AR* curve is a downward sloping from left to right. It is a steep curve.
- Marginal revenue (*MR*) curve is also downward sloping and lies below the average revenue curve. In addition, the *MR* curve falls twice the rate as *AR* curve.
- The average and marginal cost curves are conventional 'U-shaped' cost curves.

✓ The marginal conditions of equilibrium in case of monopoly are same, like perfect competition. These are:
  - *MR* = *MC* (First order condition for equilibrium – Necessary condition)
  - *MC* curve cuts *MR* curve from below (Second order condition for equilibrium – Sufficient condition.

✓ Under short run, the following cases of equilibrium determination exist:
  - Super normal profit
  - Normal profit
  - Losses

✓ In the long run, the monopolist will find his equilibrium at a point where the following conditions are satisfied:
  - *LMC* = *MR*
  - *LMC* cuts *MR* from below

✓ Price discrimination refers to the practice of selling the same product at different prices to different buyers. The person following such a practice is called a 'discriminating monopolist'.

✓ Price discrimination is of the following types:
  - Personal price discrimination
  - Geographical price discrimination
  - Price discrimination according to use

✓ Price discrimination has been defined in terms of three degrees which are as follows:
  - First degree of price discrimination
  - Second degree of price discrimination
  - Third degree of price discrimination

✓ In case of a discriminating monopolist, a profit maximizing monopolist charges different prices and supplies different quantities in the sub-markets having different price elasticities.

## Review Questions

1. Explain the short- and long-run equilibria determination under monopoly form of market structure.
2. Elaborate the price and output determination in case of monopoly.
3. What are the assumptions of monopoly form of market structure? Explain long-run equilibrium determination under monopoly.
4. Can a monopolist incur losses in short run? Explain.
5. Explain price determination in case of monopoly? How is it different from that of a perfect competitive firm?

6. Explain the statement 'In case of monopoly, the difference between firm and industry disappears. Hence, firm itself is the industry'.
7. What is price discrimination? Explain its types and degrees.
8. Compare the results of perfect/ pure competition and monopoly in respect of price, output and profit. Is monopoly price always higher price?
9. Explain the price-output determination under discriminating monopoly.
10. Who is a discriminating monopolist? Explain the price and output determination by a discriminating monopolist?
11. How price and output are determined under monopoly? Is monopoly price always higher than the competitive market?
12. Explain how the output will be determined by a monopolist who is operating his business activities in two sub-markets?
13. Explain the necessary conditions for price discrimination and also analyze the allocation of total sale by a monopolist in two different markets.

## CASE STUDY: INDELIBLE INK PROCESSED BY MYSORE PAINTS AND VARNISH LTD. (MPVL) (MARCH 22, 2019)

Indelible ink refers to the violet-coloured ink in India that is applied on a voter's forefinger after she exercises her vote. In 1962, the Election Commission in collaboration with the Law Ministry, the National Physical Laboratory of India and the National Research Development Corporation made an agreement with Mysore Paints and Varnish Ltd. to manufacture ink that couldn't be wiped off easily. Mysore Paints was founded in 1937 by Maharaja Krishnaraja Wadiyar IV. The company is the sole supplier of indelible ink for civic body, Assembly and Parliamentary polls. It also supplies ink to about 25 countries. Indelible ink remains bright for about 10 days, after which it starts fading. It is known to contain silver nitrate and is manufactured in secrecy.

*Source:* The Hindu (March 22, 2019) Retrieved From https://www.thehindu.com/opinion/op-ed/what-is-indelible-ink/article26600648.ece on November 10, 2019.

### Questions

1. Explain the above case in the context of monopoly market structure. How Mysore Paints and Varnish Ltd. enjoy monopoly in the market?
2. What attributes of monopoly market structure are found in Mysore Paints and Varnish Ltd?
3. Do you think indelible ink market would be easy or difficult to enter? Give reasons in support of your answer.
4. Explain the short-run equilibrium determination by MPVL?

# 17 Chapter

# Price and Output Decisions Under Monopolistic Competition

**Learning Objectives**

After going through this chapter, reader would be able to understand:

- ✓ The meaning and concept of monopolistic competition.
- ✓ The assumptions that formulate the base of monopolistic competition.
- ✓ Revenue and cost curves under monopolistic competition.
- ✓ The short-run price and output decisions under monopolistic competition.
- ✓ The long-run price and output decisions under monopolistic competition.
- ✓ Excess capacity hypothesis.

## 17.1 INTRODUCTION

In chapter 15 and 16, the price and output determination under perfect competition and monopoly were discussed. Now we move further to have conceptual understanding of the realistic form of market structure, namely, monopolistic competition. At first, the chapter specifies the concept of monopolistic competition. The analysis thereafter unfurls the assumptions that define the dynamics related to monopolistic competition. Further, the revenue and cost curves under monopolistic competition have been discussed. It is to be noted here that in this market form the demand curve is downward sloping from left to right, but since there are many close substitutes for the product, the demand curve (*AR*) is highly elastic. Thus, unlike monopoly which has a downward sloping steep curve, the demand curve (*AR*) in case of monopolistic competition is a flatter curve. Then we move on to the study of equilibrium analysis under monopolistic competition in both short and long runs. The short-run analysis of equilibrium specifies the occurrence of three possibilities. These are supernormal profits, normal profits and losses. However, in long run on account of existence of free entry and exit, only normal profits prevail under monopolistic competition. In the last section, excess capacity hypothesis has been discussed and elaborated. In this section, the reason for nonexistence of excess capacity in perfect competition has also been elaborated.

## 17.2 MEANING OF MONOPOLISTIC COMPETITION

Monopolistic competition is one of the forms of imperfect competition in which there are many sellers (but less than perfect competition), which sell closely related but different products to many buyers. It is a realistic form of market structure.

***For example:*** Markets of products like toothpaste, detergents, hair oils, shampoos, soaps, toothpaste, etc., are examples of monopolistic competition. In this form of market structure, the free entry and exit is allowed like perfect competition. Thus, it has features of both monopoly and perfect competition. It may be represented as an integration of monopoly and perfect competition as shown in Figure 17.1.

**Fig. 17.1** Monopolistic Competition as an Integration of Monopoly and Perfect Competition

## 17.3 ASSUMPTIONS/ FEATURES OF MONOPOLISTIC COMPETITION

**1. Large Number of Buyers and Sellers**

- In this market form, there are many sellers and buyers of a product.
- However, the number of buyers and sellers is not as large as in case of perfect competition.
- Each firm acts independently and has a limited share of the market. So, an individual firm has limited control over the market price.
- The existence of large number of firms leads to competition in the market.

**2. Product Differentiation**

It is one of the marked features of monopolistic competition. It refers to the act of differentiating the products from the suppliers of other products on the basis of shape, size, colour, packaging, etc. These differences may be real or pecuniary (artificial).

- **Real product differentiation** means creating the differences in real manner or making real improvements in the product.

  ***For example:*** The initial models of Santro car did not have power steering. Then, the company worked on the engineering and the new model was a better model as compared to the previous model. This is real product differentiation.
- **Pecuniary (artificial) product differentiation** means creating the differences in the minds of the consumers and positioning the product.

*For example:* The cosmetic soaps under the same brand name are sold to different customers on the name of pink soap composed of rose petals, white soap composed of jasmine petals and so on. The customers are also willing to pay different prices for the same product produced by different firms. Hence, each firm is in a position to exercise some degree of monopoly power (in spite of large number of sellers) through product differentiation.

**3. Freedom of Entry and Exit**

- Under monopolistic competition, firms are free to enter or exit the industry.
- When the supernormal profits exist, new firms try to enter the industry and when there are losses, they exit the industry.
- However, it must be noted here that entry under monopolistic competition is not as easy and free as under perfect competition because of competition.

**4. Presence of Selling Costs**

- Another differentiating feature of monopolistic competitive firm is the incurring of selling costs in order to promote the sales of the product.
- Selling costs refer to the costs incurred to influence the buyers to purchase a particular product against competitor's product.
- These are incurred on marketing, sales promotion and advertisement of the product.
- Thus, they constitute a substantial part of the total cost under monopolistic competition.

**5. Non-price Competition**

In monopolistic competition, non-price competition also exists. It refers to the act of competing with other firms by offering free gifts, making favourable credit terms, providing good after-sales service, etc., without changing prices of the products. This is done in order to attract customers and to promote their sales.

| Large number of buyers and sellers |
|---|
| Products differentiation |
| Freedom of entry and exit |
| Presence of selling costs |
| Non-price competition |

**Fig. 17.2** Assumptions of Monopolistic Competition

## 17.4 REVENUE AND COST CURVES UNDER MONOPOLISTIC COMPETITION

Under monopolistic competition, many firms are engaged in selling closely related but different products. This results in downward sloping demand curve (*AR* curve). It implies that a firm can sell more output only by reducing the price of its product in order to maximize profits. This has been reflected in Fig. 17.3 as follows:

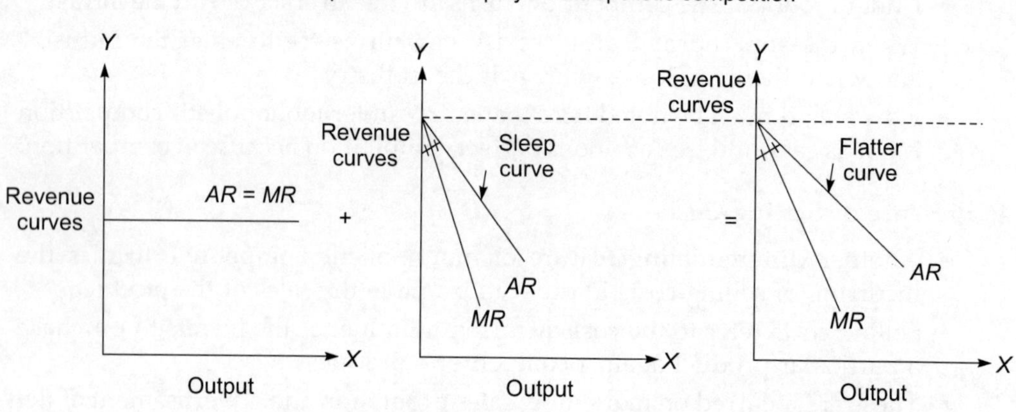


**Fig. 17.3** Revenue and Cost Curves under Monopolistic Competition

Since monopolistic competition has features of both monopoly and downward sloping flatter curve of perfect competition. In Fig. 17.3, *AR* curve is a downward sloping flatter curve from left to right. The marginal revenue (*MR*) curve is also downward sloping and lies below the average revenue curve, that is, $MR < AR$. In addition, the *MR* curve falls twice the rate as *AR* curve. Since *AR* is a flatter curve, therefore *MR* curve is also a downward sloping flatter curve as compared to monopoly form of market structure. Thus, the elasticity of demand of both *AR* and *MR* is greater than one. The monopolistic competitive firm will use these *AR* and *MR* curves along with the conventional 'U shaped' cost curves to arrive at equilibrium. The cost curves have been considered directly for equilibrium analysis under Section 17.5 and 17.6.

## 17.5 SHORT-RUN EQUILIBRIUM UNDER MONOPOLISTIC COMPETITIVE FIRM/SHORT-RUN PRICE AND OUTPUT DECISIONS UNDER MONOPOLISTIC COMPETITION

The equilibrium determination is mainly studied in consonance with two time periods: short run and long run. In monopolistic form of market structure, equilibrium determination has been shown with the help of Fig. 17.4.

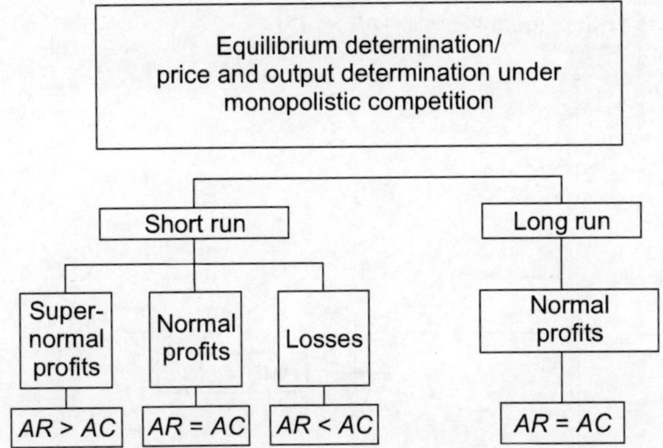


**Fig. 17.4** Equilibrium Determination under Monopolistic Competition

However, the marginal conditions of equilibrium are same, like perfect competition and monopoly. These are:

1. $MR = MC$ (First order condition for equilibrium – Necessary condition)
2. $MC$ curve cuts $MR$ curve from below (Second order condition for equilibrium – Sufficient condition)

However, the innate analysis relating to short run and long run vary among the three different market forms, namely, perfect competition, monopoly and monopolistic competition.

In monopolistic competition, under short run, the following cases of equilibrium determination exist:

**Case I:** Supernormal profit (SNP)

**Case II:** Normal profit (NP)

**Case III:** Losses

These cases have been explained under.

**Case I: Supernormal Profits ($AR > AC$)**

A monopolistic competitive firm is said to earn supernormal profits when the price ($AR$) charged by him is more than the average cost ($AC$). In such a case, $AR > AC$. The excess of revenue over the cost is known as supernormal profits.

However, in order to qualify for equilibrium the following conditions must be satisfied.

- Marginal revenue is equal to marginal cost.
- Marginal cost curve cuts marginal revenue curve from below.

The diagrammatic representation of equilibrium determination is shown in Fig. 17.5.

Case 1: Supernormal profits $AR > AC$

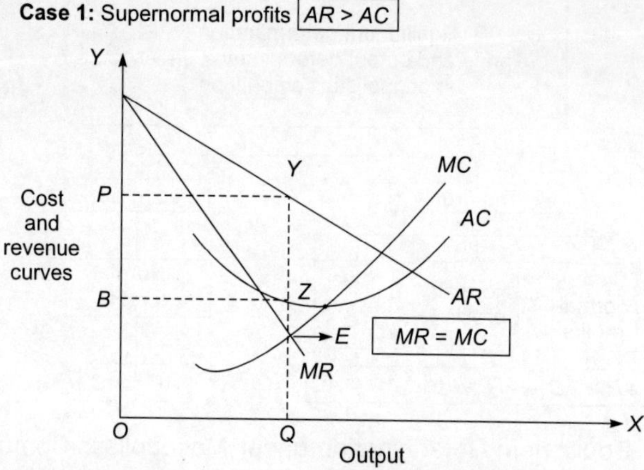


**Fig. 17.5** Determination of Supernormal Profits under Monopolistic Competition

Figure 17.5 can be explained in the following manner:

1. Under monopolistic competition, both *AR* and *MR* are downward sloping steep curves. *MR* curve falls twice the rate as *AR* curve and lies below it. *MR* is steeper than *AR* curve.
2. *AC* and *MC* are conventional short-run average and marginal cost curves of the firm.
3. The firm's equilibrium will be at point *E* when the conditions of equilibrium are satisfied.
4. A perpendicular parallel to the *Y*-axis is drawn from the equilibrium point *E* that connects the *X*-axis at *Q*. Here, equilibrium quantity (*OQ*) is determined.

## Determination of Supernormal Profits (SNP)

$$SNP \text{ per unit} = AR - AC \quad \ldots(17.1)$$

where,

$$AR = YQ = OP$$
$$AC = ZQ = OB$$

Substituting the value of *AR* and *AC* in equation (17.1), we get

$$SNP \text{ per unit} = OP - OB$$
$$= PB$$
$$\text{Total } SNP = SNP \text{ per unit} \times \text{Quantity sold}$$
$$= PB \times OQ$$
$$= PB \times BZ$$
$$= BPYZ \text{ (shaded area)}$$

**Total *SNP* = *BPYZ* (Shaded area)**

### Case II: Normal Profits ($AR = AC$)

A monopolistic competitive firm is said to earn normal profits when the price ($AR$) charged by him is equal to the average cost ($AC$). In such a case, $AR = AC$.

However, in order to qualify for equilibrium the following conditions must be satisfied.

- Marginal revenue is equal to marginal cost.
- Marginal cost curve cuts marginal revenue curve from below.

The diagrammatic representation of equilibrium determination is shown in Fig. 17.6:

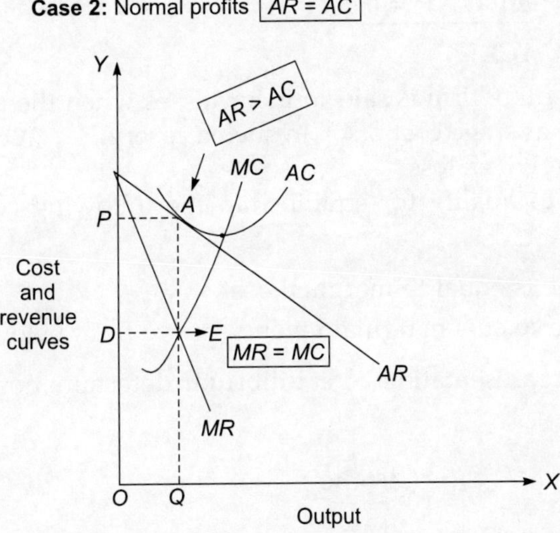


**Fig. 17.6** Determination of Normal Profits under Monopolistic Competition

Figure 17.6 can be explained in the following manner:

1. Under monopolistic competition, both $AR$ and $MR$ are downward sloping steep curves. $MR$ curve falls twice the rate as $AR$ curve and lies below it. $MR$ is steeper than $AR$ curve.
2. $AC$ and $MC$ are conventional short-run average and marginal cost curves of the firm.
3. The firm's equilibrium will be at point $E$ when the conditions of equilibrium are satisfied.
4. A perpendicular parallel to the $Y$-axis is drawn from the equilibrium point $E$ that connects the $X$-axis at $Q$. Here, equilibrium quantity ($OQ$) is determined.

### Determination of NP

$$NP \text{ per unit} = AR - AC \qquad \ldots(17.2)$$

where,

$AR = AQ = OP$

$AC = AQ = OP$

Substituting value of $AR$ and $AC$ in equation (17.2), we get

$$NP \text{ per unit} = OP - OP$$
$$= 0$$
$$\text{Total } NP = NP \text{ per unit} \times \text{Quantity sold}$$
$$= 0 \times OQ$$
$$= 0$$

**Total $NP$ = 0**

**Case III: Losses ($AR < AC$)**

A monopolistic competitive firm is said to incur losses when the price ($AR$) charged by him is less than the average cost ($AC$). In such a case, $AR < AC$. The excess of cost over the revenue is known as loss.

However, in order to qualify for equilibrium the following conditions must be satisfied.

- Marginal revenue is equal to marginal cost.
- Marginal cost curve cuts marginal revenue curve from below.

The diagrammatic representation of equilibrium determination has been shown below:

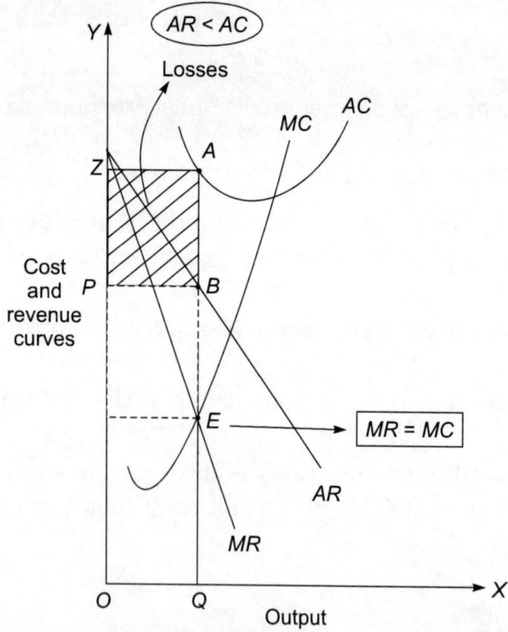


**Fig. 17.7** Determination of Losses under Monopolistic Competition

Figure 17.7 can be explained in the following manner:

1. Under monopolistic competition, both *AR* and *MR* are downward sloping steep curves. *MR* curve falls twice the rate as *AR* curve and lies below it. *MR* is steeper than *AR* curve.
2. *AC* and *MC* are conventional short-run average and marginal cost curves of the firm.
3. The firm's equilibrium will be at point *E* when the conditions of equilibrium are satisfied.
4. A perpendicular parallel to the *Y*-axis is drawn from the equilibrium point *E* that connects the X-axis at *Q*. Here, equilibrium quantity (*OQ*) is determined.

## DETERMINATION OF LOSSES

$$\text{Loss per unit} = AC - AR \qquad \ldots(17.3)$$

where,

$$AC = AQ = OZ$$
$$AR = BQ = OP$$

Substituting value of *AR* and *AC* in equation (17.3), we get

$$\begin{aligned}\text{Loss per unit} &= OZ - OP \\ &= PZ \\ \text{Total loss} &= \text{Loss per unit} \times \text{Quantity sold} \\ &= PZ \times OQ \\ &= PB \times PB \\ &= PZAB \text{ (shaded area)}\end{aligned}$$

**Total loss = *PZAB* (shaded area)**

## 17.6 LONG-RUN EQUILIBRIUM ANALYSIS AND EXCESS CAPACITY HYPOTHESIS

In the long run under monopolistic competition, there is entry and exit restriction. The firms may enter or exit the industry depending on the profits or loss conditions in the market. The adjustment process will ultimately lead to the existence of only normal profits. This can be explained as under:

**Case 1:** Suppose, the existing firms are making supernormal profits, new firms will be attracted to join the industry. With the entry of new firms, supply would increase, this will reduce the price. It will happen till the excess profits are absorbed by the existing industries and normal profits are restored.

**Case 2:** Suppose, the existing firms are making losses, existing firms will be inclined to leave the industry. With the exit of firms, supply would reduce, this will increase the price. It will happen till the losses are converted into normal profits.

This two-way adjustment process ensures that each firm earns only normal profits in the long run. Thus, all firms are in long-run equilibrium at point *E* where the following conditions are satisfied:

1. *MR* = *LMC*, and
2. *LMC* cuts *MR* from below.

In addition, the condition of normal profits has the following implications:

1. *AR* = *LAC*
2. It means that *LAC* curve is tangent to the *AR* curve (demand curve) at point *A*.

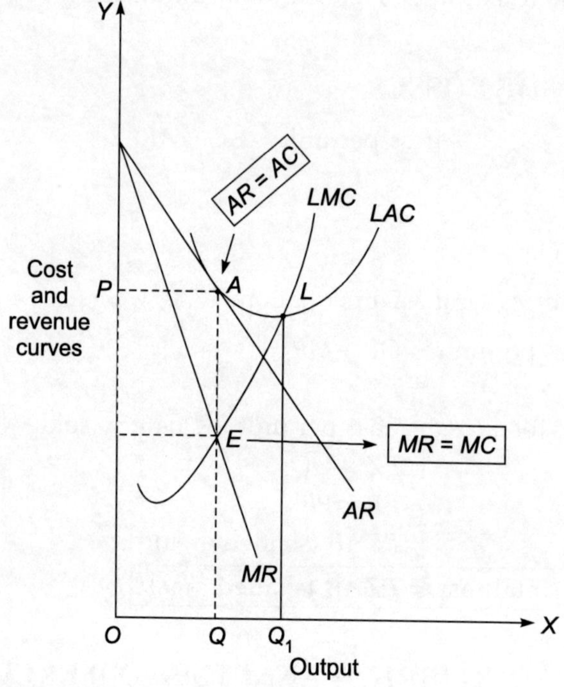


**Fig. 17.8** Long Run Equilibrium Analysis under Monopolistic Competition

Thus, conditions of equilibrium in long run are as follows:

$$MR = LMC = AR = LAC$$

## DETERMINATION OF NORMAL PROFITS IN LONG RUN

$$NP \text{ per unit} = AR - AC \quad \ldots(17.4)$$

where,

$$AR = AQ = OP$$
$$AC = AQ = OP$$

Substituting value of *AR* and *AC* in equation (17.4), we get

$$NP \text{ per unit} = OP - OP$$
$$= 0$$
$$\text{Total } NP = NP \text{ per unit} \times \text{Quantity sold}$$
$$= 0 \times OQ$$
$$= 0$$
$$\boxed{\textbf{Total } NP = 0}$$

In long run under monopolistic competition, the following points are worth noting (Fig. 17.8):

- The point of tangency between *AR* and *LAC* curve (point *A*) and minimum point of *LAC* (point *L*) do not coincide.
- *L* is to the right of point *A*, that is, the point of tangency.
- This is because the *AR* is negatively sloped from left to the right.
- Each firm under monopolistic competition has $Q$–$Q_1$ unutilized capacity (excess capacity) even in the long run. It means that each firm and the entire industry is not producing its optimum output which generates unutilized capacity (excess capacity) in monopolistic competitive firms in long run.

## EXCESS CAPACITY HYPOTHESIS UNDER MONOPOLISTIC COMPETITION OR IMPERFECT COMPETITION

### Meaning

It refers to a concept that is studied under imperfect competition, especially with reference to monopolistic competition in long run. It is to be noted here that the concept of excess capacity refers only to the long run because in the short-run market structures (including perfect competition) face departures from the ideal output as they are exposed to adjustments in the existing market conditions.

The concept of excess capacity means that the firms under monopolistic competition produce an output which is less than socially optimum or ideal output. Excess capacity has been defined in Fig. 17.9 and Fig. 17.10 as follows:

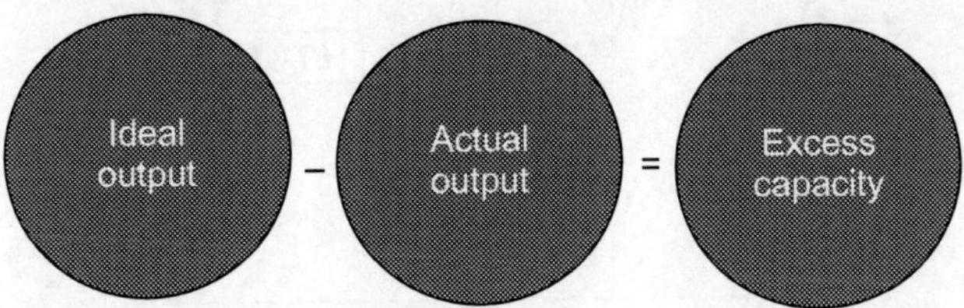


**Fig. 17.9** Excess Capacity Hypothesis

It may be written as:

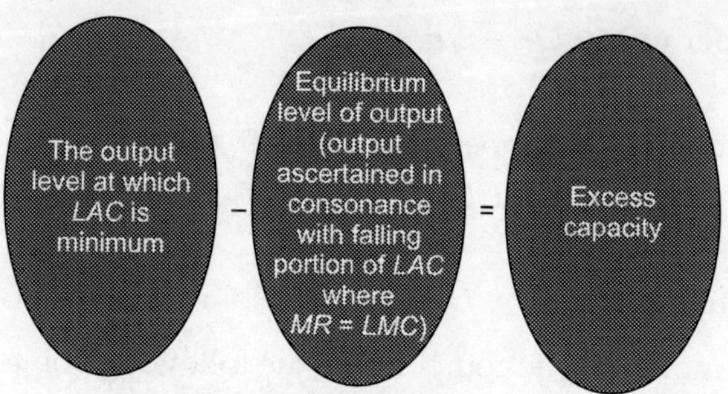


**Fig. 17.10** Excess Capacity Hypothesis (Redefined)

An important feature of monopolistic competitive market structure is that in the long run, firms operate at the point on the falling portion of long-run average cost curve (*LAC*) and do not produce at the level of output where long-run average cost is minimum. This has an important implication as it generates excess capacity hypothesis.

In long run, a firm under monopolistic competition is able to earn only normal profits due to free entry and exit of firms. Thus, the equilibrium is ascertained where average revenue curve or the demand curve becomes tangential to the long-run average cost curve. It means where $AR = LAC$ and in such a case the firm earns only normal profits.

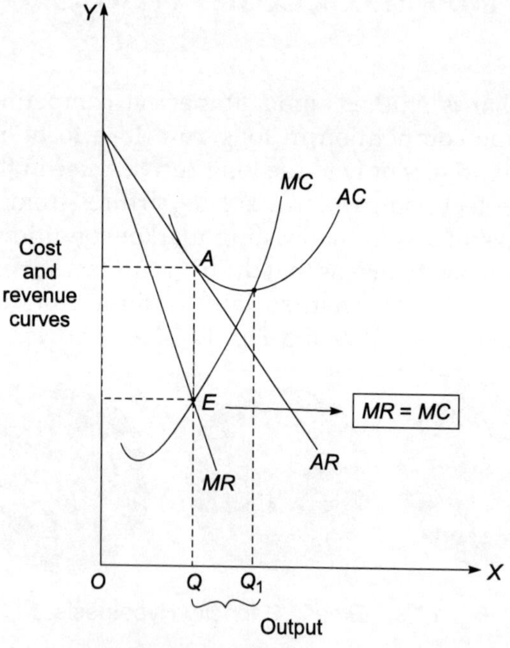


**Fig. 17.11** Extent of Excess Capacity under Monopolistic Competition

Under such circumstances, equality of marginal revenue with long-run marginal cost (*MR* = *LMC*) is attained at the level of output which is smaller than the level at which *LAC* is minimum.

In Figure 17.11, the excess capacity may be calculated as follows:

| Excess capacity (unutilized capacity) = Ideal output – Actual output |
|---|
| $= OQ_1 - OQ$ |
| $= QQ_1$ |

**No Excess Capacity under Perfect Competition**

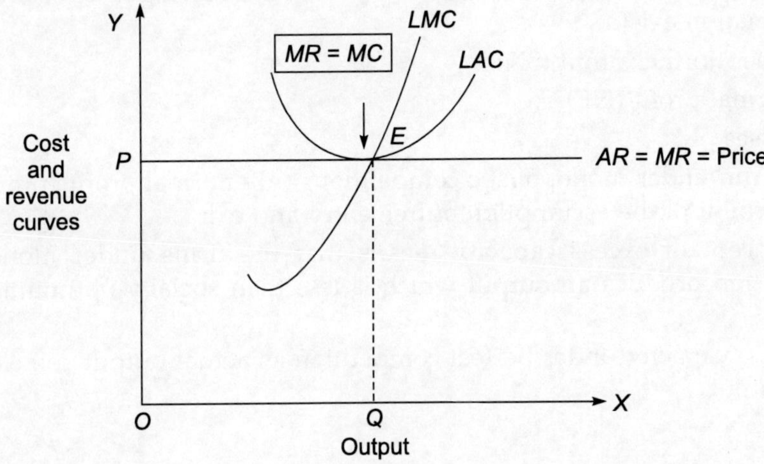


**Fig. 17.12** No Excess Capacity under Perfect Competition

In perfect competition, in long run, the following condition is satisfied:

Price = *LMC* = *LAC*

Figure 17.12 reflects that the output level at which *LAC* is minimum and where equilibrium level of output (*MR* = *LMC*) coincide. It is thus clear that firms under perfect competition produce socially ideal output. Thus, in long run, the following condition is satisfied:

Price = *LMC* = *LAC*

| Under perfect competition, |
|---|
| Excess capacity (unutilized capacity) = Ideal output – Actual output |
| $= OQ - OQ$ |
| $= 0$ |

## Summary

- ✓ Monopolistic competition refers to a market structure in which there are many sellers selling closely related but different products.
- ✓ In monopolistic competition, revenue curves take the following forms:
  - *AR* curve is a downward sloping flatter curve from left to right.
  - The marginal revenue (*MR*) curve is also downward sloping and lies below the average revenue curve.
- ✓ In monopolistic competition, the conventional 'U-shaped' average and marginal cost curves are used.
- ✓ In monopolistic competition, under short run, the following cases of equilibrium determination exist:
  - Super normal profit (SNP)
  - Normal profit (NP)
  - Losses
- ✓ In long run under monopolistic competition, only normal profits prevail. This is on account of the assumption of free entry and exit.
- ✓ The concept of excess capacity means that the firms under monopolistic competition produce an output which is less than socially optimum or ideal output.
- ✓ No excess capacity under perfect competition as actual output coincides with ideal output.

## Review Questions

1. Explain the short-run equilibrium determination under monopolistic competition.
2. Explain the price and output determination in case of monopolistic competitive market.
3. Explain the difference between monopolistic competition and perfect competition. Discuss the equilibrium of a monopolistic competitive firm in long run.
4. What are the characteristics of monopolistic competitive form of market structure? Explain the reasons for the existence of normal profits in long run?
5. Monopolistic competitive firm has features of both monopoly and perfect competition. Explain.
6. Compare and contrast characteristics of monopolistic competition with perfect competition
7. 'Monopolistic competitive firm is the integration of monopoly and perfect competition'. Explain the statement.
8. What are the wastages under monopolistic competition? Compare situation of monopolistic competition with perfect competition.

9. What is the concept of ideal output and actual output under monopolistic competition? Explain with the help of diagrams.
10. Does a monopolistic firm always make profit? Explain using appropriate diagrams.
11. How is monopolistic firm's long-run equilibrium different from short-run equilibrium?
12. Explain diagrammatically excess capacity hypothesis under monopolistic competition.
13. 'The concept of excess capacity means that the firms under monopolistic competition produce an output which is less than socially optimum or ideal output'. Explain the statement.
14. 'In long run, a monopolistic competitive firm does not produce at the level of output where long-run average cost is minimum'. Explain the statement.
15. 'There is no excess capacity under perfect competition'. Explain the statement by comparing it with the situation under monopolistic competition.
16. Write short notes on the following:
    (a) Non-price competition
    (b) Excess capacity hypothesis
    (c) Product differentiation

## CASE STUDY: MONOPOLISTIC COMPETITION: TOOTHCALM (2019)

Toothcalm is a leading company that is servicing its customers by providing toothpaste tube from past 45 years. The aim of the company was to give the consumer an excellent product with complete oral hygiene. The company is well known and has huge brand loyal customer base. It is being used and recommended generations by generations over the years for protection of teeth. It faces stiff competition from many players but the major players include Tooth Care, Dental Health, Tooth Precision, Happy Tooth, Healthy Teeth, etc. In Q1 2019, the management of the company was shocked to see that market share had declined by 38 per cent. It was for the first time since inception of the company that the company faced such a situation. The company executives conducted market research and analyzed that the share of "Homoeoneem Care", homoeopathic pharmaceutical company that was formed 5 years back utilizing traditional benefits of neem and other ingredients has increased by 17% during the same period while the shares of other rival companies who were operating for so many years had also declined.

This was a major concern for the company as it was losing its market share after the entry of "Homoeoneem Care". The company management soon started realizing that the declining market share is attributed to change in consumer taste and preferences that has led to shift from already existing brands to natural brands. In one of the board meetings, the managing director of Toothcalm Company said "We need to work on the product portfolio...Perhaps the new product with supplemented features is need of the hour." He added that "We need to work on combo of neem, clove and any other ingredient that can ensure complete oral care." He continued and stated that "Our earlier variation with clove as ingredient really worked well... Let's hope that we are able to revive our market share in toothpaste market soon". A few days later, the company reduced the prices of the existing products and started working on the promotion driven strategies.

## Questions

1. Identify the market form to which the company "Toothcalm" belongs.
2. State the assumptions on which this market form is based.
3. Considering the conventional cost and revenue curves, determine the equilibrium under this market form in the short and long run.
4. What promotional strategies the company can adopt to enhance the sales of its product?
5. What should the company do to combat competition with its competitors like 'Homoeoneem'?

# 18 CHAPTER

# Price and Output Decisions Under Oligopoly

**LEARNING OBJECTIVES**

After going through this chapter, reader would be able to understand:

- ✓ The meaning and concept of oligopoly.
- ✓ The assumptions that formulate the base of oligopoly.
- ✓ Types of oligopoly.
- ✓ Price and output under oligopoly.
- ✓ Models of oligopoly form of market structure.

## 18.1 INTRODUCTION

After understanding the equilibrium analysis of three forms of market structure in chapters 15, 16 and 17, now we move further to analyze the dynamics pertaining to the oligopoly form of market. Oligopoly is the market structure that involves the active participation of a few sellers in the market. It is the most prevalent market form in manufacturing sector of countries like India. The producers and sellers of automobiles, cement, steel, two-wheelers, airlines, etc., represent oligopolistic market. We begin the analysis and the meaning and assumptions of oligopoly. Thereafter, in order to have holistic knowledge of the concept of oligopoly, we move to understand types of oligopoly. Thereafter, indeterminate nature of price and output under oligopoly has been discussed. Thereafter, some of the most important oligopoly models have been discussed. These are Cournot Duopoly Model, Kinked Demand Model, Prisoner's Dilemma Model and Baumol's Sales Maximization Model. Cournot Duopoly Model specifies that if each firm presumes that the competitor would keep output as constant, each firm will sell 1/3 of the market . However, Paul M. Sweezy in his kinked demand model focused on indeterminate nature of *AR* curve and the price rigidity often observed in oligopolistic markets. The situation of dilemma observed by oligopolistic firms in case of production, advertisement of the product, etc., has been described by Prisoner's Dilemma model. The last model that considered is Baumol's Sales Maximization that emphasizes the revenue maximization motive of the firm and undermines the profit maximization motive. However, the model includes the profit constraint line and specifies that the firms aim to maximize sales revenue after they have earned sufficient profit to satisfy the stakeholders. However, the irony associated with these models is that they focus on a particular aspect pertaining to oligopoly and have different areas of focus. Thus, they have limited applicability.

## 18.2 MEANING OF OLIGOPOLY

The term oligopoly derives from two Greek words: 'oligi' means 'few' and 'polein' means 'to sell'. Oligopoly is a market structure that is characterized by a few sellers selling homogeneous or different products. The presence of a few sellers in the market reflects the existence of massive competition in the market. It means the actions of one firm influences the actions of the firms and is also influenced by the reaction of other firms.

While studying oligopoly a special reference is made to "DUOPOLY". It is a special case of oligopoly, which involves the existence of two sellers selling homogeneous products that have no substitutes. The best examples of duopoly are Pepsi and Coca-Cola in the soft drink market. However, it is assumed here that they do not have other substitutes like 7 Up, Miranda, Fanta, Sprite, etc.

## 18.3 ASSUMPTIONS/FEATURES OF OLIGOPOLY

The main assumptions underlying oligopoly form of market are as follows:

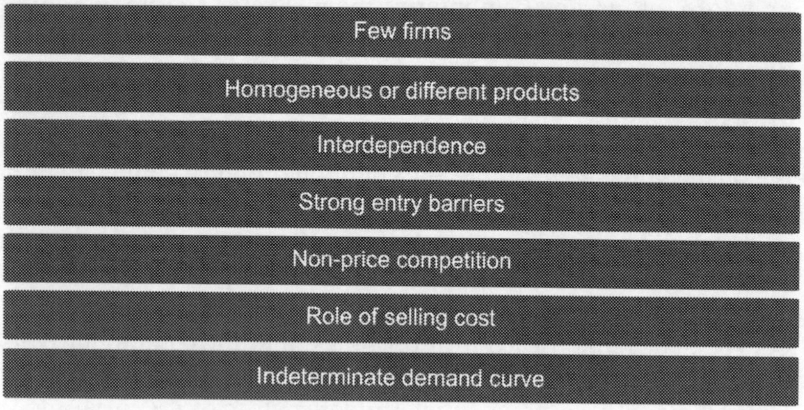

Few firms

Homogeneous or different products

Interdependence

Strong entry barriers

Non-price competition

Role of selling cost

Indeterminate demand curve

**Fig. 18.1** Assumptions of Oligopoly

1. **Few Firms**

   Oligopoly market structure has a few large firms. How many firms constitute the few, has not been defined so far. However, some economists are of the view that the minimum number of firms is 2 and maximum number may be 10 or 20. It is to be noted here each firm produces a significant portion of the total output. Each firm keeps a close eye on the behaviour of other firms and tries to outsmart each other.

2. **Nature of the Product**

   In this form of market structure, the firms may produce homogeneous or different products.

   (i) If the firms produce a homogeneous product, then industry is known as pure or perfect oligopoly.

   ***For example:*** Cement, aluminum or steel industries.

   (ii) If the firms produce different products, then industry is known as differentiated or imperfect oligopoly.

   ***For example:*** Automobiles industry, mobile manufacturing units

3. **Interdependence**

   There is a marked interdependence among the oligopolistic firms. It means that actions of one firm call for reactions of other firms. Each firm considers the action and reaction of the rival firms while determining its price and output levels.

   ***For example:*** In India, the car market is mainly ruled by major players such as Maruti, Tata, Hyundai, Ford, Honda, etc., which are a few in number. If one firm (say, Hyundai) changes prices of its product (say, I 20) will induce the competitor firms (say, Maruti, Tata, etc.) to make changes in prices of their products.

4. **Strong Entry Barriers**

   In this market form, there are strong entry restrictions or barriers for new firms. These barriers may be imposed in the form of patents, requirement of large capital, and control over crucial raw materials. There barriers make the entry of new firms a challenging task. Thus, the firms under oligopoly form of market impose string entry restrictions to discourage new entrants and thereby attempt to reduce competition.

5. **Non-price Competition**

   This is one of the marked features of oligopoly form of market structure. It means a policy that aims at calling customer's attention by sorting to methods advertising, subsidized delivery, better after-sales services. The motive is increase the demand for the product by positioning the product in the minds of the consumers by creating the product value.

   Under oligopoly, firms tend to avoid price competition on account of policy of price rigidity. It means that if a firm tries to reduce the price, the rivals will immediately react by reducing their prices. No firm is in win-win situation. However, if it tries to raise the price, other firms might not do so. It results in loss of customers for the firm, which intended to raise the price. Thus, firms prefer non-price competition.

6. **Role of Selling Costs**

   Selling costs are more important under oligopoly than under monopolistic competition. Due to intense competition and interdependence of the firms, various sales promotion techniques are used to promote sales of the product. Thus, a considerable portion of the expenditure is also allocated to enhance the sales of the product.

7. **Indeterminate Demand Curve**

   Under oligopoly, the actions of one firm are followed by the reactions of other firms. Then the reaction of second firm is affected by the action of previous firm. This leads to uncertainty and makes behaviour pattern of each producer unpredictable. Thus, any change in price by one firm may lead to change in prices by the competing firms. The demand curve (*AR* curve) keeps on shifting and it is not definite, rather it is indeterminate. Thus, in oligopoly form of market, demand curve is indeterminate (uncertain).

## 18.4 TYPES OF OLIGOPOLY

The types of oligopoly have been shown in Fig. 18.2.

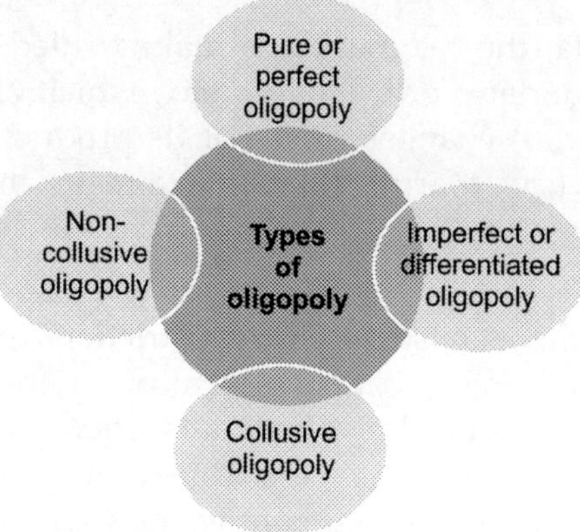


**Fig. 18.2** Types of Oligopoly

1. **Pure or Perfect Oligopoly**

   An industry that is characterized by the composition of firms that produce homogeneous or identical products is called pure or perfect oligopoly.

   ***For example:*** Cement, steel, aluminum and chemicals producing industries.

2. **Imperfect or Differentiated Oligopoly**

   An industry that is characterized by the composition of firms that produce unidentical products is called differentiated or imperfect oligopoly. The products have their own distinguishing characteristics, yet all of them are close substitutes of each other.

***For example:*** Soft drinks and automobile industry.

3. **Collusive Oligopoly**

   An industry that is characterized by the composition of firms that collide or cooperate with each other in determining price or output or both, it is called collusive oligopoly or cooperative oligopoly.

4. **Non-collusive Oligopoly**

   An industry that is characterized by the composition of firms that compete with each other, is called a non-collusive or non-cooperative oligopoly. In this type of oligopoly, the firms strongly get indulged in action and reaction pattern and vice versa.

## 18.5 INDETERMINATE PRICE AND OUTPUT UNDER OLIGOPOLY

In other forms of market structure (such as perfect competition, monopoly, and monopolistic competition), price and output are determined by taking into account revenue (*AR* and *MR*) and cost (*MC* and *AC*) curves. However, in oligopoly, the number of sellers is less with keen competition among the sellers. An action on the part of seller invites the reaction of the other producers and then it is followed by the action and then reaction and so on. If an organization lowers down its prices, its sales would increase as compared to the competitors. Thus, other organizations would also lower their prices. So, both of them sell at reduced price and receive less revenue and thus, reduced profits. If one seller increases price, then others don't increase the level of prices. Therefore, the prices and the output that would be sold in the market are indeterminate under oligopoly. Different economists have considered different aspects of oligopoly and thus, models of oligopoly came into existence. These have been explained as we move further.

## 18.6 MODELS OF OLIGOPOLY

### 18.6.1 Model 1: Cournot's Duopoly Model

Cournot's Duopoly model is based on one of the oldest theories of the behaviour of the oligopoly firm and is a model of non-collusive (non-cooperative) oligopoly.

***Assumptions***

To illustrate the model, Cournot assumed the following:

1. There are two firms producing mineral water and their waters are identical. They are selling it in the same market. Their waters are identical. Therefore, his model relates to the duopoly with homogeneous products.

2. For the sake of simplicity, the cost of production has been assumed to be nil.
3. Conventional cost and revenue curves have been assumed. It means that the cost curves are *U* shaped and the demand curves have constant negative slope.
4. Each seller acts on the assumption that the rival firm will keep its output constant, that is, it will go on producing the same amount of output which it is presently producing. This is Cournot's Behavioural or Heroic Assumption.

## Cournot's Approach to Duopoly Equilibrium

Given these assumptions, suppose there are two suppliers of mineral water, viz., Firm *A* and Firm *B*.

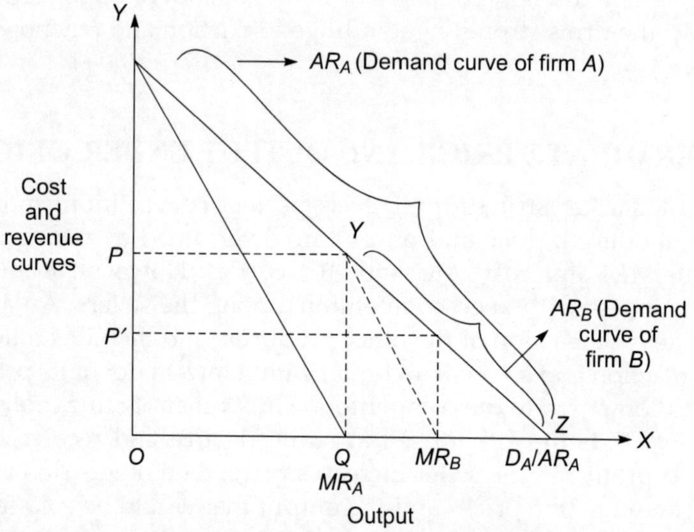


**Fig. 18.3** Cournot's Duopoly Model

Figure 18.3 explains the working of Cournot's model in the following manner:

$AR_A$ = Demand curve of firm *A* if it assumes that Firm *B* will not produce anything. Hence, it is the market demand curve.

$MR_A$ = Marginal revenue curve of firm *A*. It falls twice the rate as *AR* curve like other forms of imperfect competitive markets.

$AR_B$ = Demand curve of firm *B*.

$MR_B$ = Marginal revenue curve of firm *B*. It falls twice the rate as *AR* curve like other forms of imperfect competitive markets.

**Model**

Let us assume that the firm *A* is the first mover.

At equilibrium,

$$MR_A = MC$$

$$MR_A = 0 \text{ (because } MC = 0)$$

The marginal costs of both *A* and *B* are assumed to be zero so that they coincide with the horizontal axis (assumption 2)

Output sold by firm *A* = *OQ* = ½ Total market output

= 1/2 *OZ* = *OQ*

Here price charged by firm *A* = *OP*

Now, firm *B* reacts to firm *A*'s action. Now, firm *B* enters the market and expects that *A* will not change its output level, *OQ*. It, therefore, regards *YZ* segment of *AR* curve as its demand curve

Therefore, $AR_B = YZ$

and

$$MR_B = YB$$

For equilibrium of firm *B*,

$$MR_B = 0 \text{ (Because } MC = 0)$$

The marginal costs of both *A* and *B* are assumed to be zero so that they coincide with the horizontal axis (Assumption 2).

Therefore, price charged by firm *B* = *OP'*

Output produced by firm *B* = *QB* (1/3rd total market output). It has been further clarified in Table 18.1:

**TABLE 18.1** Cournot's Duopoly Model

| Firms → / Time Horizon ↓ | Firm *A* | Firm *B* |
|---|---|---|
| Period 1 | $\frac{1}{2}(\text{Total market}) = \frac{1}{2}(1) = \frac{1}{2}$ | $\frac{1}{2}(\text{Total market} - A\text{'s share})$ $= \frac{1}{2}\left(1 - \frac{1}{2}\right) = \frac{1}{4}$ |
| Period 2 | $\frac{1}{2}(\text{Total market} - B\text{'s share})$ $= \frac{1}{2}\left(1 - \frac{1}{4}\right) = \frac{3}{8}$ | $\frac{1}{2}(\text{Total market} - A\text{'s share})$ $= \frac{1}{2}\left(1 - \frac{3}{8}\right) = \frac{5}{16}$ |
| Period 3 | $\frac{1}{2}(\text{Total market} - B\text{'s share})$ $= \frac{1}{2}\left(1 - \frac{5}{16}\right) = \frac{11}{32}$ | $\frac{1}{2}(\text{Total market} - A\text{'s share})$ $= \frac{1}{2}\left(1 - \frac{11}{32}\right) = \frac{21}{64}$ |

*Contd.*

| Period 4 | $\frac{1}{2}$(Total market – *B*'s share) $= \frac{1}{2}\left(1 - \frac{21}{64}\right) = \frac{43}{128}$ | $\frac{1}{2}$(Total market – *A*'s share) $= \frac{1}{2}\left(1 - \frac{43}{128}\right) = \frac{85}{256}$ |
|---|---|---|
| ⋮ | ⋮ | ⋮ |
| Period *N* | $\frac{1}{3}$ of Total Market Output | $\frac{1}{3}$ of Total Market Output |

Thus, finally each duopolist sells 1/3 of the market, i.e., both the producers sell 2/3 of the total output.

### 18.6.2 Model 2: Kinked Demand Model/The Sweezy Model of Kinked Demand Curve (Rigid Prices): (By Paul M. Sweezy)

It is one of the most important models of non-collusive oligopoly that attempts to explain price rigidities often observed in oligopolistic form of markets.

#### *Assumptions*

The kinked demand curve hypothesis of price rigidity is based on the following assumptions:

(a) If one firm increases the price, other firms will not follow. It means that price increments are not followed.

(b) If one firm decreases the price, other firms will also decrease the price. Price reductions are followed.

(c) There is an established prevailing price.

(d) There is a kink in the demand curve.

#### Explanation of the Model

The model has been explained in terms of two demand curves:

(a) Perceived demand curve (*dd*)

(b) Proportional demand curve (*DD*)

#### (a) Perceived Demand Curve (*dd*) (More than Elastic Demand)

If the oligopolistic firm increases its price, its rivals will not react by following the price rise. Instead, they will keep the prices unaltered. As a result, the quantity demanded of firm who increased the price falls considerably. The decline in demand is more than the rise in price, hence, this portion of the demand curve is more than elastic or relatively elastic (Fig. 18.4).

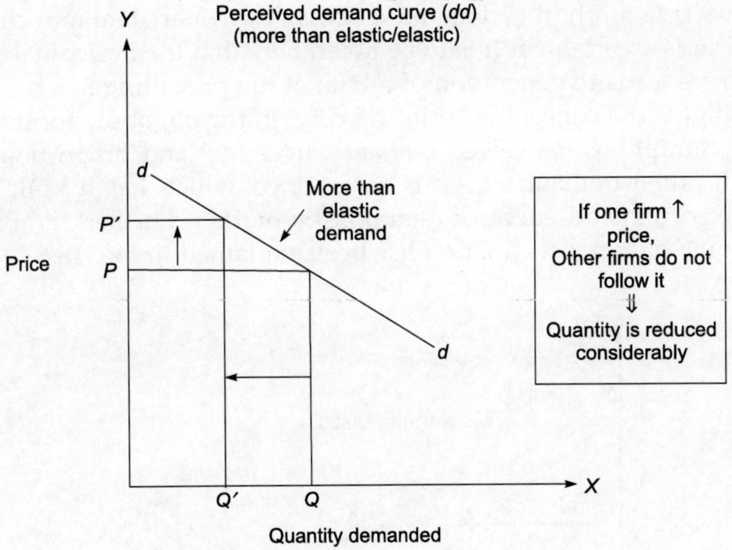


**Fig. 18.4** Perceived Demand Curve

### (b) Proportional Demand Curve (*DD*) (Less than Elastic Demand)

On the other hand, Sweezy assumes that if the oligopolistic firm reduces its price, its rivals will also reduce the price to avoid the probability of losing their customers. Thus, the firm lowering the price will be able to increase its demand but insignificantly. It means that the decline in price is more than the rise in demand, hence, this portion of the demand curve is less than elastic or relatively inelastic (Fig. 18.5).

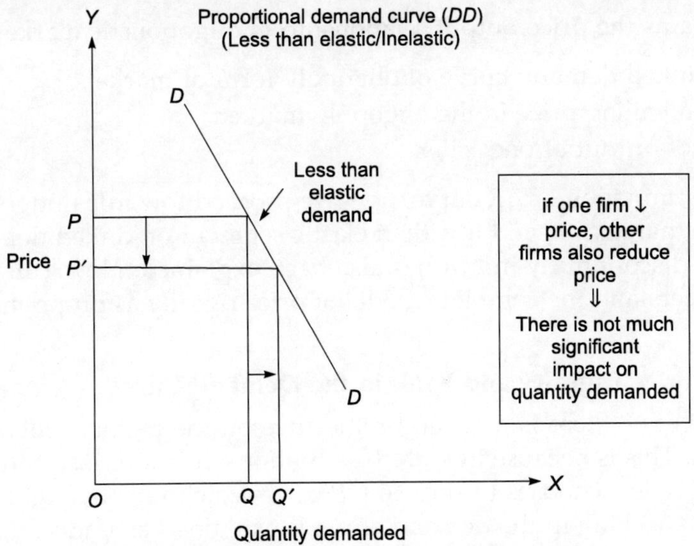


**Fig. 18.5** Proportional Demand Curve

After considering both the demand curves, the final demand curve of the oligopolistic firm is ascertained. It is to be noted here that the horizontal summation of both the curves leads to generation of a kink at the prevailing market price level. This kink highlights the concept of 'price rigidity' in the oligopoly form of market.

Given the assumptions, perceived demand curve (*dd*) and proportional demand curve (*DD*), the final demand curve is ascertained which has a kink at point *k*. *dkD* is the kinked demand curve of oligopolistic market. Further, the price-output relationship in the oligopolistic market has been explained in Fig. 18.6.

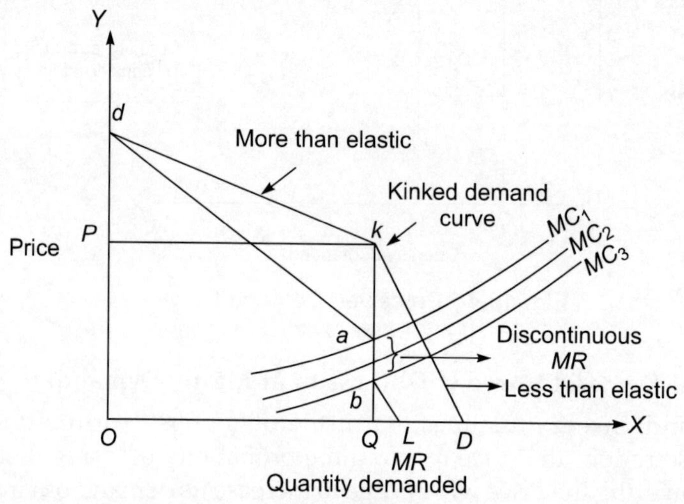


**Fig. 18.6** Price Output Relationship in the Oligopolistic Market

Fig. 18.6 explains the price-output relationship in oligopolistic market as follows:

*dkD* = the kinked demand curve of oligopoly form of market.
*OP* = the prevailing price in the oligopoly market.
*OQ* = level of output of one seller.

After the determination of *AR* curve, now we proceed towards understanding the reason for more than elastic and less than elastic segment of kinked demand model. In addition, the discontinuity in *MR* has also been explained. Now, considering Fig. 18.6, we can understand the complete model of price rigidity as propounded by Paul M. Sweezy.

### Explanation of Price Rigidity and Kink in the Demand Curve

According to Sweezy, there is a general reluctance on the part of sellers to raise or reduce the price. This is because in both the situations, it is lose-lose situation. Thus, he (oligopolistic seller) chooses to stick to *OP* price which remains rigid. The reason of price rigidity and kink in the demand curve is explained as under:

**(a) Reason for more than elastic segment of AR curve**

If the price is enhanced above *OP* which is the prevailing price, then his rivals are not expected to follow his price increase. As a result, any increase in price above *OP* will considerably reduce his sales. Hence, a slight increase in price leads to considerable decline in quantity demanded. Therefore, *dk* portion of the kinked demand curve is elastic, and corresponding to it, portion *da* of the *MR* curve is also more than elastic. Therefore, any price rise will adversely affect total sale, total revenue and profit.

**(b) Reason for less than elastic segment of *AR* curve**

If the seller reduces the price of the product below *OP* which is the prevailing price, his rivals will react by reducing their prices. They will do so in order to evade the possibility of losing their customers. Thus, the output will increase but insignificantly. As a result, revenue and profit would be less than before. Therefore, *kD* portion of the kinked demand curve is less than elastic, and corresponding to it, portion *bL* of the *MR* curve is also less than elastic and negative.

**Explanation of Discontinuity in *MR***

Under kinked demand model, the changes in costs within a certain range do not affect the prevailing price. Suppose the cost of production falls from $MC_1$ to $MC_2$. It cuts the *MR* curve in the gap *ab*. This gap *ab* reflects the discontinuity in *MR* which existed as there was a kink in *AR* curve. Thus, a kink in *AR* curve made the *MR* discontinuous at *ab* segment.

**Explanation of Operation of MC Curves**

In the discontinuous portion of *MR*, the cost of production falls from $MC_1$ to $MC_2$ and then $MC_2$ to $MC_3$, the profit maximizing output will remain *OQ* which would be sold at *OP* price which is the prevailing price. Further, the gap *ab* widens in order to accommodate any *MC* curve below point *a* and will cut the marginal revenue curve inside the gap. Finally, the same output *OQ* would be sold at the same price *OP*. In this manner, the oligopolistic sellers would make larger profits despite the existence of price rigidity.

## 18.6.3 Model 3: Prisoner's Dilemma Model

Prisoner's Dilemma Model, propounded by Von Neumann and Oskar Morgenstern, was published with title "Theory of Games and Economic Behaviour" in 1944. This is another model of oligopoly which tends to explain the strategic behaviour of oligopolistic firms under the conditions of uncertainty. It is an important model of game theory that explains how rivals behaving selfishly act contrary to their mutual or common interests. The model of Prisoner's Dilemma has been explained with the examples which were originally given while propounding this model.

**Model**

Suppose two convicts, namely, Ranga and Billa, have been caught for committing a bank robbery. However, the evidence is not enough to prove the charges against both of them unless either one or both of them confess the robbery. In order to prove the charges, they are interrogated in two separate rooms so that there is lack of communication between them and they are not in a position to decide the next step. Therefore, in each convict acts in isolation and takes independent decisions.

While interrogation of each accused, the police gave the following situations to them:

(a) If both confess (that is, cooperate with the police), each will go to jail for 5 years (reflected by upper left corner).
(b) If both do not confess (that is, do not cooperate with the police), both will go jail for 2 years ( reflected by lower right corner).
(c) If one confesses (that is, cooperates with the police) and other does not confess (keeps silent ), then the convict who has confessed will be sentenced to the prison for 1 year and the convict who committed crime but has not confessed will be sentenced to the prison for 20 years (reflected by upper right and lower left corner).

The choices or possible outcomes open to each accused are presented in payoff matrix in Table 18.2.

**TABLE 18.2** Payoff Matrix under Prisoner's Dilemma

**Prisoner's Dilemma**

| | | Ranga's choices | |
|---|---|---|---|
| | | Confess | Deny |
| Billa's choices | Confess | Ranga: 5 years<br>Billa: 5 years | Ranga: 10 years<br>Billa: 1 year |
| | Deny | Ranga: 1 year<br>Billa: 10 years | Ranga: 2 years<br>Billa: 2 years |

The above payoff mentioned in Table 18.2 matrix has the following implications:

- Each prisoner is open to two strategies or choices:
  (a) Confession
  (b) No confession or denial
- The convicts are required to work in isolation as they cannot communicate with each other while deciding their best option.
- Each prisoner faces an uncertain situation regarding how his accomplice will react to the given options, whether or not he will confess.
- Considering the probable behaviour of his accomplice, each convict has to make an independent choice regarding the confession or denial.

Now, under these circumstances prisoner behaving selfishly and working in self-interest will confess to the crime and cheat the other.

Take Ranga first. The choices under prisoner's dilemma are mentioned in Table 18.2.

**TABLE 18.3** Ranga's Choices under Prisoner's Dilemma

| Confession | Denial |
|---|---|
| Minimum sentence: 1 year | Minimum sentence: 2 years |
| Maximum sentence: 5 years | Maximum sentence: 10 years |

(a) If Ranga confesses, and Billa confesses, it is very likely that he will be imprisoned for 5 years.

(b) If Ranga confesses, he will get 1 years imprisonment if Billa does not confess he will be imprisoned for 10 years.

(c) If Ranga does not confess, and Billa also does not confesses, it is very likely that he will be imprisoned for 2 years.

The best option is to have 2 years imprisonment but that is possible if both the convicts do not confess to the crime and remain loyal to each other. But the uncertainty reading the behaviour of other convict and inspired by the self-interest, each prisoner would not opt for this option assuming that other convict may confess and get lesser imprisonment of 1 year. Thus, each prisoner works in self-interest and tries to make the "best" of the "worse outcomes" in an uncertain situation.

Thus, in the condition of uncertainty of choice of option exercised by other prisoner, each prisoner is likely to behave selfishly and in self interest. Thus, each will choose an option where his self interest would be maximized. In this case, each prisoner would choose the option of confession. As if he confesses and the other also confesses, the maximum sentence is of 5 years and if he confesses and other denies, then imprisonment is of 1 year only. Thus, they would be sentenced for 5 years, though they would have received a light sentence of only two years if they had not confessed and remained loyal to each other.

Prisoner's Dilemma of games theory is generally connected with the behaviour of oligopolistic firms that behave strategically to the competitor's disadvantage. The oligopolistic firms are unaware of the behaviour of their competitors and have to take strategic decisions considering their own interest level. They are often faced with dilemma or are in state of fix in certain situations like fixation of price, to advertise or not to advertise, etc. They are required to take these strategic decisions considering the best out of the worst situations in such a manner that their personal interests are maximized.

### 18.6.4 Model 4: Sales Maximization Model (Baumol's Revenue Maximization Model)

Sales maximization model has been propounded by W.J. Baumol, an American economist. He asserted that the main aim of any firm is to maximize the sales revenue and rather than maximization of profits. Thus, he contributed sales maximization model of oligopoly as an alternative to profit maximization model. It is one of the important managerial theories as it gives great importance to the behaviour and role of managers while managing business. The theory points that ownership and management are separate concepts. A manager has been entrusted the task of managing the business and is oriented towards pursuing his self-interest in maximizing sales than profits as his revenues are more concerned with maximization of sales revenue.

***Assumptions***

The theory is based on the following assumptions:

1. There is a single period time horizon of the firm. During that period, a firm would be interested in maximization of total revenue (Sales Revenue = Price per Unit × Quantity sold) and not physical quantities of output.
2. The main motive of each firm is to maximizing its total sales revenue in the long run.
3. The cost and revenue curves are of the conventional type. The cost curves are U shaped and the demand curve (*AR* curve) is downward sloping from left to right.

### Explanation of the Model

According to Baumol, the ownership and control have been separated from each other. The goals of managers are closely connected with rising sales revenue as it leads to higher salaries and prestige in the organization. Thus, in short as well as long run, the revenue maximization motive represents the goal of the management. The following arguments are given in support of his theory:

1. The steady performance with rising sales enhances the prestige of a business concern. Thus, a firm attaches great importance to the magnitude of sales and thus the sales revenue.
2. The compensation of employees (wages, salaries, bonus and other facilities) also depend on the sales.
3. The banks and financial institutions are interested in lending or providing loans to the firms who have rising sales. Thus, such firms are viewed favourably in provision of loans.
4. The consumers also favour a product that has more popularity and has rising sales.
5. The distributors and dealers are more interested to promote a product with rising sales.

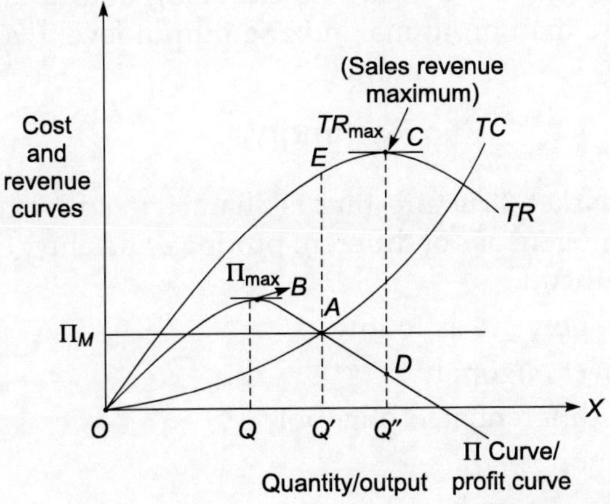


**Fig. 18.7** Baumol's Sales Maximization Model

Figure 18.8 explains Baumol's model in the following manner:

1. *TR*, the total revenue curve which is inverted U-shaped and is starting from origin.
2. *TC* is the total cost curve which is inverse S-shaped and is starting from origin.
3. Π curve is the total profit curve and is inverted U-shaped.
4. $\Pi_M$ is the profit constraint line and is parallel to X-axis.

**Profit Maximizing Output Level**

Π curve or the total profit curve is maximum at point *B*. Thus, profit maximizing output level is reflected by *OQ* that corresponds to the highest point *B* on Π curve. Thus, profit maximizing output level is *OQ*.

**Sales Maximizing Output Level**

*TR* curve is maximum at point C thus, reflects that the firm maximizes its sales revenue at this point. Corresponding to the highest point C on *TR* curve, *OQ″* output is ascertained. Thus, sales maximizing output level is *OQ″*.

**Profit Constraint Line ($\Pi_M$)**

But sales maximizing output level is subject to profit constraint (**$\Pi_M$**). The output $OQ''$ will not be able to maximize sales as the minimum profits $O\Pi_M$ are not being covered by profits $DQ''$. For sales maximization subject to profit constraint, the firm should produce at such a level where the following conditions must be satisfied:

1. Minimum profits are ensured.
2. The output level must be consistent with the highest total revenue.

This is attained at output level $OQ'$ where the minimum profits $AQ'$ ($O\Pi_M$) are consistent with highest total revenue ($EQ'$).

Thus, finally, Baumol's model reflects that the sales maximizing level of output subject to profit constraint ($OQ'$) is different from profit maximizing output level ($OQ$). It is to be noted here that the sales maximizing output level subject to profit constraint ($OQ'$) is more than profit maximizing output level ($OQ$).

## Summary

✓ Oligopoly is a market structure that is characterized by the existence of few sellers selling homogeneous or different products and entry or exit from industry is possible but difficult.

✓ The types of oligopoly are as follows:
- Pure or perfect oligopoly
- Imperfect or differentiated oligopoly
- Collusive oligopoly
- Non-collusive oligopoly

✓ The prices and the output that would be sold in the market are indeterminate under oligopoly.

✓ The Cournot's Model shows that if each firm considers the output of other firm as constant then each firm sells 1/3 of the market, i.e., both the producers sell 2/3 of the total output.

✓ Sweezy's kinked demand model emphasizes price rigidity in oligopoly form of market structure. It specifies that if one firm increases the price, other firms will not follow the price rise. It means that price increments are not followed. On the other side, if one firm decreases the price, other firms will also decrease the price. Price reductions are followed. As a result, there is a kink in the demand curve and *MR* is discontinuous.

✓ Prisoner's dilemma of games theory is generally connected with the behaviour of oligopolistic firms that behave strategically to the competitor's disadvantage. The oligopolistic firms are unaware of the behaviour of their competitors and have to take strategic decisions considering their own interest level. In such situation, they are required to take these strategic decisions considering the best out of the worst situations in such a manner that their personal interests are maximized.

✓ Baumol's sales maximization model postulates that the main motive of a oligopolistic firm is to maximize its total sales revenue after they have earned a satisfactory rate of profit. Thus, sales revenue maximization is highlighted under this model, subject to a profit constraint.

## Review Questions

1. Identify the distinguishing characteristics of oligopoly. How is this form of market different from other forms of market structure?
2. What are the features of oligopolistic form of market structure? Is price a determinate in this form of market structure?
3. What are the assumptions that delineate the base of oligopoly form of market? Also explain the types of oligopoly.
4. Compare and contrast oligopoly form of market with monopolistic competition.
5. Explain the concept of oligopoly in the light of Cournot's Model. Prove that under this model, each firm sells 1/3 of the market output.
6. 'Under Cournot's Model, each firm sells 1/3 of the market output and both the producers sell 2/3 of the total output'. Comment.
7. Explain price rigidity with the help of kinked demand curve in case of oligopolistic market.
8. What is price stickiness? Explain the concept in light of kinked demand model of oligopoly.
9. Explain Sweezy's model of oligopoly. Why there is a kink in the demand curve under this model?
10. What is prisoner's dilemma? How does it help to explain the likelihood of firms opting for suboptimal solution in oligopoly?
11. 'Prisoner's dilemma is all about taking strategic decisions considering the best out of the worst situations so that personal interests are maximized'. Comment.
12. Explain Baumol's sales maximization model of oligopoly. Is profit maximizing output level same as sales maximizing output level? If yes. Give reasons in support of your answer.
13. What is a profit constraint line? How is it used in order to explain the sales maximization model?
14. 'Each oligopolistic firm tends to maximize its total sales revenue after they have earned a satisfactory rate of profit'. Comment.

## CASE STUDY: 'BIG FOUR' ACCOUNTANCY GIANTS (NOV. 23 2018)

**London, Nov. 23 2018:** The accountancy sector's so-called "Big Four" – Deloitte, EY, KPMG and PwC – have a long-established oligopoly to advise and monitor big business, experts say. The powerful companies engage in a wide range of activities, from accounts auditing and strategy consulting to proposed mergers and acquisitions, restructuring and taxation. The Competition and Markets Authority watchdog launched a sector review in October and is expected to report back before Christmas.

The firms feel they need one of the Big Four on their side as investors usually want to see their labels when they scrutinize the quality of companies. "Firms need to placate financial markets and having a 'Big Four' badge is one easy way to do this," Professor Crawford Spence at King's College, London told AFP. "These symbolic aspects are very important." The Big Four audit all but one of the 100 companies listed on London's benchmark FTSE 100 stocks index, media reports say. "This is partly explained by the need for big listed companies to have an auditor with an international network who can deal with subsidiaries overseas, partly with issues to do with brand," added Spence.

"The Big Four – pride themselves on trying to understand the whole business of a client, not just its audit issues. This 'rounded business knowledge' is very useful for big clients." The Big Four also have more than 95 per cent of FTSE 350 businesses on their books. In reaction to their strong grip, Grant Thornton – Britain's fifth biggest accountancy firm – announced in March that it would stop bidding for new auditing contracts as it could not compete.

*Source*: *Business Today* (November 23, 2018) retrieved from https://www.businesstoday.in/pti-feed/big-four-accountancy-giants-face-uk-probe/story/293748.html

## Questions

1. Explain the above case in the context of oligopoly form of market.
2. The above-mentioned companies relate to collusive or non-collusive oligopoly? Give reasons in support of your answer.
3. Do you think that it is possible for a new firm to enter accountancy industry?
4. Give your opinion regarding the following in the context of case mentioned above:
   (a) number of buyers
   (b) number of sellers
   (c) intensity of competition
   (d) market control
   (e) independence or interdependence

# 19 CHAPTER

# Income Distribution and Factor Pricing

**LEARNING OBJECTIVES**

After going through this chapter, reader would be able to understand:

- ✓ The concept of factor pricing.
- ✓ The differences and similarities in factor pricing vs product pricing.
- ✓ Distribution of income in terms of personal and functional distribution.
- ✓ Fundamental concepts of theory of factor pricing.
- ✓ The theoretical framework of market for factor inputs under conditions of perfect and imperfect commodity market and perfect input markets.
- ✓ The concepts of economic rent, actual earning and transfer earning.

## 19.1 CONCEPT OF FACTOR PRICING

In economics, factors of production refer to the basic inputs that help in production of goods or rendering of services. These inputs are classified under four major heads, namely, land, labour, capital, and entrepreneur. The price that an entrepreneur pays to these factors in accordance with the services that are rendered by them is called factor pricing or factor remuneration. These factor rewards are in the form of rent, wages, interest, and profit that is paid for availing the services of factors such as land, labour, capital, and entrepreneur, respectively. The theory of factor pricing deals with the determination of rewards that pertain to the factors of production for their contribution in facilitating the production processes.

Figure 19.1 clearly reflects that the theory of factor pricing is concerned with the determination and distribution of respective reward of the each factor of production. It is for this reason it is also known as 'theory of distribution' or 'theory of distribution of factor rewards'. These factor rewards may be shown as:

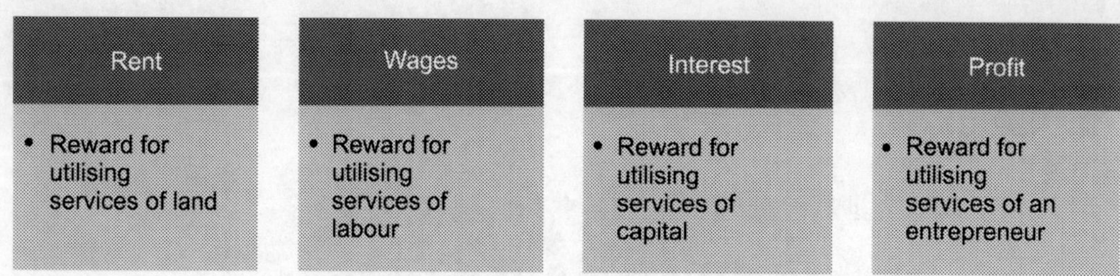


**Fig. 19.1** Distribution of Factor Rewards

## 19.2 FACTOR PRICING VS PRODUCT PRICING

Like product pricing, the factor pricing also involves the interplay of demand and supply forces. However, in case of factor pricing, demand forces work similar to demand forces in product or commodity market. However, the difference arises in case of supply side dynamics. This is due to the fact that in product market, the supply of a product is determined by its marginal cost of production. On the other hand, in factor market, it is not possible to determine the supply of factors on the basis of marginal cost.

***For example:*** In case of factors of production such as land and capital, the marginal (additional) cost of production of respective factors cannot be calculated. Moreover, the supply of factors of production such as land cannot be increased in short run. However, in case of commodity market, the supply of commodities can be varied both in short and long run.

## 19.3 DISTRIBUTION OF INCOME: PERSONAL AND FUNCTIONAL

The term 'distribution of income' refers to the distribution or allocation of rewards among various economic units. In economics, the word distribution is interpreted in two senses:

(a) Personal distribution of income

(b) Functional distribution of income

### (a) Personal Distribution of Income (Individual Share Distribution)

Personal distribution refers to the economic phenomenon that deals with the dissemination of rewards pertaining to the various individuals of an economy. The respective personal distribution of income has been described in Fig. 19.2.

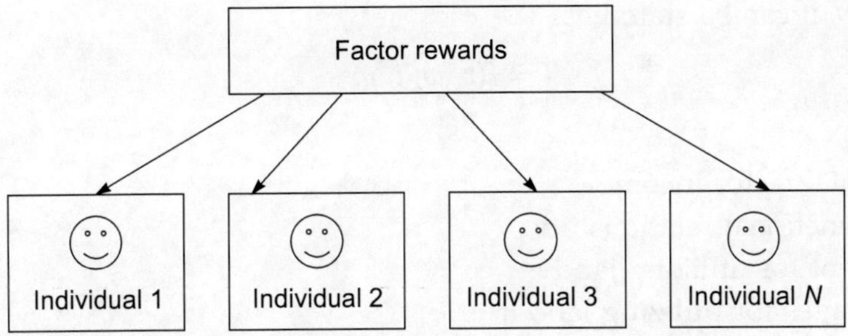


**Fig. 19.2** Personal Distribution of Income

These rewards may exist in the form of income (flow concept) or wealth (stock concept) in any economy. It tries to answer the questions in the following form:

- Why the wages of blue collar job workers are lower than the salaried employees?
- What is the reason of differential wage system with the same economic unit?
- Why is the rent of one piece of land located in same vicinity higher than the other?
- How the inequality of income impacts the lives of poor income segment of people?
- What measures can be taken to reduce the gap between haves and have-nots?

To sum up, personal distribution of income deals with the problems of inequality of income and wealth, its effects, and measures to mitigate those inequalities.

## (b) Functional Distribution of Income (Factor Share Distribution)

Functional distribution refers to the economic phenomenon that deals with the dissemination of rewards pertaining to the various factors of production in an economy. These rewards are given to the factors for their contribution in economic activities of the economy such as production of goods and rendering of services in any economy. They exist in the form of rent, wages, interest and profit. The respective functional distribution of income has been described in Fig. 19.3.

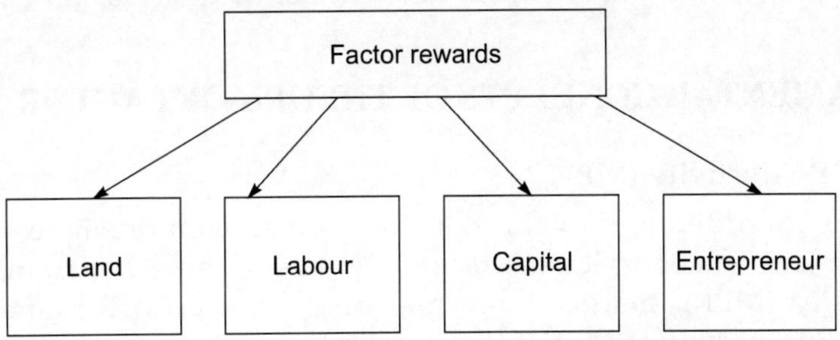


**Fig. 19.3** Functional Distribution of Income

Algebraically, it can be stated as:

$$T = f(r, w, i, p)$$

where,

$T$ = Total factor income
$F$ = Functional relationship
$r$ = Rent for utilizing land
$w$ = Wages for utilizing labour
$i$ = Interest for utilizing capital
$p$ = Profit for utilizing services of an entrepreneur

Functional distribution tries to answer the questions in the following form:

- How the reward for utilizing the services of labour will be calculated?
- What is the mechanism of determination of rent?
- How capital and entrepreneur as factors of production are remunerated?

To sum up, functional distribution of income deals with the determination and distribution of factor rewards among the factors of production. Since, it deals with the determination of factor rewards, it is for this reason it is sometimes called the 'theory of factor pricing'.

### Relationship between Personal and Functional Distribution

From the above, it can be conferred that the two concepts of distribution of income, viz., personal and functional are entirely different. However both of them are closely related. Functional distribution of income directly affects the personal distribution in an economy. If the distributions of rewards among the factors of production are just and equitable, then the receipt of personal income at individual level is also just and equitable. On the other hand, if the functional distribution of income is discriminating and involves exploitation of factors of production, the personal distribution of income would also be adversely affected. This is a bane for any economy as in this case there is depletion of economic and social welfare of masses which will, in a way, lead to regression of any economy as it results in the fight between haves and have-nots.

## 19.4 FUNDAMENTAL CONCEPTS OF THEORY OF FACTOR PRICING

**1. Marginal Productivity (MP)**

It refers to the addition to total productivity on account of employment of an additional unit of labour. It is used in three senses, namely, marginal physical productivity (MPP), marginal revenue productivity (MRP), and Value of Marginal Productivity (VMP). It is shown in Fig. 19.4.

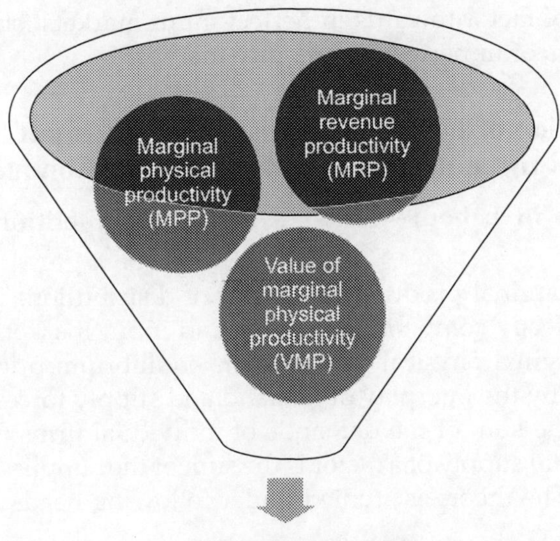


Fig. 19.4 Concept of Marginal Productivity

2. **Marginal Physical Productivity (MPP)**

   It refers to the addition in total output as a result of employment of one additional unit of labour.

$$MPP = \frac{\Delta TPP}{\Delta L}$$

3. **Marginal Revenue Productivity (MRP)**

   It refers to the addition in total output as a result of employment of one additional unit of labour.

$$MRP = MR \times MPP$$

4. **Value of Marginal Productivity (VMP)**

   It is calculated by multiplying average revenue (AR) by marginal physical productivity (MPP).

$$VMP = AR \times MPP$$

## 19.5 MARKET FOR FACTOR INPUTS

The market for factor inputs is studied under two main heads:

1. Determination of factor rewards in perfect input markets (short and long run) under conditions of perfect commodity market.

2. Determination of factor rewards in perfect input markets (short and long run) under conditions of imperfect commodity market.

### 19.5.1 Determination of Factor Rewards in Perfect Input Markets (Short and Long Run) under Conditions of Perfect Commodity Market

**{Perfect Competition in Labour Market + Perfect Competition in Commodity/ Product Market}**

It is also known as marginal productivity theory of distribution. This is on account of the fact that in perfectly competitive product and input markets, factors are paid the value of their marginal physical product. The equilibrium price of a factor (say, labour) is determined by the interplay of demand and supply forces in factor market. The total demand is the sum of the demands of individual firms for the productive factor. Similarly, the total supply of a factor is the sum of the supplies by the individual owners of the factor. The theory is studied under following heads.

**(a) Market Demand for Labour ($D_L$): (Reflects the point of view of employer)**

Demand for labour refers to the requirement of workers in order to complete a specific job requirement. There prevails an inverse relationship between wage rate and number of units of labour. At higher wages, the employers would be less inclined to employ more labour. As a result, the number of workers demanded by the employer would be less. It can be seen in Fig. 19.5 that as a result of increase in wage rate from *OW* to *OW'*, the units of labour declines from *ON* to *ON'* and vice versa.

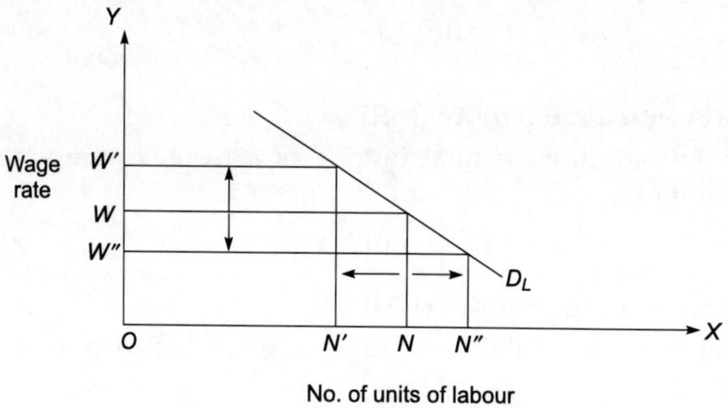


**Fig. 19.5** Demand Curve for Labour ($D_L$)

By adding the individual demand curves of labour, we arrive at market demand curve which is a downward sloping curve from left to right establishing an inverse relationship between wage rate and the number of units of labour.

**(b) The Market Supply of Labour ($S_L$)**

Supply of labour refers to the number of workers who are able and willing to work at a given wage rate, keeping the effect of other variables as constant. The predicted relation between hours of work and the wage rate is called the labour supply curve.

Generally, there prevails a direct relationship between wage rate and the number of units of labour. At higher wages, the employees would be more inclined to render services in an organization. As a result, the supply of labour would be more. Figure 19.6 shows that as a result of increase in wage rate from *OW* to *OW′*, the units of labour increase from *ON* to *ON′* and vice versa. Thus, the supply curve of labour is usually upward sloping in relation to their factor price, that is, wages.

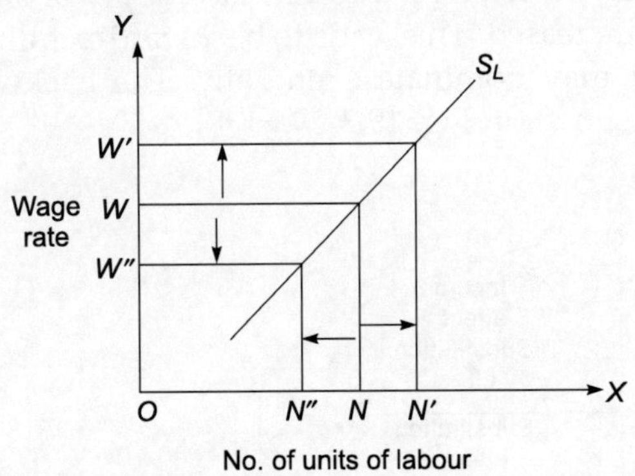


**Fig. 19.6** Supply Curve for Labour: Considering Economic Factors ($S_L$)

## Backward Bending Supply Curve for Labour

It is to be noted here that the above analysis of labour supply curve is a partial analysis. If we want to consider the entire analysis, we will have to consider two major effects.

(a) **Substitution effect** means that a higher wage encourages the workers to work more. Thus, working for more hours is a preferred alternative for workers as compared to leisure. Thus, as a result of increase in the wages or monetary rewards, the labour supply increases. This is because, the more the work, the more monetary payment they receive. As a result, the labour supply curve tends to be upward sloping till the time the workers value money more than their leisure.

(b) **Income effect** means that with higher wages, a labour can work for fewer hours and still earn same amount of money. Thus, the same target income can be earned by working for fewer hours. Therefore, income effect of the rise in wage rate which tends to increase leisure and reduce number of working hours. This leads to reduction in labour supply.

## Conditions: Income vs Substitution Effect in Labour Market

### (a) Substitution Effect is Larger than Its Income Effect (*SE* > *YE*)

At a higher wage rate, substitution effect of a rise in real wage is larger than its income effect and therefore individuals work for more hours when their wages are increased. As a result, the labour supply curve is upward sloping indicating that substitution effects are stronger initially.

**(b) Income Effect is Larger than Substitution Effect (*YE* > *SE*)**

Beyond a certain higher real wage and number of hours worked, a point comes where leisure is more desirable than rise in wages. In such a case, income effect outweighs substitution effect. As a result, the supply of labour decreases, even though wages are increased. This leads to backward-bending segment implying that income effect may dominate eventually. The backward-bending supply curve of labour is shown in Fig. 19.7.

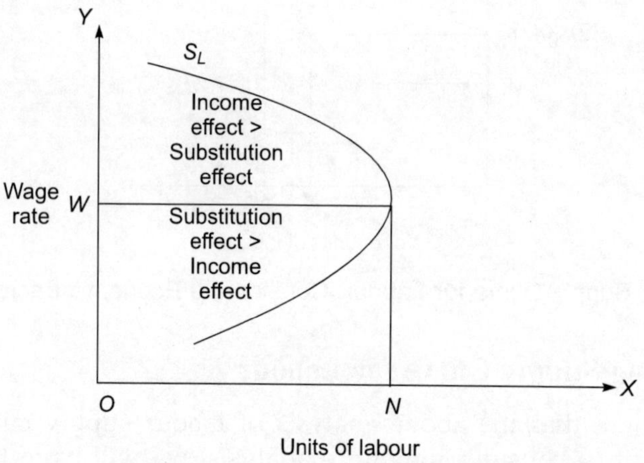


**Fig 19.7** Backward-bending Supply Curve for Labour ($S_L$)

However, for further analysis we keep non-economic factors (leisure) as constant and consider the positive slope of labour curve for deriving market labour curve.

### Derivation of the Market Labour Supply Curve from the Supply Curves of Individual Workers

The market supply curve of labour is the horizontal summation of the supply curves of individual workers. It is ascertained by adding up the hours that all persons in the economy are willing to work at a given wage rate. This has been shown in Fig. 19.8.

For the sake of simplicity of explanation, let us assume that there are two workers in the economy: worker *A* and worker *B*. The reservation wages for both of them are $w_A$ and $w_B$, respectively. When the wage is below $w_A$, no one is willing to render services as they find the wages to be too low. As the wage rises more than $w_A$, worker *A* becomes ready to supply his services and enters the labour market. This is shown by supply curve $SL_A$. At wages higher than $w_B$, worker *B* becomes ready to supply his services and enters the labour market.

This is shown by supply curve $SL_B$. Finally, the labour supply curve in the market is obtained by adding up the supply curves of all workers horizontally ($SL_A + SL_B$).

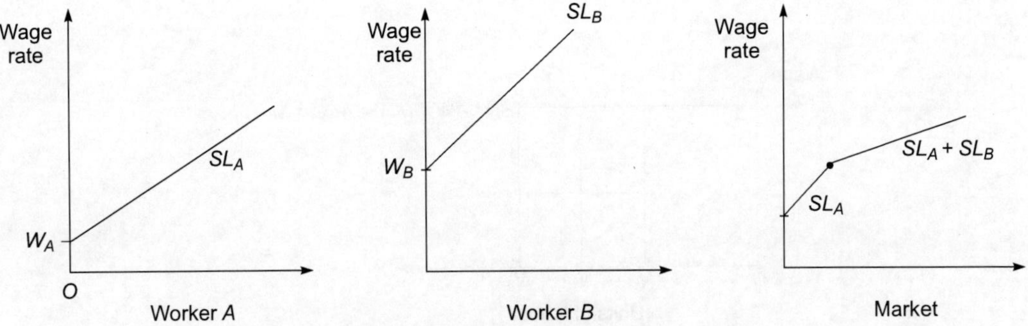


**Fig. 19.8** Derivation of the Market Labor Supply Curve

**(c) The Wage Rate (Factor Price) Determination in Perfect Markets**

In perfect market, the equilibrium wage rate is ascertained by the intersection of market demand ($D_L$) and the market supply of an input curve ($S_L$). Figure 19.9 shows that the equilibrium wage is $OW^*$ and the employment level is $OL^*$.

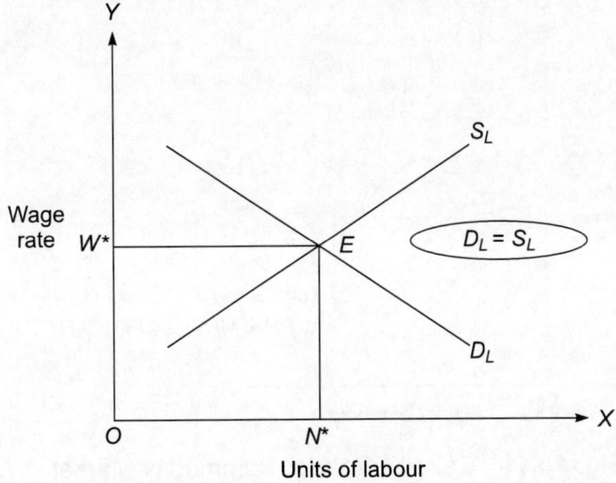


**Fig. 19.9** Wage Rate Determination in Perfect Markets

**(d) Equilibrium Determination under Perfect Commodity Market**

**(a) Considering the Case of Perfect Labour Market**

Suppose, labour is the only variable and hence its supply is perfectly elastic. It can be denoted by a straight line through $w$ parallel to the horizontal axis (Fig. 19.10).

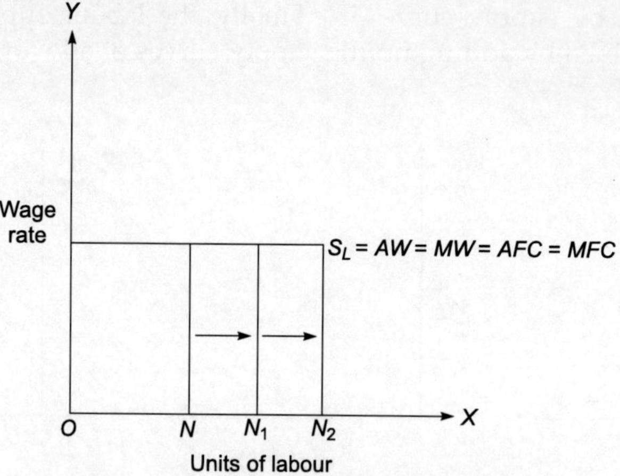


**Fig. 19.10** Case of Perfect Labour Market

Figure 19.10 clearly reveals that at prevailing wage rate the firm can employ (hire) any amount of labour it wants.

### (b) Considering the Case of Perfect Commodity Market Scenario

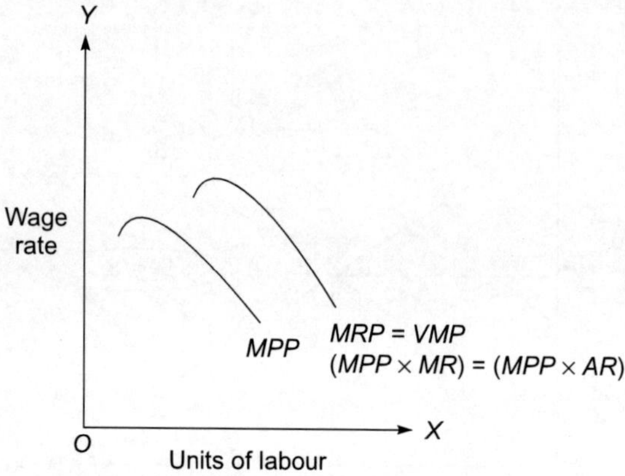


**Fig. 19.11** Case of Perfect Commodity Market

In Fig. 19.11, it can be seen that the $MPP_L$ declines at higher levels of employment, given the law of variable proportions. By multiplying $MPP_L$ at each level of employment by $AR$ curve ($P_x$), we obtain the value of marginal product curve ($VMP_L$).

Additionally, under perfect competition,

$$AR = MR \qquad \ldots(19.1)$$

Multiplying both sides of equation (19.1) by *MPP*

$$AR \times MPP = MR \times MPP$$

$$VMP = MRP$$

**(e) Equilibrium Wage Determination in Perfect Markets**

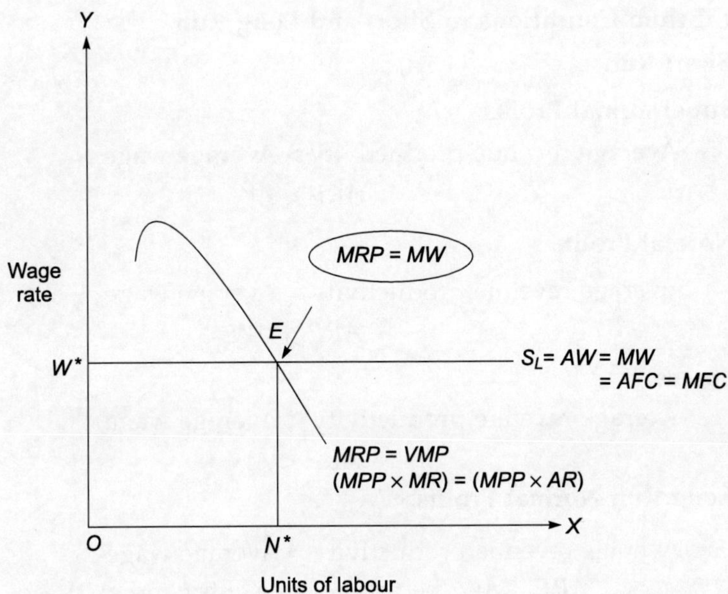


**Fig. 19.12** Equilibrium Wage Determination in Perfect Markets

The equilibrium of the firm when it is working under conditions of perfect competition in the factor market and monopoly or perfect competition in the product market is shown in Fig. 19.12. In figure 19.12, the equilibrium of the firm is denoted by *E*. At the market wage rate *OW**, the firm will maximize its profit by employing *ON** units of labour.

In this case following relations are observed:

$$S_L = AW = MW = AFC = MFC$$

where,

$S_L$ = Supply curve of labour

$AW$ = Average wage

$MW$ = Marginal wage

$AFC$ = Average factor cost

$MFC$ = Marginal factor cost

We have

$$MRP = MPP \times MR$$
$$VMP = MPP \times AR$$

Since
$$MRP = VMP$$
$$MPP \times MR = MPP \times AR$$

**(f) Equilibrium Conditions in Short and Long Run**

**1. For Short Run**

**(a) Supernormal Profits**

Average revenue productivity > Average wage

$$ARP > AW$$

**(b) Normal Profits**

Average revenue productivity = Average wage

$$ARP = AW$$

**(c) Losses**

Average revenue productivity < Average wage

$$ARP < AW$$

**2. For Long Run Normal Profits**

Average revenue productivity = Average wage

$ARP = AW$ (because of free entry and exit)

### 19.5.2 Determination of Factor Rewards/Price in Perfect Input Markets (Short and Long Run) under Conditions of Imperfect Commodity Market

**or**

### Determination of Factor Price Under Imperfect Competition (or Monopoly) in the Product Market and Perfect Competition in Factor Market

**{Perfect Competition in Labour Market + Imperfect Competition (or monopoly) in Commodity/Product Market}**

In case of imperfect competition (i.e., monopoly, oligopoly or monopolistic competition) in the product market, marginal revenue product (*MRP*) of the factor differs from the value of the marginal product (*VMP*). This is due to the fact that marginal revenue (*MR*) differs from the price (*AR*) of the product.

The determination of prices and employment of factors under imperfect competition is studied under these heads:

**(a)** Demand for Labour ($D_L$)

**(b)** Supply of Labour ($S_L$)

**(c)** Determination of the Factor Price

It is to be noted here that the explanation pertaining to the demand, supply and determination of wage rate are same as discussed in previous sections (refer subsection *A*, *B* and *C* of Section 19.5.1).

**(d) *MPP, MRP* and *VMP* curves in Imperfect Competition**

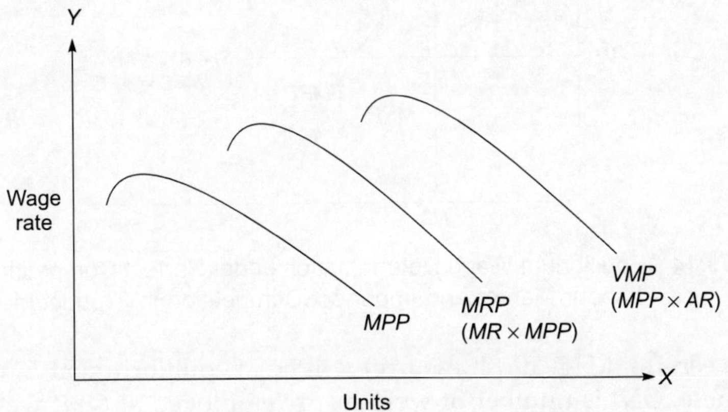


**Fig. 19.13** *MPP*, *MRP* and *VMP* curves in Imperfect Competition

Under imperfect competition (i.e., monopoly, oligopoly or monopolistic competition),

Since $AR \neq MR$

and

$$AR > MR$$

$$AR \times MPP > MR \times MPP$$

Therefore

$$VMP > MRP$$

**(e) Equilibrium Wage Determination under Perfect Competition in Labour Market and Imperfect Competition in Product Market**

The equilibrium of the firm when it is working under conditions of perfect competition in the factor market and imperfect competition in the product market has been shown in Fig. 19.14. As shown, *VMP* is greater than *MRP* when there is imperfect competition in the product market, *VMP* curve will be above *MRP* curve (for the sake of convenience, we have drawn only the downward sloping portions of *MRP* and *VMP* curves).

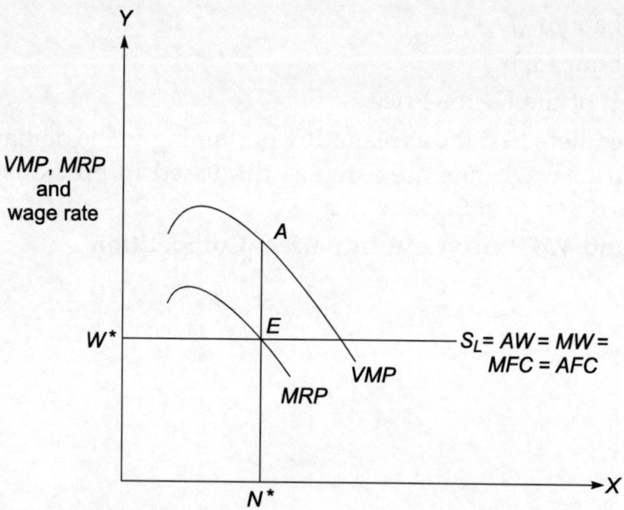


**Fig. 19.14** Equilibrium Wage Determination under Perfect Competition in Labour Market and Imperfect Competition in Product Market

It can be seen from Fig. 19.14, the firm will be in equilibrium at *E*, where *MRP* = *MW* where, *ON** is number of workers are employed at *OW** wage rate. In this case, marginal revenue product *EN** is less than its value of marginal product which is equal to *AN**. Therefore, factor gets *AE* less than the value of its marginal product.

**(f) Equilibrium in Short and Long Run**

**1. For Short Run**

**(a) Supernormal Profits**

Average revenue productivity > Average wage

$$ARP > AW$$

**(b) Normal Profits**

Average revenue productivity = Average wage

$$ARP = AW$$

**(c) Losses**

Average revenue productivity < Average wage

$$ARP < AW$$

**2. For Long Run**

**(a) Supernormal Profits**

Average revenue productivity > Average wage

$$ARP > AW$$

**(b) Normal Profits**

Average revenue productivity = Average wage

$$ARP = AW$$

**(c) Losses**

Average revenue productivity < Average wage

$$ARP < AW$$

## 19.6 CONCEPTS OF ECONOMIC RENT/RENTAL ELEMENT IN FACTOR REMUNERATION

The concept of economic rent relates to the modern theory of rent. It was first discussed by J.S. Mill and thereafter developed by economists like Jevons, Pareto, Marshall, Joan Robinson, etc.

According to the postulates of modern theory, economic rent may be defined as the payment made to a factor of production which is in excess of the minimum amount necessary to keep the factor in its present position. In other words, it is the difference between the actual payment to a factor and its supply price or transfer earning. It can be written as:

| **Economic rent = Actual earning (AE) – Transfer earning (TE)** |
|---|

where,

**Actual earning (AE)** means the actual monetary reward of a factor of production (say, labour) in his present occupation.

**Transfer earning (TE)** means expected earning of the factor from his next best occupation. It is also called opportunity cost of a factor. Thus, it reflects the minimum payment that is to be made to a factor of production (say, labour) to retain him in his current occupation.

This concept can be explained with the help of an example:

Suppose, a farmer has a piece of land which can be used for cultivation of both wheat and rice. The actual amount received by him post-cultivation is Rs. 10000. If either wheat or rice is grown there is no surplus or extra earning because there are no transfer earnings.

Now the farmer in another time period cultivates rice and earns Rs. 10000. If, however, he utilizes the same piece of land for cultivation of wheat then he could earn Rs. 6000. In this case, the **expected earning of the factor from his next best occupation** is Rs. 6000. Thus, economic rent may be calculated as:

| Actual earning: Rs. 10000.<br>Transfer earning: Rs. 6000.<br>Economic rent = Rs. 4000. |
|---|

The concept of economic rent would be clearer with the help of following cases.

### *Case 1: When Factor Supply is Perfectly Elastic*

The supply of factor (land) is said to be perfectly elastic when such a factor is available in abundance. It means that at prevailing factor cost, any amount of that factor is available. In such a case, therefore, its actual earning and transfer earning will be equal.

We know,

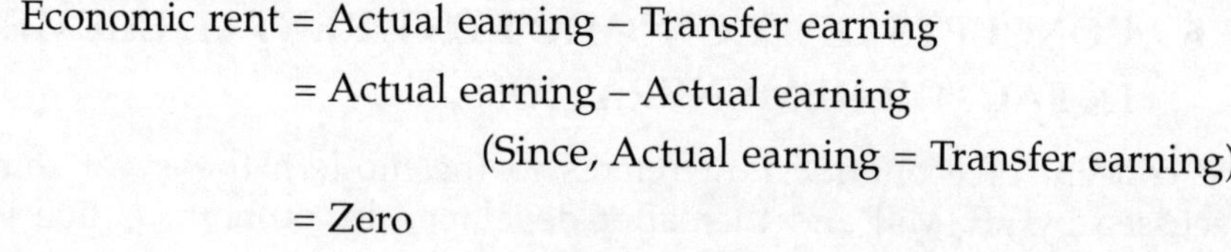

Economic rent = Actual earning – Transfer earning

= Actual earning – Actual earning

(Since, Actual earning = Transfer earning)

= Zero

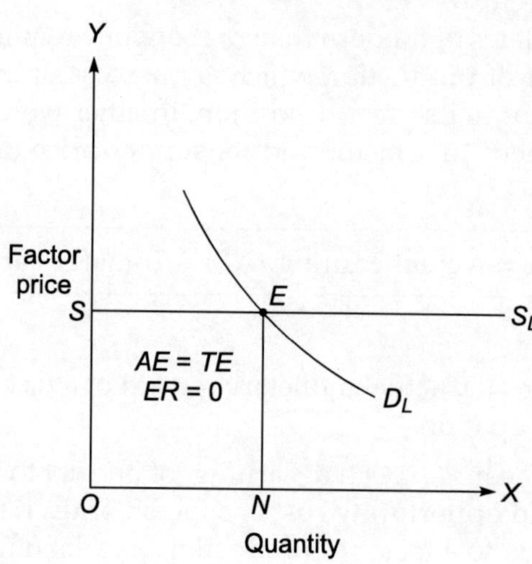


**Fig. 19.15** When Factor Supply is Perfectly Elastic

In the above figure,

*DD* = Demand curve of the factor of production. It is downward sloping from left to right exhibiting an inverse relationship between price of factor and quantity demand of it.

*SS* = Supply curve of the factor of production. It is a horizontal straight line curve parallel to X-axis. It means all factors are available at price *OS*.

Point *E* = Equilibrium point where the demand and supply curves intersect each other.

*OS* = Equilibrium price

*ON* = Equilibrium quantity (the quantity of factor used)

Now,

Actual earning = *OSEN*

and Transfer earnings = Actual earnings, i.e., *OSEN*

Therefore,

Economic rent = Actual earning – Transfer earning
= *OSEN* – *OSEN* (since, Actual earning = Transfer earning)
= Zero

***Case 2: When the Factor Supply is Perfectly Inelastic***

The supply of factor (land) is said to be perfectly inelastic when any rise or fall in factor price does not lead to change in factor supply. It indicates that if price of factor (say, land) falls to zero even then supply remains fixed. In such a case, transfer earnings (opportunity cost) of land will be zero. In the absence of transfer earning, the actual earnings will be called economic rent.

We know,

Economic rent = Actual earning – Transfer earning
= Actual earning – 0 (Since transfer earning is zero)
= Actual earning

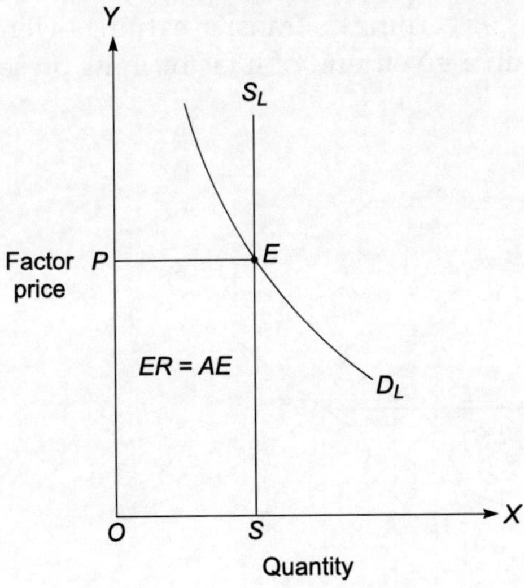


**Fig. 19.16** When Factor Supply is Perfectly Inelastic

In the above figure,

*DD* = Demand curve of the factor of production. It is downward sloping from left to right exhibiting an inverse relationship between price of factor and quantity demand of it.

$SS$ = Supply curve of the factor of production. It is vertical straight line curve parallel to $Y$-axis. It means supply of factor of production is fixed at $0S$ quantity.

Point $E$ = Equilibrium point where the demand and supply curves intersect each other.

$OP$ = Equilibrium price

$OS$ = Equilibrium quantity (quantity of factor used)

Now,

$$\text{Actual earning} = OSEP$$

and

$$\text{Transfer earnings} = 0$$

Therefore,

$$\text{Economic rent} = \text{Actual earning} - \text{Transfer earning}$$
$$= OSEP - 0 \text{ (since, Actual earning = Transfer earning)}$$
$$= OSEP$$

***Case 3: When the Supply is Less than Perfectly Elastic***

When the supply of factor is less than perfectly elastic, it means that transfer earnings of all the factor units are not equal. In order to explain the concept, Mrs. Joan Robinson used the concept of 'transfer earnings'. Transfer earnings were defined as the price which is necessary to retain a given unit of a factor in its present occupation.

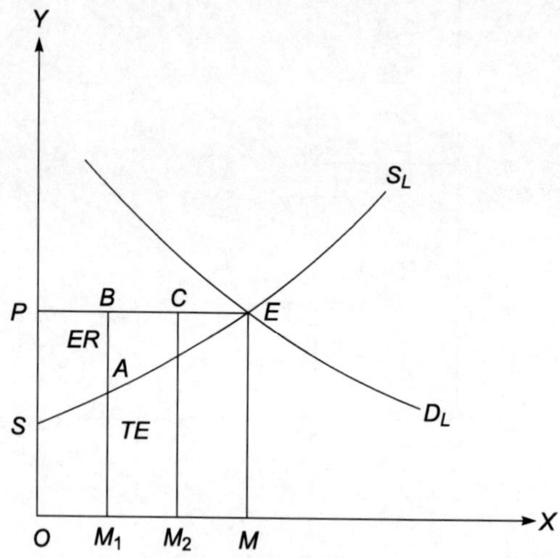


**Fig. 19.17** When Supply is Less than Perfectly Elastic

In the figure,

$DD$ = Demand curve of the factor of production. It is downward sloping from left to right exhibiting an inverse relationship between price of factor and quantity demand of it.

$SS$ = Supply curve of the factor of production. It is a positively sloped curve indicating direct relationship between price of factor and quantity supplied of it. Supply curve indicates what quantity of the factor will be available at various prices.

Point $E$ = Equilibrium point where the demand and supply curves intersect each other.

It can be seen from diagram that the transfer earning of one unit of factor is $AM_1$ while the price is $OP$.

Thus, the surplus or rent is $AB$ for unit 1. Similarly, the other units earn surplus or rent. In this manner $SEP$ will define the magnitude of economic rent.

Thus,

$$\begin{aligned} \text{Economic rent} &= \text{Actual earning} - \text{Transfer earning} \\ &= OMEP - OMES \\ &= SEP \end{aligned}$$

The above-mentioned cases may be summarized as:

**TABLE 19.1** Summary of Cases of Economic Rent

| Elasticity of Factor of Production | Actual Earning (*AE*) and Transfer Earning (*TE*) | Economic Rent (*ER*) |
|---|---|---|
| Es: Infinity | *AE* = *TE* | 0 |
| Es: Zero | *TE* = 0 | *AE* |
| Es: Less than Perfectly Elastic | *AE* > *TE* | *AE* – *TE* |

## Summary

- ✓ The factor market comprises mainly of four factors of production, namely, land, labour, capital, and entrepreneur.
- ✓ The price that is paid to the factors of production for rendering services is called factor pricing or factor remuneration.
- ✓ These factor remunerations or rewards exist in the form of rent, wages, interest, and profit that is paid for availing the services of factors such as land, labour, capital, and entrepreneur, respectively.
- ✓ The theory of factor pricing is concerned with the determination and distribution of respective reward of the each factor of production. It is for this reason also known as 'theory of distribution' or 'theory of distribution of factor rewards'.
- ✓ Like product pricing, the factor pricing also involves the interplay of demand and supply forces. However, in case of factor pricing, demand forces work similar to demand forces in product or commodity market. However, the difference arises in case of supply side dynamics.

- ✓ As far as distribution of income is concerned, there are two types, namely, personal distribution and functional distribution.
- ✓ Personal distribution refers to the economic phenomenon that deals with the dissemination of rewards pertaining to the various individuals of an economy. Whereas, functional distribution refers to the economic phenomenon that deals with the dissemination of rewards pertaining to the factors of production in an economy.
- ✓ In factor market, market demand curve for labour is a downward sloping curve from left to right establishing an inverse relationship between wage rate and number of units of labour.
- ✓ In factor market, initially there prevails a direct relationship between wage rate and number of units of labour. However, that income effect may dominate eventually which leads to backward-bending segment of supply curve.
- ✓ The market demand and supply curve of labour are horizontal summation of the demand and supply curves of individual workers.
- ✓ In labour market, the equilibrium wage rate is ascertained by the intersection of market demand ($D_L$) and the market supply of an input curves ($S_L$).
- ✓ When there is perfect competition in labour market and perfect competition in product market, in short-run supernormal profits, normal profits and losses exist. However, in long run, only normal profits exist.
- ✓ When there is perfect competition in labour market and imperfect competition in product market, there is possibility of supernormal profits, normal profits and losses both in short and long run.
- ✓ The concept of economic rent relates to the modern theory of rent. It was first discussed by J.S. Mill and thereafter developed by economists like Jevons, Pareto, Marshall, Joan Robinson, etc.
- ✓ Economic rent is the difference between the actual payment to a factor and its supply price or transfer earning.
- ✓ Actual earning (*AE*) means the actual monetary reward of a factor of production (say, labour) in his present occupation.
- ✓ Transfer earning (*TE*) means expected earning of the factor from his next best occupation. It is also called opportunity cost of a factor.

## Review Questions

1. Explain determination of factor rewards in perfect input markets in the short run and long run under conditions of perfect commodity markets.
2. Explain determination of factor rewards in perfect input markets in the short run and long run under conditions of imperfect commodity markets.
3. Why the demand curve for labour is backward bending?
4. How the non-economic factors affect the shape of supply curve of labour?

5. Highlight the similarities and differences in the determination of price of factor vs price of a product.
6. Elaborate the theory of distribution of factor rewards.
7. What is functional distribution of income? Do you find any relationship between functional and personal distribution of income? If yes, give reasons in support of your answer.
8. Explain the concept of rental element in factor remuneration.
9. How economic rent is determined? What role does transfer earnings play in determination of economic rent?
10. Explain the determination of supply curve of labour in the light of income and substitution effect in labour market.
11. Explain the interplay of demand and supply forces in determination of equilibrium in factor market.
12. Write short notes on the following:
    (a) Marginal physical product
    (b) Marginal revenue product
    (c) Value of marginal physical productivity
    (d) Economic rent
    (e) Transfer earnings

# Index

# Index

## E



## F



## G



## H



## I

## K



## L



## M

## N



## O



## P

## Q



## R



## S

## T



## U



## V



## W



## Z